The United Nations
And The Domestic Jurisdiction
of States

THE UNITED NATIONS
AND THE DOMESTIC JURISDICTION
OF STATES

Interpretations and Applications of the
Non-Intervention Principle

by

Goronwy J. Jones

CARDIFF
UNIVERSITY OF WALES PRESS
AND
WELSH CENTRE FOR INTERNATIONAL AFFAIRS
1979

©Goronwy J. Jones, 1979

British Library Cataloguing in Publication Data

Jones, Goronwy John
The United Nations and the domestic jurisdiction of states.
1. United Nations
2. Intervention (International law)
I. Title II. Welsh Centre for International Affairs
341.5'8   JX1977.2.A1

ISBN 0-7083-0717-5

Printed in Wales by South Western Printers Ltd., Caerffili, Mid-Glamorgan.

CONTENTS

PREFACE

The basic purpose of this study is to present what conclusions may be drawn from the practice of the United Nations in relation to the principle of non-intervention in matters essentially within the domestic jurisdiction of states under Article 2(7) of the Charter.

Having placed the subject in historical perspective, the book examines how far UN organs have observed or departed from the principle of non-intervention in human rights and colonial questions, peacekeeping operations, the regulation and reduction of national armaments, and economic and social questions, and assesses the impact of their decisions on the development of the UN.

I wish to thank the authorities of the Open University for granting me permission to publish the work, which was the result of my studies for a higher degree under the supervision of Professor A. Marwick, Professor of History, the Open University, and Professor H. Hearder, Professor of Modern History, University College, Cardiff, to both of whom I am indebted.

I am very thankful to the Trustees of the UNA (Wales) Trust, at the Welsh Centre for International Affairs, for providing a financial contribution to the University of Wales Press towards the publication of the book, and I very much appreciate the help given to me by Mr. John Rhys, Director of the University of Wales Press, and Mr. W.R. Davies, Director of the Welsh Centre for International Affairs.

My thanks are due to the following for giving me very useful services: the chief librarians and staff of the Reference Library of University College, Cardiff, the City of Cardiff Public Libraries, the Mid-Glamorgan County Library, the Bodleian Library, Oxford, the Library and Records Department of the Foreign and Commonwealth Office, the Public Record Office, London, and the Archives Section, United Nations, New York; the Director and staff of the United Nations Centre, London; and the Director and staff of the Welsh Centre for International Affairs, Temple of Peace, Cardiff.

I also wish to acknowledge that the late Sir Michael Wright, G.C.M.G., who was head of the British delegation at the Geneva Disarmament negotiations in the early 1960s, was kind enough to correspond with me on several issues raised in part VI of the book.

Bridgend, 1979.   Goronwy J. Jones.

FOREWORD

by

Professor H. Hearder, Ph.D.(London), Professor of Modern History, University College, Cardiff

The United Nations has survived in a difficult world for thirty-three years — appreciably longer than did the League of Nations. While it is perhaps true that the UN has never had the same zealous, even rapturous, support that the League enjoyed at odd moments in its short life, it is also the case that the League did not live long enough to be accepted as a permanent feature of the international landscape in the way that the UN has done. The UN has survived into a phase in which its abolition or demise is scarcely any longer considered a possibility. If extravagant hopes are less frequently expressed, hostile criticism is more muted. It may be dangerous to prophesy about the life-span of institutions, but it certainly begins to look as if the UN is here to stay. The subtle change which has occurred in world opinion with regard to the UN can be illustrated by a consideration of the contrasting reactions to UN intervention in the Congo in the early 1960s and to UN intervention in Lebanon in 1978. In contrast to the bitter disputes over the former, the latter has been accepted as a not unnatural development. While there are obvious factors in international politics which partly explain this contrast, they do not tell the whole story. That the prestige of the UN, in spite of set-backs, is slowly and almost imperceptibly growing, is also part of the story. It may be that, in more senses than one, the United Nations has arrived.

This being the case, the study here conducted by Mr Goronwy Jones is vital and opportune. Central to any understanding of the role and history of the UN is a consideration of Article 2(7) of the Charter — the article specifying that the UN should not 'intervene in matters which are essentially within the jurisdiction of any state'. By examining how, over the years, this article has been interpreted and applied, and by showing how it has at times inhibited, but at other times preserved, the UN, Mr Jones has performed a valuable service for anyone interested in history, international politics, or international law.

The picture of the United Nations that emerges from this careful and balanced study is of an institution capable of change, growth and development. By observing the UN in a full, historical perspective, Mr Jones reminds us that it is not simply an abstract legal construction, but that it is the product of the day-to-day drama of world politics and of the domestic politics of its members. It is already acquiring what Michael Oakshott, in his memorable inaugural lecture at the L.S.E., called the 'intimations' of society — in this case, of world society. It is beginning to develop its own traditions, and, on the occasions when it can make a positive response to a crisis, it no longer raises the sense of outrage and astonishment that it once raised in certain quarters.

Development and change in the UN could lead to a re-interpretation of Article 2(7). Mr Jones weighs meticulously, and shows clearly, how the principle of non-intervention in matters within the domestic jurisdiction of sovereign states can be — and has been — differently interpreted. He gives no rash advice on the point, and his argument is full of a sense of political realism. But beneath his sense of realism is the understanding of the immensely beneficial functions the UN can perform, even in a world in which peace has for so long been preserved by a balance of terror. An alternative method of keeping the peace must be evolved, but it can be evolved only after enquiries like the one carried out in this book have been quietly and dispassionately conducted.

I. INTRODUCTION — FROM THE CONGRESS OF VIENNA TO THE BIRTH OF THE UNITED NATIONS

Before the attempt is made to analyse the principle of non-intervention in matters essentially within the domestic jurisdiction of states under Article 2(7) of the Charter of the United Nations, and to assess the significance of its interpretation and application by United Nations organs, it is proposed to place the subject in historical perspective by examining various developments in international relations, of relevance to it, from the Congress of Vienna in 1815 to the period of the League of Nations experiment.

The Congress System

The main aims of the Allied great powers that effected the overthrow of Napoleon — Austria, Britain, Prussia and Russia — were to prevent a resurgence of French aggression without depriving France of great power status, and to create an equilibrium of power to ensure the stability of Europe. Various territorial adjustments were agreed upon to achieve these objectives, which were finalised, with French concurrence, under the Treaty of Vienna in June 1815.

The general international background which obtained for almost forty years after the Napoleonic wars was shaped by the Vienna settlement, and great power agreement on the holding of periodic congresses, in accordance with the Treaty of Chaumont which has been concluded in March 1814, to consider the affairs of Europe as a whole and to deal with issues that might disturb the peace, gave rise to the congressional form of international government — the first experiment of its kind in the history of modern Europe.[1]

The Congress system, which France joined on terms of equality at the Congress of Aix-la-Chapelle in 1818, thus came into being to protect the public law of Europe,[2] with the exception of the Turkish empire.[3] But so determined were the Continental autocracies — Austria, Russia and Prussia — to preserve the monarchical system in European states, in accordance with their Holy Alliance which they signed in 1815, that they considered it legitimate to use the Congress system as an instrument for authorising intervention in the domestic affairs of those states whose constitutional development displeased them.

To this doctrine, Castlereagh, the British Foreign Secretary, was strongly opposed. Anxious to maintain the territorial settlements of the peace treaties, he insisted that the form of government within a state was a matter within its domestic jurisdiction, outside the international jurisdiction of the Congress system. 'In this Alliance as in all other human Arrangements, nothing is more likely to impair or even destroy its real utility, than any attempt to push its duties and obligations beyond the

1

Sphere which its original Conception and understood Principles will warrant,' he declared in a state paper of 5 May 1820. 'It was an union for the Reconquest and liberation of a great proportion of the Continent of Europe from the Military Dominion of France, and having subdued the Conqueror it took the State of Possession as established by the Peace under the Protection of the Alliance: — It never was however intended as an Union for the Government of the World, or for the Superintendence of the Internal Affairs of other States.'[4] Such was Castlereagh's response to the Tsar's call for a congress to be summoned for the purpose of approving concerted intervention in Spain to put an end to the liberal constitution which had limited the power of the king through a revolution early in 1820. He considered that the Congress system should be used to authorise the joint intervention of the Powers only if a state threatened to undermine or destroy the territorial integrity and independence of another.

Though Metternich, the Austrian Chancellor, 'wanted to maintain all established governments and existing institutions because he believed that a defeat of authority in any state could lead to a collapse of order throughout Europe',[5] he joined Castlereagh on this occasion in opposing the Tsar's appeal for a congress since he was wary of the Tsar's desire to send forces to the aid of the Spanish Royalists and to secure the establishment of a Russian fleet in the Mediterranean. But he agreed to a congress when revolutions had established democratic constitutions in Portugal, Piedmont and Naples, and at the Congress of Troppau in October 1820, to which Britain sent an observer but not a plenipotentiary, he concurred in a protocol inspired by the Tsar, and issued by Russia, Austria and Prussia, which declared their intention to intervene by force, if necessary, to suppress revolutionary movements in states in which the authority of monarchs was threatened.

Castlereagh attacked this policy in a circular published in January 1821 before the Continental Powers met again at the Congress of Laibach. He conceded the right of intervention by a state or states 'where their own immediate security, or essential interests, are seriously endangered by the internal transactions of another State', but emphasised that its application should always be an exception to the general rule of non-intervention since it could be justified only by extreme necessity.[6] For the most part, then, Castlereagh believed that if the Congress system was to succeed, it was imperative that it should confine its regulative functions to those fields where the external policies of states impinged upon the territorial integrity and independence of other states. He thus called for a policy of non-intervention in matters within the domestic jurisdiction of states in opposition to the Continental Powers. It was a policy which neither aimed to facilitate political or social changes, nor to arrest such changes, but one designed to ensure the maintenance of the territorial status quo in the interest of the general peace and security of Europe.[7] But it was rejected by the other great powers. Metternich was authorised at the Congress of Laibach in January 1821, despite British protests, to re-establish absolutist regimes in Naples and Piedmont, and in March of the same year Austrian forces moved into Italy to enforce this policy.

Though Castlereagh refused to associate Britain with the decisions of the Congress of Laibach, he reached agreement with Metternich at the end of 1821 to summon a congress with the aim of preventing Alexander of Russia from intervening in the Turkish empire to assist the national revolt of the Greek Christians. To Metternich the application of the principle of non-intervention in this instance was justified because it meant supporting the cause of legitimate authority and order against a revolutionary movement; to Castlereagh such a policy was consistent with his doctrine that the Congress system should not be used to authorise intervention in matters of domestic jurisdiction mainly because of his fear of 'all the destructive confusion and discussion which such an attempt may lead to not only in Turkey but in Europe', where it 'must . . . hazard . . . the fortune and destiny of that system (of international relations) to the conservation of which our latest solemn transactions with our allies have bound to us'.[8] But before the congress met at Verona in 1822, Castlereagh was dead and had been replaced by Canning.

At the Congress of Verona the question of Spain took precedence over the Greek affair since Metternich was able to convince the Tsar Alexander at the outset of the congress proceedings that the Greek rising against the Turks was 'outside the restricted sphere over which the Quadruple Alliance played the part of Providence'.[9] The attention of the congress was thus focused on the French request to obtain the support of the other great powers to restore order in Spain, where civil war had broken out between the Royalists and the constitutionalists, and to re-establish the Spanish king as an absolute ruler. Notwithstanding the protests of Wellington, the British representative, the Continental great powers gave France their moral support, and in 1823 the latter invaded Spain, abolished its liberal constitution, and restored the absolutist status of the king.

Canning defined the British position in much the same terms as Castlereagh had done. 'Intimately connected as we are with the system of Europe,' he stated, 'it does not follow that we are therefore called upon to mix ourselves on every occasion, with a restless and meddling activity, in the concerns of the nations which surround us.'[10] The only justification for a policy of intervention in the internal affairs of other states, he contended, was 'that our interests should have been, in some way or other, affected by their condition, or by their proceedings',[11] and his antipathy to any further British involvement in the Congress system was such that in 1824 he declined to send representatives to congresses summoned to deal with the Greek revolt against Turkey and Spain's insurgent South American colonies. Instead, without consulting the other powers, he saw to it that

Britain accorded belligerent status to the Greek rebels, which involved a departure from Castlereagh's policy of non-intervention in matters within the domestic jurisdiction of Turkey, and recognised the independence of Spain's revolted colonies in line with the Monroe doctrine that America would not tolerate the intervention of European states in the affairs of the American continent. Canning thus hastened the collapse of the Congress system as envisaged under the Treaty of Chaumont, though its disintegration stemmed not only from his independent action, but also from disagreement among the four Continental powers whose meeting at Petersburg in 1825 broke up on account of dissension over the question of the Greek revolt against Turkey.[12]

This review of the Congress system indicates that 'if all the Powers began by agreeing that a new international system was needed in Europe they brought different conceptions of international organisation — and, even, different conceptions of Europe — to the task of reconstruction. It was on the rocks of these differences as to the aims and limits of an international system that the Congress foundered'.[13] In other words, its failure came about because of great power disagreement over the measure of international jurisdiction which the Congress system should possess, and the purpose for which it should be used, for it could not possibly function effectively so long as the great powers were at variance over the principle of non-intervention in matters of domestic jurisdiction. Indeed, this is a matter which it will be essential to bear in mind when we come to consider the work of the architects of the League of Nations and United Nations systems, but at this juncture let us examine the role which was assigned to the Concert of Europe that functioned mainly through *ad hoc* conferences after the collapse of the Congress system.

The Concert of Europe after the Collapse of The Congress System

It is significant that 'the failure of the Congress system marked not the end but the beginning of an age of collaboration between the Great Powers because they then fell back on the Congress system as it had been interpreted by Castlereagh',[14] the essence of which was 'the notion of a body of great powers always ready to defend the established balance of power by combining against any state which was determined to disturb the existing territorial order'.[15] In practice this meant that as far as possible the great powers attempted to maintain the status quo, and that whenever any territorial changes took place they had to be finalised in accordance with the principle of 'no annexation without ratification'.[16] It also meant that the great powers on the whole observed the principle of non-intervention in matters within the domestic jurisdiction of states, which had been so strongly advocated by Castlereagh. Certainly, during the revolutions of 1830 and 1848 the Concert of Europe was not used as an instrument to suppress or assist revolutionary movements in various states, and the extent to which some of the great powers intervened unilaterally did not upset the general European balance of power.

It was Russia's unwillingness to respect the principle of non-intervention in matters within the domestic jurisdiction of Turkey, which other great powers considered would adversely affect the European balance of power, that brought about the Crimean War in 1854. Though Britain and France had joined Russia to help the insurgent Greeks by destroying the Turkish fleet at Navarino in 1827, and forced the Sultan to accept the independence of Greece,[17] they were not prepared to permit unilateral Russian intervention in the Balkans. Several diplomatic efforts were made to induce the Tsar to abandon his claim that Russia had the sole right to protect Turkey's Christian subjects, and Britain and France declared war in March, 1854, 'after Austria and Russia had joined them in a further conference which issued a further protocol to warn the Tsar that Europe would be against him if he failed in his promises to respect Turkey's integrity and do nothing to weaken the Sultan's authority over his Christian subjects'.[18]

Though under the Treaty of Paris (1856) the concert of major European powers expressed their concern about the future treatment of the Sultan's Christian subjects in the Balkans, it recognised Turkey as a completely sovereign state within the comity of European powers and made the Sultan responsible for their welfare, and it was laid down that there should be no unilateral or collective intervention in Turkey's domestic jurisdiction. In effect, therefore, the powers of the Concert of Europe simply contented themselves with a moral appeal to the conscience of the Sultan, for 'the independence of Turkey was affirmed: no Power had the right to interfere between the Sultan and his subjects: the privileges of Moldavia, Wallachia were guaranteed, but always under the suzerainty of Turkey: "the generous intentions" of the Sultan towards his subjects "without distinction of religion or of race" were recognised, as was the "high value" of the proposals he had made in a recent Firman'.[19] Clearly, the signatories of the Treaty of Paris intended that there should be no dictatorial interference to force Turkey to observe her promises to carry out reforms to improve the condition of her Christian subjects.

That the principle of non-intervention should apply to Turkey's treatment of her Christian subjects was strongly challenged by Gladstone during the Bulgarian atrocity agitation in 1876, when he urged that the Concert of Europe, which had played no part in determining the questions of German and Italian unification, should authorise collective measures to enforce humanitarian reforms on Turkey and the granting of self-government to Christian minorities under her direct rule in the Balkans. Even though he argued that Turkey should possess 'titular sovereignty' over the self-governing territories which he desired to see established, in order to exclude foreign powers from them, what he urged required dictatorial interference in Turkish affairs because it meant that the Sultan would be required to delegate power to the oppressed peoples to enable them to operate systems of self-government. In Gladstone's view, the Concert of Europe was 'an important factor in the advance of civilisation. Its functions in this respect were to enforce international law, to preserve European peace and to relieve oppressed peoples. While the first two carried the emphasis in his thought during the eighteen fifties and sixties, the last one gained predominance in the late seventies'.[20] But in view of the rival ambitions among the great powers, the possibility of obtaining agreement to operate the Concert of Europe which Gladstone advocated was remote.

Russia had urged the concerted intervention of the great powers shortly after the outbreak of the revolt of Bosnia and Herzegovina in 1875, but though Austria and Prussia joined Russia in threatening sanctions against Turkey if she did not carry out reforms, Disraeli, suspicious of Russian designs in the Near East, rejected such a policy. It is true that Lord Salisbury attempted with the representatives of the other powers at Constantinople and London, early in 1877, to induce Turkey to undertake a programme of reforms under international supervision, but the powers of the Concert lacked the unity to agree on enforcement measures. Indeed, the Berlin Congress of 1878, which effected a settlement of the Eastern question after Russia's unilateral intervention in Turkey in 1877, 'sacrificed the national aspirations of all Balkan peoples to the avarice and rivalries of the great powers',[21] and though the arrangements which Turkey was obliged to accept deprived her of half her territory, the Sultan's promises to introduce reforms in what remained of his Balkan empire still depended on his readiness to co-operate. Thus little was done at the Congress of Berlin by the Concert of Europe to satisfy Gladstone's demand to obtain justice for the oppressed national groups in the Balkans, and during his Second Ministry (1880-85), 'when he faced Bismarck in European politics, it became clear to him that it was no longer possible to establish a diplomatic concert of the principal powers. Though he always hoped one day to see the great powers brought together for humanitarian ends, in those years he rarely advocated his idea of the European Concert'.[22]

Later in this study it will be interesting to consider how far Gladstone's concept of the Concert of Europe as an instrument for intervening in the domestic jurisdiction of states, to enable oppressed peoples to secure basic human rights, compares with the theory and practice of the League of Nations and United Nations systems. But at this point, before leaving the nineteenth century, mention must be made of Lord Salisbury's attempt to revive the Concert of Europe in the late 1890s, when Europe had become divided into two rival camps — the Triple Alliance of Germany, Austria-Hungary and Italy, and the Dual Alliance of France and Russia — and European states were in danger of collision as they extended their jurisdiction over territories in Asia and Africa as imperialist powers.

Though Salisbury had been very critical of the Concert of Europe both before and after the Congress of Berlin in 1878, in 1897 he advocated its revival because he was concerned about the arms race and the growing tension in Europe. In brief, he believed it should be used to maintain the territorial arrangements laid down in the treaties concluded by the great powers, including those that guaranteed the territorial integrity and independence of the Ottoman empire, notwithstanding the further disrepute which it had acquired through the Armenian atrocities of 1894-96. That the Concert should be used for the collective intervention of the powers in the domestic jurisdiction of states, for the humanitarian purposes which Gladstone had advocated in the eighteen seventies, formed no part of his concept. But it should be noted that Salisbury went further than to suggest a revival of the Concert of Europe which rested on no formal instrument and whose proceedings were not regulated by constitutional obligations. 'The one hope we have,' he stated in November 1897, 'is that the Powers may gradually be brought together, to act together in a friendly spirit on all questions of difference which may arise, until at last they shall be welded in some international constitution which shall give to the world, as a result of their great strength, a long spell of unfettered and prosperous trade and continued peace.'[23]

It can thus be seen that Salisbury, like Castlereagh, was 'more interested in peace than in justice. But Gladstone, moved by the suffering of oppressed peoples and inspired by the ideas of nationality and self-government, strove for justice. Castlereagh, who sometimes expressed what might be called an organic conception of the congress system, and Salisbury, who in 1897 hoped that the European Concert would lead to some sort of international constitution, countenanced organization of the society of states. But Gladstone, advocating reform and reorganization in Turkey, concentrated on civilization of barbaric governments. Castlereagh, who identified himself with the territorial arrangements of the Vienna Congress, and Salisbury, who defended the work of the Berlin Congress, based their views on a positive law of treaties. But Gladstone rested his ideas on a natural law of rights'.[24]

Such were the ideas that induced Castlereagh and Salisbury to consider it necessary to advocate a policy of non-intervention in matters within the domestic jurisdiction of states, and why Gladstone felt that the principle of non-intervention in such matters should not stand in the way of the Concert of Europe to advance the cause of human rights and social justice; and how far these concepts of international organisation influenced the architects of the League of Nations will be referred to presently. But, as further background to a study of such questions, mention must now be made of the Hague Conference of 1899 which showed the reluctance of sovereign states to surrender matters of domestic jurisdiction to the control of an international body.

Not only did the Hague Conference fail to produce an agreement on the limitation of national armaments — it merely stated that a reduction of military budgets was extremely desirable for the material and moral welfare of mankind — but the jurisdiction of the Court of Arbitration which it set up was seriously limited by 'the fact that no state bound itself to report to the Court: that no state could get assistance in bringing an unwilling state to arbitration: and that disputes involving the honour and vital interests of a state were expressly exempted from the Court's jurisdiction'.[25] Each state thus remained the sole judge of whether it would submit to the Court disputes with other states, which showed that states were unprepared to surrender a sufficient measure of their sovereignty to give the Court the necessary competence to become an effective arbitral body. Indeed, not until the world had endured the agony of the Great War was the attempt made to establish the League of Nations system whose primary aim was the settlement of international disputes which might endanger peace and security.

The League of Nations and the Principle of Non-intervention in Matters of Domestic Jurisdiction

To some extent the Covenant of the League of Nations had some features which were inherent in Gladstone's concept of the Concert of Europe as an instrument for the promotion of social justice. Thus Article 22 of the Covenant, which dealt with the mandates system, proclaimed that the well being and development of peoples not yet able to govern themselves should form a 'sacred trust of civilisation' — very much a Gladstonian phrase — and the Council of the League[26] was given supervisory powers over the administrative acts of the mandatory powers.[27] The Council was also asked to concern itself with minorities of race, language or religion who were assured protection by the League under the peace treaties. But 'in each case the League could, in practice, do little more than exert a moral pressure, relying on the unwillingness of governments to be held up, in the Council or the Assembly,[28] as having failed to carry out their treaty obligations'.[29] Moreover, although the Covenant recognised the need for peaceful change through the revision of treaties, all the Assembly could do under Article 19 of the Covenant was 'to advise the reconsideration by members of the League of treaties which became inapllicable', and not even this was attempted 'because of the ascendancy of French policies towards Germany when the latter's co-operation might have been achieved'.[30]

The fact was that the Covenant of the League was more in tune with the concept of Castlereagh and Salisbury than that of Gladstone, for the maintenance of peace through the preservation of the status quo was more important to its architects than the provision of effective means to remove injustices through imperfections in the peace treaties. Above all, as laid down in Article 10 of the Covenant, the League was designed to protect the territorial integrity and existing political independence of its members in accordance with the principle of collective security, and it was also made clear in the Covenant that the organisation was not intended to interfere dictatorially in matters within the domestic jurisdiction of states — the scope of which will be examined presently — even though such matters, eg. a state's immigration policy,[31] might give rise to international disputes.

In order to understand the principle of non-intervention in matters of domestic jurisdiction under the League of Nations system, it is necessary to examine the procedures laid down in its Covenant for the pacific settlement of international disputes and the enforcement of peace. Article 12 of the Covenant stated that if there should arise any dispute between members of the League likely to lead to a rupture, they would be required to submit the matter either to arbitration or judicial settlement, or to inquiry by the Council, and they agreed in no case to resort to war until three months after the award by the arbitrators, or the judicial decision, or the report by the Council, which had to be presented within six months after the submission of the dispute. Thus the most difficult disputes had, finally, to be brought before the Council, for if the disputants had failed to settle a dispute through diplomatic negotiations, or had not submitted it to arbitration or judicial processes under Article 13 of the Covenant, they were required to submit the matter to the Council under Article 15. If, then, the Members of the Council, *voting without* the parties to the dispute, succeeded in reaching a unanimous report on the case, no member of the League was permitted to go to war with any party that complied with the recommendations of the report. But if the Council members failed to produce a unanimous report, this condition no longer applied. Even then, however, a party to a dispute would be guilty of breaking the Covenant if it resorted to war before three months had elapsed after the report had been published, and sanctions under Article 16 could be applied.[32]

In view of the fact that 'before the Covenant was signed every nation had still an unlimited right of private war, except in so far as this had been curtailed by a certain number of arbitral treaties devoid of international sanction',[33] states signatory to the Covenant thus agreed to accept significant restrictions on their right to make private war. But it should be realised that no such restrictions applied if the League Council found that a state's claim that a dispute in which it was involved arose out of a matter within its domestic jurisdiction, such as a state's immigration policies. This was laid down in paragraph 8 of Article 15 of the Covenant, the text of which was as follows: 'if the dispute between the parties is claimed by one of them, and is found by the Council, to arise out of a matter which by international law is solely within the domestic jurisdiction of that party, the Council shall so report, and shall make no recommendations as to its settlement'.

As Sir Alfred Zimmern pointed out, the inclusion of Article 15(8) in the

Covenant meant that 'no sanction whatsoever was provided for a war arising out of such a dispute, since the sanctions of Article XVI apply only to breaches of XII, XIII and XV'.[34] And it was Zimmern's view that 'this paragraph, in fact, if pushed to its logical limit, endangers the whole peace-preserving structure of the Covenant, since, as has been pointed out, the great majority of really dangerous disputes arise out of matters which indisputably fall within the category of domestic jurisdiction and the problem of how to deal with them is the most crucial, and unfortunately also the most intractable, of all international problems'.[35]

Zimmern also emphasised that though disputes arising out of matters of domestic jurisdiction could still be raised under Article 11 of the Covenant, which stipulated that the League could take any action that might be deemed wise and effectual to safeguard the peace of nations in the event of any war or threat of war, the parties to such disputes were 'left quite free, under that article, to accept or reject any suggestion made by members of the Council'.[36] The fact was that no action could be taken by the League Council or the Assembly under Article 11 without the unanimity of their members, including those member-states party to the dispute.[37]

But though signatories to the Covenant did not accept restrictions on their right to make private war in the case of a dispute arising out of a matter of domestic jurisdiction, it was recognised in Article 15(8) of the Covenant that the claim by a state that a matter was solely within its domestic jurisdiction, i.e. that it was sole judge of the matter and so outside the international jurisdiction of the League Council, had to be tested by the criterion of international law, and could be referred by that body to the Permanent Court of International Justice for an advisory opinion.[38] One important instance of this arose in 1922 when the Court was asked to give an opinion to the League Council concerning a dispute between France and Britain over a question of nationality. France had attempted to impose French nationality and liability to military conscription upon certain British subjects in her protectorates of Tunis and Morocco, and refused to resort to arbitration on the ground that the question was solely within her domestic jurisdiction. But when Britain appealed to the League of Nations, the League Council referred the matter to the Permanent Court for an advisory opinion.

The Permanent Court pointed out that although questions of nationality were not in principle regulated by international law, this did not apply in this case because Britain could claim the validity of certain treaties which placed obligations on France that denied her the right to act as sole judge of the matter. Hence the Court concluded that the issue was not a matter solely within the domestic jurisdiction of France.[39] In effect, then, the Court maintained that a matter not regulated in principle by international law, in the absence of international treaties which placed obligations on the parties to such treaties, was solely within the domestic jurisdiction of a state.[40] 'As regards such matters,' it declared, 'each State is sole master of its decisions,' to which it added: 'The question whether a particular matter is or is not solely within the jurisdiction of a state is an essentially relative question; it depends upon the development of international relations'.[41]

During the League of Nations period the development of international relations was such that it was generally recognised that matters solely within the domestic jurisdiction of a state included its right to make private war as permitted under the quasi legal articles of the Covenant, as already explained: the nature of its government:[42] the size of its armaments and armed forces, except those of the defeated states in World War I until they defied the Versailles treaty which had imposed restrictions on their military strength: its government of the colonies it possessed, i.e., those non-self-governing territories which were not under the League system of mandates:[43] the treatment of its own subjects, which covered the whole field of human rights,[44] except the treatment of minorities under the Minorities treaties:[45] and, in the absence of international treaties, its immigration policies,[46] questions of nationality,[47] and economic policies, such as the imposition of tariffs, quotas, etc.[48] The scope of a state's domestic jurisdiction was thus very wide, and the purpose of Article 15(8) of the Covenant was to prevent the League of Nations Council from making recommendations for the settlement of disputes that arose out of matters, which, according to the criterion of international law, were still within the domestic jurisdiction of states. Furthermore, as already stated, though any war or threat of war arising from such disputes could be considered by the Council or Assembly under Article 11 of the Covenant, no action could be decided by those bodies without the unanimity of their members, including those member-states party to a dispute.

But Sir Alfred Zimmern's misgivings concerning the domestic jurisdiction limitation on the powers of the League of Nations to maintain international peace proved in practice to be unfounded. During the existence of the League 'the domestic jurisdiction of Article 15(8) was tested in its forum in very few cases, though the issue of domestic jurisdiction cropped up many times in the course of debates in the League Assembly and the Council',[49] and in none of the disputes considered by the League Council did a state successfully invoke the domestic jurisdiction provision of Article 15(8).[50] The point needs to be stressed, therefore, that the League did not fail to maintain international peace because of its lack of competence under the Covenant to deal with breaches of the peace that arose out of matters within the domestic jurisdiction of states; its failure was caused by the reluctance of its members to implement the principle of collective security in major instances of aggression, such as those committed by Japan against Manchuria in 1931 and by Italy against Abyssinia in 1935, when the domestic jurisdiction limitation under Article 15(8) could not be justifiably invoked to prevent the League Council from deciding that aggression had been committed and from authorising sanctions under Article 16 of the Covenant. Had League members used the Organisation as they were entitled under the terms of the Covenant, the Axis powers would not have been emboldened in the late thirties to pursue their aggressive policies on a wider scale.

The fact, however, that the League did not have definite responsibilities and powers under the Covenant to regulate to some extent interstate economic and financial relations — the various aspects of the economic and social policies of states remained within their domestic jurisdiction in the absence of international treaties — was a major weakness. It was because of this that, as the great economic depression of the late twenties and early thirties spread unemployment and poverty throughout the world, 'the Council and the Assembly were hardly more than spectators of a series of catastrophic events',[51] and so far as the League was concerned, 'its direct and immediate consequence was to tear down the structure of economic co-operation which was gradually being built-up. Its indirect consequence was to poison and embitter relations between Germany and France, Italy and France, and, in general, between the so-called dissatisfied powers on the one hand and the satisfied on the other; to encourage the worst forms of nationalist and bellicose ambition in Germany, Japan and Italy; to weaken the cohesion, and confuse the purposes, of the peace-loving states'.[52]

To sum up: in this introduction it has been emphasised that the Congress system of the early nineteenth century collapsed because of great power disagreement over the measure of international jurisdiction which the system should possess, and the purpose for which it should be used. The clash between those who believed that peace and stability depended upon a policy of non-intervention in matters of domestic jurisdiction, and those who wanted to use the Congress system to intervene in such matters to prevent or assist political changes, was later reflected in the conflicting policies of the great powers of the Concert of Europe towards the Eastern question, with Russia, an ambitious power anxious to intervene in Turkish affairs in the name of justice for oppressed peoples, and other powers, to a greater or lesser extent, suspicious of Russian designs and influenced by a mixture of strategic and selfish considerations. The consequence of this was a settlement of the Eastern question in 1878, at the Congress of Berlin, which ignored the nationalist aspirations of the Balkan peoples and contained the seeds of future wars.

Of particular interest to the student of international relations is the difference between the Gladstonian concept of the Concert of Europe and that of Lord Salisbury. Whereas Gladstone's concept required the intervention of the Concert in the domestic jurisdiction of Turkey to effect the implementation of human rights and the self-determination of nations, Salisbury's concept, which was similar to that of Castlereagh, stressed that the Concert of powers should aim to maintain the territorial integrity and political independence of states, and observe a strict policy of non-intervention in matters of domestic jurisdiction, even if this meant blocking the path to political and social changes to meet the demands of justice. In line with Castlereagh's concept of the Congress system, Salisbury considered that in a world of variegated states, with differing ideologies, it was impracticable for international organisation, charged with the task of maintaining peace, to be used for the advance of social justice through intervening in matters of domestic jurisdiction and that its terms of reference should be confined to preserving the independence of states against acts of aggression.

Though the principle of national self-determination, which was inherent in Gladstone's concept of the Concert of Europe as an instrument for the promotion of social justice, was a prominent feature of Woodrow Wilson's Fourteen Points, the League of Nations system, which was largely his brainchild, did not provide effective arrangements to protect the large number of new national minorities that still existed after the Treaty of Versailles — about 25 million people in all — though the treaty had granted national self-determination to 75 million people.[53] Hence the treatment of these minorities, though in theory a matter outside the domestic jurisdiction of states under the Minorities Treaties, was in practice within the control of those states in whose territories they had been placed. The fact was that the League of Nations system was more in consonance with the concept of Castlereagh and Salisbury than that of Gladstone, designed primarily to preserve against external aggression the territorial integrity and political independence of member-states of the Organisation. It failed because its members lacked the will to implement the principle of collective security when it might have succeeded without the help of isolationist America; its policy of non-intervention in disputes arising out of matters of domestic jurisdiction did not militate against its functioning as a peace-keeping organisation.

The next chapter will attempt to explain how far the architects of the Charter of the United Nations in 1945 were influenced by the theory and practice of the Concert system of the nineteenth century and the League of Nations experiment. Their main problem, of course, was that of defining the measure of international jurisdiction which the new organisation should possess, and the extent to which the principle of non-intervention should apply to matters within the domestic jurisdiction of states.

II. THE PRINCIPLE OF NON-INTERVENTION IN MATTERS ESSENTIALLY WITHIN THE DOMESTIC JURISDICTION OF STATES UNDER ARTICLE 2(7) OF THE CHARTER OF THE UNITED NATIONS

The task that challenged the architects of the Charter of the United Nations at San Francisco in 1945 was to draw up the constitution of an international organisation whose authority would depend upon the measure of national sovereignty which the nation-states, particularly the great powers, were prepared to forego in order to provide it with the necessary jurisdiction to effectuate such broad purposes as the maintenance of international peace and security, the development of friendly relations among nations based on respect for the principle of equal rights and self-determination of peoples, and the achievement of international co-operation in solving problems, of an economic, social, cultural, or humanitarian character, and in promoting respect for human rights and fundamental freedoms. In brief, they had to formulate a constitution indicating the powers which the member-states would be required to delegate to the new United Nations system, and ensure that the United Nations would not be empowered to intervene in matters which were to remain under the control or within the domestic jurisdiction of the member-states.

The principle of non-intervention in matters essentially within the domestic jurisdiction of member-states of the United Nations, which is stated in Article 2, paragraph 7 of the Charter, has given rise to such conflicting interpretations that it is proposed in this chapter to examine the subject in the light of the discussions which took place at the San Francisco Conference, as well as the great power negotiations at Dumbarton Oaks, near Washington, D.C., which paved the way for that Conference. First of all, however, it is necessary to consider the powers which the founder members of the United Nations decided to delegate to the Organisation to implement its broad purposes.

Powers delegated to the United Nations

For the purpose of maintaining international peace and security, member-states accepted two basic obligations; the obligation to seek a peaceful settlement of situations or disputes likely to endanger the peace, and the obligation to refrain in their international relations from the threat or use of force against the territorial integrity or political independence of any state. Under Chapter VI of the Charter (Pacific Settlement of Disputes), it was thus agreed that if parties to a dispute likely to endanger international peace failed to reach a peaceful settlement of the matter, they should refer it to the Security Council, the organ primarily responsible for the maintenance of international peace and security, and that body was empowered to make recommendations for pacific settlement.

Such recommendations under Chapter VI of the Charter were to have no binding effect on the parties to the dispute, however. The decisions of the Security Council were to be binding on the member states of the United Nations only if they related to measures for the enforcement of the peace under Chapter VII of the Charter, i.e. action with respect to threats to the peace, breaches of the peace, and acts of aggression. Moreover, the Security Council's ability to decide on enforcement measures was made dependent upon the unanimity of its five great power permanent members, for though at San Francisco, after much reluctance on the part of the Soviet Union, the great powers agreed to the principle that a permanent member of the Security Council, party to a dispute to be resolved through pacific methods, should not have the right to veto a recommendation of the Council, they insisted that in all decisions requiring the application of sanctions against a recalcitrant state, a permanent member, whether party to a dispute or not, was to possess the veto. This meant that each of the five great powers on the Security Council was to have the right to block the authorisation of diplomatic, economic, or military sanctions not only against itself, but also against a small state which it cared to sponsor. Indeed, this insistence on the dominant role of the great powers was less marked in the League of Nations system, for under the Covenant of the League it was possible for the Council to recommend sanctions against a great power which committed an act of aggression.[1] In this sense the United Nations system was more closely patterned on the Concert of Europe of the nineteenth century than on the League of Nations system. It should be noted, however, that the fact that the right of individual or collective self-defence was included in the Charter, under its Article 51, was a tacit admission by the architects of the Charter of 'the necessity of relying upon operations and arrangements of the balance of power system for dealing with potential threats of disorder that might be posed by great powers or states acting under their protective wings'.[2]

Unlike the Security Council, which was given the power to take mandatory decisions under Chapter VII of the Charter if approved by its five permanent and any two of its other seven temporary members,[3] the General Assembly of the United Nations, in which each state has one vote and whose resolutions on important questions require a two-thirds majority of the members present and voting, was not given the authority to make any of its decisions binding on United Nations members. Under Article 11(2) of the Charter it was authorised to discuss any question relating to the maintenance of international peace and security, and to make recommendations with regard to any such questions to the state or states concerned, or to the Security Council, or to both, provided they were not being considered by the Council. But the fact that the same article laid down that any such question on which action was necessary should be referred to the Security Council has been interpreted in different ways.[4]

15

It must also be pointed out that those responsible for drawing up the Statute of the International Court of Justice, which was annexed to the Charter, might have decided that all disputes of a judicial nature should come within the compulsory jurisdiction of the Court. On the other hand, they could have left the issue of accepting the jurisdiction or judicial authority of the Court as a purely voluntary act on the part of its signatories when a dispute to which they might be party arose. Actually the Statute of the Court was a compromise. The acceptance of the Court's jurisdiction was left to the discretion of each state in each dispute to which it might be party, and it was made optional for any state, signatory to the Statute, to accept the compulsory jurisdiction of the Court in advance, according to its Article 36, paragraph 2, viz. 'The states, party to the present Statute, may at any time declare that they recognise as compulsory, ipso facto, and without special agreement in relation to any other state accepting the same obligation, the jurisdiction of the Court in all legal disputes concerning (a) the interpretation of a treaty, (b) any question of international law, (c) the existence of any fact, which, if established, would constitute a breach of an international obligation, and (d) the nature or extent of the reparation to be made for the breach of an international obligation.' This was the equivalent of the Optional Clause of the Statute of the Permanent Court instituted under the Covenant of the League of Nations, and it was arranged that the jurisdiction of the International Court should apply to all those declarations that were made accepting the compulsory jurisdiction of the original Court. Although some forty-five states signed the Optional Clause during the history of the Permanent Court, it must be remembered, of course, that their acceptance of the clause was more often than not characterised by a number of reservations which curtailed considerably the measure of compulsory jurisdiction involved, and this was to apply under the new system.

The maintenance of international peace and security was placed as the first purpose of the United Nations in Article I of the Charter. As to the purpose stated in Article 1(2) — 'to develop friendly relations among nations based on respect for the principle of equal rights and self-determination of peoples' — it was laid down in Article 73 of Chapter XI that 'Members of the United Nations which have or assume responsibilities for the administration of territories whose peoples have not yet attained a full measure of self-government recognize the principle that the interests of the inhabitants of these territories are paramount, and accept as a sacred trust the obligation to promote to the utmost, within the system of international peace and security established by the present Charter, the well-being of the inhabitants of these territories . . .', and under paragraph (e) of the same article, 'to transmit regularly to the Secretary-General for information purposes, subject to such limitation as security and constitutional considerations may require, statistical and other information of a technical nature relating to economic, social and educational conditions in the territories for which they are respectively responsible other than those territories to which Chapter XII and XIII apply', i.e. other than those non-self-governing territories under the international trusteeship system of the United Nations. But the administering powers were not obliged to transmit to the Secretary-General information of a political nature indicating the development of self-government within their colonies, and their administration of such territories remained essentially within their domestic jurisdiction. In fact, 'Chapter XI is to be sharply distinguished from Chapters XII and XIII, which relate to the trusteeship system and provide in detail for international accountability and international supervision, but only for those territories placed under trusteeship by special agreement. Chapter XI, by contrast, makes no specific provision for international supervisory machinery; however, it applies to all non-self-governing territories from the time the Charter entered into force'.[5]

In order to implement the purposes of the United Nations stated in Article I(3) of the Charter — 'to achieve international co-operation in solving international problems of an economic, social, cultural, or humanitarian character, and in promoting and encouraging respect for human rights and for fundamental freedoms for all without distinction as to race, sex, language, or religion' — the General Assembly and the Economic and Social Council were authorised to make recommendations of a non-binding character to member-states on such matters.[6] The force of such recommendations are thus essentially of a moral nature, member-states being free to accept or reject them, and it should also be realised that the process of converting moral obligations into international legal commitments under conventions prepared by the General Assembly and the Economic and Social Council, acting under its authority, depends upon the consent of member-states of the United Nations to ratify such conventions.[7]

Some interpreters of the Charter have asserted that its signatories have accepted legal obligations with respect to the implementation of human rights.[8] But while it is true that the revulsion produced by Nazi violations of basic human rights had created a climate of opinion which impelled the drafters of the Charter to require its signatories to pledge themselves to take joint and separate action in co-operation with the United Nations to promote respect for and observance of human rights under Article 56, they made no attempt to define such rights and the measures necessary for their implementation. This was not embarked upon until after the birth of the United Nations when the UN Commission on Human Rights began its work in 1947, and until states have accepted precise legal obligations with respect to such matters through the ratification of international conventions, it is difficult to see how it can be maintained that human rights and fundamental freedoms, as well as economic and social matters not regulated by inter-state treaties, are not within the domestic jurisdiction of states. Certainly, 'there is the strong legal argument to be overcome that since the Charter does not commit Members to respect defined rights and freedoms, there is no basis for saying that a Member has violated a particular right unless it has expressly agreed to respect it'.[9]

In fact, the United Nations, a voluntary association of sovereign states with differing political, economic and social systems, and hence differing concepts of human rights, was intended to function in accordance with the general principle of non-intervention in matters essentially within the domestic jurisdiction of states, the only exception to this general principle being the competence of the Security Council to authorise enforcement measures to maintain or restore international peace, if it decided that a situation arising out of a matter essentially within the domestic jurisdiction of a state constituted a threat to the peace, breach of the peace, or act of aggression under Article 39 of Chapter VII of the Charter. This is laid down in Article 2(7) of the Charter, which is analysed below.

The Principle of Non-intervention

From the above outline of the powers delegated to the organs of the United Nations, it can be seen that 'sovereignty under the Charter must obviously mean sovereignty subject to the provisions of the Charter. It implies that the Member-States are free and sovereign within the limitations imposed upon them by the Charter. It means that they are assumed to have accepted in good faith the obligations of membership and to have delegated to the Organisation the powers that they have expressly delegated; but that the residue of the so called sovereign powers of states still remains with the Member-States themselves'.[10] In fact, to safeguard the powers which were to remain with the member-states of the United Nations, the drafters of the Charter laid down the principle of non-intervention in matters of domestic jurisdiction in Article 2(7), the text of which is as follows: *nothing contained in the present Charter shall authorize the United Nations to intervene in matters which are essentially within the domestic jurisdiction of any state or shall require the Members to submit such matters to settlement under the present Charter; but this principle shall not prejudice the application of enforcement measures under Chapter VII.*

Article 2(7) stemmed from the domestic jurisdiction reservation included in the proposals for a general international organisation agreed to by the four great powers, the United States, Soviet Union, Great Britain and China, at Dumbarton Oaks in 1944. It was stated in paragraph 7, section A, Chapter VIII, the first six paragraphs of which stipulated the procedure to be followed by the Security Council and members of the Organisation in resolving situations that might cause international friction and for the pacific settlement of disputes. Parties to a dispute, the continuance of which was likely to endanger international peace and security, were obliged to submit the matter to the Security Council if they failed to find a solution through pacific methods. But paragraph 7 stated that 'the provisions of paragraphs 1 to 6 of Section A should not apply to situations or disputes arising out of matters which by international law are solely within the domestic jurisdiction of the state concerned'.[11]

The domestic jurisdiction clause in the Dumbarton Oaks proposals was thus designed to limit the authority of the Organisation in the pacific settlement of situations or disputes arising out of a matter solely within the domestic jurisdiction of a state, such as a state's immigration policy not governed by an international treaty. As in Article 15(8) of the Covenant of the League of Nations, it laid down that international law was to be the criterion for testing whether a situation or dispute arose out of a matter within the domestic jurisdiction of a state, but it did not state, as Article 15(8) of the Covenant had done, the organ or authority which was to determine, in accordance with this criterion, whether the situation or dispute was outside the international jurisdiction of the Organisation.

This omission in the Dumbarton Oaks proposal prompted some states to submit amendments to the text agreed to by the four great powers, and prior to the San Francisco Conference Brazil, Czechoslovakia, Ecuador, Greece, Mexico, Peru and Turkey suggested it should be revised so that the International Court of Justice would be the organ to make the decision,[12] and Belgium proposed that 'any state, party to a dispute brought before the Security Council, shall have the right to ask the Court of International Justice whether a recommendation or a decision made by the Council or proposed in it infringes on its essential liberties. If the Court considers that such rights have been disregarded or are threatened, it is for the Council either to reconsider the question or to refer the dispute to the Assembly for discussion'.[13] But Norway took the view that the domestic jurisdiction clause should be deleted on the grounds that 'as long as the procedure instituted by the Security Council is one of pacific settlement of disputes, the party in whose domestic jurisdiction a matter belongs will always have the right to present this plea. Consequently, the original draft affords no real additional protection at this stage. On the other hand, the Security Council should not be prevented from recommending a procedure or method by the mere fact that a matter involved in the dispute or situation belongs in the domestic jurisdiction of a party'.[14]

As a result of preliminary discussions on the line to be taken at San Francisco, the United States delegation also desired changes in the text of the domestic jurisdiction reservation agreed to at Dumbarton Oaks. Congressional opinion in the delegation wanted it to be made clear that in a situation or dispute to be resolved through pacific settlement under Chapter VIII, Section A, of the proposals, a state which was involved should be able to decide the jurisdiction issue. This, it was decided, could be met by widening the domestic jurisdiction reservation through omitting the international law criterion, and substituting the word 'essentially' for 'solely' to describe matters of domestic jurisdiction.[15]

At San Francisco, John Foster Dulles, senior adviser to the United States delegation, defended the use of the word 'essentially' on the ground that if the term 'solely' were retained, the whole effect of the limitation on the authority of the United Nations, which was the purpose of the domestic jurisdiction reservation, would be destroyed. His argument was that although in the modern world matters of domestic jurisdiction were almost always bound to have some international repercussions, or cause some international concern, this was no justification for saying that such matters should be regarded as outside the domestic jurisdiction of states. Through the use of the term 'essentially', then, the United States delegation hoped to make the domestic jurisdiction clause apply to a much wider field of domestic matters, for though its members considered that international co-operation through the General Assembly and the Economic and Social Council was essential to promote economic and social progress and the implementation of human rights, they did not want those organs, in Dulles's words, 'to penetrate into the economic and social life of the member-states'.[16]

The British delegation also believed that there should be changes in the text of the domestic jurisdiction reservation agreed to by the four great powers at the Dumbarton Oaks meetings. Prior to the San Francisco discussions in Committee I of Commission I, which dealt with the drafting of the clause, Britain proposed to the other great powers that the Dumbarton Oaks clause (paragraph 7, Section A, Chapter VIII) should be replaced by the following provisions, which might ultimately form a separate chapter in the Charter.[17]

(1) The Charter should not confer the right on any member of the United Nations to require that a dispute or situation arising out of matters which by International Law are solely within the domestic jurisdiction of the State concerned should be submitted to the means of settlement mentioned in Section A(3).[18] Should, however, such a situation or dispute constitute a threat to the maintenance of international peace or security, or should a breach of the peace occur in consequence of such a situation or dispute, it should be open to the Security Council, acting in accordance with Section B,[19] to take such action as it may deem appropriate.

(2) The question whether a particular dispute or situation does arise out of matters which by International Law are solely within the domestic jurisdiction of the State concerned should be decided, if necessary, by the body to which it is sought to submit the dispute or situation.

This British amendment, together with a United States amendment which stated that 'the provisions of paragraph 1 to 6 of Section A should not apply to situations or disputes arising out of matters which are within the domestic jurisdiction of the state concerned' — an amendment which omitted the reference to 'international law' and the word 'solely' — was referred to a sub-committee of the four powers to produce a redraft of the domestic jurisdiction reservation. On that committee were Mr Dulles (United States), Sir William Malkin (United Kingdom), Mr Golunsky (Soviet Union), and Mr Wang Chia-chen (China), and as a result of their discussions they produced a formula on which they could all agree except for one point, viz. whether or not the international law criterion should be included. The representatives of the United States and the Soviet Union on the committee were opposed to its inclusion, those of Great Britain and China wanted its retention. Consequently, the words 'by international law' were placed in parentheses in the text when it was submitted to the delegations of the four powers under the leadership of Mr Stettinius (United States), M. Molotov (Soviet Union), Mr Eden (Great Britain), and Dr Soong (China). The redraft read as follows:

> Nothing contained in this Charter shall authorize the Organization to interfere with matters which (*by international law*) are essentially within the domestic jurisdiction of the State concerned or shall require the members to submit such matters to settlement under this Charter. Should, however, a situation or dispute arising out of such a matter assume an international character and constitute a threat to the maintenance of international peace or security, or should a breach of the peace occur in consequence of such a situation or dispute, it shall be open to the Security Council, acting in accordance with Chapter VIII, Section B, to take such action as it may deem necessary.[20]

Mr Dulles, who reported to the four powers on this redraft, stated that the subcommittee 'had agreed that the exception for domestic jurisdiction should cover not only the peaceful settlement of disputes, but should apply to the whole Charter except for threats to the peace, breaches of the peace and action with respect thereto'. As to the question of including the words 'by international law', 'the United Kingdom and China were inclined to include them, but the U.S.S.R. and U.S. representatives on the sub-committee had preferred to exclude them due to the difficulty of establishing when a matter is by international law under domestic jurisdiction'.[21] But after further discussions by the leaders of the four delegations this was resolved when Great Britain and China conceded to the Soviet Union and the United States on the question, and subsequent redrafting produced a shorter paragraph which became known as the sponsoring powers' amendment, which read as follows:

Nothing contained in this Charter shall authorise the Organization to intervene in matters which are essentially within the domestic jurisdiction of the state concerned or shall require the members to submit such matters to settlement under this Charter; but this principle shall not prejudice the application of Chapter VII, Section B.[22]

The main differences between this version and the original Dumbarton Oaks proposal may now be summarised.

(i) It did not refer to matters *solely* but *essentially* within the domestic jurisdiction of the state concerned. The reason for this change has already been explained.

(ii) The reference to *international law* as the criterion for determining whether or not a matter fell essentially within the domestic jurisdiction of a state, which had been included in the Dumbarton Oaks proposal, was not in the new version. Nor did it include any reference to the organ or authority that should determine the matter.

(iii) The new version involved the transference of the domestic jurisdiction clause from paragraph 7, Section A, Chapter VIII of the Dumbarton Oaks proposals, which dealt with the Pacific Settlement of Disputes, to paragraph 8 of Chapter II, which listed the principles of the Organisation. This modification, which was inspired by the United States, stemmed from the 'fear of the United States Government that under the expanded powers given the United Nations in the economic and social fields, the United Nations might interfere in matters that had been traditionally regarded as within the exclusive jurisdiction of states. This attitude no doubt reflected uncertainty over what might be the Senate attitude toward the Charter, in view of earlier Senate opposition to the League Covenant, if United States domestic jurisdiction in such matters as immigration, tariffs and civil rights was not protected'.[23] This is also made abundantly clear in Russell and Muther's account of the role of the United States at the San Francisco Conference.[24]

The purpose of transferring the domestic jurisdiction clause to the chapter on Principles was to make all the activities of the United Nations organs, not simply the pacific settlement of disputes, subject to the principle of non-intervention, and the only exception to this general rule was the competence of the Security Council under Chapter VIII, Section B, to authorise measures to maintain or restore international peace and security, should that body determine the existence of any threat to the peace, breach of the peace, or act of aggression arising out of a matter essentially within the domestic jurisdiction of a state. But it should be remembered that the Security Council could only make such decisions through the affirmative votes of 7 out of its 11 members, including the concurring votes of its five permanent members.

(iv) What was confusing about the new version was the use of the term *to intervene* in the first part of the paragraph. The words *to interfere* had been used in the early stage of drafting the sponsoring powers' amendment,[25] and this term did not have the same technical connotation as the term *to intervene*. As defined by Sir H. Lauterpacht, *intervention* 'is a technical term of, on the whole, unequivocal connotation. It signifies dictatorial interference in the sense of action amounting to the denial of the independence of the state. It involves a peremptory demand for positive conduct or abstention — a demand, which, if not complied with, involves a threat of, or recourse to compulsion, though not necessarily physical compulsion, in some form'.[26]

If this was what was meant by *intervention* in the sponsoring powers' amendment, United Nations organs would be prohibited, under the general rule of non-intervention stated in the first part of the article, from making dictatorial demands involving the threat to or recourse to some form of compulsion on member-states, but still competent to discuss and investigate matters essentially within the domestic jurisdiction of states, in order to make recommendations of a non-binding nature on such matters, including recommendations for the pacific settlement of situations or disputes that might arise out of them. But this does not appear to have been the intention of the four powers. In transferring the domestic jurisdiction reservation to Chapter II on Principles, the principle of non-intervention was to apply to all the operations of the organs of the Organisation except those of the Security Council when dealing with threats to the peace or breaches of the peace arising out of matters essentially within the domestic jurisdiction of states, and hence to the non-mandatory recommendations of the Security Council and the General Assembly in the pacific settlement of disputes, as well as to the resolutions and recommendations of the General Assembly and Economic and Social Council on a state's policies on economic and social matters, including human rights. It is logical to infer, therefore, that by *non-intervention* under the general rule of the article its drafters meant *no interference in any form*, as some interpreters of the article have suggested.[27] It is not without significance that in the four-power consultations to which reference has been made, 'Senator Vandenberg commented that under the new text, a state has a larger option to reserve domestic jurisdiction', and that another member of the United States delegation, Mr Pasvolksy, 'added that in the new form and location it applied even to Assembly discussion',[28] and this was not challenged by any member of the other delegations, Moreover, subsequent discussions in Committee 1 of Commission I at San Francisco, which was responsible for the final drafting of the article, reinforces this interpretation.

Committee I of Commission I Discussions

At the eighth of Committee I/1 on 17 May 1945, the Norwegian delegate reiterated the view of his government that the provision of an article on the principle of non-intervention in matters of domestic jurisdiction should be dropped. He considered that there was no reason why the Security Council should be debarred from passing recommendations for the pacific settlement of situations or disputes that might arise out of such matters.[29] On the other hand, since the Australian delegate, Dr Evatt, feared that this was still implicit in the sponsoring powers' amendment, he wanted it modified.

Dr Evatt contended that the first part of the sponsoring powers' amendment — 'Nothing contained in this Charter shall authorise the Organisation to intervene in matters essentially within the domestic jurisdiction of any state[30] or shall require members to submit such matters to settlement under this Charter' — was undone by what was stated in the second part — 'but this principle shall not prejudice the application of Chapter VIII, Section B', on the ground that since paragraph 2 of Section B stated that 'in general the Security Council should determine the existence of any threat to the peace, breach of the peace or act of aggression and should make recommendations or decide upon measures to be taken to maintain or restore peace and security', the Council would still be able to recommend terms of a settlement with respect to a dispute arising out of a matter within the domestic jurisdiction of a state.[31]

In a memorandum on the subject, Dr Evatt stated the Australian position in the following terms:

> Such a provision is almost an invitation to use or threaten force, in any dispute arising out of a matter of domestic jurisdiction, in the hope of inducing the Security Council to extort concessions from the state that is threatened. Broadly, the exception cancels out the rule, whenever an aggressor threatens to use force. This freedom of action which international law has always recognised in matters of domestic jurisdiction becomes subject in effect to the full jurisdiction of the Security Council.
>
> The Australian delegation opposes the inclusion in the Charter of any provision which produces this result. Our grounds are in no way peculiar to Australia itself. Every country represented in this Conference has its own internal problems, its own vital spheres of domestic policy, in which it cannot without forfeiting its very

existence as a state permit external intervention.

I assert that the sponsoring governments would not themselves have included in the Charter this principle of general intervention, had it not been for one significant fact. The Charter reserves to each of them an individual veto on action by the Council under Chapter VIII, Section B. They can therefore assure their legislatures that these drastic powers of intervention in domestic matters can never be put into operation against themselves. What is the position however of the remaining members of the Organisation — those 45 members who have no veto? The very argument which justifies acceptance of this proposed paragraph by the sponsoring governments destroys the case for its acceptance by the rest.[32]

Dr Evatt thus proposed that the clause, 'but this principle shall not prejudice the application of Chapter VIII, Section B', should be amended to read, 'but this principle shall not prejudice the application of enforcement measures under Chapter VIII, Section B', so that the Security Council would be prohibited from recommending terms for the settlement of a dispute arising out of a matter essentially within the domestic jurisdiction of a state, even though it had determined that a threat to the peace existed. Its action would then be limited to enforcement measures against the aggressive state.

The French delegate argued that acceptance of the Australian amendment would not allow the Security Council to intervene at the time when it should intervene. 'It can, according to this provision,' he maintained, 'intervene only when a situation is too far advanced to make such intervention really effective in preventing aggression, and it is for this reason that we cannot support the amendment.'[33] The Chinese delegate also felt that it was wrong to limit the authority of the Security Council to enforcement measures only. 'A threat to the peace may lead to a breach of the peace, and a breach of the peace may lead to acts of aggression. Recommendations may, therefore, very well precede enforcement measures, which, after all, should only be taken as a last resort. Prevention is better than cure.'[34] But to this criticism the Australian delegate, who was very anxious that there should be no interference of any kind in his country's immigration policy, and reflected the sensitivity of most delegates towards any encroachments by the Organisation in matters essentially within the domestic jurisdiction of their states, replied: 'Now why should a country's right, recognised by everybody, in that respect be prejudiced merely because a country with a demand which, in its initial stage, is wrong, follows up that demand with force or threat of force.'[35]

The Australian amendment was approved by 31 votes to 3, with 5 delegates abstaining and 11 making no response. This indicated, therefore, that there was very substantial support for the view that recommendations by the Security Council, whether under Chapter VIII, Section A, which dealt with the pacific settlement of disputes, or under Chapter VIII, Section B, which dealt with action with respect to threats to the peace, breaches of the peace, and acts of aggression, even though they were not intended to be binding on the states to whom they might be addressed,[36] should not be permitted by the United Nations in situations or disputes arising out of matters essentially within the domestic jurisdiction of states. Moreover, since the general rule of non-intervention was intended to apply to all organs of the United Nations in the sponsoring powers' amendment, it would apply to the non-mandatory recommendations of the General Assembly in the pacific settlement of disputes.

The approval of the Australian amendment by Committee I/1 meant that the text of the sponsoring powers' amendment was revised to read as follows:

> Nothing contained in this Charter shall authorize the Organisation to intervene in matters which are essentially within the domestic jurisdiction of any state or shall require the members to submit such matters to settlement under this Charter; but this principle shall not prejudice the application of enforcement measures under Chapter VIII, Section B.

This amendment, and other amendments which called for the inclusion of the international law criterion, the naming of the organ or authority that should determine whether or not a matter was essentially within the domestic jurisdiction of a state, as well as an amendment to substitute 'solely' for 'essentially' to describe matters of domestic jurisdiction, were debated in Committee I/1 at its seventeenth and final meeting on 14 June, 1945.

As the spokesman for the sponsoring powers' amendment, John Foster Dulles gave an explanation of its basic concept of non-intervention. 'I want first to make it clear, if I may, that we are dealing now with a principle, not with some technical rule of law dealing with international disputes,' he stated. 'The language of this principle is in some respects similar to the language which was found in the Covenant of the League of Nations, Article 15, and in the original Dumbarton Oaks Proposals. But in both the League of Nations Covenant and in the original Dumbarton Oaks Proposals, the language was that of a rather technical legalistic formula designed to deal with a specific subject matter, namely the settlement of disputes by the Council. The present Four-Power amendment puts the matter in a totally different aspect, and presents a new and basic principle governing the entire Organisation: that the Organisation, in none of its branches, in none of its organs, shall intervene in what is essentially the domestic life of the member States.' This had been necessary, he explained, because they were building at San Francisco an organisation which was quite different in character from the League of Nations, and indeed, from that which had been planned at Dumbarton Oaks. The difference, he added, was primarily the fact that the Organisation they were building was one which was going to have functions which they believed would enable it to eradicate the causes of war, and not simply to deal with international disputes after they had arisen. But having explained this point, Dulles was anxious to make it clear that though this would involve inter-governmental economic and social co-operation through the United Nations, this did not mean that the organs of the United Nations would be permitted 'to penetrate into the economic and social life of the member-states'. It was for this reason, he asserted, that the principle of non-intervention in matters essentially within the domestic jurisdiction of states had been laid down in the sponsoring powers' amendment as a broad directive.[37]

This statement implied, as has already been inferred from the four power consultations which had preceded the discussions in Committee I/1, that the term 'to intervene' was not be interpreted in its traditional legal sense as defined by Lauterpacht, but rather as meaning 'interference in any form'. As already explained, it had been made clear that recommendations for the pacific settlement of disputes arising out of matters essentially within the domestic jurisdiction of states would be outside the competence of the United Nations, even though they were of a non-binding character. In the light of Mr. Dulles's speech, too, it may be inferred that although the sponsoring powers looked forward to inter-governmental co-operation in solving problems of an economic and social nature through the work of the Assembly and the Economic and Social Council, they were opposed to any form of interference by those organs in the economic and social policies of states. It is reasonable to conclude, therefore, that whilst they intended that the Assembly and Economic and Social Council should function within their terms of reference by discussing economic and social matters, and addressing recommendations on such issues generally to member-states for their guidance, in order to facilitate international economic and social co-operation, they did not intend that those organs should hold discussions, institute investigations, and pass recommendations on the economic and social policies of a particular state, which would embarrass it through some form of censure or urge it to take action to effect a pacific settlement of an international dispute arising out of a matter which it regarded as a domestic question. The only exception to the general rule of non-intervention or non-interference was the Security Council's competence to authorise enforcement measures against a state, if the Council decided that a situation arising out of an economic or social matter within that state's jurisdiction, or any other matter of domestic jurisdiction, constituted a threat to or breach of international peace and security.

Mr Dulles met with no criticism because the sponsoring powers' amendment had included the domestic jurisdiction reservation as a principle in the United Nations Charter. But there was criticism of the amendment because it did not state (i) how a matter essentially within the domestic jurisdiction of a state was to be defined, and (ii) who was to be responsible for the definition. As to the question of including a reference to international law as the criterion for determinating whether or not a matter was one within domestic or international jurisdiction, which several delegates had called for, Mr. Dulles dismissed this in somewhat disparaging terms. He seemed to fear that its inclusion would lead to the erroneous belief that every subject dealt with by the United Nations would no longer be a matter of domestic jurisdiction on the grounds that the Charter would be a treaty which made international law, with the consequent danger that the whole purpose of the principle of non-intervention would be done away with. Moreover, in defence of the omission in the sponsoring powers' text of any reference to what authority should determine the issue of jurisdiction, Dulles maintained that it would not be an effective limitation on the United Nations in such matters if it were left to the Organisation to decide. As to the question being decided by the International Court of Justice, he contended that it was 'not practicable to provide, certainly in regard to nations who do not accept the compulsory clause, that the jurisdiction of the Court should be compulsory on them'.[38]

The truth was that after Dumbarton Oaks the United States and the Soviet Union had had second thoughts about the desirability of inserting the international law criterion in the domestic jurisdiction reservation. Mr Dulles, like other American officials, had run into 'the problem of traditional congressional fear that an international organisation might presume 'to dictate' to the United States on any question that it considered should not be within the purview of the agency. For this reason American officials sought at San Francisco to make the domestic jurisdiction reservation subject to the interpretation of the state concerned, rather than to the conventional standard of international law (and hence to interpretation by the Court) . . . The Soviet Union also wished the right to its own interpretation of domestic jurisdiction. This was in line with wartime Soviet insistence that its controversies with neighbouring countries were subject only to direct settlement with them'.[39]

An amendment submitted by the Greek delegate in the final meeting of Committee I/1, which urged that 'it should be left to the International Court of Justice at the request of a party to decide whether or not such situation or dispute arises out of a matter that under international law falls within the domestic jurisdiction of the state concerned', was carried by 17 votes to 14, but it failed to get the required two-thirds majority.[40] Before the vote was taken Mr Dulles intervened to assert that its approval would be tantamount to the acceptance by states of the compulsory jurisdiction of the Court. 'There are a thousand questions to every paragraph of our Charter,' he maintained, 'where the question can be raised if a dispute arises — who will settle it? And when you take all of those and roll them together, Mr. Chairman, you have the problem which the Judiciary Committee has been wrestling with throughout the life of this Conference. And they have come to the conclusion that at the present state of world development it is not possible to say that all of these questions will be referred to the World Court for settlement. It has left that for each state to determine for itself. As I pointed out before, there are a number of states who have accepted the compulsory jurisdiction clause. In the case of those states, the World Court will decide. The Council, the Assembly, the Economic and Social Council can get advisory opinions from the World Court whenever they feel that they are in doubt. Conceivably that leaves that area in this matter as it exists in almost every other matter, where differences can conceivably arise without any agreed method of settlement by the World Court. But I am very much afraid that it is not possible in this particular case, any more than in other cases, to introduce in effect the principle of compulsory jurisdiction of the World Court which another branch of this Conference after very thorough consideration has found it necessary to reject.'[41]

The Belgian delegate put forward several amendments to modify the sponsoring powers' text. His main purpose was to effect changes in the general rule of non-intervention in the first part of the article. Instead of 'Nothing contained in this Charter shall authorize the Organisation to intervene in matters which are essentially within the domestic jurisdiction of any state or shall require the members to submit such matters to settlement under this Charter', he wanted it to read as follows: 'Nothing contained in this Charter shall authorize the Organization to intervene in matters which *in the judgment of the Organization are according to international law exclusively (or solely)* within the domestic jurisdiction of any state or shall require the members to submit such matters to settlement under this Charter'. The underlined words indicate that his proposals involved three amendments to the sponsoring powers' text, but all three were defeated. Thus the text of the sponsoring powers' amendment, apart from the change which had been made to the exception stated in the second part of the article through the acceptance of the Australian amendment, remained unchanged. It was approved in Committee I/ 1 by 33 votes to 4,[42] and subsequently accepted by the Conference as Article 2(7) of the Charter.

Conflicting Interpretations of Article 2(7)

It is important to realise that there was nothing in the adopted text to indicate which organ or authority was to determine whether or not a matter was essentially within the domestic jurisdiction of a state, and this, together with the fact that the criterion of international law was also omitted, conspired to make it a subject of controversial interpretation. Besides, although it is reasonably clear, in the light of the San Francisco discussions, that the term 'non-intervention' was intended to mean 'no interference in any form', it was perhaps inevitable that controversy over this would arise because the full implications of the term were not stated in precise terms.

Goodrich and Hambro have maintained that 'while discussion does not amount to intervention, the creation of a commission of inquiry, the making of a recommendation of a procedural or substantive nature or the taking of a binding decision constitutes intervention under the terms of the paragraph'.[43] On the other hand, as already mentioned, Sir H. Lauterpacht has asserted that the passing of recommendations on matters of domestic jurisdiction does not amount to intervention. Since he contends that *intervention* is used in a strictly traditional legal sense in Article 2(7), he infers that the principle of non-intervention 'does not exclude on the part of the organs of the United Nations procedures of investigation, study, report and recommendations, seeing that they do not amount to intervention in the accepted legal connotation'.[44] According to Lauterpacht, therefore, United Nations organs are competent to address recommendations not only to states generally, but also to individual states, on matters of domestic jurisdiction, since such recommendations do not involve a threat to or recourse to compulsion in some form, if they are not complied with.

M.S. Rajan has described the Goodrich and Hambro interpretation as a 'static' one, which, if followed, would not enable the United Nations to advance the broad purposes of the Charter. 'It does not seem to attach any importance to the needs of the changing conditions of international society and is content to make a literal and restrictive interpretation of the provisions of the Charter,' he asserts. 'It has essentially a negative and static approach.' In contrast, Rajan points out, 'the Lauterpacht theory of interpretation claims to be based on general principles of international law. Its dominant purpose is to effectuate the broad purposes and functions of the United Nations according to the changing needs and conditions of international society. It also seeks to minimize the effects of indifferent or faulty drafting of the provisions of the Charter to the extent of giving meaning and purpose to ostensibly conflicting terms of some of the Charter provisions. Its approach is essentially positive and dynamic. It is therefore appropriate to call it the dynamic theory of interpretation of the term'.[45]

The interpretation of Article 2(7) in this study differs from the so-called 'dynamic' and 'static' interpretations. In the light of the discussions at San Francisco, it appears that it was the intention of those who drafted Article 2(7) that whilst United Nations organs should function within their terms of reference by discussing matters within the domestic jurisdiction of states with a view to addressing recommendations generally to member-states, in order to further inter-governmental co-operation in the political, economic, social and cultural fields, they did not intend that those organs should authorise procedures of investigation into the domestic policies of any state, or make recommendations on such matters to a particular state, which would cause embarrassment to it through expressing some form of censure or calling for some form of action.[46] In fact, it was not intended that a state's domestic policies should be discussed in United Nations organs, even though it would be obviously difficult for a United Nations organ to decide, without discussion, whether or not some matters were essentially within the domestic jurisdiction of states. Nevertheless, the discussions at San Francisco point to that conclusion, and reflect the desire of the majority of powers to make the domestic jurisdiction reservation subject to the interpretation of the sovereign state. Certainly they were opposed to the inclusion of any reference in Article 2(7) as to how and by whom matters essentially within the domestic jurisdiction of states should be defined.

In brief, it was the evident intention of those who drafted Article 2(7) of the Charter that the United Nations should observe a strict policy of non-interference in matters traditionally regarded as within the domestic juris-diction of states, such as a state's form of government,[47] the treatment of its own subjects, which covers the entire field of human rights: in the absence of international treaties, its economic policies and questions of immigration and nationality: the size of its national armaments and armed forces: internal conflicts within its territory: and its administration of non-self-governing territories, if any, not placed under the trusteeship system of the United Nations. The only exception to this general principle of non-interference in matters of domestic jurisdiction which they intended was the competence given to the Security Council to authorise enforcement measures to maintain or restore international peace and security, if it deter-mined that a situation or dispute arising out of a matter essentially within the domestic jurisdiction of a state constituted a threat to the peace, breach of the peace, or act of aggression.

As already explained, the Security Council's competence, under this exception to the general principle of non-interference, was specifically restricted to the authorisation of enforcement measures to maintain or restore international peace and security in order to emphasise that it did not possess the authority to make recommendations or decide upon the terms of a settlement of a dispute arising out of a matter essentially within the domestic jurisdiction of a state. It was feared that unless this was made clear a state would be tempted to use or threaten the use of force against another state in any situation or dispute that arose out of a matter of domestic jurisdiction, in the hope of inducing the Security Council to extort concessions from the state that was threatened or attacked.

It should be understood, therefore, that the competence of the UN Security Council under the exception to Article 2(7) differs from Glad-stone's concept of the Concert of Europe as an instrument for the enforce-ment of reforms on a state that grossly violated the basic human rights of its subjects; for whereas Gladstone believed that the Concert of Europe should have possessed the competence to intervene with force to secure justice for oppressed peoples, those who drafted Article 2(7) of the Charter considered that the Security Council should possess the competence to authorise enforcement measures to maintain or restore international peace and security if the situation arising our of a matter essentially within the domestic jurisdiction of a state constituted a threat to the peace, breach of the peace, or act of aggression.

It should be appreciated that though the term 'threat to the peace' was not defined in the Charter, the Security Council was given the competence to decide whether a 'threat to the peace' existed under Article 39 of the Charter. It was thus given the loop-hole to decide that a situation of international tension arising out of a matter essentially within the domestic jurisdiction of a state, such as might arise from a state's violation of human rights or discriminatory immigration practices, constituted a threat to international peace and security, even though the state judged guilty of such practices had not used or threatened to use force against another state, or employed other measures to undermine its territorial integrity or political independence, in contravention of Article 2(4) of the Charter.[48]

In this connection it should be noted that Committee IV(2) at the San Francisco Conference, which dealt with legal problems, anticipated that difficulties over the interpretation of the Charter would be bound to arise in United Nations practice. Consequently, it declared that 'in the course of the operations from day to day of the various organs of the Organization, it is inevitable that each organ will interpret such parts of the Charter as are applicable to its particular functions. This process is inherent in the functioning of any body which operates under an instrument defining its functions and powers. It will be manifested in the functioning of such a body as the General Assembly, the Security Council, or the International Court of Justice. Accordingly, it is not necessary to include in the Charter a provision either authorizing or approving the normal operation of this principle'.[49] This view, which was adopted by the Conference, thus gave the organs of the United Nations the loop-hole to assert their competence to decide whether or not a question was precluded from their consideration under Article 2(7) of the Charter, and to adopt resolutions on matters claimed by states as matters essentially within their domestic jurisdiction, contrary to the intentions of those who drafted the non-intervention principle.

The purpose of subsequent chapters in this study is to present what conclusions may be drawn from the practice of United Nations organs in relation to the principle of non-intervention in matters essentially within the domestic jurisdiction of states. We shall need to consider, therefore, how far they have observed or departed from the general principle of non-interference which was the evident intention of those who drafted Article 2(7) of the Charter, their interpretation and application of the exception to that general principle, and the impact of their decisions on the development of the United Nations.

III. THE APPLICATION OF THE NON-INTERVENTION PRIN-
CIPLE IN CASES OF ALLEGED VIOLATIONS OF HUMAN
RIGHTS

The revulsion caused by the flagrant violation of human rights by the
Nazi regime, before and during the Second World War, resulted in a wide-
spread feeling that the essential rights of the individual, such as freedom
from arbitrary arrest, the right to a fair trial, freedom from torture, and
freedom of speech, should be internationally protected. It was not
surprising, therefore, at the San Francisco Conference in 1945, that several
delegations put forward proposals for the inclusion of provisions concerning specific human rights in the Charter of the United Nations, so that
states signatory to it would assume definite legal obligations to treat
persons under their rule with respect for such rights.[1] But these proposals
were not accepted. Committee I/1, which drafted the Preamble, Purposes
and Principles of Chapter I of the Charter, received the proposals with
sympathy, but decided that the Conference, if only for lack of time, could
not proceed to draft an international bill of human rights for inclusion in
the Charter. It was felt that the United Nations, once formed, could better
proceed to consider the suggestion and to deal effectively with it through a
special commission or by some other method, and the Committee recommended that the General Assembly of the projected Organisation should
consider the matter and give it effect.[2] It was agreed at San Francisco,
however, that the Charter should contain various articles affirming that the
United Nations should seek to promote and encourage respect for human
rights and fundamental freedoms without defining them, and this purpose
was included in Article 1(3) of the Charter. This was reiterated in Article
55(c) in Chapter IX (International Economic and Social Co-operation),
viz. *With a view to the creation of conditions of stability and well-being
which are necessary for peaceful and friendly relations among nations
based on the respect for the principle of equal rights and self-determination of peoples, the United Nations shall promote ... universal
respect for, and observance of, human rights and fundamental freedoms
for all without distinction as to race, sex, language, or religion,* and in
Article 56 it was laid down that *All Members pledge themselves to take
joint and separate action in co-operation with the Organization for the
achievement of the purposes set forth in Article 55.*
There were some misgivings at San Francisco that the pledge required of
signatories to the Charter, under Article 56, to take not only joint but
separate action to promote respect for human rights, was in the nature of a
direct obligation which would remove a state's treatment of its own
subjects from the sphere of domestic jurisdiction. If the pledge involved
this, it was feared, the United Nations would be competent to intervene in
questions concerning human rights which most states regarded as essen-

tially within their domestic jurisdiction, and in order to remove all possible doubts about this, Committee II/3, which dealt with the question of economic and social co-operation under Chapter IX of the Dumbarton Oaks Proposals (Chapter IX and X of the Charter), including the promotion of human rights, agreed to insert in its records the following statement: *The members of Committee 3 of Commission II are in full agreement that nothing contained in Chapter IX (Chapter IX and X of the Charter) can be construed as giving authority to the Organisation to intervene in the domestic affairs of member states.*[3] Moreover, this was also made clear in the discussions that led to the drafting of Article 2, paragraph 7, of the Charter by Committee I/1 at San Francisco, as explained in the previous chapter. The principle of non-intervention in matters essentially within the domestic jurisdiction of states was intended to prevent the United Nations from interfering in any form in the economic and social policies of states, and in human-rights questions relating to their own subjects.

Moreover, it is difficult to see how the Security Council could justifiably determine that a state's violation of human rights of its own nationals constituted a threat to international peace and security, and authorise enforcement measures in accordance with the exception to the general principle of non-intervention in matters essentially within the domestic jurisdiction of states under Article 2(7) of the Charter, if the state considered guilty of such practices had not used or threatened to use force against another state, or sought to undermine its territorial integrity or political independence in some other way.

The fact is that the UN was not conceived as an instrument for the enforcement of human rights, and membership of the Organisation did not involve the acceptance by states of precise legal obligations in respect of the human rights of their subjects. It is true that UN members have pledged themselves to take joint and separate action in co-operation with the Organisation to achieve the purpose set forth in Article 55 of the Charter, viz. the promotion of universal respect for, and observance of, human rights and fundamental freedoms for all without distinction as to race, sex, language, or religion. But what this means, in effect, is that they have promised to adopt a co-operative attitude towards the non-binding recommendations of the UN Assembly and Economic and Social Council whose terms of reference in respect of human rights were defined in the following articles of the Charter.

Article 13(1b):
The General Assembly shall initiate studies and make recommendations for the purpose of ... promoting international co-operation in the economic, social, cultural, educational, and health fields, and assisting in the realization of human rights and funda-

mental freedoms for all without distinction as to race, sex, language, or religion.

Article 62 (2&3)

The Economic and Social Council . . .

2. It may make recommendations for the purpose of promoting respect for, and observance of, human rights and fundamental freedoms for all.

3. It may prepare draft conventions for submission to the General Assembly, with respect to matters falling within its competence.

Article 68:

The Economic and Social Council shall set up commissions in economic and social fields for the promotion of human rights, and such other commissions as may be required for the performance of its functions.

The drafters of the Charter thus intended that a special commission should be appointed by the Economic and Social Council to discuss and report on the best way to promote respect for, and obervance of, human rights and fundamental freedoms, and that when the Council had approved the recommendations of the commission, they should be considered and voted upon by the Assembly.

The Commission on Human Rights, which began its work in January 1947, envisaged an international bill of human rights in three parts; a declaration proclaiming general principles, the force of which would be essentially of a moral nature: a covenant, or covenants, embodying these principles which would become legally binding on states that ratified them; and measures to implement the covenant or covenants through international machinery.[4] The first part of this programme was completed when the Assembly, by a vote of 48 to 0, with 8 abstentions, approved the Universal Declaration of Human Rights on 10 December 1948.[5] Its articles consisted of individual civil and political rights, such as freedom of speech, freedom from arbitrary arrest, and the right of the individual to take part in the government of his country, directly or through freely chosen representatives, and such economic and social rights as a person's right to work and education. Proclaimed by the Assembly as 'a common standard of achievement for all peoples and all nations', it was intended as a general appeal to the conscience of rulers. But, as the Commission on Human Rights had emphasised in its report, it was not a treaty which imposed legal obligations on states, and this was reiterated by the President of the General Assembly, who said that 'the Declaration only marked a first step, since it was not a convention by which states would be bound to carry out and give effect to the fundamental human rights, nor would it provide for enforcement; yet it was a step forward in a great evolutionary process'.[6]

Only the representatives of a few states — Belgium, France, Lebanon, Panama and Chile — maintained that the Universal Declaration had a legal force, and even then not without some reservations.[7] As Castaneda has pointed out, 'the prevailing opinion is that the great majority who participated in its drafting did not intend to create a binding document, that is, to impose on states the international legal obligation to respect and guarantee the rights expressed in the Declaration, so that the states that violated them would incur an international responsibility'.[8] Indeed, the very fact that after adopting the Universal Declaration, the Assembly requested the Economic and Social Council to ask the Commission on Human Rights to prepare draft covenants on civil and political rights, and economic, social, and cultural rights, which would become legally binding on states that ratified them, substantiates the view that the force of the Universal Declaration was essentially of a moral, not a legal nature. So, too, does the fact that the General Assembly and the UN specialised agencies adopted and opened for signature and ratification a number of international conventions relating to human rights mentioned in the Declaration, such as the Convention on the Political Rights of Women in 1952. Consequently, even after the adoption of the Declaration, unless states voluntarily bound themselves to respect and observe human rights through ratifying treaties, or conventions, or the international covenants on human rights approved by the Assembly in 1966,[9] they were still legally justified in claiming that questions involving the treatment of their subjects, which covered the entire field of human rights, were essentially within their domestic jurisdiction, to which the principle of non-intervention under Article 2(7) should apply.

This is likely to be the position within the foreseeable future, for many UN members who have ratified particular conventions have done so only with important reservations, and the large majority of states have shown reluctance to ratify the comprehensive international covenants on human rights approved by the Assembly.[10] Besides, 'ratification apart, the implementation measures in most of the conventions (other than those of the I.L.O.) are of limited significance. Some provide none; others, only governmental reporting. None provides a mandatory right of an individual to make a complaint'.[11] And, as explained below, in the covenants on human rights approved by the Assembly no provision is made for an international organ to override the authority of the supreme organs of each state.

In the International Covenant on Economic, Social and Cultural Rights it is recognised that the implementation of such rights must be a long term objective for most states, and the only measure of implementation which it provides is the requirement that states which ratify it must submit progress reports to the Economic and Social Council. And though provision is made in the International Covenant on Civil and Political Rights for the states that ratify it to elect a Human Rights Committee, that body is not given the power to authorise sanctions against a state which violates any of the rights stipulated in the Covenant. All the Committee is permitted to do is to consider periodic reports submitted by the states-parties and address comments to those states and the Economic and Social Council, and to help to effect a settlement of one state's complaint against another state on a human rights issue, if both states agree in advance to such a procedure. If a settlement is not reached, the Committee would confine its report to a brief statement of the facts, and attach to the report the written sub-missions and record of the oral submissions made by the states concerned. This, too, would be the procedure adopted if the Committee set up a conciliation commission to help the disputants to find an amicable solution of the matter, except that the commission's report would include its views on the possibilities of a reasonable settlement.

No provision is thus made in the Covenant on Civil and Political Rights for the reference of a human rights dispute between states to an inter-national court, as provided for under the European Convention on Human Rights. Moreover, only if states ratify the Optional Protocol to the Inter-national Covenant on Civil and Political Rights would the Human Rights Committee be competent to consider complaints from private individuals claiming to be victims of a violation of human rights included in the Covenant, and in such cases all that the Committee could do would be to forward its views to the state party concerned and the individual complainant.

Clearly, under the International Covenants each state that ratifies them has the final word in human rights questions, and no international organ would be able to override the authority of the supreme organs in each state. Even so, the international procedures under the Covenants provide the UN with some scope to expose violations of human rights by those states that ratify them, and it is possible that states will do something to modify their domestic policies in the field of human rights if they are likely to incur the moral condemnation of world opinion for transgressing covenants which they have voluntarily ratified.

But though UN organs have recognised that states are not bound by legal obligations in respect of human rights unless they have voluntarily ratified international conventions or covenants on such matters, they have never-theless interfered in human rights questions with regard to which states have not accepted such obligations. Indeed, there have been several instances in which states accused of violating human rights have claimed that UN organs have interpreted and applied the principle of non-inter-vention in matters essentially within the domestic jurisdiction of states, as laid down in Article 2(7) of the Charter, contrary to that which was intended by those that drafted the article at San Francisco, and in-consistent with the UN approach to the implementation of human rights through the adoption of international conventions or covenants which states are free to reject or ratify. These cases are analysed below.

Cases of Alleged Violations of Human Rights

As explained in Chapter I, under the League of Nations system, if a state claimed that a dispute in which it was involved arose out of a matter within its domestic jurisdiction, the League Council was empowered to decide whether the claim was justified or not in accordance with the criterion of international law, and this it did in the few instances with which it was concerned by seeking the advisory opinions of the Permanent Court of International Justice. But those who drafted the non-intervention principle in matters essentially within the domestic jurisdiction of states, stipulated in Article 2(7) of the Charter of the UN, did not specify the organ or authority which was to determine whether or not a matter was essentially within the domestic jurisdiction of a state, or the criterion by which such a matter was to be determined. To a great extent these omissions stemmed from the desire of both the United States and the Soviet Union to make the domestic jurisdiction reservation subject to the interpretation of the state concerned. But since it was recognised at San Francisco that in the course of the day to day operations of the United Nations, each organ would interpret such parts of the Charter as were applicable to its functions, the door was left open to the political organs of the Organisation, like the General Assembly and the Security Council, to assert their competence to decide whether or not a question was precluded from their consideration under Article 2, paragraph 7, of the Charter on the ground that it was a matter essentially within the domestic jurisdiction of a state.[12] In fact, the General Assembly began to assert its competence in this connection, without taking a formal vote on the issue, at its first session in 1946, when it decided to deal with the question, *The Treatment of People of Indian Origin in the Union of South Africa.*[13]

The Indian complaint was that the South African government had enacted discriminatory measures restricting the rights of its subjects of Indian origin in regard to trade and residence under the Asiatic Land Tenure and Indian Representation Act of 1946, and that these measures were a violation of the Capetown Agreements of 1927 and 1932, and of the principle of the Charter concerning human rights and fundamental freedoms. The Indian government also contended that since South Africa had refused to settle the question by amicable means, a situation had arisen which was likely to impair friendly relations between the two states, and it had thus resolved to submit the matter for consideration by the General Assembly in accordance with Articles 10 and 14.

Under Article 10 the General Assembly may discuss any matter within the scope of the Charter and make recommendations with regard to it, provided the Security Council is not dealing with it under Article 12, and under Article 14, subject to the same proviso, the General Assembly may recommend measures for the peaceful adjustment of any situation which it deems likely to impair the general welfare or friendly relations among nations. But the competence of the General Assembly under these articles was denied by the South African delegate when the Indian complaint was brought up in the General Committee of the Assembly. He contended that since the question arose out of a matter essentially within the domestic jurisdiction of South Africa, the principle of non-intervention under Article 2, paragrpah 7, by which he meant 'no interference in any form', precluded the General Assembly from considering it. This was not accepted by the General Committee, however, and later the General Assembly in plenary session decided that its 1st (Political) and 6th (Legal) committees should discuss the matter jointly.

The delegate of India reiterated the reasons for his country's complaint against South Africa when it was discussed by the 1st and 6th committees, but the South African delegate insisted that the matter was one within the domestic jurisdiction of South Africa by contending that the Capetown Agreements did not give rise to international legal obligations since they had never been signed or registered as treaties by the League of Nations; and that his government had not violated human rights as a signatory to the Charter on the ground that since human rights were nowhere defined in the Charter, no member state could be said to have undertaken legal obligations in regard to such matters. He thus reasserted his government's claim that the General Assembly was not competent to deal with a matter within the domestic jurisdiction of South Africa. Nevertheless, he put forward a proposal, which was supported by the United Kingdom and Sweden, that the International Court of Justice should be asked for an advisory opinion as to whether or not the matter was essentially one of domestic jurisdiction.

The fact that this proposal was rejected by the General Assembly in plenary session by a vote of 31 to 21, with 2 abstentions,[14] indicated that there was a large section of opinion in the General Assembly which considered that the International Court of Justice was the most suitable organ for offering guidance under Article 96 of the Charter to a political forum, like the Assembly, on a matter which required legal interpretation. It will be recalled that when the League of Nations was in existence, the Permanent Court of International Justice had maintained that a matter not regulated in principle by international law, in the absence of international treaties which placed obligations on the parties to such agreements, was solely within the domestic jurisdiction of a state, and with this in mind several United Nations members felt that it was desirable in the dispute between India and South Africa that the International Court of Justice should advise the General Assembly whether the Capetown Agreements had the force of international treaties which placed legal obligations on South Africa and thus removed the question from the domestic jurisdiction of that state. Besides, since some states opposed India's contention that the matter was not within the sphere of domestic jurisdiction on the ground that the South African government had violated the principles of the Charter relating to human rights, they considered it necessary that the opinion of the International Court should be sought on the legal implications, if any, of the human-rights articles of the Charter. But, as already mentioned, the majority of states finally took the view that the advice of the Court was unnecessary, and the General Assembly approved a resolution, by a vote of 32 to 15, with 7 abstentions, which expressed the opinion that the treatment of people of Indian origin in South Africa should be in conformity with the international obligations under the Capetown Agreements and the relevant provisions of the Charter, and asked the two parties to the dispute to report to the next session of the General Assembly.[15] It was thus implicit in the resolution that the General Assembly did not regard the principle of non-intervention under Article 2, paragraph 7, as a denial of its authority to discuss the substance of the case and to recommend a line of approach for its pacific settlement, notwithstanding the claim by the delegate of South Africa that this was a contravention of the article and contrary to the intentions of those who had drafted it at San Francisco.

Reports submitted by India and South Africa at the second session of the General Assembly in 1947, when Pakistan became a party in the case,[16] indicated that no progress had been made to settle the question, and in subsequent sessions of the Assembly the delegation of South Africa adhered to the claim that the United Nations had no right to interfere in a matter outside international jurisdiction. This was countered by the Indian delegate's assertion in the Political Committee of the Assembly in May, 1949, that any argument based on the domestic jurisdiction reservation under Article 2, paragraph 7, of the Charter was invalidated by the right of the Assembly to discuss and make recommendations on any matter within the scope of the Charter under Article 10, provided it was not seized by the Security Council.[17] This was tantamount to claiming that the Assembly was competent to discuss and make recommendations on the matter whether or not it was within the domestic jurisdiction of a state, and in line with the interpretation of Article 2, paragraph 7, put forward by Lauterpacht, viz. that since the term *intervention* was a technical term implying a peremptory demand accompanied by enforcement, or the threat of enforcement, in the event of non-compliance, it followed that the Assembly was competent under the article not only to discuss and investigate a situation or dispute arising out of a matter essentially within the domestic jurisdiction of a state, but also to address recommendations to a state directly concerned to facilitate a peaceful settlement of the matter, since none of these procedures amounted to *intervention* in the accepted legal meaning of the term. Notwithstanding this argument, however, the Indian delegate still attempted to justify the Assembly's right to deal with the question on the ground that it was *not* a matter within the domestic jurisdiction of South Africa, for he also maintained that the contractual obligations assumed by South Africa under the Capetown Agreements, and a state's pledge under Article 56 of the Charter to take joint and separate action in co-operation with the United Nations for the promotion of respect for, and observance of, human rights and fundamental freedoms, stated in Article 55, removed the matter from the sphere of domestic jurisdiction.

The Indian delegate's interpretation of Article 56 of the Charter prompted the South African delegate to warn the Political Committee that if it accepted such a view, the door would be opened to United Nations interference not only in questions relating to human rights, but also in other matters referred to in Article 55 which involved the economic and social policies of states. Not surprisingly, therefore, the delegates of several states, including the United Kingdom and France, expressed the view that the question should be referred to the International Court of Justice for an advisory opinion, if mediation between the disputants failed to effect a solution. But the Indian delegate was clearly anxious to secure acceptance of a resolution which would assert the responsibility of the Assembly in questions involving human rights and recommend the appointment of a commission to inquire into the charge of racial discrimination against people of Indian and Pakistan origin in South Africa. This was not accepted by the Political Committee, but it approved a draft resolution sponsored by Mexico and France which recommended that the disputants should be invited to seek a settlement of the dispute through discussion at a round table conference, and take into account the purpose and principles of the Charter and the Universal Declaration which had been adopted by the Assembly in December, 1948. This was adopted by the Assembly by a vote of 47 to 1, with 10 abstentions, on 14 May 1949,[18] but the negotiations for holding a round-table conference fell through, and when India, in 1950, requested that further consideration should be given to the matter by the Assembly, that body referred it to its *Ad Hoc* Political Committee.

The debate in the *Ad Hoc* Political Committee in November 1950, dealt almost entirely with the extent to which the general rule of non-intervention under Article 2, paragraph 7, barred the Assembly from taking steps to bring about a peaceful settlement of the dispute.[19] Hitherto the Assembly had considered itself competent to decide its own competence in the matter without a formal vote, but on this occasion the chairman ruled that the discussion would proceed on both the question of competence and the substance of the item, and that a vote would be taken on the question of competence prior to voting on any proposals submitted.

The delegates of those states that argued that the Assembly was competent to deal with the question — Ecuador, India, Iraq, Lebanon, Mexico, Pakistan, the Philippines, the United States, Uruguay and Yugoslavia — attempted to do so not by advancing the Lauterpacht interpretation of Article 2, paragraph 7, viz. that the general rule of non-inter-

41

vention in matters essentially within the domestic jurisdiction of states did not preclude measures short of coercion, but by putting forward reasons why the question was outside the sphere of domestic jurisdiction, so that the general rule of non-intervention was not applicable. The points which they advanced may be summarised as follows:

(i)   A matter which threatened to impair relations between states or jeopardise international peace and security, such as the South African government's discriminatory measures against minority racial groups, ceased to be essentially within the domestic jurisdiction of a state.

(ii)   South Africa had violated certain international obligations under the Capetown Agreements.

(iii)   The obligations assumed by South Africa under the human-rights articles of the Charter of the United Nations were sufficient to establish the competence of the United Nations to consider the question and to make recommendations in accordance with Articles 10 and 14 of the Charter.

(iv)   Though the Universal Declaration of Human Rights had no legal binding force, it imposed the moral obligation on Members of the United Nations not to adopt legislative measures which violated human rights.

For these reasons it was asserted that the Assembly was competent to discuss and make recommendations on the matter to effect its pacific settlement. But the delegate of South Africa, supported by the delegates of Greece and Australia, argued that Article 2, paragraph 7, of the Charter prohibited the Assembly from dealing with the question under Articles 10 and 14 because it was a matter within the domestic jurisdiction of the South African government. They contended that it was a domestic matter for the following reasons:-

(i)   The people of Indian and Pakistan origin referred to in the case were South African citizens whose status and rights were thus within the jurisdiction of the South African government.

(ii)   The Capetown Agreements of 1927 and 1932, which defined the status of the minority racial groups concerned, did not have the force of international treaties, and therefore did not involve international legal obligations which removed the question from the sphere of domestic jurisdiction.

(iii)   That a member state of the United Nations was not obliged to carry out the human rights provisions of the Charter, including the pledge under Article 56, had been made clear by the architects of the Charter, for it had been agreed at San Francisco that 'nothing contained in Chapter IX . . . can be construed as giving authority to the United Nations to intervene in the domestic affairs of Member States'. (*UN Conference of International Organisation, 1945, Vol. 10, pp. 271-2.*)

This summary of the arguments for and against the competence of the Assembly to discuss and make recommendations on the question emphasised the need for the clarification of several controversial issues by the judicial organ of the United Nations, the International Court of Justice. Certainly, this applied to the question whether the Capetown Agreements involved the legal obligations of international treaties, and to the question whether the human rights articles of the Charter had a legal force which invalidated the South African government's claim that the treatment of persons of Indian and Pakistan origin was a matter of domestic jurisdiction. But no attempt was made to seek the guidance of the International Court of Justice, and on 18 November 1950, the *Ad Hoc* Political Committee declared itself competent to consider and vote on proposals relating to the question by a vote of 35 to 3, with 17 abstentions. This was the first occasion that a formal vote on the question of competence had been taken.

In the light of the San Francisco discussions that led to the inclusion of Article 2(7) in the Charter, the South African delegate could justifiably claim that it had not been the intention of those who had drafted the article to empower the Assembly to interfere in a matter involving a state's treatment of its own nationals. But the vote on the issue of competence in the *Ad Hoc* Political Committee of the Assembly had shown that the majority of states were determined to interpret the principle of non-intervention in accordance with their political or moral predilections, not from a legal standpoint, and the fact that they were unwilling to seek the advisory legal opinion of the International Court seemed to indicate their fear that they might receive advice which would not support their interpretation of Article 2(7). The fact was that the task assigned to the United Nations Commission on Human Rights, to formulate covenants which would transform the moral obligations of member states of the United Nations under the Universal Declaration of Human Rights into legally binding obligations, had only just begun, and no particular international convention on the elimination of all forms of racial discrimination had yet been drafted.

The fact that the Universal Declaration of Human Rights was a moral appeal to rulers to respect and observe human rights, which had not created any legal obligations, was emphasised by the South African delegate in a statement which he made to the *Ad Hoc* Political Committee after it had voted on the question of competence. Clearly, the moral principles of the Universal Declaration, which called for the elimination of all forms of discrimination against human beings, were not going to deflect his government from proceeding with its policy of *apartheid*, or racial segregation,

43

which had been introduced in South Africa, in 1950, under the Group Areas Act, for the purpose of dividing the population into three racial groups, white, native and coloured; and there were several condemnatory references to this in the meetings of the *Ad Hoc* Political Committee. In fact, the draft resolutions approved by the Commitee on the complaints by India and Pakistan against South Africa, which was adopted by the Assembly in plenary session on 2 December 1950, included a reference to the policy of *apartheid* as 'necessarily based on doctrines of racial discrimination', before recommending that the three states should hold a round-table conference 'on the basis of their agreed agenda and bearing in mind the provisions of the Charter of the United Nations and of the Universal Declaration of Human Rights'. It also recommended that if the governments concerned failed to reach agreement in the round-table conference within a reasonable time, a commission should be appointed to assist the parties in carrying out appropriate negotiations.[20]

It can thus be seen from the Assembly's handling of the case from 1946 to 1950 that it had considered itself competent, without seeking the advice of the International Court of Justice, to adopt various procedures in a case of alleged violation of human rights, notwithstanding the claim of the accused state that such procedures contravened the principle of non-intervention in matters essentially within the domestic jurisdiction of states under Article 2, paragraph 7, of the Charter. These procedures included placing the question on its agenda, discussing it, and making recommendations for its pacific settlement which had not been intended by those who drafted Article 2, paragraph 7, at the San Francisco Conference. But the Assembly had attempted to justify its competence by implying in its resolutions that the human rights question being dealt with was not a matter essentially within the domestic jurisdiction of South Africa on the grounds that (i) the disputants had entered into contractual obligations by accepting agreements which had the legal force of an international treaty: (ii) the human rights provisions of the Charter and the Universal Declaration of Human Rights imposed obligations on a member state of the United Nations to observe certain standards of conduct in the treatment of its nationals without distinction as to race, sex, language, or religion: and (iii) the situation caused by the South African government's discriminatory measures against minority groups under its rule impaired inter-state relations. Since, therefore, the Assembly did not consider that the question was essentially within the domestic jurisdiction of South Africa, it concluded that it was not contravening the general rule of non-intervention by adopting the procedures referred to above.

It is important to realise, however, that so far all that the Assembly had considered itself competent to do in the case was to exert moral pressure on the state accused of violating human rights to co-operate in achieving a pacific settlement of the matter through observing the principles relating to human rights in the Charter and the Universal Declaration of Human Rights. Though the Assembly had indicated in its resolutions that the situation caused by the policy of the South African government towards persons of Indian and Pakistan origin threatened to impair relations between the states involved in the dispute, it had not requested the Security Council to deal with the matter as a threat to international peace and security under Chapter 7 of the Charter, so that enforcement measures might be considered under the exception to the general rule of non-intervention under Article 2, paragraph 7.

After 1950 the South African government continued to deny the competence of the Assembly to deal with the question, and ignored the Assembly's call to suspend its implementation of the Group Areas Act whilst the attempt was being made to arrange a round-table conference to explore ways and means of settling the dispute. In fact, negotiations to convene the conference soon broke down, and later a UN Good Offices Commission which was appointed by the Assembly at its seventh session in 1952, to arrange and assist negotiations between India, Pakistan and South Africa,[21] was not recognised by the South African government. That government continued to pay no heed to the moral appeals of the Assembly to modify its policy towards its subjects of Indian and Pakistan origin, and insisted that Article 2(7) of the Charter prohibited all forms of interference in matters of domestic jurisdiction, except the authorisation of enforcement measures by the Security Council to deal with threats to international peace and security arising out of such matters.

The general question of race conflict alleged to have arisen from the South African government's policies of *apartheid* was first considered as a separate item by the Assembly in 1952, but before this matter is examined, it is proposed to deal with two other cases which highlighted the controversy over the interpretation and application of the domestic jurisdiction reservation under Article 2(7) of the Charter in 1948 and 1949, one in which the Soviet Union was accused of violating the rights of Soviet wives of foreign citizens who wished to leave Russia to join their husbands abroad, the other involving the alleged denial of basic human rights to certain clerics in Bulgaria, Hungary and Romania.

The question involving the alleged denial of basic rights to Soviet wives of foreign citizens, which the delegate of Chile requested to be placed on the agenda of the Assembly's third regular session in 1948, was entitled, *The Violation by the Soviet Socialist Republics of Fundamental Human Rights, Traditional Diplomatic Practices, and other Principles of the Charter.*[22] According to the Chilean complaint, the measures taken by the U.S.S.R. to prevent Soviet wives, including the daughter-in-law of the former Chilean Ambassador in Moscow, from leaving Russia to join their husbands abroad, constituted violations of the human rights articles of the Charter, as well as traditional diplomatic practices, and at its plenary meeting on 24 September 1948, the Assembly referred the question to its 6th (Legal Committee) to consider a Chilean draft resolution requiring the Assembly to recommend the withdrawal of the measures complained of, and also an Australian draft resolution which called for an advisory opinion from the International Court of Justice on two issues, the text of which read as follows: (i) *to what extent do the privileges and immunities granted to the head of a foreign mission in accordance with diplomatic practices traditionally established by international law extend to his family and to his establishment?* and (ii) *in particular, is the action of a state in preventing one of its nationals who is the wife of a member of a foreign diplomatic mission, or of a member of his family, or of his establishment, from leaving its territory with her husband, or in order to join her husband, a breach of international law?*

During the debate in the Sixth Committee it was claimed by the Chilean delegate that the measures taken by the U.S.S.R. were violations not only of the human rights articles of the Charter — the Preamble, Articles 1(3), 55 and 56 were all cited — but also of certain articles of the draft Universal Declaration of Human Rights which had been approved, at that stage, by the Third Committee of the Assembly,[23] and of a resolution of the Economic and Social Council.[24] But all these claims were refuted by the delegate of the Soviet Union on the grounds that the granting of exit visas and marriage legislation were matters of domestic jurisdiction, and the reference to human rights was irrelevant. As to the allegation that diplomatic practices had been contravened in the case of the daughter-in-law of the former Chilean Ambassador in Moscow, he maintained that diplomatic immunity did not extend to all members of a diplomat's family, and he warned the Committee that it could not deal with the question without violating the principle of non-intervention in matters essentially within the domestic jurisdiction of states under Article 2(7) of the Charter.

There was much to justify the desirability of referring the case to the International Court for Justice for an advisory opinion, as recommended by the Australian delegate, in view of the divergence of views in the Committee on the legal aspect. For instance, it was the Soviet view that under Article 15 of the Cambridge Regulations on Diplomatic Privileges adopted by the Institute of International Law on 13 August 1895, the U.S.S.R. was entitled to decide the subject of the exit of its citizens from the country, and that the matter was therefore within its dometic jurisdiction. On the other hand, the Chilean delegate maintained that by virtue of Article 12 of the provisions laid down by the Institute of International Law at Oxford in August, 1895, members of a diplomat's family, by the mere fact of living in his house, enjoyed diplomatic immunity, and thus did not come under the penal or civil jurisdiction of the state to which the diplomat was accredited. Indeed, it was because of such differences of opinion that the Australian delegate was anxious to obtain the guidance of the International Court of Justice, and in support of this approach he quoted resolution 171 which had been adopted by the Assembly in 1947, according to which it was 'of paramount importance that the Court should be utilized to the greatest possible extent in the progressive development of international law, both in regard to legal issues between States and in regard to constitutional interpretation'. But the Committee rejected the Australian draft resolution by 13 votes to 9, with 12 abstentions, a further instance of the reluctance of the majority to seek the advice of the Court as the organ most qualified to assist the political organs of the United Nations in determining whether or not a matter was essentially within the domestic jurisdiction of a state according to the criterion of international law. In fact, it was the Chilean draft resolution, to some extent modified by an amendment put forward by France, and Uruguay, that was finally approved by the Sixth Committee of the Assembly.

The French delegate had emphasised, in effect, that if the Assembly could not assume competence in the question because it was not covered by an international agreement under which the U.S.S.R. had accepted legal obligations, its competence in the matter would have to be claimed on the ground that the situation was likely to cause an impairment of friendly relations between the states directly involved, so that it could act under Article 14 of the Charter to effect a peaceful adjustment of the matter; and it is significant that the draft resolution recommended by the Sixth Committee, which was endorsed by the Assembly in plenary session by a vote of 39 to 6, with 11 abstentions,[25] took this into account. Having invoked the human rights articles of the Charter, Articles 13 and 16 of the Universal Declaration of Human Rights, and the Economic and Social Council resolution 154(VII) D, to which reference has already been made, the Assembly declared that 'the measures which prevent or coerce the wives of citizens of other nationalities from leaving their country of origin with their husbands or in order to join them abroad, are not in conformity with the Charter; and that when those measures refer to the wives of persons belonging to foreign diplomatic missions, or of members of their families or retinue, they are contrary to courtesy, to diplomatic practices and to the principle of reciprocity, and are likely to impair friendly relations among nations'. It thus recommended the Government of the U.S.S.R. to withdraw the measures which it had taken to prevent Soviet wives from leaving Russia to join their husbands abroad.

The question of the observance of human rights in Bulgaria and Hungary was requested to be placed on the agenda of the Assembly by the delegate of Australia on 19 March 1949. The item was entitled *Observance of fundamental freedoms and human rights in Bulgaria and Hungary, including the question of religious and civil liberty in special relation to recent trials of Church leaders*, and this proposal and another put forward by the Bolivian delegate that the Assembly should study the legal proceedings against Cardinal Mindszenty, Roman Catholic Primate of Hungary, in relation to Articles 1(3) and 55(c) of the Charter, were presented as a joint item at the third session of the Assembly in the following terms:

Having regard to the provisions of the Charter and of the Peace Treaties, the question of the observance in Bulgaria and Hungary of human rights and fundamental freedoms, including questions of religious and civil liberties, with special reference to recent trials of Church leaders.

Notwithstanding the opposition of certain delegations to its consideration by the Assembly for the reason that it constituted interference in the domestic jurisdiction of the two states, who were not then members of the United Nations, the Assembly referred the matter to its *Ad Hoc* Political Committee, which discussed it from 19 to 22 April 1949.[26]

The majority of delegates in the Committee took the view that since minority Communist groups had seized power in Bulgaria and Hungary, and suppressed political, civil and religious liberties in contravention of the peace treaties under which the two states had undertaken international obligations in respect of such rights, the principle of non-intervention in matters essentially within the domestic jurisdiction of states, under Article 2(7) did not apply to the case. It was also asserted that Articles 55 and 56 of the Charter brought questions involving human rights within the competence of the Assembly. But these claims were rejected by the delegates of the U.S.S.R., the Ukrainian S.S.R., the Byelorussian S.S.R., Czechoslovakia, Poland and Yugoslavia as a violation of the principle of non-interference in the internal affairs of states.

The draft resolution which was approved by the *Ad Hoc* Political Committee, and later endorsed by the Assembly in plenary session by a vote of 34 to 6, with 9 abstentions,[27] read as follows:

The General Assembly,

Considering that one of the purposes of the United Nations is to achieve international co-operation in promoting and encouraging respect for human rights and fundamental freedoms for all, without distinction as to race, sex, language or religion,

Considering that the Governments of Bulgaria and Hungary have been accused, before the General Assembly, of acts contrary to the purposes of the United Nations and to their obligations under the Peace Treaties to ensure to all persons within their respective jurisdiction the enjoyment of human rights and fundamental freedoms,

1. Expresses its deep concern at the grave accusations made against the Governments of Bulgaria and Hungary regarding the suppression of human rights and fundamental freedoms in those countries;

2. Notes with satisfaction that steps have been taken by several States signatories to the Peace Treaties with Bulgaria and Hungary

regarding these accusations, and expresses the hope that measures will be diligently applied, in accordance with the Treaties, in order to ensure respect for human rights and fundamental freedoms.

3. Most urgently draws the attention of the Governments of Bulgaria and Hungary to their obligations under the Peace Treaties, including the obligation to co-operate in the settlement of all those questions;

4. Decides to retain the question on the agenda of the fourth regular session of the General Assembly of the United Nations.

This resolution thus illustrates the point that the Assembly considered itself competent to deal with a matter claimed by states to be within their domestic jurisdiction for two reasons; that the contractual obligations assumed by Bulgaria and Hungary under the peace treaties had removed the question of ensuring human rights to their citizens from their domestic jurisdiction, and that the conduct of the two governments was contrary to the purpose of the United Nations in promoting respect for human rights though Bulgaria and Hungary were not members of the United Nations.

Later, in October 1949, after Romania had been accused of human-rights violations similar to those that had been made against Bulgaria and Hungary, and all three states had rejected the charges of treaty violation made against them by states signatory to the peace treaties, and had refused to appoint representatives to treaty commissions for the settlement of the disputes, which it was contended, was prescribed in the peace treaties, the question was considered by the Assembly's *Ad Hoc* Political Committee.[28] Since Bulgaria, Hungary and Romania denied the legal obligation to co-operate in the examination of the charges brought against them in this way, the delegates of the United States, Canada and Bolivia put forward a proposal that the following questions should be submitted to the International Court of Justice for an advisory opinion:

(i) Do the diplomatic exchanges between Bulgaria, Hungary and Romania on the one hand and certain Allied and Associated Powers signatories to the Treaties of Peace on the other, concerning the implementation of article 2 in the Treaties with Bulgaria and Hungary and article 3 in the Treaty with Romania, disclose disputes subject to the provisions for the settlement of disputes contained in article 36 of the Treaty of Peace with Bulgaria, article 40 of the Treaty of Peace with Hungary, and article 38 of the Treaty of Peace with Romania?

In the event of an affirmative reply to question (i):

(ii) Are the Governments of Bulgaria, Hungary and Romania obligated to carry out the provisions of the articles referred to in question (i), including the provisions for the appointment of their representatives to the Treaty Commissions?

(iii) If one party fails to appoint a representative to a Treaty

49

Commission under the Treaties of Peace with Bulgaria, Hungary and Romania where that party is obligated to appoint a representative to the Treaty Commission, is the Secretary-General of the United Nations authorised to appoint the third member of the Commission upon the request of the other party to a dispute according to the provisions of the respective Treaties?

In the event of an affirmative reply to question (iii):

(iv) Would a Treaty Commission composed of a representative of one party and a third member appointed by the Secretary-General of the United Nations constitute a Commission, within the meaning of the relevant Treaty articles, competent to make a definitive and binding decision in settlement of a dispute?

The U.S.S.R. delegation opposed this approach to the International Court on the ground that the text of the treaties with Bulgaria, Hungary and Romania clearly stipulated that in all questions relating to the interpretation and application of the Peace Treaties, agreement had to be reached between the representatives of the United Kingdom, the United States and the Soviet Union, and that if no agreement could be reached, no action could be taken under the peace treaties. In the present case, the Soviet delegation asserted, there was no such agreement since the Soviet Union did not recognise the existence of a dispute or violation of the Treaties. It thus considered that setting up of commissions envisaged in the Treaties was not called for, and that there was no reason to apply for an advisory opinion by the International Court of Justice. But the majority of delegates rejected this argument, and the draft resolution which was passed on to the Assembly in plenary session included the request to the Court to answer the four questions referred to above. On 22 October 1949, this was endorsed by the Assembly by a vote of 47 to 5, with 7 abstentions,[29] a procedure which it had not approved of in dealing with India's complaint against South Africa of violating the Capetown Agreements, and Chile's complaint against Russia concerning the Soviet wives of foreign citizens.

In its reply to the Assembly, the International Court of Justice made the following comment:[30]

> The Court is not called upon to deal with the charges brought before the General Assembly since the Questions put to the Court relate neither to the alleged violations of the provisions of the Treaties concerning human rights and fundamental freedoms nor to the interpretation of the articles relating to these matters. The object of the Request is much more limited. It is directed solely to obtaining from the Court certain clarifications of a legal nature regarding the applicability of the procedure for the settlement of disputes by the Commissions provided for in the express terms of Article 36 of the Treaty with Bulgaria, Article 40 of the Treaty with Hungary and

Article 38 of the Treaty with Romania. The interpretation of the terms of a treaty for this purpose could not be considered as a question essentially within the domestic jurisdiction of a State. It is a question of international law which, by its very nature, lies within the competence of the Court.

These considerations also suffice to dispose of the objection based on the principle of domestic jurisdiction and directed specifically against the competence of the Court, namely, that the Court, as an organ of the United Nations, is bound to observe the provisions of the Charter, including Article 2, paragraph 7.

The International Court also stated that 'for the purposes of the present Opinion, it suffices to note that the General Assembly justified the adoption of its Resolution by stating that "the United Nations, pursuant to Article 55 of the Charter, shall promote universal respect for and observance of human rights and fundamental freedoms for all without distinction as to race, sex, language or religion"',[31] and this statement, according to Rosalyn Higgins, signified that 'the Court clearly upheld the view that no objection could be raised to the passing of resolutions by the Assembly, on grounds of Art. 2(7), when human rights were involved; for Article 55 provided a legal basis of obligation'.[32] But it is difficult to see this, for the Assembly's resolution was no more than a request, as the Court itself stressed, 'solely to obtaining from the Court certain clarifications of a legal nature regarding the applicability of the procedure for the settlement of disputes by the Commissions provided for in the express terms of Article 36 of the Treaty with Bulgaria, Article 40 of the Treaty with Hungary, and Article 38 of the Treaty with Romania'. Surely, what the Court implied was that the Assembly's request for an opinion on the question was justified under Article 55 of the Charter, not that Article 55 imposed a legal obligation on states with regard to respect for and observance of human rights.

In reply to questions (i) and (ii) contained in the Assembly's resolution, the Court declared that a dispute did exist, and that Bulgaria, Hungary and Romania were obligated to nominate their representatives to the treaty commissions, and it set a time-limit of thirty days for the three states to comply with the opinion. Since, however, they failed to nominate representatives within the time-limit, the Court advised, in reply to question (iii), that the Secretary-General of the United Nations was not authorised to appoint the third member of each commission. In view of this, the Court stated that the reply to question (iv), which asked whether a commission of two members, one appointed by the Secretary-General and the other by a party to the dispute, would be competent to make a definitive and binding decision, was not necessary.[33]

In November, 1950, the Assembly condemned 'the wilful refusal of the Governments of Bulgaria, Hungary and Romania to fulfil their obli-

51

gations under the provisions of the Treaties of Peace to appoint representatives to the Treaty Commissions, which obligation has been confirmed by the International Court of Justice', and expressed its opinion that their violation of human rights and fundamental freedoms showed that they were 'callously indifferent to the sentiments of the world community'. It concluded its moral censure of the three states by inviting members of the United Nations, and in particular those which were parties to the Treaties of Peace with Bulgaria, Hungary and Romania, to submit to the Secretary-General all evidence which they held or which might become available in the future in relation to the question.[34]

In this case and the other two cases which have so far been examined, it may be stated that resolutions were passed by the Assembly, notwithstanding the claims of those states accused of human-rights violations that Article 2(7) of the Charter prohibited any form of interference in matters essentially within their domestic jurisdiction. The majority of states that voted for these resolutions sought to justify the competence of the Assembly by claiming that the issues considered were not matters of domestic jurisdiction mainly on the grounds that (i) the various human-rights articles of the Charter or the Universal Declaration imposed obligations on the accused states to promote respect for and the observance of human rights and fundamental freedoms, without distinction as to race, sex, language or religion, and (ii) the states accused of violating human rights had broken contractual obligations in respect of certain practices which they had agreed to observe under international treaties or customary international law. But in two of the three cases — the Indian complaint against South Africa and the Chilean complaint against the U.S.S.R. — it was also implied in the Assembly's resolutions that the likely impairment of friendly relations between states through the violation of human rights had removed the questions from the sphere of domestic jurisdiction, and thus made it possible for the Assembly to assert its competence under Article 14 of the Charter to recommend measures for their peaceful adjustment. In none of the three cases, therefore, did the Assembly attempt to justify its competence in accordance with the view advanced by Lauterpacht, namely, that the general rule of non-intervention in matters essentially within the domestic jurisdiction of states did not preclude measures short of coercion. Moreover, only in one of the three cases — the Observance of Human Rights and Fundamental Freedoms in Bulgaria, Hungary and Romania — did the Assembly request an advisory opinion from the International Court of Justice, although this procedure was clearly desirable in the interest of impartiality in the other cases.

A further point that needs to be stressed is the fact that the resolutions approved by the Assembly in the three cases were moral exhortations to the states accused of violations of human rights; they contained no request to the Security Council to consider the question of enforcement measures in the event of non-compliance of the recommendations put forward, and no attempt was made within the Assembly to initiate moves that would lead that body to recommend enforcement action against any of the states for violating human rights, a recommendation which other member states of the United Nations would be free to accept or reject.

At a later stage in its history the Assembly was to recommend economic sanctions against South Africa because of the refusal of that state to respond to moral appeals to abandon its policy of apartheid. But this did not come about until several moral exhortations addressed to the South African government had failed to bring about a change in that government's policy.

It was in September 1952 that several Afro-Asian states requested that the *Question of Race Conflict in South Africa resulting from the Policies of Apartheid of the Government of the Union of South Africa*[35] be placed on the agenda of the seventh session of the Assembly. In a memorandum submitted by these states,[36] it was alleged that policies of racial segregation in South Africa were causing an inflammatory situation which constituted a threat to international peace and a flagrant violation of the principles of human rights and fundamental freedoms laid down in the Charter, and several instances were cited of racial discrimination against the non-white population through the segregation of races under the Group Areas Act. It was thus urged that the Assembly should urgently consider the matter, and on 17 October 1952 the Assembly, by a vote of 45 to 6, with 8 abstentions, accepted its General Committee's recommendation that the question should be placed on its agenda and then referred it to its *Ad Hoc* Political Committee.[37]

In both the General Committee and plenary session of the Assembly the South African delegate had protested strongly against the matter being included as an item on the agenda. He argued that the domestic jurisdiction reservation under Article 2(7) of the Charter prohibited United Nations interference in any form, in accordance with the intentions of those who had drafted the Article at San Francisco; and when the matter was brought up at a meeting of the *Ad Hoc* Political Committee in November, 1952, he insisted that with the single exception of the application of enforcement measures by the Security Council under Chapter VII of the Charter, i.e. action with respect to threats to the peace, breaches of the peace, and acts of aggression, Article 2(7) did not permit any kind of interference in the domestic affairs of states. The points he advanced in support of his argument were as follows:-

(i)   The term 'to intervene' in Article 2, paragraph 7, was not to be interpreted in the narrow restrictive sense of dictatorial interference, but included such interference as the discussion of, and passing of resolutions by the Assembly on matters essentially within the domestic jurisdiction of a state.

(ii)   The pledge of international co-operation in Article 56 to promote respect for and observance of human rights and the economic and social objectives of Article 55, did not authorise any interference by the United Nations.

(iii)   The allegation that the policy of apartheid in South Africa constituted a threat to international peace could not be justified because it did not threaten the territorial integrity or political independence of any other state.

These points were generally supported by the delegates of Australia, Belgium, France, New Zealand and the United Kingdom, and in the light of the discussions at the San Francisco Conference in 1945 it is difficult to see how they could be refuted. But by a vote of 45 to 6, with 8 abstentions, the *Ad Hoc* Political Committee rejected a South African motion which required the Committee to admit that under Article 2(7) it had no competence to consider the question, and then proceeded to vote on two resolutions.

The first resolution which it adopted by a vote of 35 to 2, with 22 abstentions, included references to the policy of racial segregation (*apartheid*) as 'necessarily based on doctrines of racial discrimination': the establishment of a Commission, consisting of three members, 'to study the racial situation in the Union of South Africa in the light of the Purposes and Principles of the Charter, with due regard to the provision of Article 2, paragraph 7, as well as the provisions of Article I, paragraphs 2 and 3, Article 13, paragraph Ib, Article 55c, and Article 56 of the Charter, and the resolutions of the United Nations on racial persecution and discrimination, and to report its conclusions to the General Assembly at its eighth session': and an invitation to the Government of the Union of South Africa to extend its full co-operation to the Commission. It was thus implicit in the resolution, which was approved by the Assembly by a vote of 35 to 1, with 23 abstentions,[38] that the Commission should study the extent to which the human rights articles of the Charter and the principle of non-intervention under Article 2(7) might determine or affect the competence of the United Nations in the matter.

The other resolution approved by the *Ad Hoc* Political Committee by a vote of 20 to 7, with 32 abstentions, which had been originally submitted by Denmark, Iceland, Norway and Sweden, and later adopted by the Assembly in plenary session by 24 to 1, with 34 abstentions,[39] declared that 'in a multi-racial society harmony and respect for human rights and freedoms and the peaceful development of a unified community are best assured when patterns of legislation and practice are directed towards ensuring equality before the law of all persons regardless of race, creed or colour, and when economic, social, cultural and political participation of all racial groups is on a basis of equality': affirmed that 'governmental policies of Member States which are not directed towards these goals but which are designed to perpetuate or increase discrimination, are inconsistent with the pledges of the Members under Article 56 of the Charter': and solemnly called upon all Member States 'to bring their policies into conformity with their obligation under the Charter to promote the observance of human rights and fundamental freedoms'. Though couched in general terms, the resolution clearly stated that Article 56 of the Charter imposed a definite obligation on member states of the United Nations to refrain from pursuing a policy of racial discrimination, but the very large number of states that abstained from voting indicated that this was still a very controversial question.

The report of the Commission appointed by the Assembly under its other resolution (616A) was submitted to the Assembly at its eighth session. Based on a study of the legislative and administrative provisions in force in the Union of South Africa, statements by witnesses, and information supplied by some member states of the United Nations, it alleged that because of the policy of *apartheid*, 80 per cent of the population were being denied basic human rights and fundamental freedoms. But when the report was considered by the *Ad Hoc* Political Committee of the Assembly in November, 1953, the South African delegate, whose government had not recognised the Commission, maintained that it presented a distorted picture of the situation in his country, and still insisted that the Assembly did not possess the competence to consider the matter for reasons which he had stated earlier. This contention was rejected by the majority of delegates, however, and the Committee, by a vote of 37 to 10, with 9 abstentions, noted with concern that the Commission, in its study of the racial policies of the Government of the Union of South Africa, had concluded that these policies and their consequences were contrary to the Charter and the Universal Declaration of Human Rights, and requested the Commission to continue its study of the development of the racial situation in the Union of South Africa, and to suggest measures which would help to alleviate the situation and promote a peaceful settlement. The Committee also invited the South African government to extend its full co-operation to the Commission, and its resolution was endorsed by the Assembly by a vote of 38 to 11, with 11 abstentions, on 8 December 1953.[40]

Further reports submitted to the Assembly by its three-man Commission in 1954 and 1955 stressed that the policy of *apartheid* had not been revised,[41] but the South African delegate in the Assembly continued to assert that there should be no interference by the United Nations in matters within the domestic jurisdiction of his state. It was not surprising, therefore, that the African and Asian states, who regarded *apartheid* as a new form of colonialism against which they were conducting a persistent struggle in the United Nations, and whose numbers in the United Nations increased considerably in the late 1950s and early 1960s, began to show signs of wanting more positive action against the South African regime than expressions of concern by the Assembly, and the Sharpeville incident of March 1960, when seventy four demonstrators against racial discrimination and segregation were killed by South African police, intensified this trend. Within a few days of the incident, twenty nine Afro-Asian states requested the Security Council to consider the situation in South Africa which, in their view, 'had grave potentialities for international friction, which endangered the maintenance of international peace and security'. But though the Security Council rejected the South African government's claim that Article 2(7) of the Charter prohibited the matter being placed on its agenda, and recognised that if continued the situation in South Africa might endanger international peace and security, the resolution which it adopted amounted to little more than a moral appeal to the South African government to abandon its policies of *apartheid* and racial discrimination.[42] It was approved by a vote of 9 to 0, with France and the United Kingdom abstaining, the latter making it clear before the vote that anything more than a discussion of the issue would amount to a contravention of the principle of non-intervention in a matter essentially within the domestic jurisdiction of the Union of South Africa.

This Security Council resolution was an obvious disappointment to those Afro-Asian states who were anxious to obtain the approval of sanctionary measures against the South African regime. But in April 1961 the Assembly, by a vote of 96 to 1 (Portugal), with 0 abstentions, approved a resolution which reiterated the point made in its previous resolutions that 'racial policies designed to perpetuate or increase discrimination are inconsistent with the Charter of the United Nations and with the pledges of Members under Article 56 of the Charter'; noted 'with grave concern that these policies have led to international friction and their continuance endangers international peace and security'; and requested all states 'to consider taking such separate and collective action as is open to them, in conformity with the Charter of the United Nations, to bring about the abandonment of these policies'.[43] Even the United Kingdom and France, who had hitherto been opposed to anything beyond a discussion of the *apartheid* question in the Security Council and the Assembly, on the ground that this would contravene the principle of non-intervention in matters of domestic jurisdiction under Article 2(7), voted for the resolution. In fact, the United Kingdom delegate stated in the debate which preceded the vote that his government now regarded *apartheid* as being so exceptional as to be *sui generis*, which apparently implied that the practice of *apartheid* was a worse form of sin than the denial of individual civil and political rights by those states with totalitarian systems of government which supported the resolution.

Clearly, the resolution indicated that there was now overwhelming support for the view that Article 2(7) could not nullify the Assembly's competence to request its members to consider taking some form of action against South Africa. But it did not specify the kind of action that should be taken since there were differences of opinion even among the Afro-Asian states as to what should be recommended. In 1962, however, during the seventeenth session of the Assembly, when the question of *apartheid* and the treatment of persons of Indian and Pakistan origin in the Union of South Africa were considered jointly, the Afro-Asian states, with the support of the Soviet bloc, succeeded in securing the adoption of a resolution[44] which requested member-states to take action, separately or collectively, to bring about the abandonment of the policies of *apartheid* and racial discrimination by '(a) breaking off diplomatic relations with the Government of the Republic of South Africa or refraining from establishing such relations; (b) closing their ports to all vessels flying the South African flag; (c) enacting legislation prohibiting their ships from entering South African ports; (d) boycotting all South African goods and refraining from exporting goods, including all arms and ammunition, to South Africa; (e) refusing landing and passage facilities to all aircraft belonging to the Government of South Africa and companies registered under the laws of South Africa'.

These measures were recommended after the resolution had deprecated the continued and total disregard by the South African government of its obligations under the Charter and re-affirmed that the continuation of its policies of *apartheid* seriously endangered international peace and security. The resolution also requested the Security Council to take appropriate measures, including sanctions, to secure South Africa's compliance with the resolutions of the Assembly and itself on the subject, and, if necessary, to consider action under Article 6 of the Charter — the Article which states that a UN member which has persistently violated the principles of the Charter may be expelled from the Organisation by the Assembly on the Security Council's recommendation. In addition, the Assembly decided to establish a special committee to keep the racial policies of the South African government under review when the Assembly was not in session, and to report either to the Assembly or to the Security Council, or to both, as might be appropriate from time to time.

This resolution, which appears to have been based on Article 11(2) of the Charter, under which the Assembly may make recommendations on a question relating to the maintenance of international peace and security, provided it is not seized by the Security Council, and in line with the 'Uniting for Peace' procedure adopted by the Assembly in 1950,[45] was approved by a vote of 67 to 16, with 23 abstentions. It was opposed by Australia, Belgium, Canada, France, Greece, Ireland, Japan, Luxembourg, Netherlands, New Zealand, Portugal, South Africa, Spain, Turkey, United Kingdom and United States, and since four of these states (the United Kingdom, United States, France and Japan) were South Africa's leading trade partners, there was little possibility that the economic sanctions recommended by the Assembly would be effective.

During the debate on the resolution the United States delegate warned that if the coercive measures were ineffectively applied, the authority of the United Nations would be seriously weakened, and several members of the Assembly, among them the United Kingdom, United States and France, expressed doubts as to the wisdom of requesting the Security Council to consider action, if necessary, for the expulsion of South Africa from the United Nations. The United States delegate thought that expulsion would simply remove the South African government from the one place where the full weight of world opinion could be brought to bear on it.

But the Western powers laid themselves open to the criticism that though they no longer regarded the general principle of non-intervention in matters essentially within the sphere of domestic jurisdiction as an impediment to the UN's application of moral pressure on the South African government, and had gone as far as to support the Assembly's resolution 1958(XV) which had noted with grave concern that the continuance of the policies of *apartheid* endangered international peace and security, and requested states to consider taking such separate and collective action as was open to them to bring about an abandonment of those policies, they were unwilling to accept the logical consequences of those decisions by supporting the Assembly's recommendation for diplomatic and economic sanctions against South Africa. Moreover, though they supported a Security Council resolution which described the situation in South Africa as 'seriously disturbing international peace and security', and solemnly called upon UN members 'to cease forthwith the sale and shipment of equipment and material for the manufacture and maintenance of arms and ammunition in South Africa',[46] they opposed moves for the Council to authorise a general economic boycott on the ground that the practice of *apartheid* did not amount to a *threat* under Article 39 of Chapter VII of the Charter.[47] They thus exposed themselves to the charge of being inconsistent in their approach to the *apartheid* question, and it would appear that their opposition to the authorisation of coercive measures by the Security Council against South Africa was due to their concern that such action would militate against their economic and defence interests in an area in which the Soviet Union was seeking to extend its influence and naval power.

Indeed, though on 4 November 1977 the Western powers voted with all the other members of the Security Council for the imposition of a mandatory arms embargo gainst South Africa under Chapter VII of the Charter — the resolution (418/1977) stated that the Council 'determines, having regard to the policies and acts of the South African Government, that the acquisition by South Africa of arms and related material constitutes a threat to the maintenance of international peace and security'

— they vetoed other African draft resolutions which would have imposed economic and other sanctions going beyond the mandatory arms embargo.

But the fact that it is necessary to point out the inconsistency of the Western powers in this connection should not be regarded as justification for the claim, advanced by the Soviet Union and Afro-Asian states, that since the practice of *apartheid* created racial tension in an area where several states were highly sensitive to the racial discrimination being practised against the black population in the Union of South Africa, it constituted a threat to international peace; for it is difficult to see how it could be claimed that the racial policies of the South African government within its own territory could threaten the territorial integrity or political independence of other states.

Besides, it should not be overlooked that among those states which vehemently supported the demand for coercive measures against South Africa and consideration by the Security Council, if necessary, for that state's expulsion from the United Nations — a measure 'obviously conceived as a form of action going beyond the enforcement measures for the taking of which the Security Council is made responsible'[48] — there were several whose dictatorial forms of government and tyrannical practices made them ill-qualified to call for such measures. Certainly in view of the fact that the Soviet Union's violent suppression of the political rights of the Hungarian people in 1956 had demonstrated the scant respect of its government for fundamental freedoms, its attitude towards the practice of tyranny in South Africa was very hypocritical.

The history of the *apartheid* question at the United Nations thus demonstrated the inconsistency and hypocrisy of states towards the use of the Assembly and Security Council as instruments for authorising various forms of interference in a human rights issue which legally belonged to the sphere of domestic jurisdiction, and there can be little doubt that since the United Nations was weakened as a result of inter-state antagonism over the affair, it highlighted the need for the Organisation to confine its regulative functions to those matters over which it could legitimately claim to have some jurisduction, such as South Africa's disregard of its international obligations as the mandatory power in South West Africa (Namibia).

The question of South West Africa (Namibia) will be examined at a later stage in this study, but now let us consider an Assembly resolution approved by 72 votes to 35, with 32 abstentions, on 11 November 1975, which, having taken note of a resolution of the Organisation of African Unity which considered that 'the racist regime in occupied Palestine and the racist regime in Zimbabwe and South Africa have a common imperialist origin, forming a whole and having the same racist structure and being organically linked in their policy aimed at repression of the dignity and integrity of the human being', determined that 'Zionism is a form of racism and racial discrimination'.[49]

Clearly, the Assembly's *Declaration on Zionism as a Form of Racism* which was sponsored by twenty Arab states, and supported by the Communist East European countries, except Romania, a substantial number of African and Asian states, including China, and a few Latin American countries, was intended to discredit Israel as a racist state which was guilty of violating human rights in much the same way as the white minority regimes in Rhodesia and South Africa. But it was strongly condemned by the United States and members of the European Economic Community, and the substantial number of states that either voted against the resolution or abstained from voting reflected the deep division among the members of the Assembly over the question.

The United States delegate contended that 'racism' was according to Webster's Third New International Dictionary, 'a belief in the inherent superiority of a particular race and its right to domination over others', and had 'always been altogether alien to the political and religious movement known as Zionism'. Consequently, he argued, Zionism was not and could not be a form of racism.

Since the resolution referred to 'the racist regime in occupied Palestine', the United Kingdom delegate rightly warned the Assembly that it would 'undermine the right of Israel to exist'. The point needs to be stressed, therefore, that the adoption of the resolution was, in effect, another instance of the UN Assembly being used to interfere in a human rights issue that legally belonged to the sphere of domestic jurisdiction of a state which was a member of the United Nations, and ran counter to what had been intended by those who drafted the non-intervention principle under Article 2(7) of the Charter. It also needs to be emphasised that the bitter confrontations between those who took opposite sides on the question militated against the usefulness of the United Nations as a forum in which it was essential that the attempt should be made to promote a settlement of the Arab-Israeli question which recognised and guaranteed the existence of the state of Israel and the establishment of a separate state for the Palestinian Arabs.

The Application of the Non-Intervention Principle by the Economic and Social Council and its Commission on Human Rights

In 1947 the Economic and Social Council endorsed a declaration by its subsidiary organ, the Commission on Human Rights, that it had no authority to take action in regard to any complaints concerning human rights,[50] and when the question of investigating such matters as the violation of trade union rights and forced labour was raised in subsequent sessions of the Council, it was recognised that the consent of the governments concerned would be required before such inquiries could be carried out.[51] In 1959 the Council endorsed its 1947 rule that the Commission on

Human Rights was not competent to take any action with regard to human rights complaints.[52]

All these decisions were in line with the principle of non-intervention under Article 2(7) of the Charter, but this approach was modified in 1967 when the Economic and Social Council confirmed the decision of its Commission on Human Rights to give annual consideration to the question of human rights violations,[53] and the Commission established an *ad hoc* working group of experts to investigate charges of torture and ill-treatment of prisoners, detainees or persons in police custody in South Africa.[54]

At its 24th session, held from 5 February to 12 March 1968, the Commission on Human Rights examined a report by the *ad hoc* working group of experts which stated that, in all their main features, the allegations made in the various documents transmitted by the UN Assembly's Special Committee on the Policies of Apartheid by the Government of the Republic of South Africa were supported by evidence given by witnesses questioned by the group, and recommended that the South African government should reform the appalling prison conditions described in the report, and that studies be undertaken to ascertain whether the elements of the crime of genocide existed in the system prevailing in South Africa.[55]

The Commission on Human Rights endorsed the conclusions and recommendations of the *ad hoc* working group, and called upon the government of South Africa to conform to the International Standard Minimum Rules for the Treatment of Prisoners, and to ensure that the supervising authorities kept a close watch on the behaviour of the police and prison officials. But the Commission did not approve at its 24th session the recommendation of its Sub-Commission on Prevention of Discrimination and Protection of Minorities for the establishment of working groups of experts to investigate complaints concerning violations of human rights by the military junta in Greece and the Duvalier government in Haiti. In fact, during the Commission's debate,[56] differing views were expressed on whether the Commission should confine itself to discussing violations of human rights resulting from policies of racial discrimination and *apartheid* in Southern Africa, or consider violations in all parts of the world. This was not surprising in view of the fact that allegations of violations of human rights were made by various member states against the governments of Greece, Israel, the United States, the Soviet Union and the Ukrainian SSR. But though the Commission took no action on allegations of ill-treatment of Jewish minorities in certain countries of the Middle East, it expressed its distress to learn from newspapers of Israeli acts of destroying homes of the Arab population in areas occupied by the Israeli authorities subsequent to the hostilities of June 1967, and called upon the government of Israel to desist forthwith from indulging in such practices and to respect human rights and fundamental freedoms.

Subsequent sessions of the Commission on Human Rights and other organs of the United Nations[57] also demonstrated that there was little consistency in the attitude of the majority of the members of those bodies, for they were concerned almost exclusively with charges against South Africa, Israel, and (after 1970) the regime that replaced the Allende Government in Chile.[58] Their inconsistency thus further illustrated the point that had been made earlier by one writer, viz. 'Governments might be ready to assert the Organisation's authority against other governments even in despite of the precedents thereby created. They were less enthusiastic when its actions were directed towards their own state'.[59]

In 1970, in accordance with resolution 1503 approved by the Economic and Social Council, a five-man working group of the Sub-Commission of the Commission on Human Rights was set up to sort out from the numerous complaints of violations of human rights, many thousands of which had been received over the years by the UN Secretariat, those which appeared to reveal a consistent pattern of gross and reliably attested violations. Complaints of that nature, whether they were made by individuals or groups who were the victims of such violations, or submitted by non-governmental organisations, were to be passed on by the working group to the Sub-Commission to decide which should be dealt with by the Commission on Human Rights. Finally, the Commission was required to determine whether it should make a thorough study of such complaints, or appoint ad hoc committees to examine the allegations, but this could not be done without the consent and co-operation of those states against whom the complaints were made. Moreover, these procedures had to be conducted in conditions of secrecy.

It was not until March 1978, however, that the Commission listed countries on which it had held private meetings and taken confidential measures under the Economic and Social Council's resolution 1503. The countries named were Bolivia, Equatorial Guinea, Malawi, the Republic of Korea, Uganda, Ethiopia, Indonesia, Paraguay and Uruguay. But though the Commission took confidential measures in dealing with the allegations against these countries, it continued to make public appeals for ending human rights violations in South Africa, Israeli occupied Arab territories, and Chile.[60]

Conclusions

It was the evident intention of those who drafted Article 2(7) of the Charter that the United Nations should not interfere in questions involving a state's treatment of its own subjects, which covers the entire field of human rights. But in several cases of alleged violations of human rights, United Nations organs have not observed this general principle of non-interference and brushed aside claims made by states that they have not accepted international legal obligations in respect of human rights which they have been accused of violating. For instance, UN organs have addressed censures to particular states on such matters, and the Assembly has even asserted its competence to recommend the application of coercive measures against South Africa because of that state's practice of *apartheid*.

Besides, notwithstanding conflicting interpretations of the principle of non-intervention under Article 2(7) of the Charter in particular cases of alleged violations of human rights, the International Court of Justice has not been asked to give a judicial opinion on the interpretation of the principle for the general guidance of UN member states, and its advice not sought when this was certainly desirable. This has not been conducive to promoting a sense of impartiality in contentious questions.

But though substantial majorities have indicated their reluctance to permit legal considerations to modify their political predilections on controversial issues in human rights questions, the UN Assembly and the Economic and Social Council have nevertheless pursued at the same time what may be described as the legal approach to the implementation of human rights through the adoption of international conventions and covenants which states may ratify or reject in accordance with the principle of consent. Clearly, since it is implicit in this approach that states are not bound by international legal obligations in respect of human rights unless they have voluntarily ratified the international conventions or covenants, this is tantamount to admitting that the human rights of their subjects are matters essentially within their domestic jurisdiction, to which the principle of non-intervention or non-interference is applicable, until such time as they ratify such conventions or covenants.

It can thus be seen that UN organs have acted ambivalently in human rights questions, and to cease being inconsistent it is essential that they should acknowledge that the only legitimate approach to the implementation of human rights is through the legal approach, which involves the voluntary acceptance by states of legal obligations under the international conventions or covenants which have been approved by the Assembly or such specialised agencies as the International Labour Organisation, and their observance of the procedures laid down in such multilateral agreements.

That UN organs should follow this approach, and abandon their practice of interfering in human rights questions which states can legally claim as matters of domestic jurisdiction, is clearly necessary because their unwarranted interference in cases of alleged violations of human rights, with scant respect for legal considerations, has created much antagonism between member states of the United Nations, and militated against its development as an agency for dealing with matters that are legitimately within its competence under the Charter.

As to the exception to the general principle of non-intervention laid down in Article 2(7) of the Charter, under which the Security Council is competent to authorise enforcement measures to maintain or restore international peace and security if it determines that a threat to the peace, breach of the peace, or act of aggression arises out of a matter within the domestic jurisdiction of a state, it is difficult to see how this is applicable to a state's violation of the human rights of its subjects which does not endanger the territorial integrity or political independence of another state, as in the case of South Africa's practice of *apartheid*. Besides, it needs to be emphasised that those member states of the United Nations which practise some form of tyranny within their territories are ill-qualified to advocate the application of coercive measures by the United Nations against a state whose form of tyranny they happen to dislike.

Finally, it must be pointed out that such colonial issues as Algeria and Tunisia which were considered at the United Nations before the peoples of those countries gained independence, as well as the Rhodesian affair, in which questions involving human rights were significant factors, have not been mentioned in this chapter because in dealing with these matters the United Nations was primarily concerned with the collective 'right of self-determination' — a type of right 'clearly different in kind from the individual form of human rights which are normally understood under the term', and the attainment of which is not bound to lead to the realisation of individual rights.[61] These issues will be considered in the next chapter which deals with the principle of non-intervention and de-colonisation.

IV. THE UNITED NATIONS AND COLONIAL QUESTIONS CLAIMED AS MATTERS OF DOMESTIC JURISDICTION

At San Francisco in 1945 it was decided to include three chapters on dependent territories in the Charter of the United Nations: Chapter XI (Articles 73-4), which was essentially a general declaration of colonial policy by member states of the United Nations with responsibilities for the administration of territories whose peoples had not yet attained a full measure of self-government; Chapter XII (Articles 75-85), which described the basic objectives of the international trusteeship system for the administration and supervision of such territories as might be placed under that arrangement by subsequent agreements with the governments that would administer them; and Chapter XIII (Articles 86-91), which dealt with the composition, functions and powers of the United Nations Trusteeship Council that was to supervise the administration of the trust territories.

It was agreed that a basic aim of the trusteeship system would be 'to promote the political, economic, social and educational advancement of the trust territories, and their progressive development towards self-government or independence as may be appropriate to the particular circumstances of each territory and its peoples and the freely expressed wishes of the peoples concerned, and as may be provided by the terms of each trusteeship agreement' (Article 76b); and that the system would apply to (i) territories then held under Mandates established by the League of Nations after the First World War: (ii) territories detached from enemy states as a result of the Second World War: and (iii) territories voluntarily placed under the system by states responsible for their administration (Article 77). Moreover, it was laid down in Chapter XIII (Article 87) that:

> The General Assembly and, under its authority, the Trusteeship Council, in carrying out their functions, may: (a) consider reports submitted by the administering authority; (b) accept petitions and examine them in consultation with the administering authority; (c) provide for periodic visits to the respective trust territories at times agreed upon with the administering authority; and (d) take these and other actions in conformity with the terms of the trusteeship agreements.

It was thus made clear that the administering powers under the trusteeship system would be legally obliged to accept arrangements for the United Nations supervision of their administration of trust territories, and to abide by the terms of the trusteeship agreements designed to effect the self-government or independence of those peoples under their stewardship. Since, therefore, the administering powers were made legally accountable to the United Nations for the administration of trust territories, they could not claim that the policies which they pursued in such territories were matters within their domestic jurisdiction, and that the principle of non-intervention under Article 2(7) prohibited the Trusteeship Council or the Assembly from putting forward recommendations on such matters.[1]

Unlike the administering powers of trust territories, those states administering non-self-governing territories not placed under the trusteeship system were not made similarly accountable to the United Nations. The Declaration Regarding Non-Self-Governing Territories in Article 73 of the Charter did not require the colonial powers to accept the international supervision machinery of the trusteeship system; their legal obligation was limited under clause (e) of the Article to the transmission to the Secretary-General for information purposes, subject to such limitation as security and constitutional considerations might require, *statistical and other information of a technical nature relating to economic, social and educational conditions* in their colonial territories. They were not legally obligated to transmit to the Secretary-General information of a political nature indicating the development of self-government within their colonies, and in view of this, their promise under Article 73(b) — 'to develop self-government, to take due account of the political aspirations of the peoples, and to assist them in the progressive development of their free political institutions, according to the particular circumstances of each territory and its peoples and their varying stages of advancement' — was essentially a moral, not a legal obligation. It is reasonable to assume, therefore, that the architects of Article 73 intended that the timing and manner in which the colonial peoples were to advance to self-government were to be regarded as matters essentially within the domestic jurisdiction of the colonial powers. Certainly, this was the view of the United Kingdom delegation at the San Francisco Conference, for in its report summarising the work of the Conference on Colonial Policy and Trusteeship, it was stated: 'We have evolved three chapters dealing with (a) general declaration of policy: (b) a system of international trusteeship for the limited categories of territories defined at Yalta; (c) the functions of a trusteeship Council. (a) does not infringe our sovereign rights, which are protected by the overriding provisions elsewhere in the Charter relating to domestic jurisdiction'.[2] Clearly, the UK delegation assumed that the principle of non-intervention under Article 2(7) was applicable to the policies of administering powers in their colonies, and this was stressed in the British government's White Paper published shortly after the San Francisco Conference. 'The general declaration in Chapter XI is the first comprehensive statement of Colonial policy to be included in an international instrument,' it stated. 'Its inclusion is due to the initiative of the United Kingdom and Australia, who took the lead in the drafting of this Chapter. The Chapter prescribes the principles of Colonial Administration and lays special emphasis on the political, economic, social and educational advancement of the inhabitants of the territories (whose interests are recognised to be paramount), and on good neighbourliness in international relations. It does not empower the United

Nations Organisation to intervene in the application of these principles by the Powers concerned. Provision is however made for the regular supply to the Secretary-General, for information purposes, of statistical and other material relating to economic, social and educational conditions in Colonial territories.'[3]

At one stage in the discussions of the Five Power Consultative Group (The U.S.A., U.S.S.R., U.K., France and China) which, with Committee II/4 of the San Francisco Conference, was responsible for the drafting of the Declaration, the Soviet Union's delegate tried to secure provision in the text for the transmission of information by the administering powers of political matters, in addition to information on economic, social and educational conditions in colonial territories. But the delegates of Britain and France were opposed to this, the latter protesting that 'the Charter provisions on colonial questions ought to be minimal',[4] and when the Consultative Group considered the final draft of the Declaration on 18th June 1945, he made a statement to make it clear that none of the provisions submitted for the approval of that committee implied total or partial renunciation by the French Government of the right to take advantage of the article on domestic jurisdiction.[5]

It can thus be seen that the major colonial powers, Britain and France, were anxious to have it recognised that the principles laid down in the general declaration, under Article 73 of the Charter, were not meant to override the principle of non-intervention in colonial questions. Though they accepted the principle that they should ensure the political advancement of the colonial peoples, they successfully opposed the Soviet attempt to make the administering powers transmit to the Secretary-General of the United Nations information on political matters relating to their colonial territories.[6] Moreover, though they accepted the principle that 'self-government' should be developed in forms appropriate to the particular circumstances of colonial territories, they rejected 'independence' as a co-equal alternative goal for such territories, as indicated by the following account of the debates on the subject in Committee II/4 of the San Francisco Conference.

At the sixth meeting of Committee II/4 on 17 May 1945, the Chinese delegate proposed that instead of the clause 'to develop self-government in forms appropriate to the varying circumstances of each territory', the following text should be used: 'to promote development towards independence or self-government as may be appropriate to the particular circumstances of each territory'. In favour of the proposal, it was argued that 'the change did not imply that all dependent territories would necessarily attain independent status; but independence was an aim of many dependent peoples and its attainment should not be excluded by the terms of the Charter'. Against this motion, however, it was argued that 'the word "self-government" did not exclude the possibility of "independence" and represented a broad measure of agreement which it would be inexpedient to impair by the substitution of a more controversial wording. Furthermore, the word "independence" meant different things to different peoples, and its use might lead to confusion. The use of the word "independence" would cause political uncertainty, which would tend to prevent capital development and to dissuade governments from spending money on strategic works. The ultimate result would be the creation of numerous small states at a time when the interdependence of all peoples was becoming increasingly desirable'.[7] After informal consultations among the delegations concerned, however, the Chinese delegate agreed to withdraw his proposal for the insertion in the general declaration on dependent territories of a reference to independence, as an alternative goal with self-government, if independence were included among the objectives to be sought in the political development of the territories placed under the international trusteeship system,[8] and this was the formula finally accepted by Committee II/4 and the Conference as a whole.

Some delegations asserted that the acceptance of this formula would give the general impression that 'the Conference intended that territories under trusteeship, but not other dependent territories, might eventually attain independence', and that "self-determination", a more concrete word than "self-government", had been approved by Committee I/1 of the Conference for inclusion among general principles in another part of the Charter.[9] Certainly, the fact that the Charter acknowledged the principle of self-determination of peoples in Articles 1(2) and 55 of the Charter, but did not mention or re-affirm it in the declaration on colonial policy in Chapter XI, sowed the seeds for much controversy over colonial questions within the United Nations. Hence, before examining the record of the United Nations in connection with the process of decolonisation that took place after World War II, it is important that we should consider whether the architects of the Charter intended that the principle of self-determination should override the principle of non-intervention under Article 2(7) which the Colonial powers claimed was applicable to their colonial policies notwithstanding their acceptance of the Declaration Regarding Non-Self-Governing Territories in Chapter XI.

The Principle of Self-Determination

During the Second World War, E.H. Carr asserted that 'the principle of self-determination, strictly defined, required that a group of people of reasonable size desirous of constituting a state should be allowed to constitute a state'.[10] But it should be realised, as one writer has emphasised, 'at various times and various places it has been used to define the right of self-government, the right of colonial peoples to independence, the right of minority groups to determine their own fate, the right of independent states to expropriate foreign industries, and a host of variations on these themes'.[11]

Though the principle was included in Articles 1(2) and 55 of the Charter of the United Nations, no attempt was made to define it in that document. To seek light on what those who were responsible for its inclusion in the Charter intended, it is thus necessary to examine the discussions on the matter at the San Francisco Conference.

No reference was made to the principle of self-determination in the great power proposals for a general international organisation which were agreed to at Dumbarton Oaks in 1944. But at the outset of the San Francisco Conference in 1945, the foreign ministers of the United States, U.S.S.R., the United Kingdom and China decided to amend paragraph 2 of Chapter I (Purposes) of the proposals, viz. 'to develop friendly relations among nations and to take other appropriate measures to strengthen universal peace' to read as follows: 'to develop friendly relations among nations based on respect for the principle of equal rights and self-determination of peoples, and to take other appropriate measures to strengthen universal peace'. The amendment had been proposed by the Soviet Union who had emerged at San Francisco as the champion of colonial peoples, but was soon to show that it had no intention of honouring its pledge at Yalta to permit free elections of governments responsive to the will of the Eastern European countries occupied by the Soviet forces. Though 'the United States delegation felt that the Soviet proposal could be used as a cover for Soviet expansionism, it agreed that it would be difficult to oppose the principle',[12] and the other great powers, Britain and China, followed suit.

Russell and Muther have made it quite clear that in the view of the Soviet Union the principle of equal rights and self-determination required that the dependent peoples of both colonial and trust territories should be enabled to obtain national independence as soon as possible,[13] but discussions in Committee I/1, to which the sponsoring powers' amendment was referred, revealed two conflicting opinions on the principle. In the Summary Report of the Sixth Meeting of the Committee, these were described as follows:

> Concerning the principle of self-determination, it was strongly emphasised on the one side that this principle corresponded closely to the will and desires of peoples everywhere and should be clearly enunciated in the Chapter; on the other side, it was stated that the principle conformed to the purposes of the Charter only insofar as it implied the right of self-government of peoples and not the right of secession.[14]

There was no attempt to define the principle of self-determination in the first opinion referred to, but it was implied in the other opinion that in the context of Charter purposes the principle meant no more than the right of peoples in existing states, presumably national groups, to obtain self-government within the sovereignty of those states; recognition of the principle did not mean that these peoples were entitled to independent statehood. This, of course, was a substantially different interpretation of the principle from that which had been put forward by the Soviet Union, viz. that it required that nations struggling for freedom should be granted independent statehood. It may be assumed, therefore, that the difference of opinion between the anti-colonialist delegations and their opponents over the question of including 'independence' as an objective for the political development of colonial peoples in the Declaration Regarding Non-Self-Governing Territories, to which reference was made in the account of the proceedings of Committee II/4 at San Francisco, largely accounted for their differing viewpoints on the principle of self-determination in Committee I/1.

One gets the impression that had there been insistence on the inclusion of a definition of the principle in the Charter, there would have been no agreement to accept the sponsoring powers' amendment, and it was not surprising that Committee I/1's acceptance of the amendment without change was presented to Commission I with an interpretation that was couched in the following vague terms:

> The Committee after considering paragraph 2 as amended by the sponsoring governments found it satisfactory and decided to recommend it to you.
>
> The Committee understands that the principle of equal rights of peoples and that of self-determination are two complementary parts of one standard of conduct; that the respect of that principle is a basis for the development of friendly relations and is one of the measures to strengthen universal peace; that an essential element of the principle in question is a free and genuine expression of the will of the people, which avoids cases of the alleged expression of the popular will, such as those used for their own ends by Germany and Italy in later years. [15]

This statement, as Benjamin Rivlin has argued, did not answer such questions as: 'What is meant by self-determination? Does the Charter impose any obligations with regard to its exercise? To whom does the principle apply? Under what circumstances can it be invoked?' [16] Though at San Francisco several comments were made on the need for the clarification of such matters in the Co-ordination Committee which reviewed texts with the object of improving phraseology and removing inconsistencies, and it was agreed that the Chairman and Rapporteur of Committee I/1 should be asked for a clearer interpretation than had been provided, [17] the Conference finally approved the inclusion of the principle of equal rights and self-determination of peoples in Articles 1(2) and 55 of the Charter without this being done. As Sir Francis Vallat has pointed out, 'no guidance is given in the Charter whether the principle constitutes a legal right or is political in character. Nor is there any real guidance as to its intended content'.[18]

It is difficult to see, therefore, how it can be claimed that the inclusion of the principle of self-determination in the Charter gave rise to legal rights and obligations, as some writers have asserted,[19] so that the Colonial powers that signed the Charter could no longer claim that their policies relating to the political development of their colonial territories were matters essentially within their domestic jurisdiction, to which the principle of non-intervention under Article 2(7) was applicable. This was tacitly admitted by the anti-colonialist forces in the United Nations when Afghanistan, Burma, Egypt, India, Indonesia, Iran, Iraq, Lebanon, Pakistan, the Philippines, Saudi-Arabia, Syria and the Yemen proposed in 1951 that the Assembly should draw up an article on the right to self-determination for inclusion in the draft international covenants on human rights which were then being prepared by the United Nations Commission on Human Rights.[20] The adoption of the proposal by the Assembly in 1952[21] was thus a recognition of the fact that the principle of self-determination in the Charter required to be written into law. Indeed, it was not until 1955 that the Third Committee of the Assembly approved the text of an article in which 'the right of self-determination' was defined as 'the right of all peoples to freely determine their political status and to freely pursue their economic, social and cultural development, including the right of peoples freely to dispose of their natural wealth and resources'.[22] It should also be noted that the international covenants on human rights adopted by the Assembly in 1966,[23] both of which include an article on 'the right of self-determination', cannot impose precise international legal obligations on their state-signatories until they are ratified by them.[24]

The initiative taken by the anti-colonialist forces in the Assembly during the 1950s to convert the principle of self-determination into a legal right for colonial peoples and an international legal obligation for colonial powers, through the inclusion of such a right in the projected international covenants on human rights, was but one means by which they hoped to extend international jurisdiction over matters claimed by colonial powers to be essentially within their domestic jurisdiction to which the principle of non-intervention applied. Even before the drafting of the international covenants began, those states that were anxious to enlarge the competence of the United Nations in colonial questions had embarked upon the attempt to make states administering non-self-governing territories more accountable to the Organisation under Article 73 of the Charter, than had been intended by the draftsmen of Article 2(7) of the Charter at San Francisco. In fact, between 1946 and 1960 one can perceive a gradual extension of the Assembly's competence with regard to the transmission and examination of information under Article 73, and its assertion of the right to decide whether or not a territory was non-self-governing.

The Role Assumed by the Assembly under Article 73(1945-60)

As already stated, the main colonial powers considered that the general principle of non-interference under Article 2(7) applied to their administration of those non-self-governing territories not placed under the United Nations trusteeship system. They insisted that their acceptance of Article 73(b) — 'to develop self-government, to take due account of the political aspirations of the peoples, and to assist them in the progressive development of their free political institutions, according to the particular circumstances of each territory and its peoples and their varying stages of advancement' — involved no more than the recognition of general principles which they were free to interpret according to their own judgment. Certainly, their only specific commitment relating to colonial territories was laid down in clause (e) of Article 73, viz. the transmission to the Secretary-General for information purposes, subject to such limitations as security and constitutional considerations might require, statistical and other information of a technical nature relating to economic, social and educational conditions in such territories.

This interpretation of Article 73 was not acceptable to those states who wanted to make the colonial powers more accountable to the United Nations for their colonial administration. From 1946 onwards, therefore, various initiatives were taken by them to extend the competence of the Assembly with regard to the non-self-governing territories not placed under trusteeship, and the support forthcoming from that body was sufficient to enable them to achieve some success, though not sufficient to satisfy the extreme anti-colonialist states, such as the Soviet Union, most of the Afro-Asian states, and some Latin American countries.

The first controversial issue arose during the second part of the first session of the Assembly in 1946, when consideration was given to the Secretary-General's statement summarising the information transmitted under Article 73(e) which had been included in his annual report in response to the Assembly's request.[25] In his report, which enumerated the seventy four non-self-governing territories administered by eight member states of the United Nations (Australia, Belgium, Denmark, France, the Netherlands, New Zealand, the United Kingdom, and the United States), the Secretary-General suggested the need for an *ad hoc* committee to assist the Assembly in examining and making recommendations on the information provided,[26] but this suggestion was viewed with some misgivings by several administering powers.

When the question was considered by a sub-committee of the Assembly's Fourth Committee (Trusteeship, including Non-Self-Governing Territories) in December 1946,[27] four of the administering powers (Denmark, the Netherlands, the United Kingdom and the United States) proposed that the information transmitted in the course of 1947 should be summarised, analysed and classified by the Secretary-General and included in his report to the second session of the Assembly, when that body might be able to decide whether any other procedure for dealing with the information was desirable. This was approved by the sub-committee, but later rejected by the Fourth Committee, which adopted a Cuban proposal that called for the establishment of an *ad hoc* committee to examine the information transmitted under Article 73(e).

The French delegate asserted that the establishment of this *ad hoc* committee was contrary to Article 73(e), but it was approved by the Fourth Committee and endorsed by the Assembly on 13 December 1946. Under the resolution, the *ad hoc* committee, which was to consist of representatives of the administering powers and an equal number of representatives of states elected by the Assembly, was invited 'to examine the Secretary-General's summary and analysis of the information transmitted under Article 73(e) of the Charter with a view to aiding the General Assembly in its consideration of this information, and with a view to making recommendations to the General Assembly regarding the procedures to be followed in the future and the means of ensuring that its advice, expert knowledge and experience of the specialised agencies are used to the best advantage'.[28]

A year later the Assembly went a stage further when it invited its Fourth Committee to replace the *ad hoc* committee by a special committee whose terms of reference would be to report to the Assembly not only with such procedural recommendations as it might deem fit, but also with such substantive recommendations, as it might consider desirable, relating to the economic, social and educational conditions generally in colonial territories.[29] The Special Committee was thus not given the function of making recommendations to the Assembly on individual colonial territories, and though some anti-colonialist elements in the Assembly were particularly anxious to extend the committee's functions to cover political matters, this was not acceptable to the majority in the Assembly. A proposal recommending that states administering non-self-governing territories should transmit information on local government in those territories was rejected, and the Assembly resolved instead that the voluntary transmission of information on political matters and its summarization by the Secretary-General were in conformity with the spirit of Article 73 and should be duly noted and encouraged.[30] The fact was that since 1946 four out of the eight states administering colonial territories — Australia, Denmark, the Netherlands, and the United States — had voluntarily included information on government institutions in their reports, and France had transmitted information concerning changes in the constitutional status of its dependent territories. Only the United Kingdom and Belgium had restricted the information supplied to economic, social and educational conditions in their colonies. This, of course, was in strict accord with Article 73(e), since the clause did not specify that information on political matters should be transmitted. But the Soviet bloc states considered that the provision of such information was not only essential, but also a legal obligation under Article 73. In 1948, at a meeting of the special committee which had been set up by the Assembly, they argued that in the light of all the clauses of Article 73 the states administering colonial territories could not claim that the transmission of information was restricted to the economic, social and educational conditions mentioned in clause (e) of the article. But the delegates of Belgium, France, the Netherlands and the United Kingdom insisted that they were not legally obliged to submit information on political matters under Article 73(e), the only clause which made reference to their specific obligations.[31]

The majority of member states of the United Nations approached the question cautiously when the delegate of the Soviet Union put forward a formal proposal in the Fourth Committee of the Assembly, in October 1948, that it should be made obligatory for the administering powers to submit information on 'the development of organs of self-government in the non-self-governing territories and the participation of the local population in the work of these organs' and that United Nations representatives should be sent annually to the non-self-governing territories in order to make surveys on the spot. In fact, they rejected the Soviet motion,[32] and later, in December 1949, the Assembly merely expressed the hope that such of the members as had not done so might voluntarily include details on the government of non-self-governing territories in the information transmitted by them under Article 73(e) of the Charter.[33]

But though at this juncture the Assembly did not accept the Soviet view that the submission of information on institutions of government should be made compulsory, it asserted its competence to be informed of constitutional changes in a non-self-governing territory to decide whether an administering power was justified in discontinuing the transmission of information on economic, social and educational matters. There had been several instances of administering powers simply reporting that information under Article 73(e) would no longer be transmitted in respect of certain territories because they had become fully self-governing or accorded equality within the constitution of the metropolitan state, and this had prompted the delegate of India to propose in the Fourth Committee of the Assembly, in October 1948, that the Assembly should request the members concerned to communicate such information as might be relevant, 'including the constitution, legislative act, or executive order providing for the government of the territory and the constitutional relationship of the territory to the Government of the metropolitan country'.[34]

During the debate on the Indian proposal in the Fourth Committee the delegates of the United Kingdom, Belgium and Australia maintained that the motion went beyond the terms of reference of Article 73 and, if implemented, would constitute interference in the domestic jurisdiction of those states administering non-self-governing territories through making them more accountable to the United Nations than had been intended by the framers of the Charter. The delegate of New Zealand also felt that it was not within the competence of the Fourth Committee to discuss whether a particular territory had ceased to be non-self-governing and this, he feared, might well occur if the Indian draft resolution were approved. On the other hand, the delegates of Denmark and the United States were prepared to support the motion on the understanding that the information required did not infringe the right of administering powers to determine the constitutional position and status of dependent territories within their sovereignty.

The majority of delegates in the Fourth Committee supported the Indian proposal that it was essential that the United Nations should be informed of any change in the constitutional position and status of any non-self-governing territory as a result of which the responsible government concerned thought it unnecessary to transmit information of that territory under Article 73(e), and it was approved by the Assembly in plenary session.[35] During the debate preceding its adoption, however, the French delegate expressed the view of most of the administering powers when he asserted that though he was not opposed to the substance of the resolution he feared that it represented an attempt to set a definition of non-self-governing territories and that it would lead to a discussion of constitutional and political questions in such territories in the United Nations, in contravention of the principle of non-intervention in matters within the domestic jurisdiction of the administering powers.

Moves within the Special Committee which dealt with the transmission of information under Article 73(e) and the Fourth Committee of the Assembly soon confirmed the fears of the administering powers. The first move was made in 1949 when the Soviet delegate drew the attention of the Special Committee to communications which had been submitted by three administering powers explaining why they had ceased transmitting information under Article 73(e) concerning various non-self-governing territories, viz. the United Kingdom territories of Malta and Pitcairn Island; the French territories of Indo-China, French Establishments in Oceania and India, Guadeloupe and Dependencies, French Guiana, Reunion and St. Pierre et Miquelon; and the Panama Canal Zone under United States administration. For instance, the United Kingdom stated that Malta, although not yet in full control of its external affairs, had achieved full responsibility for local self-goverment on 5 September 1947, and that since economic, social and educational conditions in Malta were now the sole concern of the government of Malta, it considered the transmission of information on these matters under Article 73(e) 'inappropriate and indeed impossible'.[36]

The delegate of the Soviet Union proposed that it should be recognised that an administering state could not cease transmitting information on a particular territory until all the details concerning changes in its status had been considered by the Special Committee and that body had put forward recommendations to the Assembly regarding the cessation of such data. But though the Special Committee approved a French motion that it was not competent to consider the Soviet proposal, the Fourth Committee of the Assembly later adopted an Egyptian proposal, slightly amended by Thailand, which considered that it was within the responsibility of the Assembly to express its opinion on the principles which had guided or which might in future guide the member states concerned in enumerating the territories for which the obligation existed to transmit information under Article 73(e) of Chapter XI of the Charter, and invited any special committee which the Assembly might appoint to deal with information transmitted under that article, to examine the factors which should be taken into account in deciding whether any territory was or was not a territory whose people had not yet attained a full measure of self-government.[37]

In accordance with the terms of reference of this resolution, which was endorsed by the Assembly in December 1949 by a vote of 30 to 12, with 10 abstentions,[38] the Special Committee[39] submitted a report to the Assembly in 1951. But it was generally agreed that further study of the matter was needed, and it was not until 1953, after several discussions, that the Assembly approved a list of factors which it recommended should be used by itself and the administering powers 'as a guide in determining whether any Territory, due to changes in its constitutional status, is or is no longer within the sphere of Chapter XI of the Charter, in order that in view of the documentation provided under resolution 222(111) of 3 November 1948, a decision may be taken by the General Assembly on the continuation or cessation of the transmission of information required by Chapter XI of the Charter'.[40]

It is important to note that it was stated in the resolution, which was adopted by a vote of 32 to 19, with 6 abstentions — this was not a two thirds majority but it was decided that a simple majority would suffice — that the manner in which territories referred to in Chapter XI of the Charter could become fully self-governing was primarily through the attainment of independence, although it was recognised that self-government could also be achieved by association with another state or group of states if this was done freely and on the basis of absolute equality. Moreover, since it was also asserted that each concrete case should be decided 'in the light of the particular circumstances of that case and taking into account the right of self-determination of peoples', it may be deduced that the right of self-determination was considered not necessarily synonymous with the attainment of complete independence; in other words, a dependent people could opt for a self-governing status within the framework of another state's sovereignty in consonance with the right of self-determination.

Those states administering non-self-governing territories were strongly opposed to the Assembly being given the competence to determine whether a territory had achieved self-government, and protested against such an important question being decided by a simple majority in the Assembly. But the Assembly asserted its competence in this connection by resolving that the transmission of information under Article 73(e) by the United States no longer applied to Puerto Rico at its eighth session in 1953,[41] and re-asserted its authority with regard to Greenland in 1954 when that territory was integrated with Denmark,[42] and also with regard to Netherlands Antilles and Surinam in 1955,[43] after the Netherlands government had provided information concerning constitutional developments leading to the promulgation of a Charter for the Kingdom of the Netherlands, Surinam and Netherlands Antilles in 1954.

Later, in 1959, the Assembly resolved that Alaska and Hawaii had achieved self-government through their free integration on an equal basis into the United States, the metropolitan country, so that the latter was no longer required to transmit information under Article 73(e) in respect of those territories.[44] This again emphasised that the majority of member states of the United Nations were determined to act on the assumption that the question of deciding whether Article 73(e) applied to a particular territory was not a matter within the domestic jurisdiction of the colonial powers to which the principle of non-intervention under Article 2(7) was applicable.

It can thus be seen that although specific provision had not been laid down in Chapter XI of the Charter for the kind of international supervision and control of non-self-governing territories that was to apply to trust territories under Chapter XII, the Assembly had asserted its competence during the first decade or so of the United Nations experiment to play a supervisory role similar in some respects to that which it had been authorised to perform, in collaboration with the Trusteeship Council, with regard to trust territories. By the end of the 1950s it was generally accepted that it had the right not only to discuss and make recommendations of a general nature on economic, social and educational conditions in non-self-governing territories under Article 73, but also to decide whether or not a particular territory had ceased to be non-self-governing in order to determine whether an administering power was justified in discontinuing the transmission of information on such matters, and by the end of 1960 only Portugal, which had become a member of the United Nations in 1955, was refusing to transmit information on her African colonies, as required by the Assembly.[45]

It has to be recognised, therefore, that although the Assembly had not claimed by the end of the 1950s that it should be provided with information on the political development of the peoples of non-self-governing territories — a resolution which it adopted in 1959 referred to 'the inextricable relationship between developments in political and functional fields', but did not claim that the transmission of information on political matters was obligatory[46] — it had assumed a role which the architects of the Charter had not intended it to perform. Moreover, its intervention was not confined to the critical examination of economic, social and educational conditions in non-self-governing territories and to determining when a territory had ceased to be non-self-governing in accordance with certain criteria. From the early years of the United Nations, the Assembly, like the Security Council, had also asserted its competence to interfere in various ways in colonial conflicts, notwithstanding the claims of those colonial powers directly involved that such interference was a contravention of Article 2(7) of the Charter.

Though the United Nations did not play a very significant part in these colonial conflicts prior to 1960, with the exception of the Indonesian affair, the first case in which Article 2(7) was invoked by a colonial power to oppose interference by the United Nations, the fact that the Organisation asserted its competence to discuss and make recommendations on such questions laid the basis for its subsequent practice in the 1960s and 1970s.

United Nations Intervention in Colonial Conflicts (1946-60)

The *Indonesian affair* was brought to the attention of the Security Council by the Ukrainian S.S.R. on 21 January 1946, a few months after British troops had arrived in Indonesia, with the consent of the Allied Powers, for the purpose of accepting the surrender of Japanese troops, and on 11 October of that year, at a meeting of the Security Council,[47] the Ukrainian delegate contended that the British authorities had employed force to suppress the Indonesian nationalist movement, and that such action was a violation of the principle of self-determination under Article 1(2) of the Charter. He stressed that there was a situation in Indonesia which, under Article 34 of the Charter, threatened the maintenance of international peace and security, and appealed to the Security Council for an 'on the spot' investigation with a view to effecting a peaceful settlement of the question.

The United Kingdom delegate asserted that British forces had been obliged to defend themselves against attack by the local inhabitants, and that their task had been to restore the territory taken by the Japanese to the jurisdiction of the Netherlands, the sovereign authority in the region. He also maintained that it would be a contravention of the principle of non-intervention under Article 2(7) of the Charter for the United Nations to send an investigating commission to Indonesia on the ground that the situation in that territory was a matter essentially within the domestic jurisdiction of the Netherlands. This was reiterated by the Netherlands delegate who also argued that there was no contravention of Article 1(2) — the principle of self-determination — because Indonesia was a non-self-governing territory under Chapter XI of the Charter. He insisted that the Security Council did not possess the competence to deal with the question.

At this stage in the Indonesian affair the Security Council took no action. The Ukrainian S.S.R. proposal for the establishment of a United Nations Commission to investigate the situation was rejected. So, too, was a motion put forward by Egypt, which suggested that the Security Council should express the hope that negotiations which had started between the Netherlands government and the Indonesian national leaders would 'rapidly be concluded by a happy solution inspired by the aims and principles of the Charter and principally by the right of self-determination of peoples', and be informed in a very short time of the results of these negotiations. The President of the Council then declared the matter closed.

The negotiations which took place between the Netherlands government and the self-proclaimed Republic of Indonesia led to the conclusion of the Linggadjati Agreement in March 1947. This provided for the *de facto* recognition of the Indonesian Republic in Java, Madura and Sumatra, the establishment of a sovereign, democratic federal United States of Indonesia, consisting of the Republic and at least two other states to be formed in Borneo and the eastern islands, and the linking of the United States of Indonesia to the Netherlands in a Netherlands Indonesian Union. But the parties to the Agreement were still divided over a number of issues, such as the status and powers which the Republic of Indonesia was to possess until the Agreement was implemented, and in July 1947, the Dutch launched what was described as a 'police action' to deal with the disorders throughout Indonesia.

It was this development which prompted the Australian delegate to bring the Indonesian question before the Security Council on 30 July[48], and to propose that the Council should declare that the hostilities constituted a breach of the peace under Article 39 of the Charter and take immediate action to restore international peace. But he did not urge that the Council should authorise enforcement measures under Articles 41 and 42; instead, he recommended that it should call upon the governments of the Netherlands and the Republic of Indonesia, under Article 40,[49] to comply, without prejudice to their rights, claims or position, with the following measures: (a) the cessation of hostilities, and (b) the settlement of their disputes by arbitration in accordance with article 17 of the Linggadjati Agreement.

The Netherlands delegate strongly contested the Australian argument, which was generally supported by the delegates of the Soviet Union, Colombia, India and Syria, that the conflict was between two sovereign states. He maintained that the 'police action' being taken against the Indonesian nationalists was a matter essentially within the domestic jurisdiction of the Netherlands, which was 'sovereign in the region concerned' because the Republic of Indonesia was but one of its constituent elements. He thus argued that the Security Council did not possess the competence to intervene on the ground that it was prohibited from doing so under Article 2(7) of the Charter.

The Belgian delegate considered that the competence of the Security Council to intervene in the affair required verification, but as the debate proceeded it became clear that some delegates, particularly those of the United States and China, were anxious to avoid protracted legal arguments over the question of competence. In fact, the decision taken by the Security Council reflected the view advanced by the United States delegate that the Australian proposal should be amended to omit references to Articles 39 and 40 of the Charter, and no attempt was made to justify United Nations intervention by citing an article of the Charter. The resolution adopted simply stated that the Security Council noted 'with concern the hostilities in progress between the armed forces of the Netherlands and the Republic of Indonesia' and called upon the parties '(a) to cease hostilities forthwith, and (b) to settle their disputes by arbitration or by other peaceful means and keep the Security Council informed about the progress of the settlement'.[50]

The fact that no effort was made to seek the advisory opinion of the International Court of Justice on the competence of the Security Council in the matter, notwithstanding the claim advanced by the Netherlands that it was a question of domestic jurisdiction to which the principle of non-intervention was applicable, established the precedent that the Security Council, the main political organ of the United Nations, was competent to decide that a colonial conflict was a matter of international concern on which it could take some action, although under traditional international law colonies fell within the domestic jurisdiction of the administering power, and under the Charter the colonial powers were only required to submit information under Article 73(e). Of course, since no guidance was given in the Charter on how a matter essentially within the domestic jurisdiction of a state was to be determined, the Council was given the loophole to decide what was politically expedient without necessarily taking into account the criterion of international law or seeking the judicial opinion of the International Court of Justice.

It will be recalled that at San Francisco, John Foster Dulles, who played such an important part in the drafting of Article 2(7) of the Charter, spoke in disparaging terms about international law in order to justify its omission as a criterion for determining whether or not a matter was essentially within the domestic jurisdiction of a state. He feared that its inclusion would lead to the erroneous belief that every subject dealt with by the United Nations would no longer be a matter of domestic jurisdiction on the grounds that the Charter would be a treaty which made international law, with the consequent danger that the whole purpose of the principle of non-intervention would be done away with. Moreover, in defence of the omission of any reference to what authority should determine the issue of jurisdiction, Dulles considered that it would not be an effective limitation on the United Nations in such matters if it were left to the Organisation to decide. As to the question being decided by the International Court of Justice, it was his view that this was impracticable because it would involve the acceptance of the compulsory jurisdiction of the Court by those states that had not accepted the compulsory clause under its Statute.[51] It was somewhat ironical, therefore, that in the Indonesian affair the United States delegate sought to avoid legal factors in the debate on the course of action the Security Council should take, not to limit the authority of the United Nations as Dulles thought was necessary, but to facilitate the assertion of its competence, since the adoption of the Council's resolution implied that the question was not a matter of domestic jurisdiction. Indeed, the United States voted in favour of inviting a representative of the Indonesian Republic, after the acceptance of the cease-fire called for by the Security Council by both sides, to participate in a discussion of the question. It was approved by the Council on 12 August 1947 by a vote of 8 to 3 (Belgium, France and the United Kingdom), notwithstanding the protest of the Netherlands delegate, who claimed that the Republic of Indonesia was not a sovereign state.[52]

On 25 August the Security Council decided to establish a commission of consuls in Batavia to supervise the implementation of the cease-fire,[53] after it had rejected a Belgian proposal that the question of the Council's competence should be referred to the International Court of Justice. It also appointed a Committee of Good Offices to assist the parties to the dispute to reach a pacific settlement.[54] But though this was acceptable to both sides, and subsequent negotiations, with the help of the Committee, led to agreement on a truce and the acceptance of various principles which provided the basis for future negotiations concerning the transfer of sovereignty from the Netherlands to an independent United States of Indonesia (The Renville Agreement of January 1948), the Committee of Good Offices reported in December of that year that 'the setting-up of an interim federal government by decree of the Government of the Netherlands which is apparently to occur before 1 January 1949, will contribute further to the opinion of the Republic that the Netherlands Government has been proceeding unilaterally to establish ultimately a United States of Indonesia on its own terms and without the Republic'. The Committee concluded, therefore, that it had no confidence that even the truce could be maintained as the possibility of political agreement became more remote,[55] and when the Dutch resumed military operations in Indonesia on 19 December 1948, it reported that the Netherlands had violated its obligations under the Renville Agreement.

When the matter was considered by the Security Council on 22-24

December,[56] the Netherlands delegate still insisted that the question was outside the competence of the Council because the Charter only dealt with relations between sovereign states, that it was a matter essentially within the domestic jurisdiction of the Netherlands to which the principle of non-intervention was applicable, and that it did not endanger international peace and security. Certainly, since the negotiations under the Renville Agreement were intended to pave the way to the transfer of sovereignty from the Netherlands to an independent United States of Indonesia, there was much to support the view advanced by the delegates of France and Belgium that the Republic of Indonesia did not qualify as a state in the meaning of the Charter on a basis of international law. Though both states admitted that the action taken by the Netherlands was brutal and shocking, they argued that this could not alter the legal considerations that should be taken into account, and emphasised that though the Netherlands government had expressed its readiness to see the question of the Security Council's competence submitted to the International Court of Justice, this had not been done.

But little or no attention was given to legal factors by the majority of delegates in the debate, and it was considered politic at that juncture to approve a resolution which called for the cessation of hostilities and the release of prisoners, and asked the Committee of Good Offices to supervise the implementation of these measures.[57] Since the Netherlands government did not respond satisfactorily to the Council's resolution, steps were soon taken for more extensive intervention in the Indonesian affair. On 28 January 1949 the Council recommended the immediate resumption of negotiations with a view to the establishment of a federal, independent and sovereign United States of Indonesia, with the transfer of sovereignty not later than 1 July 1950, and resolved that the Committee of Good Offices should henceforth be known as the United Nations Commission for Indonesia and empowered to assist the parties in implementing this resolution.[58]

That the Netherlands government eventually transferred complete sovereignty over Indonesia to the Republic of the United States of Indonesia — this was done in November 1949 — demonstrated the effectiveness of United Nations intervention in the affair. But undoubtedly this was largely due to the fact that the United States, which played a leading role in determining policy in the Security Council, exerted much pressure on the Netherlands government. Before the question was resolved the United States had suspended Marshall aid to the Netherlands in Indonesia and threatened further sanctions, if it did not move in the direction which the Security Council had pointed.[59] Certainly, after the resumption of military operations by the Dutch in December 1948, it would appear that the policy pursued by the United States in the Security Council was the outcome of political and moral considerations which did not conflict. On the one hand, the United States government had to take into account the traditional antipathy in the country to colonialism, which was expressed in the Congress when 'an amendment to the Economic Co-operation Act was debated which would make it obligatory on the administration to suspend assistance wherever such assistance was deemed incompatible with the obligations of the US under Article 1(2) of the Charter — the article expressly concerned with the principle of equal rights and self-determination of peoples';[60] on the other hand, there was the realisation on the part of the US government that 'the communists were winning the war of propaganda by wedding themselves to the cause of anti-colonialism and nationalism, and were putting the US in an invidious position. The temporising attitude to such issues must be reversed, and where more fittingly than in Indonesia, where Sukarno, the Republican President, had recently suppressed a communist rebellion and executed the leaders? If the new Indonesia became an ally of the West, the defensive perimeter of the US in the South Pacific would be advanced and secured'.[61] There was thus no apparent conflict between the moral and political considerations which the United States government felt it had to take into account, since both factors required that a settlement of the Indonesian question would result in an independent United States of Indonesia, and the United States was able to pursue a policy in the Security Council which had enough common ground with the views of other members of that body to enable it to function in the way that it did.

In contrast to the extensive and significant intervention by the United Nations in the Indonesian affair, its intervention in the conflicts between France and her protectorates of Morocco and Tunisia (1951-55) was very limited and did little to influence the course of those struggles. Not surprisingly, this evoked the impatience of the extreme anti-colonialist states, particularly the Afro-Asian members of the United Nations, who appeared to regard 'the principle of self-determination' under Article 1(2) of the Charter as synonymous with the legal right of colonial peoples to independent statehood. In fact, though the Assembly decided in 1953 to include 'the right of self-determination' in the draft international covenants on human rights, it could not become a legal right until those covenants had been ratified by their signatories. Besides, it was still the majority view in the United Nations, that the granting of 'self-government' within the framework of another state's sovereignty was not at variance with the right of self-determination of peoples.

The *Question of Morocco* was first brought before the Assembly in October 1951, when six Arab states complained about 'the violation of principles of the Charter and of the Declaration of Human Rights by France in Morocco', but this request to have the item placed on the Assembly's agenda did not secure the support of the required majority. In 1952, however, when thirteen Afro-Asian states alleged that civil liberties and democratic rights had been suppressed under French rule in Morocco, and that the explosive situation in that country constituted a threat to international peace and security, the Assembly decided, without discussion, to include the question on its agenda, and to refer it to its First Committee.[62]

Before the matter was considered by the First Committee, the French Foreign Minister had contended in the opening general debate of the Assembly that since France had acquired southern Morocco as a protectorate under the Treaty of Fez, which was concluded with the Sultan in 1912, the external relations of Morocco could only be conducted through the French government, and reforms in Morocco depended upon French initiative and Franco-Moroccan collaboration. Under the Charter, he had argued, the United Nations had not been given the competence to revise treaties, and the question of Morocco was a matter essentially within the domestic jurisdiction of France to which the principle of non-intervention under Article 2(7) was applicable. He had also maintained that not only the Assembly, but also the Security Council, could not claim competence in the matter; since the question of Morocco was within French jurisdiction, the only action that could be taken by the Council was the authorisation of enforcement measures in accordance with the exception to the general rule of non-intervention under Article 2(7), if it decided that the situation in Morocco was a threat to international peace and security, but it could not be reasonably claimed that this was so. For these reasons the French Foreign Minister had informed the Assembly that the French delegation would not take part in a discussion of the question in its First Committee.

The First Committee considered the Moroccan question in December 1952, when the delegates of Ethiopia, Egypt, India, Indonesia, Iraq, Lebanon, Pakistan, Saudi-Arabia, Syria and the Yemen asserted that France had been able to impose colonial rule on the people of Morocco for the past forty years through forcing the Treaty of Fez upon the Sultan in 1912. The fact was, they maintained, that Morocco could claim to have been a sovereign state before and after the establishment of the protectorate, since the Act of Algeciras of 1906 had recognised the independence of the Sultan and the integrity of his territory, but the French government had treated it as a French colony under the control of French immigrants. They also asserted that Morocco's claim to sovereignty had been upheld by the Permanent Court of International Justice in 1922, and that in 1952 the International Court of Justice had recognised the international character of the relations between France and Morocco, so that France could not claim, according to the criterion of international law, that the situation in Morocco was a matter within French jurisdiction and outside the competence of the United Nations. The Afro-Asian states thus contended that it was the duty of the United Nations to use its good offices in inviting both parties to negotiate.

As already mentioned, the French delegation did not participate in the debate, but the delegates of Australia, Belgium, the Netherlands, the Union of South Africa and the United Kingdom argued that France was protected from United Nations intervention in the matter by the principle of non-intervention under Article 2(7). To justify the argument that the question was one of French jurisdiction, the United Kingdom delegate maintained that the International Court of Justice had recognised that the Protectorate treaty of 1912 was valid, and that under that treaty, Morocco, while retaining certain attributes of sovereignty, had agreed that the control of its external relations should belong to France. He thus argued that the situation involving France and Morocco did not have an international character which removed it from French jurisdiction, and that because it was neither an international dispute nor a threat to international peace, the Assembly did not possess the competence to discuss and make recommendations on the matter under Article 10 or 14.

The United Kingdom delegate also asserted that since Morocco was recognised as a non-self-governing territory under Article 73 of the Charter, France's only obligation was to transmit information on economic, social and educational conditions in Morocco under clause (e) of that article, and that the United Nations could not therefore intervene in Franco-Moroccan political relations. But the delegates of the states in the Soviet bloc countered this by arguing that since France had undertaken to ensure the political advancement of the people of Morocco under clause (a) of the article, the situation in Morocco was not a matter within the domestic jurisdiction of France but within the competence of the Assembly. In addition, these delegates claimed that the Assembly was competent to take measures for the solution of the Moroccan question in accordance with the principle of equal rights and self-determination under Article 1(2) of the Charter. In their view, therefore, both Articles 73 and 1(2) of the Charter could override its Article 2(7).

In view of these conflicting interpretations of the Charter, and the fact that the decisions of the International Court of Justice had been quoted by the delegates of states that took different sides in the dispute, there was much to justify a move to ask the Court to provide some clarification on the question of competence, but this was not done. Instead, the First Committee adopted a resolution which, having stated its mindfulness of 'the necessity of developing friendly relations among nations based on respect for the principle of equal rights and self-determination of peoples', and expressed 'the confidence that, in pursuance of its proclaimed policies, the Government of France will endeavour to further the fundamental liberties of the people of Morocco, in conformity with the Purposes and Principles of the Charter', as well as 'the hope that the parties will continue negotiations on an urgent basis towards developing the free political institutions of the people of Morocco, with due regard to legitimate rights and interests under the established norms and practices of the law of nations', appealed to the parties involved to settle their disputes in accordance with the spirit of the Charter.

This mild resolution, which was endorsed by the Assembly by a vote of 45 to 3, with 11 abstentions,[63] had no apparent effect on French policy, and although during the next six months the situation in Morocco became more explosive, the requisite two-thirds majority was not forthcoming in the Assembly for the adoption of a resolution that would have appealed for the reduction of tension in Morocco and urged that 'the right of the Moroccan people to free, democratic political institutions be ensured'.[64] In fact, between 1954 and 1955, when the anti-French riots in Morocco became a source of much embarrassment to the French government, the Assembly simply expressed its confidence that a satisfactory solution to the problem would be found.[65] This was realised in 1956 when Morocco achieved independent statehood and membership of the United Nations.

Though the proceedings in the United Nations had shown that the majority of states considered that the Assembly was competent to discuss and make recommendations on the conflict in Morocco, notwithstanding the claim by France and other colonial powers that it was a matter of French jurisdiction to which the principle of non-intervention was applicable, they had not been in favour of exercising the same amount of pressure which had enabled the United Nations to play a significant role in the Indonesian affair. One can only infer that too many states were influenced by diplomatic considerations which militated against such a role in the Moroccan question.

The same comment is applicable to the part played by the United Nations in the *Question of Tunisia* which was brought to the attention of the Security Council, in April 1952, by several Afro-Asian states who alleged that the situation in Tunisia was seriously endangering the maintenance of international peace and security.[66] They also asserted that the French government's violation of the Treaty of Bardo of 1881, under which it had been provided that the French military occupation of Tunisia would cease when the French and Tunisian authorities agreed that the local administration was able to maintain order, had deprived the people of Tunisia of their 'right to self-government and self-determination'.

When the Security Council discussed the question of including the issue on its agenda on 12 April, the French delegate contended that the complainants against France had presented a false picture of the situation in Tunisia, and that the Bey had consented to abide by a programme of negotiations and a plan of reforms to satisfy the national aspirations of the Tunisian people, and had given instructions for the formation of a new government. He was opposed to interference in any form by the United Nations.

A proposal to include the question on the Council's agenda failed to obtain the requisite affirmative votes of seven members. The United

Kingdom delegate voted with France against the proposal, and Greece, the Netherlands, Turkey and the United States abstained. But the question was placed on the agenda of the Assembly at its seventh session later in 1952, in response to the request by thirteen Afro-Asian states who maintained that since the Security Council had refused to place the Tunisian question on its agenda, the Assembly was competent to consider the matter under Article 11(2) of the Charter as one relating to the maintenance of international peace and security.

In the First Committee of the Assembly the delegates of Australia, Belgium, the Netherlands, the Union of South Africa and the United Kingdom questioned the competence of the Assembly to interfere in the affair on the following grounds:

(i)   Since Tunisia was recognised as a non-self-governing territory under Article 73 of the Charter, this was tantamount to recognising that the Treaty of Bardo had removed Franco-Tunisian relations from the international plane. The Tunisian question was thus within the domestic jurisdiction of France, to which the principle of non-intervention under Article 2(7) was applicable, and all that France was obliged to do under the Charter was to submit information to the United Nations on economic, social and educational conditions in Tunisia.

(ii)   The exception to the general principle of non-intervention under Article 2(7), viz. the authorisation of enforcement measures by the Security Council, if that body decided that a situation arising out of a matter within a state's domestic jurisdiction constituted a threat to international peace and security, was not applicable to the Tunisian question. This was so because it could not be reasonably claimed that the situation threatened international peace and security. In any case, the Assembly did not have the competence to authorise enforcement measures if a threat to international peace arose out of a matter of domestic jurisdiction.

(iii)   It was impolitic for the Assembly to deal with the question because discussion in that body would serve to intensify unrest and further disorder in Tunisia.

In the light of the discussions which had led to the drafting of Articles 2(7) and 73 at San Francisco, as already explained, there were sound reasons for questioning the competence of the Assembly to intervene in the Tunisian affair, as in the Moroccan question. But a large number of delegations in the Assembly considered that it was competent to do so, though not for the same reasons.

Though it was not disputed that Tunisia, like Morocco, was recognised as a non-self-governing territory administered by France, it was argued that (i) Article 73 recognised that non-self-governing territories were no longer subject to the domestic law of the metropolitan country and established an international system: (ii) the Treaty of Bardo had recognised the Tunisian state as a separate entity and made only a partial delegation of powers to France, so that Franco-Moroccan relations were governed by an international treaty which removed any issues arising from its application from the domestic jurisdiction of France: (iii) the Assembly had jurisdiction under Article 10 of the Charter which authorised it to make recommendations on any matter within the scope of the Charter if the Security Council was not dealing with it: (iv) Article 11(2) empowered the Assembly to make recommendations on any question relating to the maintenance of international peace and security, if it was not seized by the Security Council; and (v) Article 14 of the Charter authorised the Assembly to recommend measures for the peaceful adjustment of any situation subject to the same proviso.

It was also argued by some delegates that 'the right of peoples to self-determination' under Article 1(2) of the Charter prevailed over the obligations that might obtain under any other international treaty, such as the treaty of Bardo (1881), since Article 103 of the Charter stated that 'in the event of a conflict between the obligations of the Members of the United Nations under the present Charter and their obligations under any other international agreement, their obligations under the present Charter shall prevail'. But this argument assumed that the principle of self-determination under Article 1(2) of the Charter was equivalent to a legal right, which was hardly tenable; for though 'the right of self-determination' had been included in the draft international covenants on human rights in 1952, it had not yet been defined and converted into a legal right through the ratification of these covenants by states.

The arguments in favour of the Assembly's competence thus ran counter to the intentions of those who had drafted the Charter and the Assembly's own approach to the formulation of an international bill of human rights. Certainly there was need for some clarification from the International Court of Justice on matters of interpretation, but this was not asked for. There was enough support in the Assembly for that body to assert its competence by adopting a resolution which, inter alia, expressed its 'confidence that, in pursuance of its proclaimed policies, the Government of France would endeavour to further the effective development of the free institutions of the Tunisian people in conformity with the Purposes and Principles of the Charter', and 'the hope that the parties would continue negotiations on an urgent basis, with a view to bringing about self-government for Tunisians in the light of the relevant provisions of the Charter'.[67]

But this somewhat innocuous resolution did little to satisfy several anti-colonialist states in the United Nations, and at the eighth session of the Assembly in 1953, when there was much unrest in Tunisia, the representatives of Afghanistan Burma, Egypt, Indonesia, Iran, Iraq, Lebanon,

Pakistan, the Philippines, Saudi Arabia, Syria and Yemen submitted a draft resolution in the First Committee which, having expressed the conviction that 'full effect should be given to the sovereignty of the people of Tunisia by the exercise, as early as possible, of their legitimate rights to self-determination and self-government in conformity with the Charter', recommended:

(a) That all necessary steps be taken to ensure the realisation by the people of Tunisia of their right to full sovereignty and independence; and especially

(b) That the existing state of martial law and all other exceptional measures in operation in Tunisia be terminated, that political prisoners be released and that all civil liberties be established;

(c) That negotiations be undertaken without delay with representatives of a Tunisian government established through free elections held on the basis of universal suffrage and enjoying the necessary guarantees of freedom, with a view to enabling the Tunisian people to exercise all the powers arising from their legitimate rights to full sovereignty;

(d) That the Secretary-General be requested to transmit this resolution together with the record of the proceedings to the French Government and to report to the General Assembly at its ninth session.

This Afro-Asian draft resolution, which was supported by the Soviet Union, was couched in far too strong terms to gain the support of the majority of delegates.[68] Even when it was amended so that the preamble referring to 'the right of the Tunisian people to full sovereignty and independence' was omitted, paragraph (a) substituted by a new text which recommended that 'negotiations between France and Tunisia be undertaken to ensure the realisation by the people of Tunisia of their right to self-determination', and paragraph (b) deleted, the resolution was not adopted since it failed to get the requisite two-thirds majority.[69]

Thus, although the Assembly had asserted its competence to discuss and make recommendations on the Tunisian affair, it had exerted little pressure on France between 1951 and 1953. A resolution which it approved in 1954 merely expressed its confidence that Franco-Tunisian negotiations would bring a satisfactory solution,[70] and undoubtedly it was the unrest in Tunisia which impelled France to transfer full sovereignty to the Tunisians in 1956.

Clearly, the response of the United Nations to the Tunisian affair, as to the Moroccan affair, stood out in strong contrast to its very significant intervention in the Indonesian question. This was explicable by the fact that variable political factors, rather than fixed legal norms or generally accepted moral principles determined the policy of states in the Assembly and the Security Council. For example, though the United States had been prepared to advocate strong pressure against the Netherlands in 1949, it did not urge a similar approach in the Moroccan and Tunisian situations against France, probably because France was an important NATO ally and military bases in French North Africa were considered a vital interest to NATO strategy.

The United Nations response to the *Question of Algeria*, which was first brought to the attention of the Security Council by Saudi-Arabia in January 1955 and later to the Assembly by fourteen Afro-Asian states, also contrasted strongly with how it had reacted to the Indonesian affair in 1949.

When the General Committee of the Assembly considered whether the question should be included in the agenda at the tenth regular session of the Assembly in September 1955, the French delegate opposed its inclusion on the ground that Algerian affairs were essentially within the domestic jurisdiction of France because Algeria had been an integral part of Metropolitan France since 1834. But the delegates of Egypt, Iraq, Pakistan, Thailand, India and the USSR quoted Articles 1(2), 10, 11(2) and 14 of the Charter, as they had done in the Tunisian affair, to justify the competence of the Assembly to deal with the question. The present colonial status of Algeria, they asserted, was the result of Algeria's annexation by France, and the wishes of the Algerian people, denied of several rights enjoyed by French citizens, had never been consulted.[71]

The delegates of those states that supported France — the United Kingdom, the United States and New Zealand — argued that Algeria was a constituent part of the Republic of France and that the Assembly was prohibited under Article 2(7) of the Charter from intervening in French internal affairs, and this view was upheld by the majority. By a vote of 8 to 5 the General Committee decided not to recommend the inclusion of the question in the Assembly's agenda.

Though the Assembly in plenary session rejected this recommendation on 30 September 1955, it was so evenly divided over the issue — 28 to 27, with 5 abstentions — that even the delegates of those states that had supported United Nations intervention in the Algerian affair agreed later not to pursue the matter further at that session of the Assembly. A move to include the matter on the Security Council's agenda in July 1956 also failed.

Although there was sufficient support in the Assembly in February 1957 for that body to assert its competence to deal with the Algerian question, the Assembly merely expressed the hope that in a spirit of co-operation, a peaceful, democratic and just solution would be found, in conformity with the principles of the Charter.[72] An attempt by the strongly anti-colonialist states in the First Committee requesting France to recognise Algeria's 'right to self-determination', to negotiate a peaceful settlement with the nationalist leaders in Algeria, and to accept the good offices of the

Secretary-General of the United Nations, failed to win the support of the majority.

Notwithstanding the efforts of several Arab and Asian states in the Assembly to secure the adoption of recommendations that might exert greater pressure on France to negotiate a solution of the Algerian problem in consonance with the principle of self-determination, all the Assembly did at its twelfth session in 1957 was to express its concern over the situation, take note of the good offices made by the King of Morocco and the President of Tunisia, and express the wish that, in a spirit of co-operation, negotiations would be entered into and other appropriate means used to solve the problem.[73] France refused to participate in a discussion of the question when it was again included as an item on the Assembly's agenda at its thirteenth regular session in 1958 when the delegates of the USSR and several African and Asian states urged the immediate cessation of hostilities in Algeria and negotiations between French and Algerian representatives. But though the First Committee of the Assembly adopted a draft resolution sponsored by seventeen Afro-Asian states, which recommended that the Assembly should recognise 'the right of the Algerian people to independence' and urge the parties involved to negotiate with a view to reaching a solution, with a mention that the Provisional Government of the Algerian Republic was willing to do so, it was defeated in slightly amended form by the Assembly in plenary session because it did not obtain the requisite two-thirds majority.[74]

Like the Algerian affair, the *Cyprus question* illustrated the essentially insignificant role of the United Nations in colonial conflicts prior to 1960. The question came before the Assembly in 1954 when the Greek government introduced a complaint entitled 'Application, under the auspices of the United Nations, of the principle of equal rights and self-determination of peoples in the case of the population of the island of Cyprus'.[75]

The United Kingdom delegate claimed that the matter was essentially within the domestic jurisdiction of the UK since the island was a British possession, and at its regular sessions in 1954 and 1955 the Assembly did not include the item in its agenda. There can be little doubt that the fact that the Greek government was interested in removing Cyprus from the sovereignty of the United Kingdom in order to bring about its union with Greece militated against its argument for the granting of self-determination to the Cypriot people, particularly in view of the existence of the Turkish minority on the island. A draft resolution which urged negotiations between the United Kingdom and Greece to effect the self-determination of the Cypriot people failed to obtain a two-thirds majority at the 1957 session of the Assembly — the voting was 31 to 23, with 24 abstentions[76] — and in 1958, after much terrroist activity in the island and armed conflict between Greek and Turkish Cypriots and the United Kingdom had put forward various constitutional proposals for a settlement of the question, the Assembly simply expressed its confidence that the parties concerned would continue their efforts to reach a peaceful, democratic and just solution.[77]

To sum up: prior to 1960 the United Nations did not play a significant part in colonial conflicts, with the exception of the Indonesian affair. Moreover, it played no part in influencing the outcome of the colonial conflicts in Indo-China (1946-54), Malaya (1948-57), the Philippines (1945-6), and Kenya (1952-56). Nevertheless, it has been shown that the Organisation asserted its competence to discuss and make recommendations on the colonial conflicts in Morocco, Tunisia, and Algeria, even though its role in these questions was not significant, and various reasons were put forward by the protagonists of intervention to oppose the claim of France and her supporters that such matters were essentially within French jurisdiction and thus protected by the principle of non-intervention under Article 2(7) of the Charter.

Some arguments were advanced that the United Nations was competent to intervene in colonial conflicts on international legal grounds because of the existence of certain treaties, but those who put forward or opposed these claims were reluctant to seek the advisory opinions of the International Court of Justice on such matters. Some states maintained that the Declaration Regarding Non-Self-Governing Territorites under Article 73 of the Charter made the principle of non-intervention under Article 2(7) inapplicable, whilst others contended that the non-intervention principle did not apply because the violations of human rights which were taking place removed the questions from the sphere of domestic jurisdiction. It was also asserted that the Assembly was competent to deal with the questions under Article 11(2) of the Charter because the colonial conflicts were sources of international friction which were likely to endanger international peace and security, and that it had jurisdiction under Article 10 to make recommendations on any matter within the scope of the Charter. But these arguments were of a dubious nature in the light of the intentions of those who drafted the Charter. So, too, was the argument that the principle of self-determination under Article 1(2) of the Charter could override the principle of non-intervention under Article 2(7).

Above all, it has been seen that the political organs of the United Nations considered themselves competent to determine whether or not the principle of non-intervention was applicable in colonial questions, and to decide what action should be prescribed. Variable political factors thus outweighed legal factors in the determination of resolutions by the Security Council and the Assembly, though it was becoming more apparent that the Afro-Asian states, supported by the Soviet bloc, were anxious to gain general acceptance of their claim that the political organs of the UN were legally justified in discussing and making decisions on colonial conflicts solely on the ground that the principle of self-determination under Article

1(2) of the Charter could override the principle of non-intervention in such matters. It would appear that these states felt that this claim had been enhanced by the fact that in 1953 the Assembly had decided to include an article on the 'right of self-determination' in the draft international covenants on human rights, and that in 1955, the following text had been accepted in the Assembly's Third Committee, notwithstanding the opposition of several Western European states, for inclusion in both draft covenants:

All peoples have the right of self-determination. By virtue of this right they freely determine their political status and freely pursue their economic, social and cultural development.

The peoples may, for their own ends, freely dispose of their natural wealth and resources without prejudice to any obligations arising out of international economic co-operation, based upon the principle of mutual benefit, and international law. In no case may a people be deprived of its own means of subsistence.[78]

The entry of twelve former African and Asian colonies into membership of the United Nations between 1955 and 1959[79], and a further fourteen African states and Cyprus in September 1960[80], also served to strengthen the attack against colonialism in the Assembly, and to give much greater support to the doctrine that the principle of self-determination was a legal right against which the principle of non-intervention in matters essentially within the domestic jurisdiction of states was no defence. This was made manifest when the Assembly approved the Declaration on the Granting of Independence to Colonial Countries and Peoples in December 1960.[81]

The Declaration on the Granting of Independence to Colonial Countries and Peoples

This Declaration, which was adopted by a vote of 89 to 0, with 9 abstentions — Australia, Belgium, Dominican Republic, France, Portugal, Spain, Union of South Africa, the United Kingdom and the United States — seemed to indicate that the overwhelming majority of member states of the United Nations were clearly in no mood to pay attention to the contention of the United Kingdom delegate that colonialism was a necessary transitional phase on the road to self-government or independence, or to the United States view which, whilst recognising the temporary nature of colonialism, considered it necessary to plan soundly for what would replace it.[82]

The Declaration welcomed 'the emergence in recent years of a large number of dependent territories into freedom and independence', and recognised 'the increasingly powerful trends towards freedom in such territories which have not yet attained independence'. It solemnly proclaimed 'the necessity of bringing to a speedy and unconditional end colonialism in

93

all its forms and manifestations', and to that end it declared that:

1. The subjection of peoples to alien subjugation, domination and exploitation constitutes a denial of fundamental human rights, is contrary to the Charter of the United Nations and is an impediment to the promotion of world peace and co-operation.

2. All peoples have the right to self-determination; by virtue of that right they freely determine their political status and freely pursue their economic, social and cultural development.

3. Inadequacy of political, economic, social or educational preparedness should never serve as a pretext for delaying independence.

4. All armed action or repressive measures of all kinds directed against dependent peoples shall cease in order to enable them to exercise peacefully and freely their right to complete independence, and the integrity of their national territory shall be respected.

5. Immediate steps shall be taken, in Trust and Non-Self-Governing Territories or all other territories which have not yet attained independence, to transfer all powers to the peoples of those territories, without any conditions or reservations, in accordance with their freely expressed will and desire, without any distinction as to race, creed or colour, in order to enable them to enjoy complete independence and freedom.

6. Any attempt aimed at the partial or total disruption of the national unity and the territorial integrity of a country is incompatible with the purposes and principles of the Charter of the United Nations.

7. All States shall observe faithfully and strictly the provisions of the Charter of the United Nations, the Universal Declaration of Human Rights and the present Declaration on the basis of equality, non-interference in the internal affairs of all States, and respect for the sovereign rights of all peoples and their territorial integrity.

It was implicit in the Declaration, as points 3, 4 and 5 above indicate, that *complete independence* was the only status consistent with the *right of self-determination* which is given the definition that had been included in the draft international covenants on human rights not yet approved in their entirety by the Assembly, viz. the right of peoples to freely determine their political status and freely pursue their economic, social and cultural development. This represented a departure from the concept that had been recognised by the Assembly under its Resolution 742(VIII), 1953, viz. that the attainment of various systems of self-government, as distinct from independence, was not incompatible with the right of self-determination.

Under the Declaration the right of self-determination was thus synonymous with complete independence, and according to Resolution 742(VIII) the factors indicative of the attainment of independence were as follows:

A. **International status**

(i) **International responsibility**. Full international responsibility of the Territory for the acts inherent in the exercise of its external sovereignty and for the corresponding acts in the administration of its internal affairs.

(ii) Eligibility for membership of the United Nations.

(iii) **General international relations**. Power to enter into direct relations of every kind with other governments and with international institutions and to negotiate, sign and ratify international instruments.

(iv) **National defence**. Sovereign right to provide for its national defence.

B. **Internal self-government**

(i) **Form of government**. Complete freedom of the people of the Territory to choose the form of government which they desire.

(ii) **Territorial government**. Freedom from control or interference by the government of another State in respect of the internal government (legislature, executive, judiciary, and administration of the Territory).

(iii) **Economic, social and cultural jurisdiction**. Complete autonomy in respect of economic, social and cultural affairs.

Clearly, nothing less than independent statehood was considered compatible with the principle of self-determination under Article 1(2) of the Charter. The Declaration was thus in line with the Soviet view-point which had been emphasised by Molotov at the San Francisco Conference. Indeed, it was Khrushchev, in an address to the Assembly on 23 September 1960, who proposed that the Declaration should be included in the agenda of that body at its fifteenth regular session. But in assessing the role of the Soviet Union in this connection, it should not be overlooked that though its government was vociferous in its demand for the end of Western imperialism in Asia and Africa, it had prevented the application of the principle of self-determination in Eastern Europe after the defeat of Nazi Germany, and intervened to suppress the revolution against its Communist puppet regime in Hungary in 1956.

The Assembly's Approach after the Adoption of the 1960 Declaration

After the adoption of the 1960 Declaration, the Assembly acted on the assumption that the principle of self-determination was a legal right which constituted sufficient grounds to justify United Nations intervention in colonial conflicts without contravening the principle of non-intervention in matters of domestic jurisdiction under Article 2(7) of the Charter. Thus, when the Assembly resumed consideration of the Algerian question at its 16th regular session in 1961, and called upon France and the Provisional Government of the Algerian Republic to resume negotiations, it did so solely on the Algerian people's 'right to self-determination and independence'.[83]

The conflict in Algeria was approaching its end when this resolution was approved by the Assembly — Algeria gained its independence six months later — and the Afro-Asian states, with Soviet support, made it clear that they wanted the United Nations to take a more dynamic role in speeding up the process of decolonisation than it had hitherto played. This was made manifest during the debate on 'The situation with regard to the implementation of the Declaration on the Granting of Independence to Colonial Countries and Peoples', an item placed on the agenda, at the request of the Soviet Union, at the Assembly's sixteenth session.[84]

Having pointed out that 40 countries with 800 million inhabitants had obtained independence since 1946, the United States delegate maintained that the United Nations had two tasks to perform in the continuation of that process; to make specific recommendations to those administering powers that were reluctant to accept their Charter responsibilities, and in other cases to present guiding principles of action for the consideration of the member-states concerned. The United Nations, he added, should not interfere in the relations between the administering power and the indigenous leaders of a dependent territory where there was evidence of joint consultation and partnership.

But the overwhelming majority of delegates wanted a more direct approach to the elimination of colonialism than this, and the Assembly adopted a resolution which the United States delegate felt he could not oppose, though the United Kingdom, France, South Africa and Spain abstained from voting, and Portugal did not participate in the vote. This noted with regret that, with few exceptions, the provisions contained in the Declaration had not been carried out, called upon the states concerned to take action without further delay with a view to the faithful application of the Declaration, and established a special committee of seventeen members to review the situation regarding its implementation and make recommendations to the Assembly.[85]

On the basis of the work of this special committee (enlarged to 24 members at the end of 1962),[86] which took over the functions of the Committee on Information from Non-Self-Governing Territories and became the only body under the Assembly concerned with matters relating to dependent territories, with the exception of the Trusteeship Council, the Assembly addressed many resolutions to the colonial powers for the implementation of the 1960 Declaration. But the responses of the administering powers to its requests, appeals or recommendations were mixed. They were opposed to the immediate decolonisation of certain territories, and were reluctant to grant the Special Committee, which had a clear majority of anti-colonialist members, permission to send visiting missions to dependencies whose status was being investigated. In some instances, however, they agreed that the United Nations should provide supervision of elections or send representatives to participate in constitutional consultations concerning non-self-governing territories, and only Portugal and South Africa refused to keep the Special Committee of 24 informed of developments within their non-self-governing territories.

It is difficult to assess the influence of the Assembly and its Special Committee on the process of decolonisation which continued to gather momentum during the 1960s. With the exception of Portugal and South Africa, the colonial powers were not averse to granting independence or some measure of self-government to their non-self-governing territories in accordance with their own plans, but the pressure exerted by the Assembly and its Special Committee probably influenced them to give the question of decolonisation more urgent attention than they would otherwise have given it.

Within a decade after the adoption of the 1960 Declaration, twenty-six territories, with a total of 53 million inhabitants, had emerged from colonial status to independent statehood or a form of self-government which the Assembly considered compatible with self-determination, such as the free association of the Cook Islands with New Zealand in 1965 — a development which indicated that the Assembly had departed to some extent from its rigid dogma that only complete independence could be considered compatible with the exercise of a people's right of self-determination. In 1970, of the 28 million people who had not obtained self-rule, the majority — about 18 million — inhabited territories in southern Africa.[87] As to trust territories, the responsibility of the Trusteeship Council, all had achieved independence or become freely integrated with other states, with the exception of New Guinea and the Pacific Islands.

Thus in 1970, of the territories within the terms of reference of the Special Committee of 24, those under Portuguese administration (Angola, Mozambique, Portuguese Guinea and some islands off the west coast of Agrica), the former League of Nations mandate of South West Africa (Namibia) under the control of South Africa, and Rhodesia under the Smith regime, were its main problems, but though the record of the United Nations in these questions illustrated the Organisation's assertion of competence to act on the assumption that the principle of self-determination was a legal right against which the principle of non-intervention under Article 2(7) was no defence, it also showed the Organisation's limited capabilities of enforcing its decisions.

The United Nations and the Portuguese Colonies

Since the Portuguese government had refused to submit information on its non-self-governing territories under Article 73(e) of the Charter in response to the Assembly's resolution 1542(XV), on the ground that they were overseas provinces of metropolitan Portugal, it was not surprising that it ignored the Declaration on the Granting of Independence to Colonial Countries and Peoples. But this disregard for the objectives of the Declaration soon evoked in the Assembly severe censure of Portuguese policy and a demand for change.

In April 1961 the Assembly adopted a resolution which invoked the Declaration and its statement that the subjection of peoples to alien subjugation constituted a denial of fundamental human rights, and appointed a sub-committee of inquiry on Angola.[88] But a month or so later, whilst the sub-committee was conducting its inquiry, the Security Council passed a resolution which deeply deplored 'the severely repressive measures in Angola', recalled the Declaration on the Granting of Independence to Colonial Countries and Peoples, and called upon the Portuguese authorities 'to desist forthwith from repressive measures and further to extend every facility to the sub-committee to enable it to implement its mandate without delay'. But the Council did not describe the situation in Angola as a threat to international peace so that sanctions could be considered under Chapter VII of the Charter; it referred to it as one 'likely to endanger the maintenance of international peace and security',[89] and thus one suitable for pacific settlement under Chapter VI of the Charter.

In December, 1962, however, the Assembly, 'convinced that the colonial war being carried on by the Government of Portugal in Angola, the violation by that Government of the Security Council resolution of 9 June 1961, its refusal to implement the provisions of the Declaration on the granting of independence to colonial countries and peoples contained in General Assembly resolution 1514 (XV) of 14 December 1960 . . . . constitute a source of international conflict as well as a threat to world peace and security', requested the Security Council 'to take appropriate measures, including sanctions, to secure Portugal's compliance with the present resolution and with previous resolutions of the General Assembly and of the Security Council'.[90]

Although in July 1963 there was a requisite majority for the Security Council to determine that the situation not only in Angola, but also in the other Portuguese territories of Mazambique and Portuguese Guinea, was seriously disturbing peace and security in Southern Africa, it had only enough support to request that all states should refrain from offering the Portuguese government any assistance which would enable it to continue its repression of the people of those territories and to take measures to prevent the sale and supply of arms to Portugal.[91] There was insufficient support in that body for the authorisation of enforcement measures against

Portugal under Chapter VII of the Charter because three of the permanent members of the Council, France, the United States and the United Kingdom, allies of Portugal in NATO, were opposed to such a move.

Dissatisfied with the response of the Security Council to the question, many Afro-Asian states attempted to win support for sanctions against Portugal under an Assembly resolution, and in 1965 they were successful in securing approval of a motion in the Fourth Committee, which was later endorsed by the Assembly by a vote of 66 to 26, with 15 abstentions, urging member-states of the United Nations to impose a diplomatic and trade boycott on Portugal. This resolution re-affirmed 'the right of the peoples of the African Territories under Portuguese administration to freedom and independence' and recognised 'the legitimacy of their struggle to achieve the rights laid down in the Charter of the United Nations, the Universal Declaration of Human Rights, and the Declaration on the Granting of Independence to Colonial Countries and Peoples'. It also noted with deep concern 'that the activities of the foreign financial interests in these Territories are an impediment to the African people in the realization of their aspirations to freedom and independence', and referred to evidence submitted by petitioners which 'confirmed that the Government of Portugal has continued to use the aid and weapons that it receives from its military allies against the populations of Angola, Mozambique, so-called Portuguese Guinea and other Territories under its administration'; and requested 'all states, in particular the military allies of Portugal within the framework of the North Atlantic Treaty Organisation, to take all the necessary measures to prevent the sale or supply of arms and military equipment to the Government of Portugal'.[92]

But though the Assembly, guided by its Special Committee of 24, continued to pass resolutions of this nature, Portugal still adhered to its claim that the administration of its African territories was a matter within its domestic jurisdiction, and the Western powers, who denied charges that NATO supplied arms to Portugal for use in its African territories and that the activities of foreign economic and financial interests were impeding the implementation of the Declaration of Independence to Colonial Countries and Peoples, either voted against or abstained from voting on resolutions which recommended enforcement measures against Portugal.[93] Thus the application of the diplomatic and trade boycott recommended by the Assembly against Portugal was largely ineffective, and though the United Nations had asserted the claim that the peoples of Angola, Mozambique and Portuguese Guinea had the right to self-determination and independence, it lacked the enforcement capabilities to compel Portugal to relinquish control over those territories. In fact, it was the military coup against the Caetano regime in Portugal in April 1974, not enforcement measures by the United Nations, which paved the way for nationalist liberation movements to replace Portuguese rule in Guinea Bissau, Mozambique and Angola in 1975.

The UN's handling of the question of South West Africa(Namibia)

South West Africa, the territory designated as Namibia by the UN Assembly in 1968, was the only one of the seven African territories formerly held under the League of Nations mandate system, which was not placed under UN trusteeship. South Africa, the mandatory power under the League mandates system, rejected the UN Assembly's recommendations in 1946, 1947 and 1948 that the territory should be brought under the trusteeship system.[94]

In 1949 the Assembly requested the International Court of Justice to give an advisory opinion on the status of the territory, and this was given in July 1950. Though the Court did not consider that South Africa had a legal obligation to place the territory under the trusteeship system, it ruled that the mandate was still in force and that South Africa was obliged to submit reports and transmit petitions from the inhabitants of the territory to the United Nations. In fact, the Court concluded that the General Assembly of the United Nations was legally qualified to exercise supervisory functions previously exercised by the League of Nations with regard to the administration of the territory, and that the Union of South Africa was under an obligation to submit to supervision and control of the Assembly and to render annual reports to it.[95] Subsequent opinions of the Court in 1955 and 1956 reinforced the Assembly's claim to exercise supervision over the administration of the territory.[96]

During the 1950s the Assembly tried to negotiate an agreement with the South African government on some form of United Nations supervision over the territory's administration in line with the Opinions of the International Court, but these negotiations proved abortive. It still asserted its competence in the matter, however, by examining reports submitted to its Committee on South West Africa, which were based on whatever information could be gleaned on the subject.

In 1960, two members of the Organisation of African Unity, Liberia and Ethiopia, who had been members of the League of Nations, attempted a new approach to the question by instituting proceedings against South Africa before the International Court of Justice. They asked the Court to declare that South Africa had violated the terms of the League of Nations mandate by refusing to transmit to the United Nations reports on the territory and petitions from its inhabitants. But before the Court's judgment on the question appeared in 1966, the Assembly had taken steps to assert its competence in the matter.

In December 1961, a year after the adoption of the Declaration on the Granting of Independence to Colonial Countries and Peoples, the Assembly proclaimed 'the inalienable right of the people of South West

Africa to independence and national sovereignty', and called for preparations for elections to a legislative Assembly, based on universal suffrage, to be held as soon as possible under United Nations supervision, and the co-ordination of economic and social assistance by the specialised agencies of the United Nations to help the people of the territory. The implementation of the resolution was to be attained through consultations between the Assembly's Special Committee for South West Africa and the South African government,[97] but there was a negative response on the part of the latter.

The question of the legal competence of the United Nations in the affair was complicated by the International Court's judgment in July 1966, which ruled that Ethiopia and Liberia had no legal standing to petition the Court that South Africa had violated its obligations under the League mandate, since 'under the mandates system, and within the general framework of the League system, the various mandatories were responsible for their conduct of the mandates solely to the League — in particular its Council — and were not additionally and separately responsible to each and every individual State member of the League'.[98] But though the Court's judgment, which was decided by the casting vote of the president, did not deter the Assembly, by a vote of 114 to 2 (Portugal and South Africa) with 3 abstentions (France, the United Kingdom and Malawi) from resolving that the mandate exercised by South Africa was terminated and that henceforth South West Africa would be placed under the direct responsibility of the United Nations,[99] and later establishing an eleven member council to proceed to the territory to make arrangements for its independence to be attained by June 1968,[100] its decisions had no practical effect; the South African government refused the eleven member council permission to enter South West Africa.

Though in December 1967 the Assembly appealed to all states to apply economic sanctions and other measures to effect South Africa's withdrawal from South West Africa, and requested the Security Council to take steps to enable the eleven member council to carry out its functions,[101] nothing effective was done; for the Western powers were unwilling to join in the application of enforcement measures in response to the Assembly's recommendation, or vote for the authorisation of mandatory economic sanctions by the Security Council under Chapter VII of the Charter. In their view the situation could be remedied only by peaceful negotiations, as they emphasised when the Security Council dealt with the question in 1969.[102]

In July 1970, however, the United States, unlike France and the United Kingdom, voted for a Security Council resolution which, *inter alia*, asked all states to refrain from any relations with South Africa that would imply recognition over Namibia; ensure that companies owned or controlled by States cease all commercial or industrial dealings in Namibia; withhold loans and credits or other financial support that would be used by their nationals or companies from investing in Namibia; and withhold protection of such investment against claims of a future lawful government of Namibia.[103] Indeed, the United States delegate said that his government had recently announced measures that sought to discourage investment by its citizens in Namibia.

This resolution was carried by 13 votes to 0, with 2 abstentions — France and the United Kingdom. France was doubtful that the United Nations had greater powers than the League of Nations which, in its view, did not seem to have been empowered to deprive a country of its mandate; and the United Kingdom had several reservations concerning the political and juridical basis of the course of action asked for by the Security Council. Unlike the United Kingdom, however, France joined the United States in voting for a security Council resolution on 29 July 1970, which asked the International Court of Justice to give an advisory opinion on what were the legal consequences for states of the continued presence of South Africa in Namibia, shortly after Security Council resolution 276(1970) had declared 'that the continued presence of the South African authorities in Namibia was illegal and that consequently all acts taken by South Africa on behalf of or concerning Namibia after the termination of the mandate in 1966 were illegal and invalid'.[104]

The Security Council's request for an advisory opinion by the International Court was carried by 12 votes to 0, with 3 abstentions (the United Kingdom, the Soviet Union and Poland). The Soviet Union and Poland abstained because they considered that the Court's opinion was unnecessary, whilst the United Kingdom abstained on the grounds that reference of the question to the Court was based on certain legal assumptions which should themselves be examined by the Court. But in view of the Court's 1966 advisory opinion that Ethiopia and Liberia could not be considered to have established any legal right as former members of the League of Nations in the subject matter of their claims, so that it could not pass judgment on the merits of the case, it certainly appeared necessary that its opinion should be sought on the legal implications for the United Nations of the continued presence of the South African authorities in Namibia.

It was stated by the Court in its advisory opinion,[105] which was delivered on 21 June 1971, that the members of the League of Nations had not declared, or accepted even by implication, that the Mandates would be cancelled or lapse with the dissolution of the League. The last resolution of the League Assembly and Article 80, paragraph 1, of the United Nations Charter maintained the obligations of Mandatories. The Court had consistently recognised that the Mandate survived the demise of the League, and South Africa had also admitted as much for a number of years. Thus the supervisory element, which was an essential part of the Mandate, was bound to survive, the Court declared.

The Court was of the opinion, by 13 votes to 2, 'that the continued presence of South Africa in Namibia being illegal, South Africa is under obligation to withdraw its administration from Namibia immediately and thus put an end to its occupation of the Territory'; and by 11 votes to 4, 'that States Members of the United Nations are under obligation to recognise the illegality and invalidity of its acts on behalf of or concerning Namibia, and to refrain from any acts and in particular any dealings with the Government of South Africa implying recognition of the legality of, or lending support or assistance to, such presence and administration'. It was also the majority view of the Court's judges that the Security Council resolutions on Namibia were legally binding on UN member states.

In October 1971 the Security Council agreed with the Court's opinion that the continued presence of South Africa in Namibia was illegal and that it was under obligation to withdraw its administration immediately from the territory. It was carried by 13 votes to 0, with 2 abstentions — France and the United Kingdom,[106] the latter abstaining because they could not accept the premises on which most of the provisions of the Court's opinion were based, and particularly the point advanced that the Security Council's resolutions on Namibia were mandatory. Sir Colin Crowe, the British delegate, asserted that the Security Council could take decisions generally binding on member states only when the Council had made a determination under Article 39 that a threat to the peace, breach of the peace, or act of aggression existed, and that no such determination existed in relation to South West Africa or Namibia. Indeed, though the United States voted for the Security Council's resolution on the Court's opinion, it stressed that this should not be construed as reflecting any change in its position with regard to earlier resolutions approved by the United Nations on which it had abstained.

Clearly, the International Court's advisory opinion that the presence of the South African authorities in Namibia was illegal did not fundamentally alter the view of the Western powers that a settlement of the question of Namibia should be sought through negotiations with the South African government, and that it could not be sensibly remedied by the application of coercive measures under the auspices of the Security Council.

Even when, several years later, in 1974, the Security Council unanimously adopted a resolution which demanded that South Africa should make a solemn declaration to the Council that it would comply with past United Nations resolutions and with the advisory opinion given by the International Court in 1971,[107] the Western powers opposed any reference in the resolution to the application of sanctions against South Africa in case the Council was not satisfied with the response of the South African government. In fact, though they agreed that the resolution should include a declaration that in the event of non-compliance the Council would consider 'the appropriate measures to be taken under the United Nations Charter', they made it quite clear that they had no intention of supporting sanctions under Chapter VII of the Charter.

It is difficult to escape the conclusion, therefore, that though there was a sound case for the authorisation of sanctions by the Security Council against South Africa because of its intransigence over Namibia, the Western powers were afraid that the application of sanctions would not only be damaging to their economies, but also lead to a situation in southern Africa which would have given the Soviet Union greater opportunities to extend its sphere of influence.

The Western powers thus relied on diplomatic pressure to bring about a change in South Africa's policy on Namibia, and to some extent such pressure influenced the South African government, faced with the prospect of a protracted war in northern Namibia with the guerillas of the South West African People's Organisation (SWAPO), to sponsor in 1977 a scheme which involved the appointment of an Administrator-General to prepare elections for a multi-racial Namibian constituent assembly, in consultation with the political parties and a representative of the UN Secretary-General. But SWAPO, which had been recognised as Namibia's legal representative by the UN Assembly in 1973, insisted that all South African forces should be withdrawn before elections took place, and objected to the provision that a future independent Namibia would have to accept South Africa's control over the Walvis Bay enclave of 434 square miles.[108]

Towards the end of 1977 and the early part of 1978, the Western powers on the UN Security Council — Canada, France, Federal Republic of Germany, United Kingdom and United States — tried to establish the basis for a peaceful settlement of the Namibian question by engaging in negotiations with the representatives of SWAPO and the South African government, and at the end of March 1978 presented a plan to both sides which was tabled at the United Nations on 12 April 1978. This plan proposed the retention of a South African force of 1,500 men, restricted to two bases in northern Namibia, until seven days after the result of national elections for a constituent assembly to be held in 1978; the appointment of a UN representative, supported by a civilian group and a UN peacekeeping force, who would have final authority over the South African police responsible for law and order until elections had been held and an independent Namibian government installed; and the exercise of only limited powers by the South African Administrator-General during the interim period preceding elections. No mention was made of the Walvis Bay enclave which was claimed as an integral part of Namibia by SWAPO, since the Western powers considered that this question should not be allowed to impede a settlement.[109]

Subsequent developments[110]

The Western settlement plan was endorsed by the Security Council on 27 July 1978 *(SC Res.431)*, after it had been accepted by the government of South Africa and SWAPO. But the Council also declared *(SC Res.432)* that 'the territorial integrity and unity of Namibia must be assured through the reintegration of Walvis Bay within its territory', though that issue had not been included in the Western plan. Moreover, other differences soon arose between the South African appointed Administrator-General in Namibia, Justice M. Steyn, and the UN Special Representative for Namibia, Mr. Martti Ahtisaari, who had been appointed by the Secretary-General at the request of the Security Council.

Mr. Ahtisaari, who led a UN fact-finding mission in Namibia during August 1978, was not only critical of the way in which the Administrator-General had conducted the registration of voters, but also of his insistence that elections should be held to effect the establishment of a constituent assembly on 31 December 1978. He maintained that it would be impracticable for the refugees in Angola and Zambia to return to Namibia in time to participate in the elections under such an arrangement. His view on the size and composition of the UN force that would be necessary also differed from that which both South Africa and SWAPO had accepted under the Western plan.

The UN fact-finding mission left Namibia on 22 August 1978, and in a report to the Security Council based on its findings, the UN Secretary-General proposed the creation of a UN force of 7,500 military personnel to monitor the cessation of hostile acts by all parties, troop withdrawals, and the establishment of conditions that would enable the elections to be held seven months after the Security Council had given the UN operation the go-ahead. It was also proposed in the report that a UN civilian contingent of 1,500, including 360 police officers, should supervise and control all aspects of the electoral process.

The Secretary-General's proposals were generally acceptable to SWAPO, which promised to co-operate with the UN and offered to sign a cease-fire agreement with South Africa. But the latter rejected the proposals on 20 September 1978, the South African Prime Minister, Mr. Vorster, declaring that his government would go ahead with its own arrangements for elections in Namibia in December 1978.

A slightly modified version of the UN Secretary-General's plan, since it did not insist on the entry of a UN force of 7,500 military personnel if the security situation in Namibia permitted a smaller number, was approved by the Security Council on 29 September 1978 *(SC Res.435)*, but this modification was not sufficient to induce the South African government, now led by Mr. Pieter Botha, to change its position. Indeed, though on 20 October 1978 the South African government and foreign ministers of the five Western members of the Security Council agreed in Pretoria on a joint communique stating that the UN Secretary-General's Special Representative should return to Namibia to discuss arrangements for UN supervised elections in accordance with Security Council resolution 435, which provided for a ballot in about six months, the Prime Minister of South Africa made it clear in a separate statement that his government intended to proceed with its own plans to hold elections in Namibia in the coming December, and promised no more than it would use its best efforts to persuade the elected leaders to consider ways of achieving international recognition through the good offices of the UN Special Representative and the Administrator-General.

The holding of the elections in December 1978, in line with the terms of the South African authorities, was unacceptable to SWAPO and other black nationalist parties, and it soon became manifest that the electoral contest would be mainly between the white-led multiracial Democratic Turnhalle Alliance party and Aktur, a predominantly white party. The Security Council also condemned the elections, called for their immediate cancellation, and warned South Africa that failure to co-operate in the implementation of UN supervised elections under resolution 435 would 'compel the Security Council to meet forthwith to initiate appropriate actions under the Charter of the United Nations, including Chapter VII thereof . . .' The resolution — *SC Res.439*, 13 November 1978 — was carried by 10 to 0, the three permanent members (the United States, France and Britain), like West Germany and Canada, abstaining.

South Africa did not comply with the Security Council's demand for the cancellation of the December 1978 elections, but on the 22nd of that month the Prime Minister of South Africa did advise the new constituent assembly which had emerged as a result of those elections, and in which the Pretoria-supported Democratic Turnhalle Alliance had gained 41 of the 50 seats, to accept elections under UN supervision before September 1979. He still insisted, however, that some questions relating to the implementation of the Security Council's plan under its resolution *435 / 1978* would have to be cleared up by negotiations between South Africa's Administrator-General in Namibia and the UN Special Representative for the territory. Indeed, in the spring of 1979, it still remained to be seen whether the question of Namibia, further complicated by SWAPO's objections to the monitoring of its armed forces by a UN force, would be resolved through a peaceful settlement which would give the UN a significant role in effecting the birth of a new independent state of Namibia.

Though such a development was highly desirable, it needs to be stressed that more than thirty years had elapsed since the Namibian question had first been considered by the UN, and that the Organisation's handling of the affair had demonstrated its limited enforcement capabilities in an issue which, in contrast to the question of *apartheid* in South Africa, could hardly be characterised as a matter essentially within the domestic jurisdiction of that state.

In the case of Southern Rhodesia the United Nations had succeeded in authorising mandatory sanctionary measures against a regime which it condemned for pursuing a policy incompatible with 'the right of self-determination', but even in that instance the sanctionary pressure which the Organisation was able to exert was insufficient to bring about the collapse of the Smith regime. The background to this is described below.

The Question of Southern Rhodesia

In June 1962, on the recommendation of its Special Committee which was concerned with the implementation of the 1960 Declaration on the Granting of Independence to Colonial Countries and Peoples, the Assembly affirmed that Southern Rhodesia was a non-self-governing territory under Article 73 of the Charter. It also declared that the United Kingdom, the administering power, was accountable under the Charter of the United Nations and the 1960 Declaration for ensuring that the people of Southern Rhodesia would be able to exercise 'the right of self-determination' in order to attain independence, and requested the United Kingdom to call a conference to formulate a new constitution for the territory, under which the political rights of the people, on the basis of 'one man, one vote', would be guaranteed.[111]

In Southern Rhodesia, where the ruling minority of white people were operating a policy of racial discrimination against a very large majority of black people, the exercise of the right of self-determination, as the Assembly's resolution implied, meant the right of the dis-enfranchised black population to choose freely a new government responsive to their wishes, and then the transfer of full powers to this government by the United Kingdom, the administering power, in a new independent state.

The United Kingdom government maintained that since Southern Rhodesia had been a self-governing colony since 1923, not a non-self-governing territory as designated by the Assembly in 1962, the United Nations was not competent to deal with the political and constitutional developments in the territory. It thus regarded the question of formulating a new constitution a matter to be resolved through negotiations between the Southern Rhodesian and United Kingdom governments, notwithstanding the resolutions of the Assembly which censured its policy, and on 7 November 1965 condemned 'the policies of racial discrimination and segregation practised in Southern Rhodesia, which constitute a crime against humanity'.[112] As a result of the Smith regime's unilateral declaration of independence on 11 November 1965, however, the United

Kingdom changed its policy and requested the Security Council to authorise action against the illegal government in Rhodesia.

The Security Council immediately condemned the Smith regime's unilateral declaration of independence by a vote of 10 to 0, with 1 abstention (France),[113] and on 20 November 1965 called on members of the United Nations to desist from providing Southern Rhodesia with arms and military equipment, and to do their utmost to break all economic relations with it, including an embargo on oil and petroleum products. It also called upon the United Kingdom 'to quell this rebellion of the racist minority'.[114]

It was in December 1965, too, that the Assembly, by a vote of 74 to 6, with 27 abstentions, went as far as to affirm that the continuation of colonial rule, as well as *apartheid* and other forms of racial discrimination, was not only 'a threat to international peace and security,' but also 'a crime against humanity'. It also recognised 'the legitimacy of the struggle of colonial peoples to exercise their right to self-determination and independence', and invited all states to provide material and moral assistance to the national liberation movements in colonial territories.[115] Not surprisingly, therefore, the reluctance of the United Kingdom to use force against the Smith regime was severely criticised by the Assembly's Special Committee of 24, on which the large majority of members were extremely hostile to colonialism, and it was on the recommendation of that committee that the Assembly, at its regular session in 1966, called on the United Kingdom to do so. It also condemned the governments of Portugal and South Africa, as well as foreign financial and other interests, for assisting the Smith regime, and drew the attention of the Security Council to 'the grave situation prevailing in Southern Rhodesia, in order that it may decide to apply the necessary measures envisaged under Chapter VII of the Charter of the United Nations'.[116]

The United Kingdom, the United States and France abstained from voting on this resolution — it was adopted by 89 to 2 (South Africa and Portugal), with 17 abstentions — but when the Security Council met in December 1966, the United Kingdom and the United States supported the Council's authorisation of selective mandatory economic sanctions against Southern Rhodesia.[117] France and the Soviet Union abstained for different reasons; France considered that the Southern Rhodesian problem was the responsibility of the United Kingdom alone, whereas the Soviet Union shared the view of the majority of Afro-Asian states that the situation required firmer action. But their abstention did not, of course, constitute a veto.

This decision by the Security Council in 1966, by then enlarged to fifteen members, was adopted by 11 votes to 0, with 4 abstentions (France, the Soviet Union, Bulgaria and Mali), and highly significant because it was the first time in the history of the Council that it had authorised mandatory economic sanctions against a state. Since the sanctions were mandatory, failure on the part of United Nations members to comply with the decision would be a violation of Article 25 of the Charter, under which members agree to accept and carry out the Council's decisions. But not all members complied with the order. In February 1967 the Secretary-General reported to the Security Council that though there had been a significant decline in trade between Southern Rhodesia and many of her trading partners, there had been continuing traffic in certain important commodities. In fact, he pointed out that a number of states had not reported on the matter, including some which had significant trading relations with Southern Rhodesia.[118]

At the end of 1967 the Assembly declared its conviction that the sanctions adopted so far would not put an end to the illegal racist regime, and that sanctions, in order to achieve their objective, would have to be comprehensive, mandatory, and backed by force, and it condemned the governments of South Africa and Portugal, as well as foreign financial and other interests, for assisting the government in Southern Rhodesia.[119] In a subsequent resolution it drew the attention of all states to 'the grave consequences of the development in southern Africa of the *entente* between the Governments of South Africa and Portugal and the illegal racist minority regime of Southern Rhodesia, the activities of which run counter to the interests of international peace and security', and called upon them, 'particularly the main trading partners of the *entente*, to withhold any support or assistance to the members of the *entente*',[120]

Though the Security Council decided in 1968 to widen economic sanctions to include all exports to and imports from Southern Rhodesia, with the exception of medical, educational and, in particular circumstances, foodstuffs,[121] these measures were ineffectively applied by UN member states and failed to bring about the collapse of the Smith regime, and thus encouraged what Richard A Falk has described as 'strategies of violent implementation' by those whose claims to justice could not be met by the action of the United Nations.[122]

In March 1976, when Mozambique closed its border with Rhodesia, it was reported that there were a thousand African nationalist guerillas inside Rhodesia and twelve to fifteen thousand along the borders of Mozambique and Zambia in training camps.[123] And though Dr. Kissinger announced in his Lusaka speech on 27 April 1976 that the United States would provide aid to Mozambique to help compensate for its closure of the border with Rhodesia and take steps to uphold completely economic sanctions against Rhodesia,[124] he did not propose that military sanctions should be authorised by the UN Security Council. Not surprisingly, therefore, the measures which he proposed were not regarded by such African states as Tanzania and Zambia as lessening the need for the intensification of guerilla activity in Rhodesia.

Anglo-American proposals for a peaceful settlement of the Rhodesian question, put forward in August 1977,[125] were based on '(i) the surrender of power by the illegal regime and a return to legality; (ii) an orderly and peaceful transition to independence in the course of 1978; (iii) free and impartial elections on the basis of universal adult suffrage; (iv) the establishment by the British Government of a transitional administration with the task of conducting the elections for an independent government; (v) a United Nations presence, including a United Nations force, during the transition period; (vi) an Independence Constitution providing for a demo-cratically elected government, the abolition of discrimination, the protection of individual human rights and the independence of the judiciary; and (vii) a Development Fund to revive the economy of the country which the United Kingdom and the United States view as predicated upon the settlement as a whole'.

It was stated that the British government would place before the Security Council their proposal for the Independence Constitution and also their proposal for the administration of the territory of Rhodesia during the transition period leading up to independence, and that the latter would comprise (a) the appointment of a Resident Commissioner to administer the country, to organise and conduct the general election which, within a period not exceeding six months, would lead to independence for Zimbabwe, and to take command as Commander-in-Chief, of all armed forces in Rhodesia, apart from the UN Zimbabwe Force; (b) the appoint-ment by the Secretary-General of the United Nations, on the authority of the Security Council, of a Special Representative whose role would be to work with the Commissioner and to observe that the administration of the country and the organisation and conduct of the elections were fair and impartial; (c) the establishment by resolution of the Security Council of a United Nations Zimbabwe Force whose role might include 'the super-vision of a cease-fire, support for the civil power, and liaison with the existing Rhodesian armed forces and with the forces of the Liberation Armies'; (d) the appointment of a Commissioner of Police by the Resident Commissioner, to whom he would be responsible for the maintenance of law and order during the transition period by the police forces under his command; (e) the formation, as soon as possible after the establishment of the transitional administration, of a new Zimbabwe National Army which would in due course replace all existing armed forces in Rhodesia; and (f) the establishment by the Commissioner of an electoral and boundary commission to carry out the registration of voters and the holding of a general election.

On 29 September 1977, in response to the Anglo-American proposals, the Security Council requested the Secretary-General to appoint, in consultation with Council members, a representative to enter into discussions, with the British Resident Commissioner Designate (Lord Carver) and with all the parties, concerning the military and associated arrangements that were considered necessary to effect the transition to majority rule in Rhodesia.[126] But the conversations which the UN representative (Major-General Prem Chand of India) and Lord Carver had with the Rhodesian Prime Minister resulted in no agreement. This was not surprising, for the latter had earlier maintained that the Anglo-American plan was 'a very cunning scheme' to get the Patriotic Front guerilla movements of Mr. Joshua Nkomo and Mr. Robert Mugabe into power, and that the idea that the guerillas fighting against his government should form the basis of the future security forces was 'a crazy suggestion'. In fact, Mr. Smith took strong exception to the proposal that he should surrender power to a British Resident Commissioner during an interim administration leading to a majority-rule government.[127]

But though he rejected the Anglo-American plan, Mr. Smith modified his policy dramatically in November 1977. On the 24th of that month he told the press that after conversations with the leaders of Rhodesia's internal black nationalist groups — Bishop Muzorewa (United African National Council), the Rev. Sithole (African National Council), and Chief Chirau (Zimbabwe United People's Organisation of tribal leaders) — he was prepared to accept their demand for a settlement of the Rhodesian problem on the principle of one-man, one-vote, on condition that safeguards for the white minority population could be agreed.[128]

That the security situation had become more serious through the increase in guerilla activity was no doubt one of the factors which influenced the Rhodesian Prime Minister to change his position. Another factor was the marked deterioration in the state of the economy caused by the fall in Rhodesia's earnings from the export of commodities whose prices had declined in the world market, compounded by sanctions, as Mr. Smith himself admitted to *The Times* correspondent in Salisbury on 1 March 1978, when he said that he saw no benefit in delaying the final outcome.[129]

The settlement signed in Salisbury by Mr. Smith and the three internal black nationalist leaders on 3 March 1978 involved agreement on the drafting of a new constitution which would provide for majority rule on the basis of universal adult suffrage by the end of 1978, with safeguards for the white minority which was promised a referendum on the final terms of the constitution. It was thus agreed that in a new legislative assembly the white minority would have 28 out of the 100 seats for at least ten years, which would be more than sufficient to prevent the passage of a bill designed to change a provision in the constitution, since any change would require 78 votes. A declaration on the rights of individuals and recognition of the independence of the judiciary were to be included in the new constitution, which would be drafted by a transitional government consisting of (i) an Executive Council (the Prime Minister and the black nationalist leaders engaged in the negotiations) whose decisions would be reached by consensus; and (ii) a Ministerial Council, composed of equal numbers of black and white ministers, whose decisions for initiating legislation or supervising the preparation of legislation as directed by the Executive Council would be by majority vote. Other functions of this transitional government would be to bring about a cease-fire, and to deal with the composition of the future military forces, including those members of the nationalist forces who wished to take up a military career, the release of detainees, and procedures for the registration of voters with a view to the holding of free and democratic elections at the earliest possible date.[130]

The Patriotic Front guerilla leaders, Mr. Nkomo and Mr. Mugabe, condemned the internal settlement. They saw no choice but to escalate the war, notwithstanding the willingness of the parties to the settlement to accept their participation in its implementation, and in New York on 8 March 1978, a few days after the UN Security Council had begun discussion of the question, Mr. Nkomo maintained that the agreement bore no relation to what the guerillas were fighting for, and that provision for separate representation for blacks and whites under the terms of the settlement would entrench apartheid.[131] Later, on 14 March, both he and Mr Mugabe rejected the proposal made by Dr. David Owen, the British Foreign Secretary, as suggested earlier by the United States President, Mr. Carter, that they should join in a conference to negotiate their differences with the parties to the internal settlement. Instead, they urged Dr. Owen to resume discussions on the Anglo-American plan, which had been adjourned in Malta in February 1978.[132]

The majority of the Security Council members supported the guerilla leaders' condemnation of the internal settlement. On 14 March 1978 the Council adopted a resolution which declared that any internal settlement of the Rhodesian question under the auspices of the Smith regime was illegal and unacceptable. The resolution, introduced by African states, was accepted by 10 votes to 0, with 5 abstentions. The United States, United Kingdom and other Western powers on the Security Council abstained.[133]

The United States and United Kingdom governments hoped to persuade the architects of the internal settlement and the Patriotic Front leaders to negotiate a compromise formula within the framework of the Anglo-American plan. Without such a settlement they feared that there would be an intensification of the military struggle which would involve neighbouring states and facilitate Soviet-Cuban intervention.[134] But though the Patriotic Front leaders eventually accepted the proposal for an all-party conference, they insisted that its terms of reference would have to take into account a modification of the Anglo-American plan so that it gave the Patriotic Front guerilla alliance, not the British Resident Commissioner, the dominant role in the control of security during the transition period preceding independence.[135] As for the leaders of the new interim administration in Rhodesia, they declared their determination to stand by their internal settlement and re-iterated their readiness to accept the participation of the Patriotic Front leaders in its implementation.[136]

Thus in the spring of 1978 the prospects of a peaceful solution to the Rhodesian problem appeared bleak, with neither the Patriotic Front leaders nor the architects of the internal settlement prepared to accept the Anglo-American proposals for which the Security Council had shown a preference in September 1977, when it appointed a UN representative to work with the Resident British Commissioner Designate for a cease-fire and other matters necessary to effect the transition to majority rule in Rhodesia.

To sum up: the intervention of the UN in the Rhodesian question was not a contravention of the non-intervention principle under Article 2(7) of the Charter, since the United Kingdom, whose permission was necessary for constitutional changes in Rhodesia, requested the Security Council to authorise action against the Smith regime. But a review of the part played by the UN has shown (a) that though the sanctionary economic pressure which the UN was able to exert was insufficient to bring about the collapse of the Smith regime, it contributed with other factors — the adverse effect of the world recession on the Rhodesian economy and the impact of the guerilla war — to impel the Smith government in November 1977 to seek a settlement with the internal black nationalist leaders; and (b) that after such an agreement had been reached in March 1978, there was no immediate prospect that the parties to the internal settlement and the Patriotic Front guerilla leaders would be prepared to accept a compromise formula for a peaceful settlement, and little hope of a consensus being reached in the Security Council to prevent a continuation of the conflict.

Summary and Conclusions

The colonial powers which participated in the formulation of the Charter of the United Nations at San Francisco in 1945 assumed that under Article 73 of the Charter their legal obligation was restricted to transmitting to the Secretary-General for information purposes, subject to such limitation as security and constitutional considerations might require, statistical and other information of a technical nature relating to economic, social and educational conditions in those non-self-governing territories not placed under the UN trusteeship system. With the exception of this commitment, they claimed that the timing and procedures of granting self–government or independence to the peoples of those non-self-governing territories under their administration belonged to the sphere of their domestic jurisdiction, to which the principle of non-intervention under Article 2(7) of the Charter applied. They understood 'non-intervention' to mean 'non-interference in any form', and they assumed that 'the principle of equal rights and self-determination of peoples', referred to in Article 1(2) of the Charter, did not have the force of a legal right for colonial peoples and an international legal obligation for colonial powers. Consequently, they believed that questions pertaining to the administration of their colonies, involving the timing and manner in which political and constitutional developments were to be effected, remained essentially within their domestic jurisdiction, and thus outside the international jurisdiction of the United Nations.

The history of the United Nations has demonstrated that the main political organs of the Organisation have rejected these assumptions in several ways and on a variety of grounds. Both the Security Council and the Assembly have generally disregarded the intentions of those who drafted the Charter and the accepted rule of traditional international law that colonial questions were solely within the domestic jurisdiction of the administering powers unless governed by specific international treaties. Instead, they have taken the view that provided resolutions were supported by the requisite majority vote, in accordance with the voting procedures laid down in the Charter, they were competent to determine whether or not the domestic jurisdiction reservation was applicable to colonial questions. This has meant that variable political factors have generally outweighed legal factors in the determination of resolutions by both the Security Council and the Assembly.

It has been shown that between 1946 and 1960 the Assembly asserted its competence not only to receive, examine and make recommendations on the information provided on economic, social and educational conditions in non-self-governing territories not placed under the United Nations trusteeship system, but also to determine whether or not a territory was non-self-governing under Article 73 of the Charter, and that with few exceptions the administering powers accepted this measure of accountability to the United Nations. The Assembly was thus able to play a supervisory role similar in some respects to that which it had been authorised to perform, with the aid of the Trusteeship Council, with regard to trust territories, and by making such inroads into the domestic domain of the colonial powers helped to weaken their claim that colonial questions were governed by the principle of non-intervention under Article 2(7) of the Charter.

Though the United Nations played a significant role in the Indonesian affair because of the willingness of the United States to apply pressure against the Netherlands in support of the Security Council's policy of decolonising Indonesia, in other colonial conflicts between 1946 and 1960 it either played no part, or in those in which it did intervene, such as the conflicts in Morocco, Tunisia and Algeria, its role was restricted to that of exercising moral pressure for just solutions of those problems in very subdued terms. Indeed, in such instances it would appear that the overthrow of colonialism was caused by the determination of national liberation movements to adopt violent measures which made it difficult for the colonial powers, weakened by the Second World War, to maintain control. Nevertheless, the fact that the political organs of the United Nations asserted their competence, prior to 1960, to discuss and make recommendations on such questions as the conflicts in Morocco, Tunisia, Algeria and Cyprus, established the practice that it was for the United Nations to decide whether the principle of non-intervention should apply to colonial issues, not the colonial power directly involved.

After the Assembly's 1960 Declaration on the Granting of Independence to Colonial Countries and Peoples, which manifested the intense desire of the Afro-Asian states, most of them former colonies, to accelerate the process of decolonisation, that body acted on the assumption that it could intervene in colonial questions solely on a colonial people's 'right to self-determination and independence'.

Though it needs to be stressed that the Soviet Union's strong support for the anti-colonialist cause in the Assembly was not consistent with its reluctance to respect the principle of self-determination of peoples in Eastern Europe, it was understandable that colonial peoples anxious to be rid of the yoke of imperialism, or those subjected to oppressive conditions by white minority regimes in southern Africa, should have looked to the United Nations to assist them in their struggle for liberation, and resorted to 'strategies of violent implementation' when the Organisation could not effectively help them to achieve their objective.

It is difficult to assess the extent to which the work of the Committee of 24, upon which the Assembly's resolutions were based, influenced colonial powers to yield control over non-self-governing territories — almost thirty of them — during the decade that followed the adoption of the 1960 Declaration. But it seems reasonable to assume that the pressure which was exerted on the administering powers influenced most of them to deal with the problems of decolonisation with a greater sense of urgency than they would otherwise have done. Indeed, it would appear that by asserting their competence to discuss and make recommendations on colonial questions which administering powers claimed as matters of domestic jurisdiction, the political organs of the United Nations, both before and after the 1960 Declaration, exposed those powers to the wind of change.

Thus, though it has to be recognised that the United Nations lacked the enforcement capability to compel states to implement the principle of self-determination of peoples, as illustrated by its failure to enforce South Africa's obedience to Assembly and Security Council resolutions on Namibia, or its inability to do anything effective when Russia intervened in Hungary in 1956 and in Czechoslovakia in 1968, this study appears to justify the conclusion that the Organisation provided a platform for anti-colonialist propaganda which influenced most of the colonial powers to speed up the process of decolonisation.*

* The UN and the Palestinian question is reviewed in IV, note 137.

V. THE NON-INTERVENTION PRINCIPLE AS AN ISSUE IN PEACEKEEPING OPERATIONS WITH UN FORCES

In this chapter we shall consider how the principle of non-intervention in matters essentially within the domestic jurisdiction of states has been an issue in peacekeeping operations with UN forces, but in order to place the subject in perspective some mention must be made of the assumptions that influenced the great power approach to the problem of maintaining international peace and security at the San Francisco Conference in 1945, and how this approach was modified as a result of great power disunity.

At San Francisco the architects of the Charter envisaged the maintenance of international peace and security primarily in terms of great power unanimity. Though it was agreed under Article 27 of the Charter that a permanent great power member of the Security Council, party to a dispute to be resolved through pacific settlement under Chapter VI of the Charter, should not possess the right to veto a resolution before the Council, it was given the right of veto in the field of enforcement action under Chapter VII (Action with respect to threats to the peace, breaches of the peace, and acts of aggression). The implementation of this concept of security was thus based on the assumption that the five permanent members of the Security Council — the United States, Soviet Union, China, United Kingdom and France — would neither pursue aggressive policies themselves nor sponsor the aggressive policies of lesser states.

Within this context it was agreed at San Francisco that member-states of the UN would make available to the Security Council the armed forces necessary for maintaining international peace and security, in accordance with special agreements under Article 43 of the Charter, and a Military Staff Committee would assist the Security Council on all matters relating to military requirements under Article 47. But the hostile relations between the Soviet Union and the Western powers made it impossible to ensure great power agreement on the implementation of Article 43,[1] and, as one writer has stated, 'deprived of its cornerstone the UN enforcement system remained a theoretical construction as nations entrusted their defence to military coalitions of like-minded allies'.[2]

That the Security Council was able to recommend enforcement action against North Korea in 1950 was fortuitous, since this was made possible by Russia's absence from the Council in protest at the recognition of Taiwan, not Communist China, as the rightful holder of the China seat at the United Nations, the requisite majority taking the view that because of its absence, Russia was not entitled to exercise its veto. Having determined on 25 June that 'the armed attack upon the Republic of Korea' constituted 'a breach of the peace', and called upon the North Korean authorities to withdraw their forces to the 38th parallel,[3] which the latter ignored, the Security Council recommended on 27 June 'that the Members of the

116

United Nations furnish such assistance to the Republic of Korea as may be necessary to repel the armed attack and to restore international peace and security in the area'.[4] On 7 July it further recommended 'that all Members providing military forces and other assistance pursuant to the aforesaid Security Council resolutions make such forces and other assistance available to a unified command under the United States'.[5]

The majority in the Security Council thus took the view, as subsequently asserted by Rosalyn Higgins, that there was 'a clearly defined *de facto* frontier' dividing North and South Korea, and 'two different authorities', and that 'what was at issue was an external attack by one authority upon the territory under the control of the other'.[6] But the Soviet Union contended that United Nations intervention in Korea — military forces were provided by sixteen states under the unified command of the United States and other forms of assistance by twenty-one states — was a violation of the principle of non-intervention in a domestic matter. 'As regards the war between the North and South Koreans, it is a civil war and therefore does not come within the definition of aggression, since it is war, not between two States, but between two parts of the Korean people temporarily split into two camps under separate authorities,' argued Mr. Malik, the Soviet delegate, on his return to the Security Council early in August 1950. 'The conflict in Korea is thus an internal conflict. Consequently rules relating to aggression are just as inapplicable to the North and South Koreans as the concept of aggression was inapplicable to the northern and southern states of America, when they were fighting a civil war for the unification of their country.'[7]

In view of the Soviet Union's opposition to United Nations intervention in Korea, the return of its delegate to the Security Council prevented that body from adopting any further resolutions on the Korean question, but action against North Korea under United Nations auspices proceeded as had been recommended, and in order to circumvent an inactive Security Council if it was hamstrung by the veto in the event of further acts of aggression on the Korean model, the United Nations Assembly adopted the 'Uniting for Peace' plan which contained the following provisions: (i) the calling of an emergency session of the Assembly within twenty four hours if the Security Council, because of lack of unanimity of its permanent members, failed to exercise its primary responsibility for the maintenance of international peace and security in any case where there appeared to be a threat to the peace, breach of the peace, or act of aggression. The Assembly would consider the matter immediately with a view to making appropriate recommendations to member-states for collective measures, including in the case of a breach of the peace, or act of aggression, the use of armed force when necessary to maintain or restore international peace and security: (ii) the setting-up of a Peace Observation Commission under the auspices of the Assembly to observe and report on the situation in any area where there was international tension, the continuance of which was likely to endanger international peace and security: (iii) the earmarking by each member of the United Nations within its national armed forces elements, so trained, organised and equipped that they would promptly be made available, in accordance with their constitutional processes, for service in United Nations units in the event of a breach of the peace or act of aggression: and (iv) the establishment of a Collective Measures Committee to study and report on methods which might be used to maintain and strengthen international peace and security, in accordance with the purposes and principles of the Charter, taking account of collective self-defence and regional arrangements under Article 51 and 52 of the Charter.[8]

The protagonists of the 'Uniting for Peace' resolution argued that it was possible for matters veto-bound in the Security Council to be transferred to the Assembly by a procedural vote of any seven members, i.e. one not subject to a permanent member's veto, and for the Assembly to make recommendations on security questions under Article 10 or Article 11(2) of the Charter, provided such matters were not currently seized by the Security Council under Article 12; and that if such a procedure were adopted, it would then be possible for the Assembly to make appropriate recommendations to member-states for collective measures, including in the case of a breach of the peace, or act of aggression, the use of force if necessary. Though members of the United Nations are not legally bound to carry out the Assembly's recommendations, the sponsors of the 'Uniting for Peace' resolution considered it likely that states would respond in order to maintain international peace and security.

The Soviet Union asserted that the resolution was illegal under the Charter on the ground that only the Security Council possessed the competence to authorise enforcement measures, and that under Article 11(2) 'any such question on which action is necessary shall be referred to the Security Council by the General Assembly either before or after discussion'. It thus insisted that the Council was competent to accept or reject a recommendation by the Assembly for collective measures, such as those envisaged under the 'Uniting for Peace' resolution, and that it was to the Council to which armed forces should be made available under Article 43 of the Charter.[9]

The Soviet views were rejected by a large majority in the Assembly, and it was in line with the 'Uniting for Peace' resolution that the Assembly recommended an embargo on the shipment of arms and materials of strategic value to Communist China and North Korea in May 1951.[10] But enthusiasm for implementing the 'Uniting for Peace' plan soon declined, as indicated by the weak response to the recommendation that states should take action to maintain elements in their armed forces, so trained, organised and equipped that they could promptly be made available for service as United Nations units. 'Sixty member states were polled.

Seventeen states failed to respond; two merely acknowledged the inquiry; and twenty-one replies were negative to non-committal. Of the remaining twenty replies, some were hedged, and only four (Denmark, Norway, Greece and Thailand) actually set aside any forces then in existence without a great many strings attached'.[11] As Gabriella Rosner has pointed out, although the Collective Measures Committee set up under the 'Uniting for Peace' scheme 'made extensive studies of the question and submitted a number of significant proposals on the matter to the General Assembly, it was soon evident that most Member States were unwilling to undertake specific commitments for the future. The failure of the Security Council to establish an effective system of collective security had caused many of them to provide for their mutual defence by means of special arrangements for collective self-defence and hence they were anxious to determine their future course of action in the light of these commitments and the circumstances of the particular situation'.[12]

But despite the failure of the United Nations, apart from its fortuitous intervention in the Korean affair, to function as an agency for the enforcement of peace under the authority of the Security Council, or through the implementation of the Assembly's 'Uniting for Peace' scheme, the Organisation was not rendered totally incapable of slowing down the impetus of conflict or effecting a cessation of hostilities in some troubled areas. During its early years UN commissions, established either by the Security Council or the Assembly, were able to exercise a moderating influence on various parties in conflict, and military observer groups, consisting of unarmed officers made available to the United Nations by member-states considered impartial by the parties, began to operate in the Balkans in 1946, in Palestine in 1947, and on the Kashmir cease-fire line in 1948.

Since these military observer groups, which had the task of observing and reporting on the maintenance of cease-fire arrangements and, in the Balkans, of supervising the withdrawal of guerilla forces from Greece into Albania, Bulgaria and Yugoslavia, were established with the consent of those states in whose territories they carried out their duties,[13] their presence was not a contravention of the principle of non-intervention in matters essentially within the domestic jurisdiction of states under Article 2(7) of the Charter. This also applied to the stationing and operation of the United Nations Emergency Force which was established on Egyptian territory with the consent of the Government of Egypt in 1956.

The United Nations Emergency Force (UNEF) — 1956-67

The Suez crisis of 1956 resulting from the invasion of Egypt by Israel, France and Britain was a situation in which several factors combined to motivate the majority of United Nations members to decide at a special session of the Assembly,[14] as provided in its 'Uniting for Peace' resolution of 1950, to establish an international peacekeeping force. As Evan Luard has explained: 'Like the Korean invasion it was one of the few cases the Organization had met in which there occurred a clear and flagrant case of external attack against the territory of a member. Next it was a situation calculated to arouse the wide body of anti-colonialist sentiment within the Organization. Finally, it was a case where active fighting was not likely to be required by the forces set up.'[15]

The international peacekeeping force which the Assembly established was not designed for the enforcement of international peace; it was a non-coercive force, consisting of paramilitary units contributed by ten states on a voluntary basis,[16] and generally equipped only with weapons of self-defence, to secure and supervise the cessation of hostilities and to take up a position between the forces of Egypt and Israel in accordance with the Armistice Agreements of February 1949.[17]

There were various Status of Forces agreements with the host state, Egypt, according privileges and immunities to UNEF personnel, and the Force was given freedom of movement within its area of operations, and such facilities regarding access to that area and communications as were necessary for the successful completion of its task. But UN personnel were not permitted in any sense to be party to internal conflicts or used to enforce any specific political solution of pending problems.

It should also be noted that the Commander of the Force was responsible for the discharge of his task to the Assembly, but under instructions from the Secretary-General on the basis of the executive authority for the operation vested in him by the Assembly; the cost of the operation was allocated among member-states of the United Nations in accordance with the normal scale of budgetary contributions; and that the Assembly established under its resolution 1001(ES-1) of 7 November 1956 an advisory committee of seven representatives of member-states, under the chairmanship of the Secretary-General, which was required not only to assist the Secretary-General in the planning and operation of the Force, but also to request the convening of the Assembly and to report to that body whenever matters arose which, in its opinion, were of such urgency and importance as to require consideration by the Assembly itself.

The importance of the principle of consent as a guiding principle in the establishment and operation of the UNEF was dealt with by the Secretary-General in his second and final report on his plan for the Force,[18] which was approved by the Assembly on 7 November 1956.[19] 'Functioning as it would, on the basis of a decision reached under the terms of the resolution 337(V) 'Uniting for Peace',[20] the Force, if established, would be limited in its operations to the extent that consent of the parties concerned is required under generally recognised international law,' he stated. 'While the General Assembly is enabled to *establish* the Force with the consent of those parties which contribute units to the Force, it could not request the Force to be *stationed* or *operate* on the territory of a given country without the consent

120

of the Government of that country.'[21]

Clearly, the establishment of UNEF was not at variance with the principle of non-intervention in matters essentially within the domestic jurisdiction of states since the Assembly could only recommend, not order, UN members to contribute units to the Force, and the Force could not be stationed or operate on the territory of a state without its consent. In fact, though the Soviet Union did not accept the constitutional basis on which the Force was established, on the ground that only the Security Council, under Chapter VII of the Charter, not the Assembly, had the competence to set up a UN peacekeeping force — the fact that UNEF was a non-coercive force made no difference to the Soviet argument — it abstained from voting on the establishment of the force, rather than vote against it, because Egypt was prepared to consent to the stationing of the force on its territory.[22]

The question whether it was a matter within the domestic jurisdiction of the Egyptian government to *terminate* the presence of UNEF at a time of its own choosing was the subject of delicate negotiations between Hammarskjold and the Egyptian government, but the *Aide-memoire* on the basis for the presence and functioning of UNEF in Egypt which was agreed to by the Government of Egypt after Hammarskjold's discussions with Nasser in Cairo (16-18 November 1956),[23] was noted with approval by the Assembly on 24 November 1956.[24] This contained the following declarations by the Government of Egypt and the United Nations:

> The Government of Egypt declares that, when exercising its sovereign rights on any matter concerning the presence and functioning of UNEF, it will be guided, in good faith, by its acceptance of General Assembly resolution 1000 (ES-1) of 5 November 1956.[25]

> The United Nations takes note of this declaration of the Government of Egypt and declares that the activities of UNEF will be guided, in good faith, by the task established for the Force in the aforesaid resolution; in particular, the United Nations, understanding this to correspond to the wishes of the Government of Egypt, reaffirms its willingness to maintain UNEF until its task is completed.

Hammarskjold outlined in general terms the implications of the *Aide-memoire* in his Summary Study of the experience derived from the establishment and operation of the Force, the text of which was as follows:[26]

> The consequence of such a bilateral declaration is that, were either side to act unilaterally in refusing continued presence or deciding on withdrawal, and were the other side to find that such action was contrary to a good-faith interpretation of the purposes of the operation, an exchange of views would be called for towards harmonising the positions. This does not imply any infringement of the

sovereign right of the host Government, nor any restriction of the right of the United Nations to decide on the termination of its own operation whenever it might see fit to do so. But it does mean a mutual recognition of the fact that the operation, being based on collaboration between the host Government and the United Nations, should be carried on in forms natural to such collaboration, and especially so with regard to the questions of presence and maintenance. ✗

It is implicit in this statement, as M.H. Gagnon has maintained that the host government having consulted fully with the United Nations, can then properly insist on the withdrawal of the force whether or not the United Nations approves. A pledge of good faith puts the host state under obligation to act reasonably; it may well set up a duty to consult with the United Nations on all matters, but it does not by itself set up a duty to agree. Any more stringent interpretation would entail an exercise of United Nations authority inconsistent with the meaning of consent as the basis of the operation and appropriate only to Security Council enforcement action'.[27] But according to a personal memorandum written by Hammarskjold — it was dated 5 August 1957, a year or so before the publication of his Summary Study referred to above[28] — the Egyptian government had accepted a more definite obligation than the 'good faith' agreement seemed to imply. Hammarskjold asserted that Nasser had accepted a legal obligation to reach agreement on the question whether the tasks of UNEF had been completed before he could legitimately decide to terminate the presence of the Force on Egyptian territory, and consequently limited Egypt's jurisdiction in regard to this question.

Indeed, Hammarskjold gives special emphasis to this in the account of his discussions with Nasser in Cairo on 17 November 1956. 'The device I used,' he states, 'meant only that instead of limiting their rights by a basic understanding requesting an agreement *directly concerning withdrawal,* we created an obligation to reach agreement on the fact that the tasks were completed, and, thus, *the conditions for a withdrawal established.*'[29] In fact, Hammarskjold stated in his personal memorandum that 'to shoot the text through in spite of Nasser's strong wish to avoid this, and his strong suspicion of the legal construction, — especially of the possible consequences of differences of views regarding the task — I felt obliged, in the course of the discussion, to threaten three times, that unless an agreement of this type was made, I would have to propose the immediate withdrawal of troops. If any proof would be necessary for how the text of the agreement was judged by President Nasser, this last mentioned fact tells the story'.[30]

But according to U Thant, who as Secretary-General had to deal with the United Arab Republic's demand[31] for UNEF's withdrawal in May 1967, Hammarskjold's personal memorandum, which was never published as a

United Nations document, — it was released in The New York Times on 20 June 1967 by a former United States representative to the United Nations and one of Hammarskjold's legal consultants — had 'no standing beyond being a purely private memorandum of unknown purpose or value, in which Secretary-General Hammarskjold seems to record his own impressions and interpretations of the discussions with President Nasser. This paper, therefore, cannot affect in any way the basis for the presence of UNEF on the soil of the United Aráb Republic as set out in the official documents, much less supersede these documents'.[32] Certainly, this was a valid point, as M.H. Gagnon admits,[33] but she is nevertheless justified in criticising U Thant for the 'slight regard' which he paid to the 'good faith' agreement under the *Aide-memoire* of 20 November 1956, when the United Arab Republic requested UNEF's withdrawal 'without consultation or even a statement of reasons'. As Gagnon asserts, 'the day before the request was made the Secretary-General protested the buildup of Arab troops in the buffer zone and included, without comment, a copy of the 1956 good faith agreement, but when the request arrived, he made no further protest on grounds of good faith (UN Document A/6669, paragraphs 2, 6-7)'.[34] In fairness to U Thant, however, it must be pointed out that he did follow the procedure which had been suggested by Hammarskjold, as explained below.

It was on 18 May 1967, at 12 noon (New York time) that U Thant received the message from the Foreign Minister of the United Arab Republic stating that his government had 'decided to terminate the presence of the United Nations Emergency Force from the territory of the United Arab Republic and the Gaza strip', and requested 'that the necessary steps be taken for the withdrawal of the Force as soon as possible'.[35] Even before this communication was received, U.A.R. forces had taken over UNEF's posts in Sinai, Sharm el Sheikh and Ras Nasrani, and the Secretary-General made known to the permanent representative of the U.A.R. at the United Nations his 'deep misgivings about the likely disastrous consequences of the withdrawal of UNEF' and his intention 'to appeal urgently to President Nasser to reconsider his decision'.[36] Later in the day, however, he was informed that 'such a request would be sternly rebuffed',[37] and there can be no doubt that the United Arab Republic's unreasonable conduct was not in the spirit or the letter of the good faith agreement of 20 November 1956.

In the circumstances, U Thant followed the approach which had been suggested by Secretary-General Hammarskjold ten years earlier when Israel's Foreign Minister Eban had asked whether the Assembly would be given notice before UNEF was withdrawn. 'An indicated procedure,' Hammarskjold had stated, 'would be for the Secretary-General to inform the Advisory Committee on the United Nations Emergency Force, which would determine whether the matter should be brought to the attention of the Assembly'.[38] Such an approach was consistent with paragraph 9 of the General Assembly resolution 1001(ES-1) of 7 November 1956, which stated that 'the Advisory Committee, in the performance of its duty, shall be empowered to request through the usual procedures, the convening of the General Assembly and to report to the Assembly whenever matters arise which, in its opinion, are of such urgency and importance as to require consideration by the General Assembly itself'.

In accordance with this procedure Secretary-General U Thant met with the UNEF Advisory Committee at 1700 hours (New York time) on 18 May 1967, before replying to the United Arab Republic's demand. The representatives of three countries not members of the Advisory Committee but providing contingents to UNEF, were also present at the meeting, and in his account of that meeting, the minutes of which have not yet been released by the United Nations, U Thant made the following disclosure:

> No proposal was made that the Advisory Committee should exercise the right vested in it by the General Assembly resolution 1001(ES-1) to request the convening of the General Assembly to take up the situation arising from the United Arab Republic communication. At the conclusion of the meeting, it was understood that the Secretary-General had no alternative other than to comply with the United Arab Republic's demand, although some representatives felt the Secretary-General should previously clarify with that Government the meaning in its request that withdrawal should take place "as soon as possible". The Secretary-General informed the Advisory Committee that he intended to reply promptly to the United Arab Republic, and to report to the General Assembly and to the Security Council on the action he had taken. It was for the Member States to decide whether the competent organs should or could take up the matter and to pursue it accordingly.[39]

Immediately after the meeting of the Advisory Committee, at approximately 19.00 hours (New York time) on 18 May, U Thant informed the Foreign Minister of the United Arab Republic, through that state's permanent representative at the United Nations, that his Government's request would be complied with;[40] and since his special reports to the Assembly and Security Council were presented later,[41] the official United Nations response to the United Arab Republic's request for UNEF's withdrawal was made before these organs could take any move to dissuade the government of that state to change its mind.

Since it was the responsibility of the Advisory Committee under the chairmanship of the Secretary-General to determine whether the matter should have been referred to the Assembly in accordance with the Assembly's resolution 1001(ES-1), and the need for such action was obviously desirable in view of the serious consequences that might follow from UNEF's withdrawal, the failure of that Committee to request the

Assembly to consider the matter justified censure. Even if the Assembly did not possess the competence to decide that the withdrawal of UNEF should not take place, since the question of terminating the presence of the Force on United Arab Republic territory was a matter within the domestic jurisdiction of that state, it had the competence under the good faith agreement of 20 November 1956 to call for further consultations on the matter, and to make a recommendation which reflected its moral judgment on the matter. The Assembly would not have been contravening the principle of non-intervention in matters within the domestic jurisdiction of the United Arab Republic had this procedure been followed.

In defence of the part which he played in the affair, U Thant argued that he did not believe that any useful purpose would be served by his seeking a meeting of either the Assembly or the Security Council, nor did he consider that there was a basis for him to do so at the time.[42] But since he stated in his report to the Security Council on 19 May 1967 that the situation in the Middle East was 'extremly menacing',[43] he had a basis under Article 99 of the Charter on which to ask the Security Council to consider the question of UNEF's withdrawal as a threat to international peace and security.

Under Article 99 'the Secretary-General may bring to the attention of the Security Council any matter which in his opinion may threaten the maintenance of international peace and security',[44] and the exercise of this prerogative would not have been at variance with the principle of non-intervention in a matter essentially within the domestic jurisdiction of the United Arab Republic. Even though it was unlikely that the Security Council would have been able to decide that the situation constituted a threat to international peace under Article 39 of the Charter, because 'the Soviet Union could have been relied upon to stand by Egypt',[45] such a move would have dramatised the need for fresh initiatives in the search for a political settlement of the Arab-Israeli question, which was long overdue.

It would appear that U Thant's defeatist attitude was a reflection of the general malaise affecting UN's peacekeeping role at the time. Certainly, the morale of the Organisation had been lowered by the controversy over the financing of peacekeeping operations by the Assembly, which stemmed from the insistence of the Soviet Union and France that only the Security Council could authorise United Nations peacekeeping forces, such as UNEF, even though an advisory opinion of the International Court of Justice had upheld the Assembly's competence to recommend the establishment of non-coercive peacekeeping forces under Article 11(2) of the Charter.[46]

Though the United Nations Operation in the Congo (ONUC) was established in July 1960 by the Security Council, the Soviet Union's objection to the political direction of the Force resulted in its refusal to share in that peacekeeping operation, and intensified the financial and constitutional controversies within the United Nations on the question of peacekeeping.

Besides, and of special relevance in this study, the interpretation and application of the principle of non-intervention in the domestic affairs of the Republic of the Congo was a basic issue in the Congo affair, and before we consider the second United Nations Emergency Force which was established in the Middle East in October 1973, after the third Arab-Israeli war, it is proposed to examine the United Nations peacekeeping operation in the Congo and other peacekeeping operations involving UN forces which were launched in the 1960s.

The United Nations Operation in the Congo (ONUC).[47]

Like UNEF, ONUC was a peacekeeping force which was established with the consent of the host state, the newly formed Republic of the Congo. But unlike UNEF, ONUC was authorised under a resolution of the Security Council, not the Assembly, in response to Secretary-General Hammarskjold's initiative under Article 99 of the Charter, following a cable from President Kasavubu on 12 July 1960, which requested military assistance to protect the territory of the Republic of the Congo against Belgian aggression,[48] and a second cable from the President and the Prime Minister, Lumumba, on 13 July, which threatened to look for help outside the United Nations if there was no UN response.[49]

Belgian forces, stationed on bases in various parts of the Congo under the Belgo-Congolese Treaty of Friendship, had intervened to quell disorders and to protect Europeans following the mutiny of Congolese troops of the Force Publique against their Belgian officers, and their attempt to restore order was interpreted by the leaders of the central government in Leopoldville as an encouragement for secessionist movements in the provinces of Kasai and Katanga. In fact, on 11 July, the Prime Minister of Katanga, Moise Tshombe, who had asked for the intervention of Belgian troops in Elisabethville, announced the secession of Katanga. There was thus the danger that if the new Congolese government did not obtain United Nations assistance, that military aid would be forthcoming from states whose intervention might turn the Congo into an international cauldron.

The Security Council considered the question on 13 and 14 July, and the Soviet Union's attempt to characterise the situation as an issue of external aggression by Belgium and to get the Council to call for the immediate withdrawal of Belgian troops was defeated. Instead the Council adopted a Tunisian proposal, the text of which in its operative part read as follows:

1. **Calls upon** the Government of Belgium to withdraw their troops from the territory of the Republic of the Congo;

2. **Decides** to authorise the Secretary-General to take the necessary steps, in consultation with the Government of the Republic of the Congo, to provide the Government with such military assistance as may be necessary, until, through the

efforts of the Congolese Government with the technical assistance of the United Nations, the national security forces may be able, in the opinion of the Government, to meet fully their tasks;

3. **Requests** the Secretary-General to report to the Security Council as appropriate.[50]

In his First Report to the Security Council (18 July 1960),[51] Secretary-General Hammarskjold characterised the breakdown of law and order in the Congo as a situation which represented a threat to international peace and security, and stated that the aim of the UN Force was to assist the Congolese government to restore law and order and facilitate the withdrawal of Belgian forces. He was able to report that elements of ONUC were already in place, and that the following rules and principles applied to the establishment and operation of the Force: (i) the stationing of the Force on Congolese territory was based on the consent of the host state, the Republic of the Congo: (ii) the use of military personnel and equipment by the UN depended on the consent of the contributing states: (iii) the Force would not include contingents from any of the permanent members of the Security Council, but consist of forces mainly from African states and some recruited from other states: (iv) the Force was not to interfere in internal conflicts or enforce any specific political solution of pending problems: (v) freedom of movement within its area of operations was essential for the Force, and this involved the negotiation of agreements with the Republic of the Congo: (vi) the Force was restricted to military action in self-defence, which prohibited UN forces from taking the initiative in the use of armed force: (vii) the Force would be under the exclusive command of the United Nations, and its Commander responsible for the discharge of his task to the Security Council, but under instructions from the Secretary-General on the basis of the executive authority for the operation vested in him by the Security Council: and the cost should be undertaken by member-states according to the normal scale of budgetary contributions.

On 22 July the Security Council commended the Secretary-General for the prompt action that he had taken, invited the specialised agencies of the United Nations to render him such assistance as he might require, and requested him to report further as appropriate. It did not make a formal finding that the situation in the Congo was a threat to international peace and security, but 'considering that the complete restoration of law and order in the Republic of the Congo would effectively contribute to the maintenance of international peace and security', called upon the Government of Belgium 'to implement speedily the Security Council resolution of 14 July 1960, on the withdrawal of their troops', authorized the Secretary-General 'to take all necessary action to this effect', and requested all states 'to refrain from any action which might tend to impede the restoration of law and order and the exercise by the Government of the Congo of its authority and also to refrain from any action which might undermine the territorial integrity and the political independence of the Republic of the Congo'.[52]

The two Security Council resolutions (14 and 22 July 1960) were mentioned in the basic agreement between the Republic of the Congo and the United Nations,[53] which recognised that the establishment of ONUC in the Congo was based on the consent of the host state, but also made fairly clear, in contrast to the basic agreement between Egypt and the United Nations on UNEF, that the question of the termination of ONUC's presence in the Congo was a matter which the United Nations was competent to decide. This agreement, which was concluded on 27 July 1960, was as follows:

> The Government of the Republic of the Congo states that, in the exercise of its sovereign rights with respect to any question concerning the presence and functioning of the United Nations Force in the Congo, it will be guided, in good faith, by the fact that it has requested military assistance from the United Nations and by its acceptance of the resolutions of the Security Council of 14 and 22 July 1960; it likewise states that it will ensure the freedom of movement of the Force in the interior of the country and will accord the requisite privileges and immunities to all personnel associated with the activities of the Force.

> The United Nations takes note of the statement of the Government of the Republic of the Congo and states that, with regard to the activities of the United Nations Force in the Congo, it will be guided, in good faith, by the task assigned to the Force in the aforementioned resolutions; in particular the United Nations reaffirms, considering it to be in accordance with the wishes of the Government of the Republic of the Congo, that it is prepared to maintain the United Nations Force in the Congo until such time as it deems the latter's task to have been fully accomplished.

Presently it will be seen that the question of ONUC's freedom of movement and termination, referred to in the Basic Agreement, became matters of dispute between the Congolese government and the UN Command in the Congo under the general direction of the Secretary-General, but the main disagreement that emerged at an early stage of the UN operation was over the application of the principles of self-defence and non-intervention in internal conflicts, which were basic to Hammarskjold's concept of how the peacekeeping operation should be conducted, as he had emphasised in his first report to the Security Council. As already stated, this report was commended by the Security Council, but the dispute between Hammarskjold and Lumumba over the application of the two principles was highlighted in August 1960, after the Secretary-General had asked the Security Council for fresh instructions because the entry of UN troops into Katanga was likely to be opposed by force.[54]

Hammarskjold pointed out to the Security Council on 8 August that since the principle of self-defence governing the operation of ONUC prohibited UN forces from taking the initiative in the use of armed force, their entry into Katanga by the use of force was not permissible. But he did not ask the Security Council to widen ONUC's mandate by giving it the right to use enforcement measures; he was obviously anxious that ONUC should still operate in accordance with the self-defence principle, for all that he recommended was that the Council should stress the need for UN forces to enter Katanga and not be used to intervene in the internal conflicts in the Congo in order to influence their outcome.[55]

It can thus be seen that Hammarskjold considered that the secession of Katanga was a domestic question to which the general principle of non-intervention under Article 2(7) of the Charter was applicable, so that ONUC should not be used to influence the outcome of the conflict between Katanga and the central government. Moreover, since ONUC was also governed by the principle of self-defence, which prohibited UN forces from using enforcement measures, it was implicit in Hammarskjold's policy that the exception to the general principle of non-intervention under Article 2(7), which permits enforcement measures under Chapter VII of the Charter (Articles 41 and 42) if the Security Council should determine that a threat to international peace arises out of a domestic question, could not be invoked to enable ONUC to apply enforcement action against Tshombe's Katanga to end its secession.

The principle of non-intervention in internal conflicts between political factions and the principle of self-defence were thus closely linked in determining Hammarskjold's approach to the problem of Katanga, and explains why he considered that the constitutional basis for the Security Council's resolutions on the Congo affair was to be found in Article 40 of the Charter,[56] though neither that article nor any other article had been mentioned in the Council's resolutions. It would appear that Hammarskjold's view was based on the assumption that the Security Council had already recognised that the Congo situation was a threat to international peace and security under Article 39 of the Charter, but instead of making recommendations or deciding under Article 39 what enforcement measures should be taken in accordance with Article 41 or 42 to maintain or restore international peace and security, had preferred to act under Article 40, viz. 'in order to prevent an aggravation of the situation, the Security Council may, before making the recommendations or deciding upon the measures provided for in Article 39, call upon the parties concerned to comply with such provisional measures as it deems necessary or desirable. Such provisional measures shall be without prejudice to the rights, claims, or position of the parties concerned. The Security Council shall duly take account of failure to comply with such provisional measures.' Certainly, since provisional measures under Article 40 are not enforcement measures, it may be claimed that the operation of ONUC in accordance with the principle of self-defence was not at variance with Article 40, and that the exception to the general principle of non-intervention under Article 2(7) could not be invoked, since that specifically refers to enforcement measures.

In his speech to the Security Council on 8 August 1960 it was obvious that Hammarskjold was anxious that provisional measures under Article 40, as distinct from enforcement measures under Article 42, should be applied to prevent an aggravation of the situation in the Congo. But this approach was criticised by the delegate of the Soviet Union who contended that the intervention of Belgian forces in the province of Katanga was a case of external aggression against the Republic of the Congo, and maintained that the UN Force had the authority to apply enforcement measures against those who resisted its entry into Katanga.[57]

The Security Council rejected the measures proposed by the Soviet Union and adopted a resolution[58] which reflected the view of Hammarskjold. The operative parts of this resolution were as follows:

1. **Confirms** the authority given to the Secretary-General by the Security Council resolutions of 14 July and 22 July 1960 and requests him to continue to carry out the responsibilities placed on him thereby;

2. **Calls upon** the Government of Belgium to withdraw immediately its troops from the Province of Katanga under speedy modalities determined by the Secretary-General and to assist in every possible way the implementation of the Council's resolutions;

3. **Declares** that the entry of the United Nations Force into the Province of Katanga is necessary for the full implementation of this resolution;

4. **Reaffirms** that the United Nations Force in the Congo will not be party to or in any way intervene in or be used to influence the outcome of any internal conflict, constitutional or otherwise;

5. **Calls upon** all Member States, in accordance with Articles 25 and 49 of the Charter, to accept and carry out the decisions of the Security Council and to afford mutual assistance in carrying out measures decided upon by the Security Council;

6. **Requests** the Secretary-General to implement this resolution and to report further to the Security Council as appropriate.

In a memorandum on paragraph 4 above, Hammarskjold asserted that this meant that though the United Nations had no right to prevent the central government in Leopoldville from taking independent action against Katanga, the United Nations Force could not be employed on behalf of the central government to force the provincial government in Katanga to accept a particular solution of the constitutional problem posed by Katanga's secession.[59] But this interpretation was disputed by Lumumba who, in a letter to Hammarskjold,[60] maintained that the implementation of Security Council resolutions required the use of ONUC to overthrow the rebel government of Katanga. Moreover, the fact that Hammarskjold had reached agreement with Tshombe on 12 August 1960 for the immediate entry of ONUC contingents into Katanga and the withdrawal of Belgian troops from the province by the end of August, without involving Lumumba in the negotiations, or including his forces in the Katanga operation, 'had dealt a blow to Lumumba's pride, and Lumumba had decided to seek military help directly from the Soviet Union'.[61]

In response to Lumumba's criticism of his handling of the Katanga question, Hammarskjold asked for a meeting of the Security Council, but when the Council met on August 21-22 no resolution was adopted by that body. Though the Soviet Union, supported by Poland, proposed that a group of states contributing contingents to the United Nations Force should be set up to ensure the implementation of Security Council resolutions, in accordance with Lumumba's interpretation, the Secretary-General's insistence that ONUC's role should be governed by the closely linked principles of 'self-defence' and 'non-intervention in internal conflicts, constitutional or otherwise,' was supported by Ceylon, China, Ecuador, France, Italy, United Kingdom and the United States.[62] Thus, although Hammarskjold established at this juncture an Advisory Committee, representative of the eight states contributing units to the UN Force, with which he could consult as occasion demanded, he was still able to conduct the peacekeeping operation in the Congo in accordance with the basic principles which he had formulated.

Having failed to secure the use of ONUC to enforce Katanga's submission to the central government, Lumumba ordered his Congolese soldiers into Kasai province to prepare for an attack against the secessionist provice, for which he sought assistance from the Soviet Union. Their massacre of tribesmen of the Baluba secessionist movement, soon after their entry into the province, moved Hammarskjold to depart from a literal interpretation of the principle of non-intervention in internal conflicts. 'Prohibition against intervention in internal conflicts cannot be considered to apply to senseless slaughter of civilians or fighting arising from tribal hostilities,' he cabled Cordier, who had replaced Bunche as his special representative in the Congo, and after consulting with his Advisory Committee, 'he instructed Cordier, on September 2, to recommend strongly to Foreign Minister Bomboko that immediate steps be taken to control and discipline the army in Kasai. He also authorised the interposing of UN troops, using force if necessary to stop the massacre.'[63]

Hammarskjold was also greatly alarmed by the threat to international peace and security posed by Soviet military assistance to Lumumba. Already Lumumba's forces had been helped by Soviet transport planes, trucks and technicians, and on 5 September shortly after the Soviet Union had announced its support for Lumumba without recognising Kasavubu as President of the Republic of the Congo, Kasavubu dismissed Lumumba from his post and appointed Joseph Ileo in his place. In response to this Lumumba declared that Kasavubu was no longer President. But though the Congolese parliament would not ratify the dismissal of either Lumumba or Kasavubu, the bitter contest for power between the rival political leaders brought to an end the effective functioning of the parliamentary system of government.

In view of the constitutional crisis in the Congo, Hammarskjold advised Cordier to use his own discretion in handling the complex situation. 'In such a situation,' he cabled, 'responsible people on the spot might commit themselves to what the Secretary-General could not justify doing himself — taking the risk of being disowned when it no longer mattered;'[64] and Cordier took the view that the only legitimate constitutional authority in such a chaotic situation was the President. He thus acceded to President Kasavubu's requests that ONUC should become responsible for maintaining law and order throughout the Congo and that all airfields should be closed to all except ONUC aircraft. On his own initiative Cordier also decided on 6 September to close down the Leopoldville radio station in order to prevent inflammatory political broadcasts, but 'Cordier and his advisers did not know that Kasavubu, through his Bakongo contacts and his friendship with the Abbé Youlou across the river in Brazzaville, would be given access to the even more powerful transmitters of Radio Brazzaville. Thus what was intended to be a general ban on political broadcasts put Lumumba at a considerable disadvantage, especially since Lumumba was a far more effective demagogue than Kasavubu, whose normal reaction to any crisis was to lock himself in his house and go to bed . . . The closing of the airports also had a greater effect on Lumumba than on Kasavubu, who had no Soviet or other aircraft at his disposal, and was in any case not engaged, as Lumumba was, in shuttling troops about the country for military purposes'.[65] Not surprisingly, Cordier's action brought forth a storm of protest from Lumumba and his supporters and exposed him to the charge of interfering in the situation in order to influence the outcome of the internal conflicts.

Rajeshwar Dayal, who replaced Cordier as the Secretary-General's representative in the Congo on 8 September, admitted the difficulty of conducting the ONUC operation without alienating one or other of the internal factions, a few days after he had taken over from Cordier.[66] But his problem became even more intractable when Colonel Mobutu, the Congolese Army Chief of Staff, announced on 14 September that parliament was to be dissolved, and that the Army was to take over control of the country, while still accepting Kasavubu as President. Though Ileo did not challenge this coup d'état, Lumumba did, and he soon had to accept the protection of ONUC to avoid arrest.

On the same day as Mobutu announced his military coup, the Security Council was meeting to consider the claims of two rival Congolese delegations, one accredited by President Kasavubu, the other by Lumumba. A Polish proposal to seat the Lumumba delegation was supported only by the Soviet Union and Ceylon, but no decision was taken on the matter, and the Security Council turned its attention to the Fourth Report of the Secretary-General, which appealed to all states to refrain from any action which might tend to impede the restoration of law and order;[67] but a draft resolution which expressed the view that no state should interfere unilaterally in the domestic affairs of the Congo, and that all aid to the Congo should be channelled through the United Nations, as advocated by Hammarskjold, was vetoed by the Soviet Union.[68]

Since the Security Council was rendered impotent by the Soviet veto, the United States proposed the convening of an emergency special session of the Assembly under the 'Uniting for Peace' procedure. This was approved by the requisite seven votes, and the Assembly began consideration of the Congo question on 17 September. Three days later it adopted a resolution, sponsored by seventeen Afro-Asian states, which, by requesting the Secretary-General to continue to take vigorous action in accordance with the Security Council resolutions of 14 and 22 of July and 9 August 1960, virtually endorsed his political direction of the Congo operation. The resolution requested all states, *inter alia*, not to interfere in internal affairs of the Congo and to provide all forms of assistance through the United Nations, and appealed to all Congolese 'to seek a speedy solution by peaceful means of all their internal conflicts for the unity and integrity of the Congo, with the assistance, as appropriate, of Asian and African representatives appointed by the Advisory Committee on the Congo, in consultation with the Secretary-General, for the purpose of conciliation'.[69]

But the Assembly's appeal met with no response as the Congo became more fragmented by rival factions. The Mobutu regime, which was recognised by President Kasavubu, whose delegate was authorised by the Assembly to occupy the Congo seat at the UN after much lobbying by the Western powers,[70] had uneasy control over the provinces of Leopoldville and Equateur; Antoine Gizenga, formerly Lumumba's deputy prime minister, exercised some authority over Kivu and Orientale province from his base in Stanleyville; Albert Kalonji was at the head of a secessionist movement in South Kasai; and Tshombe had declared himself the head of an independent state in Katanga. To add to the confusion caused by the conflicts between the rival factions, the violent acts of indisciplined soldiers of the Armee Nationale Congolaise (A.N.C.) against civilians and ONUC personnel created a menacing situation.

In these circumstances Hammarskjold and Dayal found it impossible to secure acceptance of what they regarded as a neutral political posture in accordance with the principle of non-intervention in internal conflicts. Their attempt to reconcile Kasavubu and Lumumba with a view to restoring a central government at Leopoldville, which could function under parliamentary procedures, alienated Mobutu whom they refused to recognise, and incurred the criticism of those Western powers that supported the Kasavubu-Mobutu regime. At the same time the Soviet Union, in a bitter condemnation of Hammarskjold's policy, demanded that ONUC forces should disarm 'Mobutu's bands of terriorists' and liberate Lumumba,[71] though the latter had decided to forego the protection of the ONUC before he was arrested by Mobutu's soldiers on 2 December 1960. At this juncture, too, some states with contingents in ONUC — Ceylon, Guinea, Indonesia, the United Arab Republic, and Yugoslavia — expressed their dissatisfaction with Hammarskjold's direction of the UN operation by declaring their intention to withdraw their troops from ONUC.

In this situation of domestic factionalism, in which the various factions were being aided and abetted by outside powers, Hammarskjold was still anxious to maintain the neutral political posture which he had hitherto claimed to have observed in accordance with the principle of non-intervention in internal conflicts. But he now realised that if ONUC was to prevent a worsening of the situation in the Congo, it was necessary that the Security Council should provide ONUC with a stronger mandate that required a modification of the self-defence principle that 'men engaged in the operation may never take the initiative in the use of armed force, but are entitled to respond with force to an attack with arms, including attempts to use force to make them withdraw from positions which they occupy under orders from the Commander', as laid down in the Secretary-General's First Report to the Security Council (S/4389 and Add.1-6) and approved by that body on 22 July 1960 (S/4404).[72] It was not until 21 February 1961, however, shortly after the murder of Lumumba had made the Congo situation more explosive, that the requisite majority vote emerged in the Security Council to give ONUC a wider mandate, as advocated by Hammarskjold.[73]

Having characterised the situation in the Congo as a threat to international peace and security, section A(1) of the Security Council's resolution urged 'that the United Nations take immediately all appropriate measures to prevent the occurrence of civil war in the Congo, including arrangements for cease-fires, the halting of military operations, the prevention of clashes, and the use of force, if necessary'.[74] This involved a departure from the principle of self-defence which had hitherto governed the functioning of ONUC, since the Force was urged to use enforcement action if circumstances warranted it. It was thus given a wide enough mandate to use force to protect the civilian population against attacks by armed units if it considered such action was necessary, and to regard enforcement action permissible under section A(2) of the resolution which urged 'that measures be taken for the immediate withdrawal and evacuation from the Congo of all Belgian and other foreign military and para-military personnel and political advisers not under the United Nations Command, and mercenaries'.

Section B of the resolution, which was mainly addressed to the Congolese leaders, did not authorise the enforcement of a political settlement of the conflicts between the various factions competing for power. Having recognised 'the imperative necessity of the restoration of parliamentary institutions in the Congo in accordance with the fundamental law of the country, so that the will of the people should be reflected through the freely elected Parliament', the Security Council confined itself to two non-mandatory recommendations which urged 'the convening of the Parliament and the taking of necessary protective measures in that connexion', and 'that Congolese armed units and personnel should be re-organised and brought under discipline and control, and arrangements be made on impartial and equitable bases to that end with a view to the elimination of any possibility of interference by such units and personnel in the political life of the Congo'.

At first President Kasavubu, who had formed a government with Joseph Ileo as Prime Minister on 9 February 1961, reacted with hostility to the Security Council resolut on on the ground that it contravened the principle of non-intervention in the domestic affairs of the Congo.[75] There were armed attacks against ONUC units in Leopoldville,[76] and Kasavubu went as far as to appeal to Tshombe to make common cause with him in opposing ONUC's mission.[77] Early in March an attack by troops of the A.N.C. (Armée Nationale Congolaise) against Matadi, one of ONUC's vital links in communications, which caused the withdrawal of UN forces, prompted Hammarskjold to protest to Kasavubu that this involved not only a violation of ONUC's right to freedom of movement under the Basic Agreement between the United Nations and the host state, but also a disregard of the Security Council resolution on 9 August 1960 which had called on all member states, 'in accordance with Articles 25 and 49 of the Charter to accept and carry out the decisions of the Security Council and to afford mutual assistance in carrying out measures decided upon by the Council'. In fact, Hammarskjold contended that the relationship between the United Nations and the Government of the Republic of the Congo was not merely a contractual relationship in which the Republic could impose its conditions as host state and thereby determine the circumstances under which the United Nations operated. It was rather a relationship governed by mandatory decisions of the Security Council. The consequence of this

135

was that no government, including the host government, could by unilateral action determine how measures taken by the Security Council in this context should be carried out. Such a determination could only be made by the Security Council itself or on the basis of its explicit delegation of authority. It was of special importance that only the Security Coucil could decide on the discontinuance of the operation.[78] Certainly, since the Security Council had made a formal finding under its resolution of 21 February 1961 that the situation in the Congo was a threat to international peace and security, it was now within its competence to determine how ONUC should operate and when it should be withdrawn, even though the Force had entered the Congo initially at the request of the Republic of the Congo. On the other hand, it must be conceded that the Security Council's recommendations for the convening of the Congolese Parliament and the reorganisation of Congolese armed units, though not mandatory decisions, did constitute interference in the domestic affairs of the Congo, in contravention of the principle of non-intervention under Article 2(7) of the Charter.

Though in March 1961 Kasavubu's relations with the United Nations were very strained, he soon responded, however, to the diplomatic efforts of a three-man conciliation commission set up by the Advisory Committee on ONUC, as suggested by Hammarskjold, and to the exhortations of the Assembly.[79] On April 17 he agreed to accept the Security Council's resolution of 21 February 1961,[80] and early in August 1961 a constitutional government, with Cyrille Adoula as Prime Minister, had been re-established at Leopoldville, so that the whole of the Congo, except for Tshombe's Katanga, was again under a central government, with Kasavubu as President.

With the financial support of the Union Miniere, the largest mining company in the Congo, the encouragement of much of the press and financial interests in Britain, France, the United States and Belgium, as well as the active support of the government of the Union of South Africa and Sir Roy Welensky's in the neighbouring Federation of Rhodesia and Nyasaland,[81] Tshombe was determined to maintain the secession of Katanga with the help of his Belgian and other foreign military and paramilitary personnel and political advisers, and mercenaries. Thus he was emboldened to ignore the Leopoldville government's Ordinance of 24 August 1961 for the expulsion of foreign elements in the Katangese forces, and made no positive response to the appeals of Conor Cruise O'Brien, Hammarskjold's special representative in Katanga, to enter into talks with the central government.[82]

Since Hammarskjold was anxious to adhere to the principle that ONUC should not be party to, or in any way intervene in, or be used to influence the outcome of any internal conflict, as laid down in the Security Council's resolution of 9 August 1960, he was opposed to UN forces being used to assist the central government to subdue Katanga. Nevertheless, he interpreted section A(2) of the Security Council's resolution of 21 February 1961 to mean that ONUC was authorised to expel by force, if necessary, the foreign officers and mercenaries from Katanga.[83] Consequently, he instructed O'Brien to inform Tshombe that if these foreign military elements were not removed by his orders, UN forces would use force, if necessary, to apprehend and expel them.[84]

The operation which O'Brien launched on 28 August resulted in the arrest of eighty one officers, but he agreed to the request of consular officials in Elisabethville that the Belgian consul should attend to the repatriation of the remainder. It was soon made manifest, however, that this enabled many hundreds of officers and mercenaries, upon whom the defence of Katanga so much depended, to evade arrest. As to the second operation directed by O'Brien, which began on 13 September 1961, this aimed not only to effect the round up of the foreign officers and mercenaries who had gone into hiding, but also the arrest of Tshombe and four of his ministers, and the symbolic take-over of the Administration by a representative of the central government. For this task, which was obviously designed to end Katanga's secession, O'Brien was briefed by Mahmoud Khiary, head of the UN's civilian operations in the Congo, who planned the scheme without its authorisation by Hammarskjold.[85] The operation thus ran counter to the principle of non-intervention in internal conflicts and to Hammarskjold's approach to solving the Katanga problem through peaceful diplomatic means, and restricting the use of force to apprehending the foreign military elements.

When the operation was set in motion on 13 September UN forces met stiff resistance in Elisabethville from the mercenary-led Katangese gendarmerie. The attempt to arrest Tshombe and other ministers in the Katangese government proved a failure, and the fighting in Elisabethville soon spread to other parts of Katanga. Not surprisingly, therefore, Hammarskjold, who arrived at Leopoldville when the fighting in Elisabethville was in progress, was subjected to much pressure by the British and other western governments opposed to the UN action,[86] and it was whilst on a flight to Ndola in Northern Rhodesia on 17 September, in the hope of negotiating a cease-fire with Tshombe, that he met his death.

Though a provisional cease-fire between the ONUC authorities and Tshombe was arranged on 20 September, fighting soon broke out between Katangese forces and troops of the central government which was opposed to the cease-fire, and ONUC was again faced with the difficult task of preventing an extension of civil war. But the general consensus of opinion in the United Nations was veering towards the conviction that the only solution to the Congo affair was to put an end to Katanga's secession. The United States now tended to be more in line with the Afro-Asian states on this approach because it feared that if the moderate Adoula government failed to make progress in its struggle to overthrow the Tshombe regime it would be to the advantage of the extreme left wing elements led by Antoine Gizenga whose secessionist movement in Stanleyville had re-asserted itself.[87] Consequently, when the Security Council met to deal with the Katanga question in November 1961, the United States was prepared to take a harder line against the Tshombe regime, and this undoubtedly influenced Britain and France to take a less pronounced pro-Tshombe attitude.

It is significant that though the Security Council's resolution of 24 November 1961[88] did not specifically authorise the use of enforcement measures to end Katanga's secession, it indicated a distinct departure from the principle of non-intervention in the internal conflicts of the Congo, which it had more or less observed when Hammarskjold was responsible for the political direction of the UN operation. Not only did it declare 'that all activities against the Republic of the Congo are contrary to the Loi fondamentale and Security Council decisions', but also specifically demanded 'that such activities which are now taking place in Katanga shall cease forthwith', and urged all member states 'to lend their support, according to their national procedures, to the Central Government of the Republic of the Congo, in conformity with the Charter and the decisions of the United Nations'. It also stated clearly that the Secretary-General was authorised 'to take vigorous action, including the requisite measure of force, if necessary, for the immediate apprehension, detention pending legal action and/or deportation of all foreign military and para-military personnel and political advisers not under the United Nations Command, and mercenaries . . .'

Tshombe reacted to the Security Council's resolution as a declaration of war on Katanga, and in December 1961 there was heavy fighting between UN forces and the mercenary-led Katangese forces who had cut ONUC's line of communications between its headquarters and strategic points.[89] Though U Thant, then Acting-Secretary-General, described the UN action as a defensive operation to regain and assure ONUC's freedom of movement,[90] the scale of the action, which involved attacks by UN planes against airports at Jadotville and Kolwezi, was bound to be regarded by Tshombe, in the context of the Security Council's resolution of 24 November 1961, as a major move towards ending Katanga's secession. In fact, ONUC's action was sufficient to impel Tshombe to seek, through the good offices of the United States and the United Nations, a pacific settlement with Adoula, the Prime Minister of the central government. Under the Declaration of Kitona (21 December 1961) he recognised Kasavubu as President of the Republic of the Congo and the authority of the central government, and also agreed that Katangese representatives should participate in the national parliament at Leopoldville and in a commission to deal with constitutional issues.[91] But the Katanga question was to remain unresolved for some time yet because Tshombe maintained that the Kitona agreement could not be implemented until it had been ratified by the Katanga parliament.

It is important to realise that the UN action which had led to the Kitona agreement had shown that U Thant regarded the Security Council resolution of 24 November 1961 as permitting ONUC to intervene in the internal conflicts of the Congo to influence their outcome, and that in practice there was little difference between measures taken by ONUC to ensure its freedom of movement and coercive interventionist measures. Of course, since this interventionist policy by the United Nations was desired by the central government in Leopoldville to end Katanga's secession, there was no objection from that quarter that it contravened the principle of non-intervention in Congolese domestic affairs.

Though ONUC's intervention in Katanga had not yet brought about the downfall of the Tshombe regime, its intervention was a decisive factor in effecting the defeat of Antoine Gizenga's secessionist movement in Orientale province early in 1962. Its action against the local gendarmerie in Stanleyville, who were supporting Gizenga in his struggle with the central government, was justified by U Thant on the ground that UN forces had the right to assist the central government to maintain law and order and prevent civil war, but 'it had not, in fact, been clearly authorized to take action of the kind which felled Gizenga: the resolution of 21 February 1961 did not obviously imply that the right to prevent civil war by force was tantamount to giving the UN an equivalent right in respect of secession'.[92] Besides, though the Security Council's resolution of 24 November 1961 had declared 'that all secessionist activities against the Republic of the Congo are contrary to the *Loi fondamentale* and Security Council decisions' and specifically demanded 'that such activities which are now taking place in Katanga shall cease forthwith', it had not authorised the use of enforcement measures to end secessionist activities. Nevertheless, U Thant was not given any corrective by the Security Council for the enforcement action that had been taken by ONUC

During 1962 it also became manifest that U Thant was not to be prevented by the Security Council from attempting to put an end to Katanga's secession by forcible means if Tshombe did not respond to diplomatic pressures. In August 1962, after negotiations between the Tshombe regime and the central government had failed to produce a formula for Katanga's reintegration into a unified Congo, the Secretary-General put forward his 'Plan for National Reconciliation'. This provided for a federal system of government, the division of revenues and foreign currency between the central and provincial governments, the formation of a national army, and freedom of movement for ONUC throughout Katanga which would ensure that the Katanga government would not be able to control tax revenues from the mines by exporting ores through exit points under its control. The plan also contained provision for an economic boycott against any party to the arrangement that failed to abide by its terms.[93]

Both the central government and the Katangan authorities accepted U Thant's plan by September 1962, but since the Tshombe regime made no attempt to implement it, the Secretary-General endorsed plans for ONUC to achieve freedom of movement throughout Katanga by force, if this proved necessary,[94] and these were put into effect when the tension that had developed between the UN authorities and the Tshombe regime led to fighting against ONUC positions in Elisabethville in December 1962. The clearing of road blocks to secure freedom of movement for UN troops in the city was the prelude to UN military action which resulted in the occupation of other towns north of Elisabethville,[95] and on 14 January 1963 Tshombe had little alternative but to announce the end of Katanga's secession and his readiness to grant freedom of movement to UN forces throughout Katanga.[96] Clearly, as Gagnon has emphasised, 'in the case of Katanga the right to enforce freedom of movement necessarily meant the right to end the Katangese secession, and thus in effect to determine the internal political structure of the Congo'.[97]

Tshombe's readiness to end Katanga's secession heralded the phased withdrawal of UN forces from the Congo, but the political unity which ONUC had brought about in the Congo was more apparent than real. Indeed, when the last contingents of ONUC left the country in June 1964, there was further eruption of violence, and the irony of the new situation was that Tshombe was then the head of the Congolese government who had the task of trying to maintain the unity of the states by quelling secessionist movements in various provinces, particularly in Orientale province.

To sum up: United Nations intervention in the Congo in July 1960 was the sequel to a request by the new Congolese government for military assistance 'to protect the national territory of the Congo against the present external aggression which is a threat to international peace and security'. But the Security Council did not characterise the situation as one of external aggression by Belgian forces against the Congolese state, which necessitated enforcement measures under Article 42 of the Charter. It called for the withdrawal of Belgian forces and authorised the establishment of a non-coercive peacekeeping force, under the general direction of the Secretary-General, to assist the Congolese government to restore order, 'considering that the restoration of law and order in the Congo would effectively contribute to the maintenance of international peace and security'.

Though the establishment of the UN force was not a contravention of the principle of non-intervention in matters of domestic jurisdiction, since it came into being with the consent of the Republic of the Congo, it soon became clear that its operation in accordance with the principles of self-defence and non-intervention in internal conflicts, constitutional or otherwise, conflicted with the demand of the central government in Leopoldville that UN forces should be used to end Katanga's secession. Hammarskjold maintained that the legal basis of the Security Council resolutions under Article 40 involved the application of provisional measures of a non-coercive nature, not enforcement measures as under Article 42. He insisted, as laid down in Article 40, that the United Nations should only authorise measures which were not prejudicial to the rights, claims, or position of the parties involved in the domestic conflict, and was not empowered to authorise the use of enforcement action to end Katanga's secession through invoking the exception to the general principle of non-intervention under Article 2(7) of the Charter, viz. 'but this principle shall not prejudice the application of enforcement measures under Chapter VII'.

There were several reasons why Hammarskjold may be criticised for being so firmly attached to the view that the question of Katanga's secession was a domestic issue. In addition to the fact that the Tshombe regime depended upon the intervention of foreign elements, 'there is considerable doubt', as D.W. Bowett has stressed, 'whether, in a situation where there exists a threat to international peace, there is any justification for so general a reliance on the "domestic jurisdiction" limitation on the powers of the United Nations. A threat to *international peace* can never, by definition, be a purely domestic matter'.[98] Besides, Katanga's secession could hardly be justified by the principle of self-determination since 'Tshombe's mandate to speak for the whole of Katanga was questionable. He was the leader of the Lunda tribe, one of several tribes in Katanga, and one that is a minority in numbers and that occupies less than half the land area of the former Katanga Province. Tshombe was strongly opposed to the Baluba tribe in the north. In the only popular election in Katanga, his party gained only twenty-five seats in a sixty seat Assembly. The parliamentary group that supported him was a rump parliament lacking adequate Baluba representation.'[99]

But it was Hammarskjold's hope that the problem of Katanga could be solved peacefully, and that once Belgian forces had been withdrawn from the whole of the Congo, ONUC's presence would help to restore law and order and prevent the Congo from being turned into an international cockpit through the intervention of outside powers. But though Belgian troops, with the exception of those in Katanga, were soon withdrawn, the disruption of the central government through the clash between Prime Minister Lumumba and President Kasavubu created a situation of domestic strife in which the operation of the UN Force in accordance with the principle of non-intervention in internal conflicts proved extremely difficult. Hammarskjold's attempt to adopt a neutral posture in relation to the various Congolese factions, implicit in this principle, was invariably under attack by one or other of these factions, or by outside powers that supported particular factions. This seemed to indicate as one writer has asserted, that 'the promotion of law and order in a setting of domestic factionalism is not compatible with the idea of neutrality and impartiality. It requires that a choice be made among competing prescriptions for law and order, and competing candidates for the order giving function'.[100]

With the establishment of a unitary central government under Cyrille Adoula in August 1961, the problems of ONUC became less complex, but the question of Katanga's secession still remained. The prelude to its solution was made when the Security Council decided under its resolution 5002 (24 November 1961), shortly after the death of Hammarskjold, 'that all secessionist activities in the Republic of the Congo are contrary to the *Loi fondamentale* and Security Council decisions', demanded 'that such activities which are now taking place in Katanga shall cease forthwith', and urged all members states 'to lend their support, according to their national procedures, to the Central Government of the Republic of the Congo, in conformity with the Charter and the decisions of the United Nations'. This signified the UN's abandonment of the principle of non-intervention in the internal conflicts of the Congo, and for obvious reasons this was not considered a contravention of the principle of non-intervention in matters of domestic jurisdiction under Article 2(7) of the Charter by the central government in Leopoldville.

Thus, after the adoption of the November 1961 resolution, Secretary-General U Thant felt free to pursue a tougher interventionist policy which helped to crush Gizenga's secessionist movement, and to put an end to Katanga's secession. Though he maintained that the action by UN forces in December 1962 was intended to secure ONUC's freedom of movement throughout Katanga, under the terms of the basic agreement that governed the operation of the Force, such action approximated more to enforcement measures under Article 42 of the Charter than to provisional measures to prevent an aggravation under Article 40 which Hammarskjold had attempted to observe.

Had enforcement measures under Article 42 of the Charter been applied against Katanga in July 1960, which was what Lumumba and Kasavubu wanted before their quarrel led to a disruption of the central government, it is reasonable to assume that the political re-unification of the Congo might have been achieved at that time, and much of the conflict during the years that followed might have been avoided. Of course, such a policy would have required a clear decision by the Security Council that the situation in the Congo constituted a threat to international peace and security under Article 39 of the Charter, and the authorisation of enforcement measures under Article 42. Certainly, if the requisite political consensus had existed in the Security Council to authorise such measures in July 1960, there would have been no question of the United Nations contravening the principle of non-intervention in the domestic affairs of the Congo, since enforcement action initiated under Articles 39 and 42 of the Charter is permissible not only in cases of external aggression, but also in domestic matters that constitute a threat to international peace and security under the exception to the general principle of non-intervention laid down in Article 2(7) of the Charter.

The fact was that the constitutional basis under the Charter for UN action, which finally put to an end Katanga's secession, was not specified in a Security Council resolution, and our analysis of the ONUC operation has indicated that though the Force was originally established with the consent of the legal central government of the Congo, from time to time there were clashes between the central government and the UN Secretary-General over the proper functions of the Force under its original mandate. Indeed, there were several occasions when the central government in Leopoldville under the presidency of Kasavubu was bitterly opposed to Hammarskjold's direction of ONUC on the ground that its operations contravened the principle of non-intervention in matters which it claimed were essentially within its domestic jurisdiction.

The Peacekeeping Operation in West Irian

The smoothness of the peacekeeping operation by UN observers and UNSF (United Nations Security Force) in West New Guinea (West Irian), in 1962, stood out in strong contrast to the complexity of the ONUC operation in the Congo. This was mainly because the UN operation in West Irian was based on a clear mandate and designed to assist in the implementation of an agreed pacific settlement of the dispute between Indonesia and the Netherlands. Before we consider this, however, it is necessary to make brief mention of the background to the dispute.[101]

Under the Hague Agreement of 2 November 1949 it was not only laid down that the Netherlands should transfer complete sovereignty over Indonesia to the United States of Indonesia, but also agreed that the future of West New Guinea, peopled by 700,000 Papuans, should be decided by negotiations between the Netherlands and Indonesia within a year. This question defied solution for more than a decade, though the matter was considered by the United Nations Assembly in 1954, 1955, 1956, 1957, and 1961. Indeed, in December 1961 it caused the outbreak of hostilities between the Netherlands and Indonesia.

At this juncture, largely through the initiative of Secretary-General U Thant, who appointed an American diplomat, Ellsworth Bunker, as a mediator, an agreement between the parties to the dispute was reached on 15 August 1962. This stipulated that the administration of West Irian would be transferred to Indonesia in accordance with the procedure stated in the following articles of the Agreement.[102]

Article 1

After the present Agreement between Indonesia and the Netherlands has been signed and ratified by both Contracting Parties, Indonesia and the Netherlands will jointly sponsor a draft resolution in the United Nations under the terms of which the General Assembly of the United Nations takes note of the present Agreement, acknowledges the role conferred upon the Secretary-General of the United Nations therein, and authorises him to carry out the tasks entrusted to him therein.

Transfer of Administration

Article II

After the adoption of the resolution referred to in article I, the Netherlands will transfer administration of the territory to a United Nations Temporary Executive Authority (UNTEA) established by and under the jurisdiction of the Secretary-General upon the arrival of the United Nations Administrator appointed in accordance with article IV. The UNTEA will in turn transfer the administration to Indonesia in accordance with article XII.

United Nations Administration

Article IV

A United Nations Administrator, acceptable to Indonesia and the Netherlands, will be appointed by the Secretary-General.

Article XII

The United Nations Administrator will have discretion to transfer all or part of the administration to Indonesia at any time after the first phase of the UNTEA administration. The UNTEA's authority will cease at the moment of transfer of full administrative control to Indonesia.

Article VII

The Secretary-General will provide the UNTEA with such security forces as the United Nations Administrator deems necessary; such forces will primarily supplement existing Papuan (West Irianese) police in the task of maintaining law and order. The Papuan Volunteer Corps, which on the arrival of the United Nations Administrator will cease being part of the Netherlands armed forces, and the Indonesian armed forces in the territory will be under the authority of, and at the disposal of, the Secretary-General for the same purpose. The United Nations Administrator will, to the extent feasible, use the Papuan (West Irianese) police as a United Nations security force to maintain law and order and, at his discretion, use Indonesian armed forces. The Netherlands armed forces will be repatriated as rapidly as possible and while still in the territory will be under the authority of the UNTEA.

In addition to the UN Security Force (UNSF) which was to be established under Article VII referred to above, military observers were

144

appointed under Annex A of *Related Understandings to the Indonesia-Netherlands Agreement*.[103] Their task was to assist in the securing of a cease-fire in West Irian before UNTEA took over its temporary administration of the territory and the UN Security Force (UNSF) was placed at its disposal to supplement the Papuan police in the task of maintaining law and order.

The work of the military observers was soon accomplished, and on 21 September 1962 the UN Assembly noted with appreciation the successful efforts of the Secretary-General in bringing about a pacific settlement of the dispute, and authorised him to carry out the tasks entrusted to him under the Indonesia-Netherlands Agreement. Its resolution was adopted by a vote of 89 to 0, with 14 abstentions,[104] and though France abstained from voting without explanation, the Soviet Union, like Britain, China and the United States, voted for the resolution despite the fact that it ran counter to her view that the establishment of a UN peacekeeping forces was contrary to Article 11(2) of the Charter and that the Secretary General's authority in directing peacekeeping operations should be curbed.

As to the task of the UN Security Force in maintaining law and order in the territory while UNTEA proceeded with its administrative responsibilities, this was carried out successfully by its 1,500 Pakistani forces who were supported by Canadian and American airforce contingents; and by 1 May 1963 when administrative control was transferred to Indonesia in accordance with Article XII of the Indonesia-Netherlands Agreement of 15 August 1962, the UN peacekeeping forces were being replaced by incoming Indonesian troops.[105]

In assessing the peacekeeping operation in West Irian, the following points need to be stressed. Like UNEF in the Middle East and ONUC in the Congo, the UN Security Force in West Irian was established with the consent of the states directly involved, so that its presence in the territory did not contravene the principle of non-intervention in matters within the jurisdiction of those states. But the Secretary-General who was entrusted with its general direction did not have to face the sort of claim by Egypt in the case of UNEF that the withdrawal of the Force was a matter to be determined by the host state at an unspecified time, nor the kind of challenges made by Congolese leaders at various stages in the operation of ONUC that the mandate governing its functions was being mis-interpreted and mis-applied. As Rosalyn Higgins has pointed out, '... where the mandate is ambigouous, or where political circumstances change after the initial agreement upon a mandate, the government and the UN Secretariat may develop divergent views as to the proper functions of the UN force ... Such factors were mercifully absent in West Irian. The basis upon which the UN acted was not a mere brief resolution by a UN organ, but a detailed agreement (the result of long negotiations) between the interested parties. Both Indonesia and the Netherlands were anxious to facilitate the observers' task of securing a cease-fire. Moreover, the UN presence in West Irian was not primarily military at all; it was administrative, and the function of UNSF was the maintenance of law and order within a fairly stable quasi-governmental framework.'[106] In brief, the UN Security Force in West Irian was able to fulfil its function successfully because, in supporting the temporary UN administration in the territory, there was no question of the United Nations usurping the jurisdiction of the host state.

The United Nations, Peacekeeping Force in Cyprus (UNFICYP)

What we have been principally concerned about in our analysis of UN peacekeeping operations is the extent to which the United Nations has observed or contravened the principle of non-intervention in matters essentially within the domestic jurisdiction of states under Article 2(7) of the Charter. It has been indicated that since UNEF in the Middle East, ONUC in the Congo, and UNSF in West Irian came into being with the consent of both the host states and those states that contributed contingents, their establishment did not contravene Article 2(7). But though UNEF and UNSF did not depart from the terms of reference which had been accepted by the host states under particular mandates approved by the competent UN organs, in accordance with the principle of consent, there were several instances in the operation of ONUC in the Congo when the Secretary-General's interpretation of the mandate given to the Force conflicted with that of the legal government of the Congolese state, which the latter claimed was a violation of the principle of non-intervention in matters essentially within its domestic jurisdiction. It should be noted, however, that though the action taken by ONUC, after the death of Hammarskjold, to put an end to Gizenga's secessionist movement and Katanga's secession in 1962, constituted intervention in the domestic affairs of the Congolese Republic, such action was welcomed by the host government because it was calculated to unify the state under its jurisdiction.

Before we examine the establishment and operation of the UN force in Cyprus (UNFICYP) in relation to the principle of non-intervention in matters essentially within the domestic jurisdiction of states, let us consider briefly the developments which led to its formation in March 1964.[107]

Under the Zurich-London agreements of 1959, Cyprus was declared a sovereign republic: Britain was allowed to retain sovereignty over two military bases: Greece and Turkey were permitted to station small numbers of troops in the island, and both these states and Britain were given the right to act separately or collectively to guarantee the status of the new states: the constitution of the Republic gave executive power to a Greek Cypriot president and a Turkish Cypriot vice-president, each with the right to veto important measures, and provided for a Council of Ministers, consisting of seven Greek and three Turkish Cypriots, the same ratio of representation being applicable to the membership of a House of Represen-

.tatives: and provision was also made for separate Turkish and Greek Cypriot assemblies for communal affairs in various towns.

The Zurich-London agreements were put into effect on 16 August 1960, and in the following September Cyprus became a member of the United Nations. But the Greek Cypriots soon became dissatisfied with the provision of the constitution which gave the Turkish Cypriot vice president the right to veto significant matters, and the system of government designed under the Zurich-London agreements became unworkable.

In November 1963 President Makarios proposed several amendments to the constitution which were intended to lessen the power of the Turkish Cypriot minority in order to produce a more unified state. But these proposals aroused such antagonism that the Turkish Cypriot members of the government withdrew from office, and early in December fighting broke out inthe island. Tension increased when Turkey announced that it would intervene if the fighting continued, and to prevent a deterioration of the situation President Makarios permitted the British, Greek and Turkish forces on the island to form a temporary peacekeeping force.

Subsequent discussions between the representatives of the Greek and Turkish Cypriot communities led to no change in the attitudes of both sides, and in January 1964 the British government proposed the formation of a NATO force to maintain order in the island and the appointment of a mediator. Though President Makarios rejected these proposals, he was not averse to a United Nations presence on the island, and as fighting between Greek and Turkish Cypriots developed in Limassol and Turkey again threatened to intervene, Britain decided to place the question before the Security Council on 15 February 1964. On the same day the Cyprus government also requested a meeting of the Security Council to consider the threat of intervention by Turkey.

On 4 March 1964 the Security Council unanimously adopted a resolution recommending the establishment of a UN peacekeeping force and a mediator to help the parties towards a pacific settlement of their differences. The text of the resolution was as follows:-[108]

> The Security Council,
>
> **Noting** that the present situation with regard to Cyprus is likely to threaten international peace and security and may further deteriorate unless additional measures are promptly taken to maintain peace and to seek out a durable solution,
>
> **Considering** the positions taken by the parties in relation to the Treaties signed at Nicosia on 16 August 1960,
>
> **Having in mind** the relevant provisions of the Charter of the United Nations and its Article 2, paragraph 4, which reads: 'All Members shall refrain in their international relations from the threat or use of force against the territorial integrity or political independence of any

State, or in any other manner inconsistent with the Purposes of the United Nations',

1.   **Calls upon** all Member States, in conformity with their obligations under the Charter of the United Nations, to refrain from any action or threat of action likely to worsen the situation in the sovereign Republic of Cyprus, or to endanger international peace:
2.   **Asks** the Government of Cyprus, which has the responsibility for the maintenance and restoration of law and order, to take all additional measures necessary to stop violence and bloodshed in Cyprus;
3.   **Calls upon** the communities in Cyprus and their leaders to act with the utmost restraint;
4.   **Recommends** the creation, with the consent of the Government of Cyprus, of a United Nations peace-keeping force in Cyprus. The composition and size of the force shall be established by the Secretary-General, in consultation with the Governments of Cyprus, Greece, Turkey, and the United Kingdom. The commander of the force shall be appointed by the Secretary-General and report to him. The Secretary-General, who shall keep the Governments providing the force fully informed, shall report periodically to the Security Council on its operations;
5.   **Recommends** that the function of the force should be, in the interest of preserving international peace and security, to use its best efforts to prevent a recurrence of fighting and, as necessary, to contribute to the maintenance and restoration of law and order and a return to normal conditions;
6.   **Recommends** that the stationing of the force shall be for a period of three months, all costs pertaining to it being met, in a manner to be agreed by them, by the Governments providing the contingents and by the Government of Cyprus. The Secretary-General may also accept voluntary contributions for that purpose.

Since the Security Council recommended the creation of a UN peace-keeping force with the consent of the government of Cyprus, its establishment did not involve a contravention of the principle of non-intervention in matters essentially within the domestic jurisdiction of that government. But though the Cyprus government led by President Makarios was recognised by the Security Council as the host government to the UN force, the agreement between the United Nations and the Cyprus government on the status of UN forces, which was concluded on 31 March 1964,[109] laid down that whereas the security forces of the government would assist UNFICYP if so requested, the commander of UNFICYP was not obliged to meet a request for assistance by the government's security forces. This gave the commander of UNFICYP a sound basis on which to reject any attempts by the host government to secure UN assistance to enforce its authority over the Turkish Cypriots.

The Status of UN forces agreement also stipulated that UNFICYP was to have freedom of movement throughout Cyprus, and covered such matters as the privileges and immunities of UN personnel. But shortly after the conclusions of the agreement, on 11 April 1964, the Secretary-General, in response to various inquiries from governments who wished for a clarification of UNFICYP's mandate, made available to them an *aide-memoire* concerning certain aspects of the function and operation of the force.[110] Its main points were as follows:

(i) The United Nations had exclusive control and command over the force.

(ii) The force would 'avoid any action designed to influence the political situation in Cyprus except through contributing to a restoration of quiet and through creating an improved climate in which political solutions may be sought'.

(This was similar to the Security Council's affirmation on 9 August 1960 that the UN force in the Congo would 'not be party to or in any way intervene in or be used to influence the outcome of any internal conflict, constitutional or otherwise'.)

(iii) The force would undertake no function inconsistent with the definition of the function of the force set out in paragraph 5 of the Security Council's resolution of 4 March 1964, viz. 'that the function of the force should be, in the interest of preserving international peace and security, to use its best efforts to prevent a recurrence of fighting and, as necessary, to contribute to the maintenance and restoration of law and order and a return to normal conditions'.

(iv) The use of armed force by the UN force was permissible only in self-defence, which included the defence of UN posts, premises and vehicles under armed attack, and the support of UNFICYP personnel under armed attack. When UN forces were acting in self-defence, the principle of minimum force would always be applied, and armed force would be used only when all peaceful means of persuasion had failed. If units of UNFICYP arrived at the scene of an actual armed conflict between the members of the two communities, the commanders on the spot would immediately call on the leaders of both communities to break off the conflict and arrange for a cease fire. UN forces would not take action likely to bring them into direct conflict with either the Greek or Turkish Cypriot communities.

Significant constraints were thus imposed on UNFICYP, and in his report on the situation in Cyprus on 29 April 1964,[111] a month after the force had become operational with a strength of approximately 6000 men which had been contributed by Austria, Canada, Sweden, Finland, Ireland, and the United Kingdom,[112] Secretary-General U Thant proposed the progressive evacuation and removal of all fortified positions held by Greek and Turkish Cypriots, with priority given to Nicosia, the examination of the problems arising from the divisions that had taken place in the Cyprus police between members of both communities, and the negotiation of necessary measures for the progressive re-integration of Turkish Cypriot officials in the Cyprus administration. He also proposed the progressive disarming of all civilians other than the regular police gendarmerie, and that UNFICYP, if requested, would assist in facilitating and verifying the disarming and the storage of arms under conditions of security.

The fact that UNFICYP did not possess the authority to arrest or disarm Cypriots, except the power to arrest those who were committing offences on its premises, was a great restriction on its capacity to maintain law and order. Nevertheless, notwithstanding its limited powers, it had the right to insist on its freedom of movement throughout Cyprus, and no member of the Security Council challenged the Secretary-General's rejection of the claim made by the Makarios government, the host government to the force, that the Turkish Cypriots should be regarded as an illegal group of dissidents, so that UNFICYP should be used to assist the government to enforce its authority on them.[113]

It has been explained that in the Congo affair Hammarskjold insisted that ONUC should not be used to enforce the authority of the host government on secessionist Katanga, in line with the principle of non-intervention in internal conflicts, constitutional or otherwise. After his death, however, Katanga's secession was brought to an end when ONUC, under U Thant's direction, carried out 'defensive' operations to regain and assure its freedom of movement throughout Katanga. Such action, as already asserted, approximated more to enforcement measures under Article 42 of the Charter than provisional measures under Article 40 to prevent an aggravation of the situation, and were designed to assist the host government in Leopoldville to enforce its authority on the province of Katanga.

In contrast to the use of ONUC in this way in the Congo affair, UNFICYP has not been directed by the Secretary-General to assist the host government led by President Makarios to enforce its authority on the Turkish Cypriot minority. In effect, what it appears to have done during the past decade is to operate in accordance with Article 40 of Chapter VII of the Charter by taking provisional measures to prevent an aggravation of the situation in Cyprus, without prejudicing the rights, claims or position of the parties concerned. But the Security Council has not formally declared that the situation constitutes a threat to international peace and security under Article 39, nor cited Article 40, and it should be noted, as

Goodrich, Hambro and Simons have commented, 'there would appear to be considerable agreement that the parties concerned are obligated to comply with resolutions specifically adopted under Article 40, that other members are obligated to assist in carrying out such resolutions, and that the Council can adopt any measures it deems necessary to ensure compliance with such resolutions, subject to the general limitations of the Charter ... there is considerable less agreement as to whether these obligations are applicable, if the Council fails to cite Article 40 and/or fails to make a formal determination under Article 39 that a threat to the peace, breach of the peace, or act of aggression exists'.[114]

Neither Article 39 nor Article 40 has been cited by the Security Council when dealing with the Cyprus affair. But the legal basis for the establishment and operation of the UN Force in Cyprus has rested on the consent of the host government in response to a Security Council recommendation, and it must be stressed that since the agreement between the United Nations and the Government of the Republic of Cyprus concerning the status of UNFICYP did not oblige the Commander of the force to meet a request for assistance by the government's security forces, the United Nations was given a legal basis to reject attempts by the Makarios government to enforce its authority over the Turkish Cypriot minority, which was to be treated as a separate party.

In practice, UNFICYP, whose life has been extended from time to time since its inception,[115] has endeavoured to contain violence in Cyprus by such methods as patrolling in towns and villages where tension was high, interposing its units between armed hostile groups, helping to arrange agreements on lines of demarcation such as the one dividing Nicosia, and negotiating for the dismantling of fortifications. In the early years, restrictions imposed on its freedom of movement in a number of areas, not only by the host government, but also by armed Turkish Cypriots, greatly impeded its peacekeeping efforts, and the serious outbreaks of intercommunal violence in July 1964 and November 1967 rendered it ineffective. But for several years after the violent eruption in 1967 the force functioned with much success in accordance with the terms of its mandate, and helped to effect a return to reasonably tolerable conditions in the island.

In July 1974, however, the situation in Cyprus changed dramatically when a coup against Makarios by a militant *enosis* group resulted in the appointment of Nicos Sampson as President and the Turkish invasion of the island on 20 July. Indeed, but for the collapse of the Colonels' regime in Greece, it is probable that there would have been war between Greece and Turkey, and the fragile nature of the UN peacekeeping operation in Cyprus was again exposed.

On 20 July 1974 the Security Council unanimously adopted a resolution which called upon all parties to the fighting to accept a cease-fire and demanded the withdrawal without delay from the Republic of Cyprus of foreign military personnel not authorised under international agreements. It called on Greece, Turkey and the United Kingdom, the guarantors of the 1960 Zurich-London Agreements, under which an independent Cyprus had been established, to enter into negotiations for the restoration of peace in the area and constitutional government in Cyprus, and also on all parties to co-operate fully with UNFICYP to enable it to carry out its mandate.[116]

A cease-fire was agreed to on 22 July, but within hours after the agreement had been reached Turkish forces occupied Kyrenia and were involved in fighting the Greek Cypriot National Guard near Nicosia international airport which UN forces took over with much difficulty. In fact, though the Foreign Ministers of Britain, Turkey and Greece agreed in Geneva on 30 July that a buffer zone should be marked out by a mixed commission along the lines reached by Turkish forces on 22 July, that only UN forces should be permitted to enter this zone and similar zones surrounding the Turkish Cypriot enclaves, and that UNFICYP should police the villages of mixed Turkish and Greek Cypriot population, fighting continued as the Turks expanded their area of occupation and insisted on acceptance of their proposals for a single federal government in Cyprus, with Turkish Cypriot cantons possessing a large measure of autonomy. Clearly, within such a context the UN force of a few thousand men, authorised to play the role of arbiter in inter-communal clashes and to use armed force only in self-defence, could do little to restore and maintain peace in Cyprus, and several of its members were killed and wounded through being involved in dangerous situations.[117]

Towards the end of August 1974, by which time the Turks had established themselves in the northern third of Cyprus in defiance of the Security Council, but finally complied with its call for a cease-fire arrangement, Secretary-General Waldheim reported to the Security Council that UNFICYP's functions would soon have to be redefined, as the situation that now obtained was not the one in which the original mandate of the force had been established in 1964. There was, by no means, full agreement among the parties as to how, or with what objectives, UNFICYP should function, he stated, and the nature of the hoped-for negotiated settlement would also be a decisive factor in its future role.[118]

Whatever political settlement of the Cyprus question is ultimately agreed to, it would appear that unless a UN peacekeeping force, which is authorised to play the role of arbiter in inter-communal clashes, is also given the authority and military capability to enforce the peace when necessary, it is unlikely to prove effective. But such a force, as *The Observer* has emphasised, 'would require two political conditions; first, that both the super-Powers agree to let it happen; secondly, that the majority of other states give it their general goodwill'.[119] Moreover, the constitutional basis for enforcement action by such a force would have to be Article 39 of the

Charter under which the Security Council is authorised, without contravening the non-intervention principle in matters of domestic jurisdiction, to determine the existence of any threat to the peace, breach of the peace, or act of aggression, and to decide what measures should be taken in accordance with Article 41 or 42 to maintain or restore international peace.

The Second UN Emergency Force in the Middle East

Like the first UNEF which operated in the Middle East from 1956 to 1967, the second UNEF, which was established by the Security Council after the Arab-Israeli war of October 1973,[120] was designed to function in accordance with the principle of self-defence in a buffer zone separating the parties concerned. Like the first UNEF, too, its creation depended on the consent of the parties to the conflict, and appropriate agreements on the status of the force had to be concluded between them and the United Nations to enable the force to enjoy freedom of movement and communication and other facilities necessary for the performance of its tasks.

Since the Security Council decided that the force should be established for an initial period of six months, and that it should continue in operation thereafter 'provided the Security Council so decides',[121] it appeared that the question of determining its withdrawal was within the jurisdiction of the Council, and not an issue to which the principle of non-intervention in matters of domestic jurisdiction under Article 2(7) of the Charter was applicable, in contrast with the case of the first UNEF's withdrawal in 1967. In practice, however, diplomatic moves have shown that the Security Council has not asserted its competence to extend UNEF's mandate without Egyptian consent,[122] and that both Syria and Israel must give their approval to extensions of the mandate of UNDOP (United Nations Disengagement Observation Force) on the Golan Heights, which the Council established with their consent in May 1974.[123]

Though Israel and Egypt concluded a new Sinai disengagement agreement in September 1975 — this provided for the withdrawal of Israeli forces from 12 to 26 miles in Sinai, with the vacated area becoming the buffer zone controlled by the UN Emergency Force: the establishment of electronic warning posts in the key Mitla and Giddi passes under the supervision of United States personnel; and the withdrawal of Israel from the Abu Rudeis oilfields[124] — the presence of the UNEF in the Middle East must be regarded as a fragile instrument of peacekeeping which is unlikely to prevent a recurrence of hostilities if no significant progress is made towards a comprehensive political settlement of the Arab-Israeli question which includes Israel's withdrawal from occupied territories, the establishment of a Palestinian state which will remove most of the grievances of the displaced Palestinians, and the acceptance of Israel's sovereignty by the Arab nations.

This also applies to the *United Nations Interim Force in the Lebanon (UNIFIL)* whose establishment was the sequel to Israel's military move into south Lebanon to destroy the Palestinian guerilla bases in the area. Israeli forces had entered south Lebanon on 14 March 1978, a few days after a Palestinian terrorist attack on the main Haifa to Tel Aviv highway had resulted in the killing of 37 civilians and the wounding of 82.

The Security Council resolution authorising the establishment of the UN force was proposed by the United States on 18 March and approved by the Council on the following day by 12 votes to nil. The Soviet Union and Czechoslovakia abstained from voting, and China declined to participate, so no permanent member of the Council applied the veto to prevent the establishment of the Force.[125]

The text of the resolution was as follows:

The Security Council,

Taking note of the letters of the Permanent Representative of Lebanon (S/12606) and the Permanent Representative of Israel (S/12607),

Having heard the statement of the Permanent Representatives of Lebanon and Israel,

Gravely concerned at the deterioration of the situation in the Middle East, and its consequences to the maintenance of international peace,

Convinced that the present situation impedes the achievement of a just peace in the Middle East,

1. Calls for strict respect for the territorial integrity, sovereignty and political independence of Lebanon within its internationally recognised boundaries.

2. Calls upon Israel immediately to cease its military action against Lebanese territorial integrity and withdraw forthwith its forces from all Lebanese territory,

3. Decides, in the light of the request of the Government of Lebanon, to establish immediately under its authority a United Nations Interim Force for Southern Lebanon for the purpose of confirming the withdrawal of Israeli forces, restoring international peace and security and assisting the Government of Lebanon in ensuring the return of its effective authority in the area, the Force to be composed of personnel drawn from States Members of the United Nations.

4. Requests the Secretary-General to report to the Council within twenty-four hours on the implementation of this resolution.

As stated in the third operative clause of the resolution, the decision to set up UNIFIL was taken by the Security Council 'in the light of the request of the Government of the Lebanon'. It was thus made clear that the establishment of the Force depended upon the consent of the Lebanese Government, and was not a contravention of the non-intervention principle in matters essentially within the domestic jurisdiction of the Lebanon. It was also stated in the Secretary-General's report to the Security Council on the implementation of the resolution,[126] which was approved by the Council, that UNIFIL 'cannot and must not take on responsibilities which normally fall under the Government of the country in which it is operating. These responsibilities must be exercised by the competent Lebanese authorities. It is assumed that the Lebanese Government will take the necessary measures to co-operate with UNIFIl in this regard'.

It was suggested in the Secretary-General's report that the Force would initially be stationed in southern Lebanon for a period of six months, but the question whether the termination of the presence of the Force in Lebanon was a matter within the jurisdiction of the Lebanese Government or the UN Security Council was not dealt with. The report simply stated that the Force was being established 'on the assumption that it represented an interim measure until the Government of Lebanon assumes its full responsibilities'.

The fact was, however, that the Lebanese Government had not been able to exercise authority over southern Lebanon for some years, and in order to ensure the return of its effective authority in the area, in accordance with the Security Council's resolution, it was necessary that the UN Force should possess sufficient military strength to deal effectively with armed Palestinian groups or Israeli forces who challenged its authority.

But though the self-defence principle on which the Force was instructed to operate did not exclude 'resistance to attempts by forceful means to prevent it from disharging its duties under the mandate of the Security Council', in line with the recommendation of the Secretary-General, the defensive weapons with which UN forces were provided when they began to operate in South Lebanon were inadequate to deal with such forms of resistance. Indeed, as Mr. Kemel Assaud, Speaker of the Lebanese Parliament, stated in a message to the Secretary-General on 3 April 1978, 'the United Nations Interim Force in Lebanon will fail in its mission if the force is not strengthened', and he appealed to the UN to bolster the size and equipment of its forces.[127]

The UN force was later increased from 4,000 to about 6,000 men, but since it was required to operate with weapons of very limited fire-power, it was a very fragile instrument for the purpose of 'confirming the withdrawal of Israeli forces, restoring international peace and security, and assisting the Government of Lebanon in ensuring the return of its effective authority in the area', as decided by the Security Council. Indeed, the UN force was unable to establish its presence in territory which Israel handed over to local Christian militiamen who were determined to prevent the reinstatement of regular Lebanese troops in the area. There was thus an obvious need for it to be transformed into a force capable of taking effective enforcement action under Chapter VII of the Charter, for within that context there could be no question of action by the UN contravening the non-intervention principle under Article 2(7) of the Charter, and no need for the Organisation to conclude agreements with the parties to the conflict to enable UNIFIL to enjoy freedom of movement and other facilities that were necessary for the performance of its tasks.[128]

Summary and Conclusions

If, under Chapter VII of the Charter, the Security Council determines the existence of a threat to the peace, breach of the peace, or act of aggression, and authorises enforcement measures against a state to maintain or restore international peace and security, such action does not contravene the principle of non-intervention in matters essentially within the domestic jurisdiction of states under Article 2(7) of the Charter. But the Security Council cannot act in this way if one of its five permanent members applies its right of veto under Article 27, and the fact that military action was recommended by the Security Council against North Korea in 1950 was made possible only because the Soviet delegate was not present in the Council at that time to exercise the veto.

Under the 'Uniting for Peace' resolution of 1950 the Assembly claimed the competence to recommend the application of appropriate measures, including military sanctions, if the Security Council, because of lack of unanimity among its five permanent members, failed to exercise its primary responsibility for the maintenance of international peace and security, and in its resolution of 1 February 1951 the Assembly called upon all states to lend assistance to the United Nations action in Korea. This indicated that at the time the majority of UN members considered that an Assembly recommendation for military measures against an aggressor, in consonance with the 'Uniting for Peace' resolution, was not a contravention of the principle of non-intervention in matters of domestic jurisdiction under Article 2(7) of the Charter. But the scheme requiring states to earmark elements of their national forces for service with the United Nations, under the 'Uniting for Peace' resolution, proved a failure. Several UN members opted to provide for their mutual defence by means of regional security arrangements, and, as the Hungarian affair of 1956 demonstrated, it was considered impracticable for the UN Assembly to recommend military sanctions against a super-power.

In 1956, however, the 'Uniting for Peace' resolution was invoked to authorise the establishment of the United Nations Emergency Force (UNEF) to keep the peace as an interposition force between the forces of Egypt and Israel. But in contrast to the peacekeeping forces envisaged under Chapter VII of the Charter for the enforcement of peace, UNEF was a non-coercive force designed to operate in accordance with the principle of self-defence, and thus essentially as an umpire in cases where the cease-fire was infringed. Besides, the establishment of UNEF, to which units were contributed by UN members, excluding the great powers, on a voluntary basis, depended on the consent of the parties to the conflict and the willingness of the host state, Egypt, to permit UN forces to operate on its territory, and was thus not at variance with the non-intervention principle in matters of domestic jurisdiction under Article 2(7) of the Charter.

The fact that the UN Secretary-General U Thant and the Advisory Committee on UNEF complied with Egypt's request for the withdrawal of UNEF in 1967 without referring the matter to the Assembly — a decision accepted without challenge in the political organs of the United Nations — was a recognition that the question of terminating the presence of the force was within the domestic jurisdiction of the host state. This demonstrated the fragile nature of UN peacekeeping by consent and the failure of the United Nations to persuade the parties concerned to accept a political settlement of their differences whilst the UN force was supervising a cessation of hostilities.

Though the establishment of the second UNEF in 1973 depended on the consent of Egypt and Israel, Security Council resolution 341(1973) implied that the question of terminating the presence of the force in Sinai was a matter within the jurisdiction of the Council, since it laid down that extensions of the force's mandate would depend on decisions by the Council. But in practice the Council has been reluctant to exercise its competence in this respect. Besides, it has been recognised that both Syria and Israel must give their approval before the Security Council can decide on extensions of UNDOP's mandate for supervising a cessation of hostilities on the Golan Heights. Consequently, the continued presence of UNEF and UNDOP, small sized forces armed only for self-defence, must be regarded as precarious, and without significant progress towards a comprehensive settlement of Arab-Israeli differences, the recurrence of hostilities in the Middle East is the most likely result.

Indeed, it is difficult to avoid the conclusion that the Middle East will remain a storm centre until the great powers, particularly the United States and the Soviet Union, are prepared to exert diplomatic and economic pressure on the parties concerned to accept a political settlement, and to transform the existing non-coercive UN peacekeeping forces into forces with effective enforcement capabilities to ensure the observance of such a settlement and maintain international peace. Certainly, it is in the interest of the great powers to adopt such an approach, for it is a means by which they can avoid direct confrontation with each other through competing for influence in areas of conflict outside their military defence systems.

The establishment of a UN force with effective enforcement capabilities was not necessary for the maintenance of peace in the Congo after the conflict with Tshombe's Katanga had been resolved. But it is significant that an end to the conflict was not possible until after the Security Council had authorised the Secretary-General to take measures against Katanga's forces which approximated more to enforcement measures under Article 42 of the Charter than to provisional non-enforcement measures under Article 40 which Hammarskjold had attempted to apply by requiring ONUC to function in accordance with the principles of self-defence and non-intervention in internal conflicts, constitutional or otherwise.

In the next chapter we shall consider the question of peacekeeping by UN forces within the context of an agreed system of international disarmament based on the international control and inspection of national armaments, and the extent to which this would require a diminution of the domestic jurisdiction of states.

VI. THE DOMESTIC JURISDICTION LIMITATION ON THE COMPETENCE OF THE UNITED NATIONS TO INTERVENE IN MATTERS RELATING TO THE REGULATION AND REDUCTION OF ARMAMENTS

The architects of the Charter of the United Nations envisaged the regulation and reduction of armaments within the context of a security system whose effective functioning depended upon the unanimity of the five permanent members of the Security Council, the organ primarily responsible for the maintenance of international peace and security. Since each permanent member of the Council was given the right to veto the application of any form of sanctions, 'the security scheme of the Charter, then, was conceived as an arrangement for collective action against relatively minor disturbers of the peace, in cases where the great powers were united in the desire to permit or take action'.[1]

The implementation of this limited form of collective security, which required member states of the United Nations, under Article 43 of the Charter, 'to make available to the Security Council, on its call and in accordance with a special agreement or agreements, armed forces, assistance, and facilities including rights of passage, necessary for the purpose of maintaining international peace and security', proved impossible because of the differences between the Soviet Union and the Western powers. They disagreed on such matters as the strength and composition of the military contributions to be made by member states of the United Nations, and the deployment of forces that should be placed at the disposal of the Security Council.[2] Consequently, there was no security framework in which to implement Article 26 of the Charter on the international regulation of armaments, viz. 'in order to promote the establishment and maintenance of international peace and security with the least diversion for armaments of the world's human and economic resources, the Security Council shall be responsible for formulating, with the assistance of the Military Staff Committee, referred to in Article 47, plans to be submitted to the Members of the United Nations for the establishment of a system for the regulation of armaments'. Furthermore, the Military Staff Committee, consisting of the Chiefs of Staff of the permanent members of the Security Council or their representatives, never assumed its role, under Article 47 of the Charter, of advising and assisting the Security Council 'on all questions relating to the Security Council's military requirements for the maintenance of international peace and security, the employment and command of forces placed at its disposal, the regulation of armaments, and possible disarmament'.

Failure to bring into being the limited collective security system of the Charter, and the regulation of armaments within that structure, thus meant that states could still claim that the size and nature of their armaments and armed forces were matters essentially within their domestic jurisdiction, and thus protected from interference in such matters by the United Nations under the terms of Article 2(7) of the Charter.

During the early years of the United Nations, however, even before the attempt to reach agreement on the limited collective security arrangement under the Charter had proved abortive, the General Assembly which has the competence under Article 11(1) of the Charter to make recommendations on the principles of co-operation governing disarmament and the regulation of armaments to UN members or the Security Council, took the initiative to give these matters greater priority than had been accorded them under the Charter. In fact, the Assembly's first resolution, in January 1946,[3] established an Atomic Energy Commission, composed of one representative from each of those states represented on the Security Council, and Canada when that state was not a member of the Council,[4] to make specific proposals to the Security Council 'for extending between all nations the exchange of basic scientific information for peaceful ends; for control of atomic energy to the extent necessary to ensure its use only for peaceful purposes; for the elimination from national armaments of atomic weapons and of all other major weapons adaptable to mass destruction; and for effective safeguards by way of inspection and other means to protect complying states against the hazards of violations and evasions'.

Discussions in the *Atomic Energy Commission*,[5] which first met in June 1946, indicated the differing views of the Soviet Union and the Western Powers on the measure of domestic jurisdiction that should be surrendered to make possible the establishment of a system for the international control of atomic energy to ensure nuclear disarmament.

The plan put forward by Mr. Bernard Baruch for the United States in the Atomic Energy Commission proposed that an international authority should own all uranium and thorium mined, as well as own and manage atomic energy plants dangerous to international security. Though national governments would be allowed to carry out non-dangerous atomic energy activities under licence from the international authority, the latter would have the right to inspect and supervise those national plants at every stage of atomic energy manufacture. It was made clear that an effective system of international control of all phases of development and use of atomic energy must be in operation before the United States, which then had exclusive possession of atomic weapons, released the secrets of atomic energy manufacture and eliminated its stockpile of atomic weapons.

It was thus considered essential by the United States that an international atomic development authority, governed by the terms of a multilateral treaty, should have the rights of continuous inspection and control, and the power to take provisional measures, such as the closure of a particular atomic plant, in the case of violations or evasions of the international agreement under which it operated. It was also insisted that there must not be a veto to protect states that violated their solemn agreements not to develop or use atomic energy for destructive purposes. Hence it was laid down in the United States plan that the voting procedure based on the principle of great power unanimity, which obtained in the Security Council, should not apply to the operations of the proposed international authority; its decisions would be determined by the majority of its members.

As to the question of enforcement action against a violator of the agreements envisaged under the plan, who embarked on aggressive action, the United States position was as follows: 'In the event of an occurrence within the area of the Authority's jurisdiction constituting a threat to the peace, breach of the peace or act of aggression, such occurrence should immediately be certified by the Authority to the Security Council, the Assembly, and the signatory States. The treaty should establish this category of offences and the conditions surrounding them. For purpose of illustration, they might include violations . . . such as: (a) Illegal possession or use of an atomic bomb; (b) Illegal possession, or separation, of atomic material suitable for use in an atomic bomb; (c) Seizure of any plant or other property belonging to, or licensed by the Authority; (d) Wilful interference with the activities of the Authority; (e) Creation or operation of dangerous projects in a manner contrary to, or in absence of, a licence granted by the Authority.'[6] But though the United States justifiably maintained that in such situations the controls established under the multilateral treaty would be of no avail if enforcement action could be prevented by the veto of a state signatory to it, it did not advocate that the atomic bombs which it possessed should be placed at the disposal of a United Nations peacekeeping force to deter or coerce an aggressor in accordance with a recommendation of the UN Assembly if the Security Council was hamstrung by the veto of a permanent member of that body. Instead, the United States proposed that in certain cases the inherent right of individual or collective self-defence under Article 51 of the Charter would be applicable. 'Interpreting its provisions with respect to atomic energy matters, it is clear that if atomic weapons were employed as part of an "armed attack", the rights reserved by the nations to themselves under Article 51 would be applicable,' it was stated. 'It is equally clear that an "armed attack" is now something entirely different from what it was prior to the discovery of atomic weapons. It would therefore seem to be both important and appropriate under present conditions that the treaty define "armed attack" in a manner appropriate to atomic weapons and include in the definition not simply the actual dropping of an atomic bomb, but also certain steps in themselves preliminary to such action'.[7]

But if enforcement action under Article 51 was to be applied to coerce a state found guilty by the international control agency of manufacturing atomic weapons in violation of the multilateral treaty, it is difficult to see

161

how such action could be effective if, after the international control system had come into operation, no state other than the violator of the treaty possessed atomic weapons. The fact was that the question of enforcement action against a potential aggressor was not realistically faced, though the possibility of a state illegally possessing or using atomic bombs was not ruled out after the international control system had been set up.

Besides, the fact that under the Baruch plan the question of preventing the use of atomic energy for war purposes was considered independently of the regulation of conventional armaments and armed forces was hardly realistic, though not at variance with the terms of reference of the Atomic Energy Commission set up under the UN Assembly's resolution, which was supported by all the great powers. As Dr. Andrew Martin has pointed out, the hope of eliminating atomic weapons in advance of a general regulation of armaments 'was tantamount to ignoring the old experience that every disarmament conference is a bargaining counter. The A.E.C. could not serve as such while the United States had the virtual monopoly of atomic weapons. For the Soviet Union to surrender the right of independent research into the production of atomic weapons (as the Americans demanded) would have been a unilateral concession. For the United States to destroy immediately her stockpile of atomic bombs (as the Russians demanded) would have been an equally bad bargain, unless the Soviet Union was prepared to trade in its superior armaments on land, but negotiations in that direction were outside the Commission's terms of reference'.[8]

In brief, then, the Baruch plan was based on the doctrine that the development and use of atomic energy should be removed from the sphere of domestic jurisdiction of all states and brought under the jurisdiction of an agency which had the basic features of a supra-national authority whose decisions would be arrived at by majority voting, not subject to the veto of any state. But though the plan proposed this measure of supra-nationalism, it did not envisage the formation of a supra-national force possessing nuclear weapons, though this would be necessary if it was to be an effective deterrent to a would-be violator of the agreement not to manufacture atomic weapons.

The Atomic Energy Commission's first report to the Security Council on 31 December 1946, which was adopted by 10 votes in favour (Australia, Brazil, Canada, China, Egypt, France, Netherlands, Mexico, United Kingdom, United States) — the Soviet Union and Poland abstained —[9] was, in general, an endorsement of the Baruch plan. It rejected the Soviet Union's proposal that states should accept an international convention banning the national production, possession and use of atomic weapons, before negotiation on the setting up of international control machinery commenced. In the view of the majority such a convention would not ensure that atomic energy would be used only for peaceful purposes, or protect complying states against the hazards of violations of such an agreement.

Subsequently, in June 1947, after several months of discussion in the Atomic Energy Commission, the Soviet Union modified its earlier position to some extent by proposing that in order to prevent violations of the convention for banning the use of atomic weapons, strict international control should be established simultaneously over all facilities for the production of atomic energy. The new Soviet plan stipulated that raw materials and atomic plants would remain under national ownership and management, but subject to control based on periodic inspection. The Soviet delegate declared that the so-called veto should not apply to the day to day activities and operations of the International Control Commission suggested in the Soviet plan; but such a commission would, he explained, only make recommendations to the Security Council in respect of violations of any convention that should be drawn up. Punishments for serious violations should always be subject to decisions of the Security Council. He emphasised that the rule of unanimity of the permanent members of the Council was a basic principle of the Charter, and that the Soviet Union could never agree to a violation of such a principle.[10]

The Western powers criticised the Soviet plan not only because it permitted a great power to veto the application of sanctions against a state found manufacturing atomic energy for war purposes, but on the ground that there must be continuous as opposed to periodic inspection. Not surprisingly, further discussions in the Atomic Energy Commission in 1948 did nothing to bridge the fundamental differences between the Soviet and Western plans, and the Commission reported on 17 May 1948 that it had failed to prepare a draft treaty on the international control of atomic energy. The report stated that the majority plan had been rejected by the Soviet Union 'either as a whole or in separate parts, on the ground that such a plan constituted an unwarranted infringement of national sovereignty', and that the majority of the Commission was fully aware of the impact of its plan on traditional prerogatives of national sovereignty, but in the face of the realities of the problem it saw no alternative to the voluntary sharing by nations of their sovereignty to the extent required by its proposals.[11]

The question of the extent to which the domestic jurisdiction of states would have to be surrendered for the establishment of an essentially supranational control of atomic energy occasioned some discussion in the First Committee of the Assembly, in September 1948,[12] after the majority plan of the Atomic Energy Commission had been vetoed by the Soviet Union in the Security Council. The Soviet delegate asserted that implementation of the majority recommendations would give the opportunity to the staff of an international authority to carry out large scale espionage, and the Ukrainian S.S.R. delegate stated that, far from representing a sacrifice, the

U.S. plan was a manifestation of the supra-nationalism which was poisoning international life and preventing all co-operation.

Clearly, the essentially supra-national approach of the majority to the question of controlling the use and development of atomic energy was unacceptable to the Soviet Union on the ground that it would constitute unwarranted and intolerable intervention in matters essentially within the domestic jurisdiction of states. But though the Soviet attitude was considered obstructionist by the majority of UN member states, and the Assembly approved the recommendations of the majority plan in the reports of the Atomic Energy Commission,[13] it may be argued, as Evan Luard has done, that the effect of implementing the plan 'would have been to place the Soviet Union in a position of permanent inferiority. For even if the United States had in fact destroyed her existing weapons, and the Soviet Union could have been satisfied of this, there was no means of destroying the capacity to resume manufacture in the case of world war or even in the case of a breakdown in the agreement. The United States would thus have held permanent technological superiority in case of emergency. The Soviet Union, therefore, as the catching-up power, proceeded to frustrate any attempt to reach agreement in this field'.[14]

If this argument is accepted, it may also be contended that it was unrealistic to expect the Soviet Union to accept the majority view that conventional armaments should be considered separately from atomic weapons and other weapons of mass destruction, which was a major issue of disagreement in the Commission for Conventional Armaments[15] that had been set up by the Security Council early in 1947 in response to the Assembly's request that it should give prompt consideration to formulating measures for the general regulation of armaments and armed forces.[16] However, the attempt was made to resolve the matter in 1952, by which time the Soviet Union was building up her own stockpile of nuclear weapons, through the establishment by the Assembly of a single Disarmament Commission 'to prepare proposals to be embodied in a draft treaty (or treaties) for the regulation, limitation and balanced reduction of all armed forces and all armaments, for the elimination of all major weapons adaptable to mass destruction, and for effective international control of atomic energy to ensure the prohibition of atomic weapons and the use of atomic energy for peaceful purposes only'.[17]

The establishment of the *Disarmament Commission*, which was representative of the members of the Security Council and Canada, thus implied that agreement on disarmament depended on finding a way of balancing the West's superiority in atomic weapons with the Soviet Union's superiority in conventional armaments and ground forces. But though the search for agreement on a comprehensive and co-ordinated plan of disarmament by the Commission from February 1952 to April 1954, and its sub-committee of Canada, France, Soviet Union, United Kingdom and the

United States, from May 1954 to September 1957,[18] narrowed to some extent the gap between the Soviet Union and the Western Powers, there were still differences between them because of their divergent views on the degree of intervention that should be permitted in matters of domestic jurisdiction to enable an international control body to function with adequate powers of inspection and verification of national armaments and to initiate measures to prevent and suppress violations of a disarmament treaty.

Though the Soviet Union agreed in 1952 to the principle of continuous inspection in favour of the periodic inspection which it had previously accepted,[19] it was reluctant to define how the international control system, which it suggested should come into being simultaneously with the prohibition of nuclear weapons, should function. Indeed, it was not until May 1955 that the Soviet Union made some attempt to define the kind of international control system it envisaged.

The control system which the Soviet Union proposed was one of the main features of a plan which called for a two-stage disarmament programme corresponding to the years 1956 and 1957 which involved (1) the acceptance of the ceilings for the armed forces of the great powers and other states, as proposed by the Western Powers in March 1955, and the elimination of foreign bases; and (2) the postponement of the prohibition of nuclear weapons until after 75% of the reduction of armed forces had been carried out. During the first stage of the disarmament programme, the international control organ would have the authority to station observers at railway junctions, large ports, highways and aerodromes in the territories of all states concerned, the right to request information from states on the implementation of measures of reduction of armaments and armed forces, and the right to inspect national records on military expenditure. As to measures of prevention and suppression of violations of the agreements entered into, it was proposed that the control organ could only make recommendations to the Security Council.[20]

The Soviet plan was unacceptable to the Western Powers. There was objection to the control system which it had proposed on the ground that it would not have sufficient powers of inspection. The United States insisted that inspection on the ground should be supplemented by aerial inspection to meet the possibility of large scale surprise attacks, a matter highlighted by President Eisenhower at the Summit Conference at Geneva in July 1955. There was also opposition to the Soviet proposal that the control agency should not possess the authority to take any measures in the event of violations of the proposed disarmament agreements, other than to make recommendations to the Security Council which was governed by the great power veto.[21]

Negotiations on a formula for the regulation, limitation and balanced reduction of all armed forces and all armaments were also greatly complicated by the fact that there was no known method of detecting hidden stocks of nuclear weapons. The Soviet Union pointed out in its May 1955 proposals that since the production of atomic energy for peaceful purposes provided possibilities for evading international control, security could not be ensured because the door would be open to a potential aggressor to accumulate stocks of atomic and hydrogen bombs for a surprise attack. Indeed, it was mutual recognition of this that influenced both the Western Powers and the Soviet Union to admit the advisability of trying to reach agreement on partial measures of arms control or disarmament, as distinct from a comprehensive general disarmament plan. This was demonstrated in the 1956 and 1957 sessions of the Sub-Committee of the Disarmament Commission, consisting of France, the Soviet Union, the United Kingdom, the United States and Canada. 'All members of the Sub-Committee appear to agree on the need to seek a partial rather than a comprehensive agreement,' it was stated in the British Foreign Secretary's Report on the Disarmament Talks to Parliament in July 1957, 'though there is still considerable divergence between the Western and Soviet view of what a partial agreement should contain.'[22]

In November 1957 the UN Assembly urged that priority should be given to such partial measures, or collateral measures as they are sometimes called, as the immediate suspension of testing of nuclear weapons, the cessation of the production of fissionable materials for weapons purposes, the reduction of armed forces and armaments through adequate safeguard arrangements, and the progressive establishment of open inspection with ground and aerial components to guard against the possibility of surprise attack.[23] But the only partial measure on which agreement was reached prior to 1959 was the *Antarctic Treaty*, signed by the Soviet Union, the United States, France, the United Kingdom and eight other powers on 1 December 1959, which provided, among other things, for the demilitarisation of Antarctica.[24]

The Antarctic Treaty laid down that 'any measures of a military nature, such as the establishment of military bases and fortifications, the carrying out of military manoeuvres, as well as the testing of any type of weapons' should be prohibited in Antarctica, (Article 1) and that 'all areas in Antarctica, including stations, installations and equipment within these areas, and all ships and aircraft at points of discharging or embarking cargoes, or personnel in Antarctica' should be open at all times to inspection by any obervers of the contracting parties. (Article VII) Furthermore, Article VII stipulated that 'aerial inspection may be carried out at any time over all areas of Antarctica by any of the Contracting Parties having the right to designate observers'.

Though Article IV stated that nothing in the Treaty involved 'a renunciation or diminution by any Contracting Party of any basis of claim to territorial sovereignty in Antarctica which it may have whether as a result of its activities or those of its nationals in Antarctica, or otherwise', it was significant that the contracting parties were prepared to relinquish some measure of their jurisdiction to facilitate the work of inspection by the observers designated by any of the parties. (Article VIII) It was also stipulated in Article XI of the Treaty, which was open for accession by any member state of the United Nations or any other state invited by the contracting parties that 'if any dispute arises between two or more of the Contracting Parties concerning the interpretation or application of the present Treaty, those Contracting Parties shall consult among themselves with a view to having the dispute resolved by negotiation, inquiry, mediation, conciliation, arbitration, judicial settlement or other peaceful means of their own choice', and that 'any dispute of this character not so resolved shall, with the consent, in each case, of all parties to the dispute, be referred to the International Court of Justice; but failure to reach agreement on reference to the International Court shall not absolve parties to the dispute from the responsibility of continuing to seek to resolve it by any of the peaceful means referred to in paragraph 1 of this Article'.

Although the Antarctic Treaty was negotiated outside the United Nations, it exemplified the kind of partial or collateral measure, involving a diminution of some measure of domestic jurisdiction over the deployment of national military forces and armaments, which the Assembly of the United Nations hoped would help to build the confidence necessary to facilitate agreement on a comprehensive plan of disarmament. But though progress towards the conclusion of agreements on other partial measures was extremely slow, the Assembly impatiently requested a resumption of negotiations on general disarmament in November 1959.[25]

A joint statement issued by J.J. McCloy (United States) and V.A. Zorin (Soviet Union) on 20 September 1961, during the sixteenth session of the UN Assembly, the outcome of many months of discussions, recommended several principles as a basis for new negotiations on 'general and complete disarmament' which, as stated in the text,[26] quoted below, was designed to ensure that states would have at their disposal only those armed forces and conventional armaments essential for internal order and the security of their citizens.

1.   The goal of negotiations is to achieve agreement on a programme which will ensure:

(a)   That disarmament is general and complete and war is no longer an instrument for settling international problems, and

(b)   That such disarmament is accompanied by the establishment of reliable procedures for the peaceful settlement of disputes and effective arrangements for the maintenance of peace in accordance with the principles of the Charter of the United Nations.

2.	The programme for general and complete disarmament shall ensure that States will have at their disposal only such non-nuclear armaments, forces, facilities and establishments as are agreed to be necessary to maintain internal order and protect the personal security of citizens; and that States shall support and provide the agreed manpower for a United Nations peace force.
3.	To this end, the programme for general and complete disarmament shall contain the necessary provisions, with respect to the military establishment of every nation, for:
(a)	The disbanding of armed forces, the dismantling of military establishments, including bases, the cessation of the production of armaments as well as their liquidation or conversion to peaceful uses;
(b)	The elimination of all stockpiles of nuclear, chemical, bacteriological and other weapons of mass destruction, and the cessation of the production of such weapons;
(c)	The elimination of all means of delivery of weapons of mass destruction;
(d)	The abolition of organisations and institutions designed to organize the military effort of States, the cessation of military training, and the closing of all military training institutions;
(e)	The discontinuance of military expenditures.
4.	The disarmament programme should be implemented in an agreed sequence, by stages, until it is completed, with each measure and stage carried out within specified time-limits. Transition to a subsequent stage in the process of disarmament should take place upon a review of the implementation of measures included in the preceding stage and upon a decision that all such measures have been implemented and verified and that any additional arrangements required for measures in the next stage are, when appropriate, ready to operate.
5.	All measures of general and complete disarmament should be balanced so that at no stage of the implementation of the treaty could any State or group of States gain military advantage and that security is ensured equally for all.
6.	All disarmament measures should be implemented from beginning to end under strict and effective international control as would provide firm assurance that all parties are honouring their obligations. During and after the implementation of general and complete disarmament, the most

thorough control should be exercised, the nature and extent of such control depending on the requirements for verification of the disarmament measures being carried out in each stage. To implement control over the inspection of disarmament, an international disarmament organization including all parties to the agreement should be created within the framework of the United Nations. This international disarmament organization and its inspectors should be assured unrestricted access without veto to all places as necessary for the purpose of effective verification.

7. Progress in disarmament should be accompanied by measures to strengthen institutions for maintaining peace and the settlement of international disputes by peaceful means. During and after the implementation of the programme of general and complete disarmament, there should be taken, in accordance with the principles of the United Nations Charter, the necessary measures to maintain international peace and security, including the obligation of States to place at the disposal of the United Nations agreed manpower necessary for an international peace force to be equipped with agreed types of armaments. Arrangements for the use of this force should ensure that the United Nations can effectively deter or suppress any threat or use of arms in violation of the purposes and principles of the United Nations.

8. States participating in the negotiations should seek to achieve and implement the widest possible agreement at the earliest possible date. Efforts should continue without interruption until agreement upon the total programme has been achieved, and efforts to ensure early agreement on and implementation of measures of disarmament should be undertaken without prejudicing progress on agreement on the total programme and in such a way that these measures would facilitate and form part of that programme.

It should be noted, however, that on the day that this joint statement of principles was issued to all members of the United Nations, a report on an exchange of views between McCloy and Zorin was also released, which indicated an important difference between the Soviet Union and the United States on the question of armaments control. The United States representative stated that, in the view of his government, it was 'implicit in the entire joint statement of agreed principles that whenever an agreement stipulates that at a certain point certain levels of forces and armaments may be retained, the verification machinery must have all the rights and powers necessary to ensure that those levels are not exceeded'. But to this the

Soviet delegate was opposed. He maintained that 'while strongly advocating effective control over disarmament and wishing to facilitate as much as possible the achievement of agreement on this control, the Soviet Union is at the same time resolutely opposed to the establishment of control over armaments'.[27] Clearly, this meant that it could not be proved by the verification system advocated by the Soviet Union whether the agreed level of a particular category of armaments was being observed after a certain percentage of those armaments had been destroyed. But it should also be realised that there was a major difficulty in implementing the principle that verification should ensure that not only agreed limitations or reductions should take place, but also that retained armaments did not exceed agreed levels at any stage; for there was no known scientific method of detecting hidden stocks of nuclear weapons, and the conversion of air-liners for the delivery of such weapons could be arranged without much difficulty even if an inspection system were in operation.[28]

Notwithstanding these problems, the Soviet Union and the United States went ahead with the drafting of treaties on 'general and complete disarmament' based on the joint statement of agreed principles, and sub-mitted their draft treaties for the consideration of the Eighteen-Nation Disarmament Committee,[29] which met in Geneva in 1962.

The Soviet draft treaty — *USSR Draft Treaty on General and Complete Disarmament under Strict International Control*[30] — required that the states parties to it should carry out a disarmament programme in three stages over a period of five years. A three stage programme was also proposed in the United States draft treaty — *Outline of Basic Provisions of a Treaty on General and Complete Disarmament in a Peaceful World*[31] — two stages of three years each, and the third stage whose duration would be settled when the treaty was signed.

But though both the United States and Soviet draft treaties recognised that the implementation of a phased disarmament programme required institutions within the framework of the United Nations for control and inspection by an international disarmament organisation, procedures for the pacific settlement of disputes, and the establishment of a United Nations peacekeeping force, there were marked differences between them over the amount of domestic jurisdiction that should be surrendered to enable the United Nations, or institutions linked to it, to have the necessary authority and strength to implement their common objective of general and complete disarmament.

The United States draft treaty, unlike the Soviet draft treaty, laid down that verification procedures for the reductions of armed forces and arma-ments should also ensure that retained forces and armaments should not exceed agreed levels at any stage of the disarmament process. This was stipulated in the clauses on 'Verification of the International Disarma-ment Organisation'[32] and it was suggested that this might be accomplished by dividing the territory of a party to the treaty into an agreed number of zones for inspection, so that once a zone had been inspected it would remain open for further inspection while verification was being extended to additional zones.[33]

But the Soviet Union was opposed to the inspection of remaining stocks of armaments at a given stage of disarmament, and to the zonal system suggested by the United States. During the debate on the draft treaties in the First Committee of the Assembly in December 1962, the Soviet delegate maintained that the aim of the United States proposals was to secure information useful to the NATO intelligence services, which would be able to collect all the pertinent data about the Soviet defence system long before the completion of the first stage of the US disarmament plan and when the Western powers were still in a much stronger military position.[34]

These comments by the Soviet delegate laid the Soviet Union open to the criticism, voiced by the British delegate, Mr. J.B. Godber, that the kind of verification system it advocated could not prove that 100% of the stock of a certain category of weapon had been destroyed.[35] But the British delegate did not mention that since it was impossible to determine scientifically whether stocks of nuclear weapons, or fissionable material for weapon purposes, had been shielded from detection and discovery, there could be no assurance, even under the United States system of inspection, that agreed levels of nuclear armaments were being exceeded through the secret retention of nuclear weapons. After all, as stated earlier, this problem had been openly recognised by both the Soviet Union and the Western powers since 1955. Indeed, on 20 March 1957 Mr. Harold Stassen, for the United States, had asserted that 'a disloyal government could either keep a part of existing stocks or divert without the knowledge of the inspectors, a quantity of fissionable material from which 20, 40, or even 50 multi-megaton bombs could be fabricated. All of this could be carried out without discovery by inspectors, and without the knowledge of other nations, until it was completely accomplished'.[36] Besides, even if all forms of military delivery systems were eliminated at some stage of a disarmament programme, civil aircraft could be converted for nuclear delivery purposes with little possibility of discovery by international inspectors, as already mentioned.

It would appear that these possibilities were not discounted in the United States draft treaty. Since it contained provision for the establishment of a United Nations Peace Force with 'sufficient armed forces and armaments so that no State could challenge it',[37] in contrast to the Soviet plan for a United Nations Peace Force with 'contingents of police (militia) equipped with light firearms'[38] whose use could be vetoed by a permanent member of the Security Council, it did not rule out the need for a United Nations force strong enough to deter or coerce a great power, armed with a secret stock of nuclear weapons, which might violate the disarmament treaty. In fact, the

United States draft treaty stipulated that 'the parties to the Treaty would undertake to develop arrangements during stage I for the establishment in stage II of a United Nations Peace Force. To this end, the Parties to the Treaty would agree on the following measures within the United Nations: (a) Examination of the experience of the United Nations leading to a further strengthening of United Nations forces for keeping the peace; (b) Examination of the feasibility of concluding promptly the agreements envisaged in Article 43 of the United Nations Charter; (c) Conclusion of an agreement for the establishment of a United Nations Peace Force in stage II, including definitions of its purpose, mission, composition and strength, disposition, command and control, training, logistical support, financing, equipment and armaments'.[39] Later, in stage III, 'the Parties to the Treaty would progressively strengthen the United Nations Peace Force established in stage II until it had sufficient armed forces and armaments so that no state could challenge it'.[40]

The United States draft treaty also laid down that 'parties to the Treaty would undertake to accept without reservation, pursuant to Article 36, paragraph (1) of the Statute of the International Court of Justice, the compulsory jurisdiction of that Court to decide international legal disputes';[41] that they would agree to accept rules of international conduct related to disarmament, which would become effective three months after circulation to all parties unless a majority disapproved;[42] and that 'in the light of the study of indirect aggression and subversion conducted in stage I, the Parties to the Treaty would agree to arrangements necessary to assure States against indirect aggression and subversion'.[43]

It can be seen, therefore, that the United States scheme for 'complete and general disarmament' required the surrender of a very large measure of domestic jurisdiction to the United Nations or institutions that might be linked to it. Indeed, Mr. Arthur H. Dean, the United States delegate, emphasised in the First Committee of the UN Assembly in November 1962, that full disarmament would not come until there was a change in existing practices and institutions, a new international law had been built up, and measures taken to strengthen the United Nations and its various peace-keeping roles, in mediation, conciliation, in observation and in defence against aggression. The Soviet plan, he asserted, ignored the need for such changes.[44] Certainly, it is difficult to see how a treaty for general and complete disarmament could ensure security to states if its enforcement depended on the kind of United Nations force advocated by the Soviet Union, and if its operation was subject to the veto of a great power in the Security Council, which was also insisted upon by the Soviet Union.

It may be inferred, therefore, that the terms of the United States draft treaty which, with the Soviet draft treaty, have been the basis for negotiations on general and complete disarmament in the Geneva Disarmament Committees since 1962, 'look toward a transformation of the nation-states into something approximating a world federal system', as Arthur I. Waskow has pointed out. 'Whatever the legal and constitutional arrangements, the existence of a peace force so strong that 'no state could challenge it' would be likely to transfer the power to make many political decisions from the nations to the complex of world institutions . . . In addition, the existence of such a powerful peace force would almost certainly require the establishment of a highly effective quasi-governmental institution to control the peace force itself'.[45]

One must readily admit, however, as Waskow emphasises, 'the unlikelihood of achieving among the present conflicting interests in the world a sufficient political consensus on which to construct either a government or a series of peacekeeping institutions with quasi-governmental authority to manage a large army and settle political disputes between nations'.[46] We have seen in the previous chapter that so far it has only been possible to achieve a political consensus within the United Nations in support of the establishment of peacekeeping forces with very limited functions and, with the exception of their use in the Congo affair on certain occasions, for non-enforcement action. Such forces have served a useful purpose in a world of conflicting interests, but bear little resemblance to the kind of United Nations Peace Force required to make implementation of the United States plan for general disarmament a practicable proposition.

Clearly, the creation of a United Nations peacekeeping force, equipped with sufficient nuclear and conventional armaments to deter or coerce a state or group of states that violated a multilateral treaty on general disarmament with the purpose of committing aggression, and without which parties to such a treaty could obviously not be afforded adequate security, must therefore be regarded as a Utopian concept. This being so, it has to be recognised that it is unrealistic to regard general and complete disarmament as a serious objective for the foreseeable future; and that the only practicable objectives, in the present context of international politics, are partial or collateral measures of arms control which, in view of the failure to implement the concept of security based on great power unanimity under the Charter, may help to stabilise the balance of power which is, as one writer has stated, 'for better or worse, the operative mechanism of contemporary international politics'.[47] Indeed, this has been tacitly recognised for some time in the Geneva Disarmament Committees,[48] for since 1963, when it had been made clear that there was no hope of reconciling the differences between the Soviet Union and the United States on the question of general and complete disarmament, the negotiations in Geneva have been almost exclusively devoted to partial or collateral measures.

We shall now consider the extent to which agreements on partial measures of arms control in the field of nuclear armaments have limited the domestic jurisdiction of states, with special reference to the role of the United Nations.

The first of these agreements — *the Partial Nuclear Test Ban Treaty*[49] — which prohibited nuclear tests in the atmosphere, in outer space, and under water, but not underground, was signed in Moscow on 5 August 1963 by the Soviet Union, the United States, and the United Kingdom. It gained wide-spread approval in the United Nations Assembly,[50] but was not accepted by France. China, not then a member of the United Nations, began testing in the atmosphere in 1964.

First, it should be noted that this treaty did not require an international system of control and inspection because the testing of nuclear weapons stipulated in the agreement could be verified by external nationally controlled methods,[51] without the need for 'on-site' inspections in the territories of states, which are essential to detect the underground testing of nuclear weapons.[52]

Secondly, since it was stipulated in the treaty that 'each party shall in exercising its national sovereignty have the right to withdraw from the Treaty if it decides that extraordinary events, related to the subject matter of this Treaty, have jeopardized the supreme interests of its country,[53] its signatories were entitled to claim that the resumption of testing nuclear weapons in the atmosphere, in outer space, and under water was a matter within their domestic jurisdiction, and thus outside the competence of the United Nations in accordance with the general principle of non-intervention under Article 2(7) of the Charter.

Though the treaty has been observed by the United States, the Soviet Union and the United Kingdom, it has been ignored by France and China, and underground tests of nuclear weapons, not covered by the treaty, have been conducted by all the nuclear powers. And though under Article 1 of the *Treaty on the Limitation of Underground Nuclear Weapons Tests*, signed by the Soviet Union and the United States in Moscow on 3 July 1974, each party undertook 'to prohibit, to prevent, and not to carry out any underground nuclear weapon test having a yield exceeding 150 kilotons at any place under its jurisdiction or control, beginning March 31, 1976',[54] it should be appreciated that 'the figure of 150 kilotons is still more than seven times the power of the bomb which hit Hiroshima...'[55] Moreover, Article V(2) of the treaty stipulated that 'each party shall, in exercising its national sovereignty, have the right to withdraw from this treaty if it decides that extraordinary events related to the subject matter of this treaty have jeopardized its supreme interests'.

A similar reservation was included in the Outer space Treaty — *Treaty on Principles Governing the Activities of States in the Exploration and Use of Outer Space, including the Moon and Other Celestial Bodies*[56] — which was unanimously adopted by the UN Assembly on 14 December 1966[57] after it had been signed in London, Moscow and Washington. Under

Article IV of this treaty, which came into force in January 1967, states parties to it undertook 'not to place in orbit round the earth any objects carrying nuclear weapons or any other kinds of weapons of mass destruction, install such weapons on celestial bodies, or station such weapons in outer space in any other manner'. But the treaty did not contain international arrangements for verifying compliance with this prohibition, though both the United States and the Soviet Union had made provision in their 1962 draft treaties on general and complete disarmament for pre-launch inspection of all space vehicles and missiles by an international disarmament organisation.[58]

The Sea Bed Treaty banning the emplacement of nuclear weapons and other weapons of mass destruction on the sea bed outside a 12 mile coastal zone,[59] which was commended by the UN Assembly in December 1970[60] and entered into force on 18 May 1972 when the three Depositary Governments (USSR, USA and UK) deposited their instruments of ratification, contains verification procedures, unlike the Outer Space Treaty. Under Article III each party to the treaty has the right to verify through observation the activities of the other parties, provided that such observation does not infringe rights recognised under international law. Verification may be undertaken by any state party using its own means, or with the assistance of any other state party, or through appropriate procedures within the framework of the United Nations and in accordance with its Charter; and complaints concerning the violation of the treaty may be referred to the Security Council, which may take action in accordance with the Charter.

Like the other partial arms control agreements, to which reference has already been made, however, the Sea Bed Treaty contains the domestic jurisdiction reservation concerning the right of a state, party to the treaty, to withdraw from it 'if it decides that extraordinary events related to the subject matter of this Treaty have jeopardized the supreme interests of its country'. In such circumstances, 'it shall give notice of such withdrawal to all other States Parties to the Treaty and to the United Nations Security Council three months in advance. Such notice shall include a statement of the extraordinary events it considers to have jeopardized its supreme interests'.[61]

The domestic jurisdiction reservation is stated in precisely the same terms in Article X of the *Treaty on the Non-Proliferation of Nuclear Weapons*,[62] which entered into force on 5 March 1970, about two years after it had been approved by a large majority in the UN Assembly.[63] And even if it is assumed that this clause will not be invoked by any state that has ratified the treaty, the fact that several non-nuclear weapon states, capable of producing nuclear bombs from the by-products of nuclear reactors designed for peaceful purposes, have not even signed the treaty,[64] militates against its basic aim of preventing the spread of nuclear weapons. Further attention will be given to this question presently, but first let us examine the main provisions of the treaty.

Article I contains an undertaking on the part of the nuclear-weapon states party to the treaty, viz. 'not to transfer to any recipient whatsoever nuclear weapons or other nuclear explosive devices or control over such weapons or explosive devices directly, or indirectly; and not in any way to assist, encourage, or induce any non-nuclear weapon State to manufacture or otherwise acquire nuclear weapons or other nuclear explosive devices, or control over such weapons or explosive devices'.

Article II contains a reciprocal undertaking by non-nuclear-weapon states signatory to the treaty, viz. 'not to receive the transfer from any transferor whatsoever of nuclear weapons or other nuclear explosive devices or of control over such weapons or explosive devices directly, or indirectly; not to manufacture or otherwise acquire nuclear weapons or other nuclear explosive devices; and not to seek or receive any assistance in the manufacture of nuclear weapons or other nuclear explosive devices'. Consequently, each non-nuclear-weapon state party to the treaty, who is permitted under Article IV 'to develop research, production and use of nuclear energy for peaceful purposes without discrimination . . ' and 'to participate in the fullest possible exchange of equipment, materials and scientific and technological information' for such purposes, undertakes under Article III 'to accept safe-guards, as set forth in an agreement to be negotiated and concluded with the International Atomic Energy Agency in accordance with the Statute of the International Atomic Energy Agency and the Agency's safeguards system, for the exclusive purpose of verification of the fulfilment of its obligations assumed under this Treaty with a view to preventing diversion of nuclear energy from peaceful uses to nuclear weapons or other nuclear explosive devices . . .'[65]

At the end of the first conference held to review the Non-Proliferation Treaty, which met in Geneva on 5-30 May 1975, 94 states had ratified the treaty, but 15 non-nuclear-weapon states which had signed had not ratified. Indeed 37 states had not even signed, though several of these non-signatories, such as Argentina, Brazil, Chile, Israel, Pakistan, Saudi-Arabia and Spain were considered capable of becoming nuclear powers within the next two years.[66]

We thus return to the point with which we began, viz. that even if non-nuclear weapon states which have ratified the treaty do not exercise their domestic jurisdiction reservation to withdraw from it, there are several non-nuclear-weapon states, which have not signed it, capable of producing nuclear weapons from the by-products of nuclear reactors used for peaceful purposes. The fact is, as Secretary-General U Thant pointed out before the conclusion of the Non-Proliferation Treaty, 'the dangers of nuclear proliferation are very real and very grave, more so than may be generally recognised. The use of nuclear reactors produces plutonium which, when processed in a separation plant, can be used to make nuclear weapons by techniques that are no longer secret. According to some estimates, by 1980 nulcear power reactors throughout the world will produce more than 100 kilogrammes of plutonium every day. It is always possible that cheaper and simpler methods of producing fissionable material may be discovered and that their availability for warlike purposes will increase astronomically. The risks that now exist of the further spread of nuclear weapons hold such peril for humanity that international safeguards should be established not only over nuclear power reactors but also over other nuclear plants which produce, use or process significant quantities of fissionable materials'.[67]

This question was highlighted in May 1974, when India, who had not signed the Non-Proliferation Treaty, exploded its first nuclear device. As one expert stated: 'it has demonstrated that today any government with a modest nuclear power prgramme, a reasonable industrial base, well-trained scientists, and concerned more with its regional than its global position, can obtain primitive but highly dangerous nuclear weapons on the quiet and on the cheap.'[68]

Indeed, it was not until 12 January 1978 that the fifteen countries supplying plant and materials intended for commercial atomic power programmes, the so called Nuclear Suppliers' Group, published a set of rules requiring purchaser states to agree henceforth to international inspections and to give assurances that no explosive devices would be produced or nuclear supplies re-exported. Though this attempt to prevent the proliferation of nuclear weapons was a step forward, the new rules did not require a recipient state to accept international inspection of its complete nuclear programme. As *The Times* asserted in its leader, 'Brakes on the Nuclear Spread', on 16 January 1978, 'this concept of bringing the complete nuclear programme of a country under inspection, and not just a specific installation or batch of material, was behind the attempt to improve safeguards which produced the Non-Proliferation Treaty. The rules of the Nuclear Suppliers' Group are comparable with the old original International Atomic Energy measures. Of course the French are not signatories to the Non-Proliferation Treaty, whereas they have formed a powerful nulear exporting industry. In fact the modesty of the restraints imposed by the suppliers' group largely reflects French attitudes'.

In the immediate future, then, it is possible that several non-nuclear-weapon states which have not signed the Non-Proliferation Treaty, as well as states that have ratified the treaty if they decide to exercise their domestic jurisdiction to withdraw from it on the ground that extraordinary events have jeopardised their national interest, may embark on nuclear arms programmes.

There are various reasons why a non-nuclear weapon state may be tempted to produce nuclear armaments. It could be motivated by the fear that its national security would be placed in jeopardy unless it possessed a nuclear capability to deter a hostile state. On the other hand, it may regard the acquisition of nuclear weapons as a means of exerting pressure on another state whose national interests conflict with those of her own. It is possible, too, that a state may decide in favour of a nuclear arms programme in the belief that it would enhance its prestige and give it greater bargaining power in international diplomacy. It is reasonable to assume, however, that a non-nuclear-weapon state would be glad to refrain from pursuing a nuclear arms programme if it was more convinced that ratification of the Non-Proliferation Treaty would give it a greater sense of security.

Unfortunately, several non-nuclear-weapon states are reluctant to sign or ratify the Non-Proliferation Treaty because they are not convinced that it would afford them sufficient security, notwithstanding the security assurances given by the Soviet Union, the United States and the United Kingdom under Security Council resolution 255 of 19 June 1968.

This resolution, in line with declarations of intent made by the Soviet Union, the United States and the United Kingdom when the Security Council was considering the matter,[69]

1. **Recognizes** that aggression with nuclear weapons or threat of such aggression against a non-nuclear-weapon state would create a situation in which the Security Council, and above all its nuclear-weapon State permanent members, would have to act immediately in accordance with their obligations under the United Nations Charter;

2. **Welcomes** the intention expressed by certain states that they will provide or support immediate assistance, in accordance with the Charter, to any non-nuclear-weapon State Party to the Treaty on the Non-Proliferation of Nuclear Weapons that is the victim of an act or an object of a threat of aggression in which nuclear weapons are used.

3. **Reaffirms** in particular the inherent right, recognized under Article 51 of the Charter, of individual and collective self-defence if an armed attack occurs against a Member of the United Nations, until the Security Council has taken measures necessary to maintain international peace and security.[70]

France did not join the three permanent members of the Security Council that sponsored the resolution because it took the view that the only solution to the nuclear arms menace was the ending of the production of nuclear arms and the destruction of existing stocks of such weapons, but it promised that it would behave exactly as if it were a party to the Non-Proliferation Treaty. China (then a non-nuclear power represented by the Taiwan government), Canada, Denmark, Paraguay, Senegal and Ethiopia supported the resolution because the security assurances offered by the USSR, USA and UK seemed the best obtainable in the prevailing situation. But it was criticised by four non-nuclear-weapon states on the Council (Algeria, Brazil, Pakistan and India) on the grounds that the only real hope of security for non-nuclear weapon states was through nuclear disarmament, that the security guarantees of the three powers applied only to parties to the Non-Proliferation Treaty, and that such guarantees should apply to all kinds of aggression, not only aggression with nuclear arms.

At the Conference of Non-Nuclear-Weapon States in Geneva (August-September 1968), several states expressed their doubts concerning the adequacy of the security assurances given by the USSR, USA and UK under Security Council resolution 255 (1968). Ceylon, Ecuador, Pakistan and Syria asked for more specific and juridical commitments, enshrined in a binding treaty or some other international document. The need for assurances from nuclear states against aggression with conventional armaments was also stressed by many non-nuclear-weapon states. In fact, the Declaration of the Conference, which embodied the main conclusions of the non-nuclear weapon states, stressed 'the necessity of further steps for an early solution of the question of security assurances in the nuclear era'.[71]

From a study of the statements of many non-nuclear-weapon states in the Conference referred to above and in the UN Assembly,[72] it would appear that those non-nuclear-weapon states, which have not signed or ratified the Non-Proliferation Treaty, might be induced to do so if the general declaration of intent under Security Council resolution 255 (1968) were converted into a more positive commitment and included in the treaty itself, in line with the following suggested text: 'The nuclear-weapon states, signatory to this treaty, will provide immediate assistance to any non-nuclear-weapon state, party to this treaty, that is a victim of an act or an object of a threat of aggression in which nuclear weapons are used. To that end they will act in accordance with a resolution approved by the Security Council; but if the Security Council is prevented from taking action in the event of an armed attack in which nuclear weapons are used against a non-nuclear-weapon state, the nuclear powers signatory to this treaty will provide or support immediate assistance to that state, in accordance with the inherent right, under Article 51 of the Charter, of individual and collective self-defence, until the Security Council has taken measures necessary to maintain international peace and security'.

The inclusion of such an article in the Non-Proliferation Treaty, which may be amended under its Article VIII, would provide a more positive commitment on the part of the nuclear power signatories than their security assurances under Security Council resolution 255 (1968). Since collective defence under Article 51 is only permissible in the event of an armed attack against a state — it does not apply to threats of aggression — it is difficult to see how the nuclear power signatories to the Non-

Proliferation Treaty could give a more positive commitment than this if they are to abide by the existing terms of the Charter. Such a commitment, however, should serve as a powerful deterrent to a potential aggressor with nuclear arms.

Besides, if the Non-Proliferation Treaty is to have a more lasting significance, its signatories should recognise that the question of a state's withdrawal from it should not be a matter within their domestic jurisdiction to which the principle of non-intervention by the United Nations is applicable under Article 2(7) of the Charter. Article X of the treaty should therefore be deleted.

Since the Treaty on the Non-Proliferation of Nuclear Weapons is open to amendment, and its operation subject to review at intervals of five years from its entry into force in 1970, it is desirable that its nuclear power signatories, particularly the Soviet Union and the United States, the two super powers, should give serious attention to such questions. They should recognise that since the non-proliferation of nuclear weapons is a means of stabilising their preponderance of power, it is imperative that they should make their security assurances to non-nuclear-weapon states as firm as possible and initiate moves to remove the domestic jurisdiction reservation concerning withdrawal from the treaty.

Moreover, since the non-nuclear-weapon states, parties to the Non-Proliferation Treaty, have accepted a self-denying ordinance not to acquire nuclear arms, they have the right to expect that the nuclear powers, parties to the treaty, should make a more determined effort to put an end to their nuclear arms race, in accordance with their pledge under Article VI of the treaty.

Though the United States and the Soviet Union reached agreement in July 1974 to limit the deployment of antiballistic missiles to one apiece in their territories,[73] their Strategic Arms Limitations Talks on such strategic nuclear weapons as land-based inter-continental ballistic missiles and submarine-launched ballistic missiles, have achieved little. At Vladivostok in November 1974 they agreed to permit themselves 2,400 nuclear delivery systems, 1,320 of which might be equipped with multiple independently targeted reentry vehicles (MIRVS),[74] and the slow pace of their negotiations to reduce these enormously high 'ceilings' in subsequent SALT talks have dismayed the non-nuclear-weapon parties to the Non-Proliferation Treaty.[75]

Greater progress by the two super powers towards achieving significant agreements on strategic arms limitation would certainly help to produce a better atmosphere for the implementation of the Non-Proliferation Treaty. So, too, would the signing and ratification of the treaty by France and China, for without the co-operation of these states the Security Council cannot act in accordance with the principle of great power unanimity to prevent small or middle-sized powers from engaging in conflicts that might involve the use of nuclear weapons in the future, if the policy of non-proliferation does not succeed.

It is to be regretted that China and France have not signed the *Convention on the Prohibition of the Development, Production and Stockpiling of Bacteriological (Biological) and Toxin Weapons and on their Destruction,*[76] which was signed in London, Moscow and Washington on 10 April 1972, after being commended by the UN Assembly in 1971. This treaty, which at the end of 1973 had been signed by 110 states and ratified by 30,[77] was an important step towards the elimination of existing biological weapons.

Like the Treaty on the Non-Proliferation of Nuclear Weapons, this Convention on Biological Weapons makes provision for the intervention of the Security Council of the United Nations in case of violations of its terms. Article VI stipulates:

1.   Any State Party to this Convention which finds that any other State Party is acting in breach of obligations deriving from the provisions of the Convention may lodge a complaint with the Security Council of the United Nations. Such a complaint should include all possible evidence confirming its validity, as well as a request for its consideration by the Security Council.

2.   Each State Party to this Convention undertakes to co-operate in carrying out any investigation which the Security Council may initiate, in accordance with the provisions of the Charter of the United Nations, on the basis of the complaint received by the Council. The Security Council shall inform the States Parties to the Convention of the results of the investigation.

Article VIII states:

Each State Party to the Convention undertakes to provide or support assistance, in accordance with the United Nations Charter, to any Party to the Convention which so requests, if the Security Council decides that such Party has been exposed to danger as a result of the violation of the Convention.

It can be seen that complaints about violations of the Convention would have to go to the Security Council, so that it would be possible for a permanent member of that body to veto investigation of any complaint. The great power veto could also be used to prevent assistance to a party exposed to danger as a result of a violation of the Convention, which underlines the need for the collaboration of France and China in this, as in other partial arms control or disarmament treaties. France agreed to participate in the new UN disarmament committee which replaced the Conference of the Committee on Disarmament as a result of a decision of the UN Assembly, at its special session on disarmament in June 1978. This was because the chairmanship of the new committee, whose membership was to be open to the nuclear-weapon states and 32 to 35 other states, would rotate among all its members on a monthly basis, instead of being restricted to the United States and the Soviet Union, as obtained in the previous committee. But China, unlike France, did not take up its seat in the new disarmament committee when that body held its first meeting in Geneva in January 1979.

As in other treaties on partial measures of arms control and disarmaments that have been referred to in this chapter, the domestic jurisdiction reservation on withdrawal, if a state decides that 'extraordinary events, related to the subject matter of the treaty, have jeopardized the supreme interests of its country', is contained in Article XIII of the Biological Weapons Convention. Consequently, its implementation is based on the assumption that states parties to it will not invoke that clause.

As yet, agreement on a convention on the prohibition of the development, production and stockpiling of chemical weapons, and the elimination of existing supplies of such weapons, has not been attained. The development of chemical weapons is far more advanced than biological weapons, and several states, including the United States and the United Kingdom, are not prepared to accept a draft convention presented by the Soviet Union, which followed almost exactly the terms of the Biological Weapons Convention. This is because the Soviet Union has not been prepared to accept a system of strict international verification to ensure that the terms of such a treaty would not be violated. Thus Mr. David Ennals, for the United Kingdom, argued on 9 July 1974, that since 'chemical weapons are of considerable military importance... a State which possessed them would have a potential military advantage over a State which did not. Any State which commits itself to renounce CW under an international agreement must be satisfied that other states would not be able to contravene that agreement. A comprehensive prohibition which did not cater for the need of the signatories to be assured of other States' compliance would bring risks of military instability and might have results of the utmost gravity'.[78]

It should be noted, however, that the communique issued by the Soviet Union and the United States on 3 July 1974, stated that 'both sides reaffirmed their interest in an effective international agreement which would exclude from the arsenals of states such dangerous instruments of mass destruction as chemical weapons. Desiring to contribute to early progress in this direction, the USA and the USSR agreed to consider a joint initiative in the Conference of the Committee on Disarmament with respect to the conclusion, as a first step, of an international convention dealing with the most dangerous, lethal means of chemical warfare'.[79]

Conclusions

The history of the United Nations has shown that it has only been possible to achieve a political consensus in support of peacekeeping forces with limited functions, which bear little resemblance to the kind of United Nations Peace Force that would be necessary to enforce a treaty providing for large scale general disarmament. Even if, under such a treaty, states were permitted to retain only limited armed forces with light firearms to maintain internal order, a very powerful United Nations force would still be required because it has not been possible to devise an effective system of international inspection to detect hidden stocks of nuclear weapons, which could be used by a potential aggressor. 'What is inexorably certain,' as Sir Michael Wright, the leader of the British delegation to the Geneva Disarmament Conferences from 1959 to 1963, has asserted, 'is that a peace-keeping force of the kind so far advocated by the Soviet Union, composed of national contingents and with no integrated international structure, with a veto at the troika command level, a veto in the Security Council upon its use, and debarred in advance from possessing any nuclear weapons, would be wholly ineffective'[80]

Sir Michael Wright has pointed out that 'on the face of it there are at least three possible alternatives to leaving to the Security Council, as at present constituted and with its present voting system, the power to use and direct a peace-keeping force in a disarmed world. The first is to amend the Charter so that in this context the Security Council could take a decision by a two-thirds or conceivably a majority vote, without the power of veto for any state. The second possibility is to place the responsibility upon the U.N. Assembly, perhaps by a two-thirds vote. This again would presumably involve amendment of the Charter since it would mean giving to the Assembly responsibilities placed by the Charter on the Security Council. The third alternative would be to agree upon some specially constituted body. This would entail by-passing the existing provisions of the United Nations Charter and perhaps even the U.N. Organization altogether'.[81] But it has to be recognised, as he has emphasised, that 'the United States and the United Kingdom have shown themselves willing to explore the various possibilities involved, while the Soviet Union has so far set its face rigidly against any amendment of the Charter, or any by-passing of the Charter which would involve the abolition or the weakening of the Soviet power of veto. Yet without agreement on precisely this, the whole concept of general and complete disarmament carried out in three consecutive and uninterrupted stages is most unlikely to be realized, and it is misleading to pretend otherwise'.[82]

In brief, then, great power agreement on the means of transforming the United Nations into a political institution with sufficient powers to control a peacekeeping force so strong that no state could challenge it, as proposed in the United States 1962 draft treaty on general and complete disarmament, and without which the parties to such a treaty could not be afforded adequate security, must be regarded as outside the range of practical politics. Consequently, large scale general disarmament must be considered a remote objective, and it is sensible to recognise that the only practicable objectives that can be envisaged are partial measures of arms control and disarmament. Indeed, this has been tacitly recognised by the U.N. Assembly, and the disarmament committees linked to it, for the past decade, since negotiations in Geneva during this period have been devoted almost exclusively to partial measures.

Under some of the agreements which have been concluded, the United Nations Security Council, or institutions linked to the United Nations, have been given the competence to exercise certain powers, though in all the treaties which have come into force, states parties to them can still exercise their domestic jurisdiction to withdraw from them if they decide that their national interests are jeopardised. This is a basic weakness in such agreements, and particularly so in the important Treaty on the Non-Proliferation of Nuclear Weapons, for not only does it give a loophole to any non-nuclear-weapon state, party to it, to embark on a nuclear arms programme if it decides that its national interest dictates such a course of action, but also provides a means for any nuclear power, party to the treaty, to evade its obligation not to transfer nuclear weapons to a non-nuclear-weapon state or to assist that state in the manufacture of such weapons. It is desirable, therefore, that the domestic jurisdiction reservation on withdrawal from the treaty should be deleted.

It is also important that the security assurances under Security Council resolution 255 (1968) should be included in the Non-Proliferation Treaty itself in order to inspire confidence that great power protection would be forthcoming to non-nuclear weapon states in the event of aggression with nuclear arms or the threat of such aggression. This may help to induce those non-nuclear-weapon states, who have not ratified the treaty, or not entered into agreements with the International Atomic Energy Agency on safeguards to take such steps.

The safeguards agreements between the International Atomic Energy Agency and non-nuclear-weapon states, parties to the Non-Proliferation Treaty on Nuclear Weapons, which involve the use of the Agency's inspectors to verify whether such agreements are being complied with, may well serve as a pattern for verification procedures in other possible arms control agreements. Certainly, the services of an international agency would be necessary to negotiate safeguards agreements with parties to a convention on chemical weapons, and such agreements should provide that states take the necessary steps to ensure that the international agency's inspectors could effectively discharge their functions. Only in this way would it be possible for the Security Council to have reliable information on evasions and violations of the convention.

Of course, the limited moves to detente between the Soviet Union and the United States have made possible the partial arms control treaties which have hitherto been concluded, and there must be a further easing of tension if these agreements are to be improved and new agreements entered into. Moreover, it is essential that all the permanent members of the UN Security Council should be parties to them and actively interested in their implementation. Their co-operation must be forthcoming if we are to see the realisation of that limited form of collective security, based on the unanimity of the permanent members of the Security Council, which the architects of the Charter regarded as the framework for the regulation and reduction of national armaments.

VII. THE ROLE OF THE UN AND ITS SPECIALISED AGENCIES IN THE ECONOMIC, SOCIAL AND RELATED FIELDS, WITH SPECIAL REFERENCE TO THE NON-INTERVENTION PRINCIPLE

The Competence of the UN and its Specialised Agencies in the Economic, Social and Related Fields

At the San Francisco Conference in 1945 it was agreed that member-states of the United Nations should pledge themselves to take joint and separate action, in co-operation with the Organisation, to promote higher standards of living, full employment, and conditions of economic and social progress and development.[1] This did not mean that member-states were required to accept international legal obligations which would have removed matters in the economic and social fields from their domestic jurisdiction. In fact, in order to dispel doubts about this, the members of Committee II(3) of the San Francisco Conference declared that nothing contained in Chapter IX of the Charter (International Economic and Social Co-operation) or in Chapter X (The Economic and Social Council) could be construed as giving authority to the United Nations to intervene in the domestic affairs of member-states;[2] and, as explained earlier,[3] it was decided at San Francisco that in order to safeguard member-states from any form of UN interference in their economic and social policies, the principle of non-intervention in matters essentially within the domestic jurisdiction of states should be included as Article 2(7) of the Charter. Moreover, under the exception to the general principle of non-intervention laid down in Article 2(7), the competence of the Security Council was restricted to authorising enforcement measures to maintain or restore international peace and security if it determined that the situation arising out of the economic or social policy of a state, or any other matter essentially within its domestic jurisdiction, constituted a threat to the peace, breach of the peace, or act of aggression.

There has been some controversy over the question whether the costs of the UN's operations in the ecnomic and social fields may be considered expenses of the Organisation under Article 17 of the Charter, and thus subject to binding apportionment by the Assembly, the organ empowered to consider and approve the UN budget.[4] In practice, however, the major activities of the UN in the economic and social fields have been financed from the voluntary contributions of member-states, a matter which will be referred to later in this chapter.

The competence of the Assembly, the organ vested with the main responsibility for promoting international economic and social co-operation under Article 60 of the Charter, in which each state has one vote and whose decisions on substantive matters are arrived at by a simple majority or a two-thirds majority according to the importance of the question,[5] is limited under Article 13 to initiating studies and making non-mandatory recommendations on economic and social matters over which UN members have legislative powers. No reference is made in the Article to whom the Assembly's recommendations may be made, but in the light of the discussions in Committee I/1 of the San Francisco Conference, it would appear that those who drafted the principle of non-intervention in matters essentially within the domestic jurisdiction of states did not intend that the Assembly should be competent to make recommendations on economic and social matters that would cause embarrassment to particular states. Recommendations addressed to UN member-states in general, to promote international economic and social co-operation, were the kind apparently envisaged.[6]

Under Article 62 of the Charter, the Economic and Social Council, which is designed to promote economic and social welfare under the authority of the Assembly, and to arrive at its decisions by a majority of members present and voting,[7] with each member having one vote,[8] has the authority to make or initiate studies and reports with respect to international economic, social, cultural, educational, health, and related matters: to make recommendations with respect to any such matters to the Assembly, to the members of the United Nations and to the specialised agencies concerned: to make recommendations for the purpose of promoting respect for, and observance of, human rights and fundamental freedoms for all: to prepare draft conventions for submission to the Assembly, with respect to matters falling within its competence: and to call, in accordance with the rules prescribed by the United Nations, international conferences on matters falling within its competence.

The question of the Economic and Social Council's competence to make recommendations for the purpose of promoting respect for, and observance of, human rights and fundamental freedoms for all, as well as UN practice in that field, was discussed in a previous chapter.[9] But two points need to be mentioned concerning matters connected with Article 62.

First, unlike Article 13, which does not state to whom the Assembly may make recommendations on economic, social and related matters, Article 62 stipulates that recommendations on such matters may be made not only to the Assembly and specialised agencies, but also to member-states of the United Nations. This presumably implies that recommendations may be addressed by the Economic and Social Council to particular states, but in the light of the discussions that led to the formulation of Article 2(7) of the Charter at San Francisco, such recommendations would not be permissible if they were intended as a censure on a state's economic or social policies. Secondly, the acceptance by states of international legal obligations under conventions drawn up by the Economic and Social Council and approved by the Assembly, depends upon their ratification of such conventions, in consonance with the principle of consent, otherwise the principle of non-intervention in matters essentially within their domestic jurisdiction would be contravened.

The obligations accepted by member-states of the various specialised agencies which have been brought into relationship with the United Nations, in accordance with Articles 57 and 63 of the Charter, are also based on the principle of consent, since these agencies are the products of multilateral treaties to which states are not obliged to be parties.[10] The decisions taken by the organs of such inter-governmental institutions, some of which may be binding on their members under agreed constitutional procedures, do not, therefore, conflict with the principle of non-intervention essentially within the domestic jurisdiction of states.

Under Article 63(2) of the Charter the Economic and Social Council is empowered to 'co-ordinate the activities of the specialised agencies through consultation with and recommendations to such agencies and through recommendations to the General Assembly and to the Members of the United Nations'. In brief, then, 'the United Nations was committed to the concept of a "hub" organization and a group of autonomous "Specialized Agencies", looking to the United Nations proper for co-ordination and guidance but enjoying essential freedom of action in their respective fields'.[11]

To a greater or lesser extent the specialised agencies, which have been brought into relationship with the United Nations through special agreements under Article 63 of the Charter, possess more effective powers than the essentially recommendatory competence of the United Nations Assembly and the Economic and Social Council,[12] and the following examples indicate the limitations on the domestic jurisdiction of states which membership of some of these institutions entails.

Some specialised agencies, such as the World Health Organisation (WHO), have the authority to issue regulations of a mandatory character which give them, in effect, a legislative function. For instance, under Article 21 of WHO's constitution, the Health Assembly of that agency has the power to adopt regulations concerning sanitary quarantine requirements and other procedures to prevent the international spread of disease. These regulations are binding on members after due notice has been given of their adoption by the Health Assembly, except for such members as may notify the Director-General of rejection or reservations within the period stated in the notice, as laid down in Article 22.[13] Despite the fact that members may opt out of the regulations concerned, it is still permissible to refer to them as mandatory regulations, and it may be asserted that 'to attribute to international organs power to take regulatory action of mandatory character is to invest them in effect with legislative functions, and to run counter to the principle of state sovereignty'.[14]

Under its Articles of Agreement which were drawn up at Bretton Woods in 1944,[15] the International Monetary Fund was given a significant role to promote exchange stability and to maintain orderly exchange arrangements among its members.

It was stipulated in Article IV of the Articles of Agreement that each member undertook to establish and maintain an agreed par value for its currency and to consult the Fund on any change in excess of 10 per cent of the initial parity; and under Article III it was laid down that the subscription of each member, payable partly in gold and partly in the member's own currency, would be equal to an assigned quota that would determine its voting power and the amount of foreign exchange that could be drawn from the Fund when faced by temporary balance of payments difficulties. But at various stages in the history of the Fund, reviews of the members' quotas have led to general and selective increases in subscriptions, and various expedients have been used to provide additional resources for members in temporary balance of payments difficulties.[16] Moreover, 'hardly a single rule created by the Fund at Bretton Woods and after for governing international monetary behaviour has not had to be changed or bent in some degree during the Fund's career as an organization for rule supervision'.[17] For instance, the Fund has had to allow members with no par values to use its resources, and to tolerate fluctuating or 'floating' exchange rates.[18]

Nevertheless, it must be appreciated that in accepting the Articles of Agreement of the International Monetary Fund, its member-states may be faced with significant limitations of their domestic jurisdiction over monetary matters provided the procedures laid down in the constitution are followed. Article XII (Section 2g) stipulates that 'the Board of Governors, and the Executive Directors to the extent authorised, may adopt such rules and regulations as may be necessary or appropriate to conduct the business of the Fund'; and under Article XV (Section 2a) 'if a member fails to fulfil any of its obligations under this Agreement, the Fund may declare the member ineligible to use the resources of the Fund'. Furthermore, under Article XVIII(a), 'any question of interpretation of the provisions of this Agreement arising between any member and the Fund or between any Members of the Fund shall be submitted to the Executive Directors for their decision . . .'; and under (b) of the same article, 'in any case where the Executive Directors have given a decision under (a) above, any member may require that the question be referred to the Board of Governors, whose decision shall be final . . .' Indeed, under Article XV (Section 2b) a member may be required to withdraw from membership in the Fund by a decision of the Board of Governors which, like the Board of Executive Directors, is empowered to operate in accordance with the system of weighted voting and thus provides the largest contributors to the Fund a proportionate influence over the policy of the organisation.

Under an amendment to the Articles of Agreement, which was approved by the IMF's Board of Governors in 1968, it was agreed to establish Special

Drawing Rights in the Fund.[19] These Special Drawing Rights (SDRs) were a form of international currency which could be used by states in settling balance of payments deficits as a substitute for gold, for the supply of gold, relative to the monetary needs of states, had declined, and it was recognised that the expansion of credit through this means was necessary.

The first allocation of SDRs equivalent to 3.5 billion dollars was made to 104 participants in the Special Drawing Account on 1 January 1970, when their valuation was based on gold at the rate of .888671 grains per SDR. Later their valuation was defined as a basket of the 16 currencies of countries that did 1 per cent or more of world trade.

It should be noted that the introduction of these Special Drawing Rights increased the quotas of the members of the International Monetary Fund without any additional subscription either in gold or in national currencies, but the decision by the IMF regarding the allocation and size of SDRs required an 85% majority of voting power of the participating states. Moreover, of special importance was the fact that with the allocation of SDRs by the International Monetary Fund, the total stock of international reserves as well as its rate of growth reflected 'deliberate international decisions', rather than their determination 'solely by the availability of gold for offical reserves and the accumulation of reserve currencies'.[20] Indeed, in January 1976, the inter-ministerial committee of the IMF agreed at Kingston, Jamaica, to end the official role of gold in the IMF and its replacement at the centre of the monetary system by the special drawing right.[21]

The International Bank for Reconstruction and Development (IBRD), whose Articles of Agreement,[22] like those of the International Monetary Fund, were formulated at Bretton Woods in 1944, was established, as stated in Article 1:

> to assist in the reconstruction and development of territories of members by facilitating the investment of capital for productive purposes, including the restoration of economies destroyed or disrupted by war, the reconversion of productive facilities to peacetime needs and the encouragement of the development of productive facilities and resources in less developed countries.

> to promote private foreign investment by means of guarantees or participations in loans and other investments made by private investors; and when private capital is not available on reasonable terms, to supplement private investment by providing, on suitable conditions, finance for productive purposes out of its own capital, funds raised by it and its other resources.

In brief, the International Bank obtains its financial resources from the subscriptions of its member-states, from borrowings in the capital markets of the world, and from the earnings that it acquires from its lending operations, as explained in Articles II, III and IV. It is authorised to make loans to any member-state, or any political division thereof, and any business, industrial, and agricultural enterprise in the territories of a member, when it is 'satisfied that in the prevailing market conditions the borrower would be unable otherwise to obtain the loan under conditions which in the opinion of the Bank are reasonable for the borrower', and subject to other conditions stipulated in Article III (Section 4).

Voting rights of the member-states are related to their subscriptions to the capital stock of the Bank, as stipulated in Article V (Section 4), and under Article V (Section 2), 'the Board of Governors, and the Executive Directors to the extent authorized, may adopt such rules and regulations as may be necessary or appropriate to conduct the business of the Bank'. Moreover, under Article IX the Board of Governors has the right of final decision in respect of any question of interpretation of the Articles of Agreement between any member and the Bank or between any members of the Bank, and this applies to its affiliates, the International Finance Corporation (IFC) and the International Development Association (IDA), to which reference will be made later in this chapter. The organs of these agencies thus possess the competence to make decisions that are legally binding;[23] and under Article VI, Section 2, 'if a member fails to fulfil any of its obligations to the Bank, the Bank may suspend its membership by decision of a majority of the Governors, exercising a majority of the total voting power'.

From these examples illustrating some of the powers of specialised agencies in the economic and social fields, it can be seen that several of these institutions were designed to operate under constitutions which invested them with greater authority than the essentially recommendatory competence of the UN Assembly and Economic and Social Council. Clearly, whilst the general principle of non-intervention in matters essentially within the domestic jurisdiction of states was included in the Charter to prohibit the Assembly and the Economic and Social Council from taking binding decisions on economic and social matters, it was nevertheless recognised in the Charter that it was desirable for its state-signatories to co-operate in autonomous agencies which might possess the competence to take mandatory decisions to enable the process of international economic and social co-operation to be conducted more effectively. Of course, since the obligations accepted by states through the membership of such agencies had to depend on their ratification of multilateral treaties, in accordance with the principle of consent, they had no reason to complain that any limitations of their domestic jurisdiction as members of such institutions would conflict with the principle of non-intervention under Article 2(7) of the Charter.

It should be appreciated that the legal obligations of member-states of some specialised agencies are considerably more limited than those assumed by states that belong to the international financial agencies referred to above. For instance, 'the legal obligations of member states immediately under the constitution of UNESCO are few and slight. To a certain extent, the functions of the institution are exercised by the conclusion of international conventions on specific subjects. The procedure prescribed is that the General Conference adopts the text of the convention which member states must then submit to the competent national authorities with a view to ratification. This legal technique is modelled on that of the I.L.O., although not yet developed to the same degree of efficiency as in that institution'.[24] Above all, however, it must be realised that implementation of the conventions adopted by the Conferences of specialised agencies or special international conferences depends on the consent of national authorities to ratify them.

The Abortive International Trade Organisation

Though the Soviet Union was represented at the United Nations Monetary and Financial Conference at Bretton Woods in 1944, it did not consent to ratify the Articles of Agreement for the establishment of the International Monetary Fund and the International Bank for Reconstruction and Development, which were designed to play important roles in achieving international solutions to economic and monetary problems in the post-war world. The Soviet Union 'did not take the same interest in the economic and social aspects of the new organization's work as in the political. This was certainly understandable in the light of the Communists' view of the nature of capitalism and their conviction of the inevitability of its destruction'.[25]

In contrast to the Soviet Union, the United States was prepared to participate as the principal subscriber to the International Bank and the International Monetary Fund, though under the system of weighted voting in those institutions it was assured a major influence in their decision making processes. But the United States did not ratify the Havana Charter for the establishment of an International Trade Organisation which many states hoped would be able to deal not only with the question of tariffs and other trade barriers, but also with several other issues connected with international trade, employment, and the economic development of states.

The Havana Charter, which was signed by fifty-three states in March 1948 at the conclusion of a United Nations Conference on Trade and Employment — the Soviet Union did not particpate — outlined the objectives of the projected International Trade Organisation in its first chapter, as follows:[26]

> to assure a large and steadily growing volume of real income and effective demand, to increase production, consumption, and exchange of goods, and to contribute to a balanced and expanding economy;

to promote industrial and general economic development, particularly of those countries which are still in the early stages of industrial development, and to encourage the international flow of capital for productive investment;

to further the enjoyment of all countries on equal terms, of access to the markets, products, and productive facilities which are needed for their economic prosperity and development;

to promote on a reciprocal and mutually advantageous basis the reduction of tariffs and other barriers to trade and the elimination of discriminatory treatment in international commerce;

to enable countries, by increasing the opportunities for their trade and economic development, to abstain from measures which disrupt world commerce, reduce productive employment, or retard economic progress;

to facilitate the solution of problems relating to international trade in the fields of employment, economic development, commercial policy, business practices and commodity policy.

The International Trade Organisation was thus envisaged as a specialised agency with the broad purpose of achieving a balanced and expanding world economy based on a system of multilateral trading affording the fullest and freest exchange of goods and services. It was designed to deal with a wide range of economic matters, including the reduction of tariffs, quotas and related trade barriers, the maintenance of high levels of employment, inter-governmental commodity agreements to stablilise price fluctuations of primary products, restrictive business practices such as some practices of international cartels, the various aspects of foreign investments, the reconstruction of war-devastated countries and economic development, particularly of under-developed countries, and the settlement of trade disputes.

That such matters as inter-governmental commodity agreements and the economic development of under-developed countries were included in the terms of reference of the projected International Trade Organisation, indicated the influence of the thirty or so developing countries that participated in the drafting of the Havana Charter. Their ecnomic growth, upon which their social progress so much depended, required stable and adequate prices for their exportable primary products to ensure a steady return of foreign exchange earnings. They were also particularly interested in the expanded flow of international capital for productive investment to enable them to diversify their economies.

As provided in the Havana Charter, it was intended that the projected International Trade Organisation would work through a Conference, consisting of representatives of its member-states, vested with the final authority to determine the policies of the organisation: an Executive Board composed of eighteen members — eight representative of those states of chief economic importance and ten selected by the Conference to represent states at different levels of economic development; and a Secretariat headed by a Secretary-General. The voting procedure for the Conference and the Executive Board, unlike the weighted voting system that obtained in the International Bank and the International Monetary Fund, was based on the principle of one vote per member, and decisions were to be determined by a simple majority unless a greater majority was called for under the constitution, e.g. a decision by the Conference to waive, in exceptional circumstances, an obligation imposed on a member under the rules of membership, required a two-thirds majority. As to the settlement of trade disputes, it was laid down that if a party to a dispute did not wish to carry out a decision of the International Trade Organisation, it could withdraw from the Organisation, but in so doing it would be no longer entitled to the benefits that the members extended to one another.

Though the United States Administration signed the Havana Charter for the establishment of the International Trade Organisation, it did not submit the Charter to the Congress for ratification, since the latter was sharply divided over its provisions — 'the traditional protectionist lobbies objected to its free trade content, while the free traders objected to its protectionist elements'.[27] Besides, the fact that the projected International Trade Organisation's voting system was not based on the weighted voting system of the IMF and the IBRD militated against its birth, since the leading trading countries, particularly the United States, would not have had such a dominant position in the decision making process, and might well have been obliged to implement unpalatable decisions on matters which membership of the organisation had removed from the sphere of their domestic jurisdiction.

But though the establishment of an international trade organisation, with wide responsibilities for facilitating the solution of problems in the fields of employment, economic development, commodity and commercial policies, etc., proved abortive, twenty three states that participated in the negotiations for the reduction of tariffs in Geneva in 1947, under the sponsorship of the Preparatory Committee appointed by the Economic and Social Council to prepare the draft of the Havana Charter, became the original contracting parties to the General Agreement on Tariffs and Trade (GATT).[28]

Under this multilateral treaty,[29] which embodied reciprocal rights and obligations, it was laid down that trade should be conducted on a non-discriminatory basis. Thus tariff reductions granted by one of the contracting parties to another had to be extended to all other parties in accordance with the most-favoured nation clause. The use of import quotas as a means of protecting domestic industries was prohibited, except for certain purposes, such as their use to assist a country faced with balance of payments difficulties. But the circumstances in which they could be employed were governed by strict conditions in order to minimise any damage to the trade of other countries. Provision was also made in the Agreement to limit the freedom of governments to grant export subsidies and to prevent dumping by permitting importing countries to levy anti-dumping duties. But Part IV of the Agreement, designed to expand the trade of less-developed countries, facilitating the growth of their export earnings, and thus promoting more rapid economic development, was not included until 1965.

The obligations accepted by the contracting parties to GATT constituted an agreed code to govern their trading relationships, and representatives of the parties were required to meet periodically to deal with matters that called for joint action, including the conciliation of disputes. In fact, they were empowered, if conciliation failed, not only to make a recommendation or give a ruling in a dispute, but also to authorise the withdrawal of concessions enjoyed by a disputant if it refused to accept a ruling approved by a majority of the contracting parties, on the basis of one vote per member.

But though the establishment of the GATT system in 1948 was an important development in the liberalisation of international trade, it 'did not contain the comprehensive provisions on commodity agreements, foreign investment, and restrictive business practices that had been contained in the ITO Charter, and the less developed countries became convinced that their interests required the creation of a forum for the comprehensive review of trade and development policy. Perhaps even more important was the fact that the developing countries considered the preoccupation of GATT with the reduction of trade barriers and the elimination of discrimination as largely irrelevant to — or even inconsistent with — their interests in development'.[30]

Boyd Orr's Advocacy of a World Food Board

Undoubtedly, the lack of a comprehensive international trade organisation was but one of the deficiencies of the UN system of institutionalised international co-operation in the economic and social fields which soon became apparent during the early years of the Organisation. Though the financial agencies, the International Monetary Fund and the International Bank, possessed more effective powers of control over their members than those exercised by the UN Assembly and the Economic and Social Council, they were handicapped by the limited financial resources placed at their disposal by those states that could afford to provide more and the non-involvement of the Soviet Union. Other agencies, such as the Food and Agriculture Organisation, were restricted in their work of advancing the economic and social objectives of the Charter, not only because of scant financial resources, but also because their competence was not much greater than the essentially recommendatory competence of the UN Assembly and Economic and Social Council.

It was because of these deficiencies that Sir John (later Lord) Boyd Orr, the first Director of the Food and Agriculture Organisation (FAO), urged in 1946 the creation of a World Food Board, consisting of representatives of the FAO itself, the International Bank for Reconstruction and Development and other specialised agencies, and the Economic and Social Council, with wide enough powers and sufficient financial resources to effect an increase in the total production of food and to stablilise prices at equitable levels to both producers and consumers. Provision was made in his plan for the World Food Board to have funds available to purchase surplus food stocks in years of good harvests so that it would have reserve or buffer stocks which it could distribute, in times of scarcity, to needy countries at special prices.[31] As Lord Boyd Orr commented on his plan: 'Such a global food plan would have given ample scope for all the powers of modern science to be applied to constructive ends. The great expansion of agriculture called for in the proposals would have created a demand for vast quantities of agricultural equipment and other industrial products for irrigation, flood control, measures to stop soil erosion. This would have brought about the rapidly expanding world economy needed to provide full employment in all countries'.[32]

Though the Boyd Orr proposals were accepted with American support when they were first presented, and a preparatory commission was set up to report on measures for their implementation, they were rejected by the United States delegate at a meeting of the commission in Washington at the end of October 1946. As G.D.H. Cole pointed out at the time, '. . . as in the course of 1946, the United States swung back violently to an uncontrolled economy, the American attitude changed, both because they were felt to involve too much state intervention and because it was realised that the main task of financing the scheme would necessarily fall on the United States'.[33]

Thus, the attempt to establish a World Food Board, with the power and funds to purchase and hold surplus food stocks which could be distributed to needy countries at low prices, as occasion demanded, was abandoned early in 1947, and all that was agreed to was the setting up of a World Food Council with the authority to advise exporting states who retained their right of independent action with regard to the sale and distribution of food surpluses. Moreover, after the rejection of the World Food Board plan, progress towards inter-governmental agreements on primary food products was 'slow, painful and piecemeal, much of it conducted outside the UN'.[34]

The Soviet Union, which was not a member of the Food and Agriculture Organisation, did not participate in the discussion of proposals for a World Food Board. As already mentioned, at that time the Soviet government showed no desire to become involved in the UN system of international econmic and social co-operation, and in the atmosphere of the 'cold war' the UN's Economic Commission for Europe played a minor role in the re-construction of the war-devastated countries of Western and Eastern Europe. Besides, the participation of East European countries in the Marshall plan was opposed by Stalin, though the plan was originally intended for the whole of Europe, and it was implemented by the Organisation for European Economic Co-operation (OEEC), outside the framework of the UN system. Furthermore, since the rival great powers treated aid to non-aligned countries very largely as a means of extending their spheres of influence or improving their systems of defence, the amount of technical and financial assistance to developing countries on a bilateral basis, i.e. from one government to another, far exceeded the assistance given on a multilateral basis through the UN and its specialised agencies. In fact, in the early 1970s only about 10% was handled by the UN and related institutions, including the International Bank,[35] and this should be borne in mind in our appraisal of the UN's role in helping the economic and social development of underdeveloped countries, with special reference to the principle of non-intervention in matters essentially within the domestic jurisdiction of states, which we shall now consider.

The UN System of International Aid to Developing Countries in Practice

Before we appraise the main landmarks in the UN system of aiding developing countries to accelerate their economic and social progress, it is necessary to examine in greater detail the fiscal powers of the UN Assembly under Article 17 of the Charter, and to assess whether these powers negate the principle of non-intervention in matters essentially within the domestic jurisdiction of states under Article 2(7) of the Charter.

It is laid down in Article 17 of the Charter that 'the General Assembly shall consider and approve the budget of the Organization' and that 'the expenses of the Organization shall be borne by the Members as apportioned by the General Assembly'. Thus, since no distinction is made in these clauses between the administrative expenses of the Organiszation, on the one hand, and the expenses of peacekeeping operations of a non-coercive nature or operational activities in the economic, social and related fields, on the other hand, it has been argued that the Assembly has the competence, by two-thirds majority vote, to apportion the expenses for its operational programmes as legally binding obligations on the entire membership of the UN. Indeed, this was asserted in the interpretation put forward in 1962 by the majority of judges of the International Court of Justice on the competence of the Assembly with regard to the financing of UN's peacekeeping operations; and to reinforce this argument it was pointed out in the majority opinion that from the inception of the UN, expenses for its operational programmes of technical assistance, advisory social welfare and human rights services, narcotic drug control, etc. had been borne by member-states as apportioned by the Assembly under the regular budget, in accordance with the two-thirds majority rule.[36] It should be noted, however, that these operational programmes were of a minor character which did not involve large scale payments by UN members, and that the financing of the major operational programmes, such as the United Nations International Children's Emergency Fund (UNICEF), approved by the Assembly in 1946,[37] and the Expanded Programme of Technical Assistance established in 1949,[38] had been financed from voluntary contributions outside the normal budget of the UN.

In effect, therefore, the majority opinion of the International Court asserted that the principle of non-intervention in matters essentially within the domestic jurisdiction of states, under Article 2(7) of the Charter, did not prohibit the Assembly from making binding decisions, if approved by a two-thirds majority, on how the expenses for the UN's operational activities in the economic and social fields should be borne by all member-states, whether such programmes were of a major or minor character.

This interpretation of the powers of the Assembly was opposed by some of the judges of the International Court. For instance, President Winiarski maintained that since the Assembly's resolutions approving operational activities had only recommendatory force, they did not impose legal obligations on states to participate in them or to share in their cost. Certainly it is difficult to see how this view can be refuted, otherwise the Assembly would be competent to impose large scale taxation on states that were not in favour of major operational programmes in the economic and social fields, which would be difficult to reconcile with the principle of non-intervention in matters essentially within the domestic jurisdiction of states.

In practice, as already mentioned, except for some minor items financed under the regular UN budget, the operational activities of the UN in the economic and social fields have depended upon the voluntary contributions of member-states, so that the question of determining the amount of aid to developing countries under the auspices of the UN has been regarded as a matter essentially within the domestic jurisdiction of states, and largely depended upon the generosity of the wealthy economically advanced countries. Moreover, under the system of weighted voting in the organs of the International Bank, the wealthy states have possessed the voting power to determine the size of the loans and the rates of interest to developing countries.

During the early years of the UN, the financial resources at the disposal of the Organisation and its specialised agencies for waging the battle against hunger, disease, poverty and ignorance were very limited. The Expanded Technical Assistance Programme (EPTA) established by the Assembly in 1949, which depended on extra-budgetary funds contributed voluntarily by members of the UN or the specialised agencies, amounted to only about 25 million dollars per annum during the period 1950-59, though the programme was intended to provide expert assistance in such varied fields as health, education, special training in modern techniques, transport and communication.[39]

Such technical assistance to the developing countries was an essential prelude, of course, to new schemes of economic and social development. But, as Mr. Santa Cruz, the Chilean delegate at the Assembly's 4th regular session in 1949, pointed out, 'the most extensive natural resources and the most perfect techniques could not develop a country if it had not sufficient capital to increase productivity', and he emphasised the need for a new, bold approach to the problem of financing economic development.[40]

At this time the International Bank had very limited funds, and poor under-developed countries found it difficult, if not impossible, to borrow at the commercial rates of interest called for. Moreover, 'in its early days it was firm doctrine that the only kind of project which the Bank would even look at was a specific piece of fixed capital investment showing a measurable rate of return',[41] and this prevented developing countries from obtaining loans to meet the capital costs of roads, communications, schools, hospitals, and other non-revenue earning projects for their economic and social development. Consequently, moves were made within the UN to effect the establishment of a capital development fund, and in 1952 an expert committee was appointed by the Secretary-General to report on the matter to the Assembly.

The SUNFED Scheme

The report of the Committee, which appeared in 1953,[42] recommended the creation of a Special United Nations Fund for Economic Development to provide grants and long-term, low interest loans for the financing of suitable projects in developing countries. It proposed that those states prepared to contribute to the fund should meet annually to pledge their contributions in their own currencies, and that the fund should not be established until the equivalent of 250 million dollars had been pledged for an initial two-year period. Furthermore, it was stressed in the report that the fund should not be operated to permit interference in the internal affairs of the recipient countries.

It is significant that the expert committee did not recommend that the proposed SUNFED should be financed out of UN's regular budget, as decided by the Assembly and apportioned by that body as a legally binding decision on the membership under Article 17 of the Charter, which the majority opinion of the International Court in 1962, as explained earlier, implied was not a contravention of the principle of non-intervention in matters essentially within the domestic jurisdiction of states. What the committee recommended was that SUNFED should be financed as an operational programme out of extra-budgetary funds, like EPTA and UNICEF, so that the financial contributions of UN member-states would be voluntary.

But most of the developed countries, whose support was vital for the financing of a capital development fund from voluntary contributions, were not prepared to participate in the SUNFED scheme. Their delegates in the Economic and Social Council and the Assembly stated that their countries were not in a position at that juncture to assume any additional financial burdens. United States spokesmen declared that the U.S. would be prepared to increase its financial contrbutions to establish a UN capital development fund when savings had been made possible through international agreement on disarmament, and doubt was expressed in the statements of Soviet delegates whether much could be achieved by the creation of SUNFED. It was the Soviet view that foreign financial aid should only be used to supplement domestic resources and earnings from more favourable terms of international trade for developing countries.[43]

At the end of the debate on the SUNFED scheme in the Assembly, a resolution was approved by a large majority which reflected the American view,[44] and the President of the Economic and Social Council, with the assistance of the Secretary-General of the UN, was asked to consult with governments with a view to making recommendations to facilitate the creation of a capital development fund, as circumstances permitted.[45] The question of establishing SUNFED from voluntary contributions was thus shelved.

The Special Fund

The setting-up of the International Finance Corporation, an affiliate of the International Bank, to advance the economic development of developing countries through investing in private enterprises where sufficient capital was not available, did not lessen the agitation of those countries for the creation of a UN capital development fund to provide grants and long-term, low interest loans for major investment projects. But though this agitation did not succeed in influencing the developed countries to co-operate in establishing such a fund, a consensus did emerge in the Assembly, in 1958, for the creation of the UN Special Fund to finance pre-investment projects in developing countries, such as surveys of natural resources and research schemes.[46]

Under the rules of the Special Fund, for which the equivalent of approximately 26 million and 38½ million dollars were pledged in 1959 and 1960 respectively,[47] the conditions on which the pre-investment projects were to be undertaken were laid down in basic agreements signed by the Special Fund's representatives and the governments that requested assistance. It was also stipulated in the rules that the approval of projects recommended by the Special Fund's Managing Director required a two-thirds majority in the Fund's Governing Council, which consisted of the representatives of nine donor and nine recipient countries appointed by the Economic and Social Council. But though the donor countries had sufficient voting power to prevent a two-thirds majority, in practice 'the Governing Council of the Fund never voted but carried out its business by arriving always at a consensus'.[48] It was thus recognised, in effect, that the UN's principle of non-intervention or non-interference in matters essentially within the domestic jurisdiction of states should govern the operation of the Special Fund, for the financial contributions to the Fund depended on the consent of the contributing states, and the UN had no authority to impose the services provided under the terms of the Fund on the developing countries.

The Assembly's 'Development Decade' Resolution

Since the Special Fund was limited to the financing of pre-investment projects and research schemes, its establishment did little to lessen the agitation of the developing countries for large scale UN assistance to finance investment projects to speed up their economic and social development.

Though the International Development Association (IDA), an affiliate of the International Bank, was set up in 1960 to provide developing countries with long term loans on easier terms than those being made by the International Bank, the new agency 'fairly quickly ran through most of the not very large sum of money with which it had initially been endowed'.[49] Besides, though the Assembly, in 1961, unanimously approved a resolution designating the 1960s as the UN Development Decade with the aim of effecting in each developing country a minimum annual growth rate of 5% in aggregate national income by the end of the Decade, and called upon the members of the UN, *inter alia*, 'to pursue policies designed to enable the less developed countries and those dependent on the export of primary commodities to sell more of their products at stable and remunerative prices in expanding markets, and thus to finance increasingly their own economic development from their earnings of foreign exchange and domestic savings',[50] the response of the developed countries did not match up to what was required of them under the resolution.

Of course, though the unanimous adoption of the Assembly's resolution was an expression of the moral commitment of the economically advanced countries to provide the developing countries with greater financial aid and better terms of trade, it imposed no legal obligations upon them to carry out such policies. Since the Assembly did not possess the authority to legislate or enforce measures of economic and social co-operation, the implementation of the resolution was dependent on the consent of states, in consonance with the principle of non-intervention in matters essentially within the domestic jurisdiction of states.

A report prepared by the Secretary-General of the UN on proposals for the intensification of action in the fields of economic and social development by the UN system of organisations, which was requested by the Assembly under its 'Development Decade' resolution, was considered by the Economic and Social Council at its mid-1962 session.[51] The report advocated that the total flow of capital assistance to the developing countries should reach and maintain the level of 1% of the national income of the advanced countries, as recommended by the Assembly in 1961, and that the advanced countries should reduce barriers to the entry of imports from the less developed countries and extend to them advantages not necessarily requiring full reciprocity, i.e. by granting them tariff preferences. It also considered that the Economic and Social Council could play a part in promoting the expansion of international trade through its Commission on International Commodity Trade.

This Commission had reported to the Economic and Social Council that the adverse terms of trade of developing countries producing primary products had caused a decline in their export earnings, and that it had therefore appointed an expert group to study systems of compensatory financing to offset losses caused by such factors. This line of approach was endorsed by the Economic and Social Council, and approved by the Assembly in December 1962, with the request that the expert group's report be sent to the Preparatory Commission of the UN Conference on Trade and Development,[52] the main impetus for the holding of which had come from the developing countries who wanted to create new machinery within the UN to exert pressure on the developed countries to meet their demands for better terms of trade.

The UN Conference on Trade and Development (UNCTAD)

The developing countries considered that though the GATT organisation had done much in liberalising trade among the industrialised market economies by means of reductions of tariff and other trade barriers, it had proved inadequate to meet their trade needs. Indeed, as Richard N. Gardner has asserted, 'the late 1950's and early 1960's were years of growing frustration for the less developed countries, years in which the dreams of rapid economic development to follow in the wake of independence were rudely shattered. There was a marked decline in the prices of some key primary commodities on which developing countries rely for their export earnings. At the same time foreign aid failed to increase as rapidly as the less-developed countries had hoped, and new aid was increasingly offset by repayment of principal and interest from past loans. Among the developing countries there was a growing conviction that nothing short of a fundamental reshaping of the world trading system could deal with their desperate and urgent problems'.[53]

Attention was focused on these problems at the United Nations Conference on Trade and Development (UNCTAD) which was held in Geneva in 1964.[54] It was attended by the representatives of 120 states, 77 of which were representatives of the developing countries of the 'Third World', a much larger group than the group of Soviet bloc countries or the group of mainly Western states with developed economies.

The Conference recommended that measures should be taken to assist the developing countries increase and stabilise their earnings from commodities, expand their exports of manufactured products, and obtain the capital needed for development. It was also proposed that the Conference itself should be established as an organ of the UN Assembly to be convened at intervals of not more than three years: that the permanent executive organ of the Conference should be known as the Trade and Development Board and consist of 55 members elected by the Conference from among its membership, with regard for both equitable geographical distribution and the desirability of continuing representation for the principal trading states: and that for the effective discharge of its functions the Board should establish subsidiary committees on such matters as commodities, manufactures, and invisibles and financing related to trade. In brief, the new institution was envisaged as a body with the competence to make recommendations on matters relating to trade and development, and to co-operate with the Assembly and the Economic and Social Council in co-ordinating the activities in such fields of other institutions within the UN system.

As to the voting procedure in the Conference and the Trade and Development Board, it was recommended that 'each State represented at the Conference should have one vote. Subject to provisions to be determined by the General Assembly at its nineteenth session after consideration by it of a report and proposals to be made by a Special Committee to be appointed by the Secretary-General of the United Nations, decisions of the Conference on matters of substance should be taken by a two-thirds majority of the representatives present and voting, and decisions of the Board by simple majority. The task of the Special Committee would be to prepare proposals for procedures, within the continuing machinery, designed to establish a process of conciliation to take place before voting, and to provide an adequate basis for the adoption of recommendations with regard to proposals of a specific nature for action substantially affecting the economic or financial interests of particular countries'.[55]

Details of the conciliation procedures referred to above — the compromise formula accepted by the developing and developed countries to facilitate the adoption of recommendations by consensus instead of by majority voting — were worked out by the Special Committee appointed by the Secretary-General of the UN, and incorporated in a resolution approved by the Assembly in December 1964, which embodied the proposals of the Conference.[56] Provision was made for the process of conciliation to take place before voting on proposals of a specific nature for action substantially affecting the economic or financial interests of particular countries, if requested by a comparatively small number of members — ten in the Conference, five in the Board, and three in committees — or if initiated by the President of the Conference or Chairman of the Board.

As to the procedure within a conciliation committee, it was laid down that 'the conciliation committee shall begin its work as soon as possible and it shall endeavour to reach agreement during the same session of the Conference or the Board,. No vote shall take place in the conciliation committee. In the event that the conciliation committee is unable to conclude its work or fails to reach agreement at the same session of the Conference or the Board, it shall report to the next session of the Board or to the next session of the Conference, whichever meets earlier. However, the Conference may instruct the conciliation committee appointed by it to submit its report to the following session of the Conference, in the event that the committee shall not have concluded its work or shall have failed to reach agreement during the same session of the Conference'.

Without this form of conciliation procedure, the minority of developed countries would have found it difficult to restrain the majority group of developing countries from passing recommendations of a specific nature for action on such matters as their tariff or monetary policies, or their policies of economic assistance. The developed countries, it may be stated, regarded the conciliation procedure as necessary because they considered that the adoption by a majority vote of recommendations which called for specific action by them, despite their opposition to such action, as tantamount to interference in matters essentially within their domestic jurisdiction, even though such recommendations would not be binding decisions.

As already mentioned, the adoption of recommendations on economic and social matters, addressed to particular states or groups of states, was a form of UN interference which the drafters of Article 2(7) of the Charter had apparently sought to prevent; and in defence of their stand on this question at the UN Conference on Trade and Development in 1964, the governments of developed countries could argue that 'public opinion in the developed countries would react adversely to recommendations passed over the opposition of the developed countries but calling for action by them. Moreover, the currency of the resolutions, as well as the prestige of the UN, would be debased by the passage of resolutions that were not followed by action. What was wanted, in the last analysis, was not voting but results'.[57]

The governments of the developing countries showed some appreciation of this in accepting the conciliation procedure with regard to majority voting in UNCTAD organs. Indeed, 'in practice the formal conciliation procedure has never been used, but the concept of prolonged consultations rather than summary votes has been widely employed in UNCTAD, even in some procedural cases where it was technically not necessary'.[58] The developing countries thus recognised that UNCTAD decisions, though of a recommendatory, non-mandatory nature, should be arrived at by consensus if the co-operation of the developed countries was to be gained, and this was also true of their attitude in the Governing Council of the United Nations Development Programme (UNDP), which was formed as a result of the merger of the Expanded Programme of Technical Assistance and the Special Fund in 1965.[59] Though the developing countries had a built-in majority of two on the thirty-seven member UNDP Council, they recognised that decisions should be taken by consensus, in consonance with the principle of non-interference in matters of domestic jurisdiction, since the developed countries provided most of the funds on a voluntary basis.[60]

Dissatisfaction with the Approach by Consensus

Towards the end of 1966, however, the developing states rebelled to some extent against the 'approach by consensus' when they used their voting strength in the Assembly to establish the UN Industrial Development Organisation (UNIDO) as an autonomous body within the UN for the purpose of promoting and accelerating the industrialisation of their countries in the manufacturing sector. Expenses for the administration and research schemes of the new organ were to be financed out of the UN's regular budget, and provision was made for the holding of annual pledging conferences as a means of obtaining its source of funds for carrying out such projects as surveys of industrial development possibilities and operations to develop the marketing techniques of developing countries.[61]

But at the first UNIDO pledging conference in December 1968, the majority of rich, developed countries were not prepared to make separate contributions to UNIDO since they considered that its operational activities should be given only limited financial support from the UN Development Programme (UNDP) which was then 'moving toward an expenditure of close to 200 million dollars a year, with the United States providing 40% of the funds'.[62] In fact, only 2½ million dollars were pledged for UNIDO's operational activities,[63] and the attempt of the developing countries to obtain large scale financial support from developed countries for UNIDO, whose establishment had come about as a result of a majority vote in the Assembly which did not represent a consensus between the developed and developing states, was unsuccessful.

The developed countries reacted in similar fashion when the developing countries used their greater voting power in the Assembly to establish the United Nations Capital Development Fund as an organ of the Assembly to assist them in the development of their economies by supplementing existing sources of capital assistance by means of grants and loans, particularly long-term loans made free of interest or at low interest rates.[64]

Some developed countries, particularly the leading Western powers, were opposed to the creation of the UN Capital Development Fund on the ground that the existing specialised agencies, the International Bank and its affiliates, the International Finance Corporation and the International Development Association, were the appropriate institutions for the disbursement of multilateral aid, and the Soviet Union and France expressed opposition to the administrative expenses of the Fund being financed out of the regular budget of the UN.[65] It was not surprising, therefore, that the developed countries were not represented at the first Capital Development Fund Pledging Conference in 1967, when only about $1^1/_2$ million dollars were pledged by twenty-two countries.[66] Clearly, the establishment of the UN Capital Development Fund by a majority vote in the Assembly, without the support of the developed countries who would be required not only to accept the main burden of the administrative expenses, but also the grants and long-term loans free of interest or at low interest rates, was doomed to failure.

This again served to emphasise the point that any attempt by the developing countries to pressurise the developed countries into participating in UN aid schemes through the adoption of resolutions in the Assembly by majority vote, which did not reflect the consensus between the developing and developed states, was regarded by the latter, in effect, as using the UN to interfere in matters essentially within their domestic jurisdiction in contravention of Article 2(7) of the Charter, and was thus unacceptable to them.

The UN's International Development Strategy for the Second Development Decade

It is significant that the General Assembly's resolution on the UN's International Development Strategy for the Second Development Decade was arrived at by a consensus of all UN member-states[67] — it was adopted unanimously without a formal vote in 1970 — and could not therefore be construed as a form of interference in matters essentially within the domestic jurisdiction of states.

'On the threshold of the 1970's, Governments dedicate themselves anew to the fundamental objectives enshrined in the Charter of the United Nations twenty-five years ago to create conditions of stability and well-being and to ensure a minimum standard of living consistent with human dignity through economic and social progress and development', it was stated in the preamble to the Strategy. 'The launching in 1961 of the First United Nations Development Decade marked a world wide endeavour to give concrete substance to this solemn pledge. Since then attempts have continued to be made to adopt specific measures and to fashion and employ new institutions of international co-operation for this purpose. However, the level of living of countless millions of people in the developing part of the world is still pitifully low. These people are often still under-nourished, uneducated, unemployed and wanting in many other basic amenities of life. While a part of the world lives in great comfort and even affluence, much of the larger part suffers from abject poverty, and in fact the disparity is continuing to widen. This lamentable situation has contributed to the aggravation of world tension.'

Though it was recognised in the preamble that the primary responsibility for the development of developing countries rested upon themselves, it nevertheless maintained that 'however great their own efforts, these will not be sufficient to enable them to achieve the desired development goals as expeditiously as they must unless they are assisted through increased financial resources and more favourable economic and commercial policies on the part of the developed countries'.

Among the objectives of the Strategy were the following:

The average annual rate of growth in the gross product of the developing countries as a whole during the Second United Nations Development Decade should be at least 6 per cent, with the possibility of attaining a higher rate in the second half of the Decade to be specified on the basis of a comprehensive mid-term review . . .

The average annual rate of growth of gross product per head in developing countries as a whole during the Decade should be about 3.5 per cent with the possibility of accelerating it during the second half of the Decade in order at least to make a modest beginning towards narrowing the gap in living standards between developed and developing countries. An average annual growth rate of 3.5 per cent per head will represent a doubling of average income per head in the course of two decades. In countries with very low incomes per head, efforts should be made to double such incomes within a shorter period.

The target for growth in average income per head is calculated on the basis of an average annual increase of 2.5 per cent in the population of developing countries, which is less than the average rate at present forecast for the 1970s. In this context, each developing country should formulate its own demographic objectives within the framework of its national development plan.

An average annual rate of growth of at least 6 per cent in the gross product of developing countries during the Decade will imply an annual average expansion of: (a) 4 per cent in agricultural output; and (b) 8 per cent in manufacturing output.

As the ultimate purpose of development is to provide increasing opportunities to all people for a better life, it is essential to bring about a more equitable distribution of income and wealth for promoting both social justice and efficiency of production, to raise substantially the level of employment, to achieve a greater degree of income security, to expand and improve facilities for education, health, nutrition, housing and social welfare, and to safeguard the environment. Thus, qualitative and structural changes in the society must go hand in hand with rapid economic growth, and existing disparities — regional, sectoral and social — should be substantially reduced. These objectives are both determining factors and end-results of development; they should therefore be viewed as integrated parts of the same dynamic process and would require a unified approach . . .[68]

These objectives, it was pointed out, called for a continuing effort by all peoples and Governments to promote economic and social progress in developing countries by the formulation and implementation of a coherent set of policy measures, which included the following:

International Trade[69]

All efforts will be made to secure international action before 31 December 1972, including, where appropriate, the conclusion of international agreements or arrangements on commodities mentioned in resolution 16(II) of 26 March 1968, adopted by the United Nations Conference on Trade and Development at its second session . . . (*The commodities mentioned in the UNCTAD resolution were sugar, oil-seeds, oils and fats, rubber sisal and henequen (Hard fibres), jute, bananas, citrus fruit, cotton, tungsten, tea, wine, iron ore, tobacco, manganese ore, mica, pepper, shellac and phosphates.*)[70]

Efforts will be made to reach agreement, before the third session of the United Nations Conference on Trade and Development, on a set of general principles on pricing policy to serve as guidelines for con-sultations and actions on individual commodities. As one of the priority aims of pricing policy particular attention will be paid to securing stable, remunerative and equitable prices with a view to increasing the foreign exchange earnings from exports of primary products from the developing countries.

Special attention will be given to the expansion and diversification of the export trade of developing countries in manufactures and semi-manufactures, particularly for enabling them to attain increased participation, commensurate with the needs of development, in the growth of international trade in these commodities.

Arrangements concerning the establishment of generalised, non-dis-criminatory, non-reciprocal preferential treatment to exports of developing countries in the markets of developed countries have been drawn up in the United Nations Conference on Trade and Development and considered mutually acceptable to developed and developing countries. Preference-giving countries are determined to seek as rapidly as possible the necessary legislative or other sanction with the aim of implementing the preferential arrangements as early as possible in 1971. Efforts for further improvements of these preferential arrangements will be pursued in a dynamic context in the light of the objectives of resolution 21(II) of 26 March 1968, adopted by the Conference at its second session.

Financial Resources for Development[71]

Each economically advanced country should endeavour to provide by 1972 annually to developing countries financial resource transfers of a minimum amount of 1 per cent of its gross national product at market prices in terms of actual disbursements having regard to the special position of those countries which are not importers of capital. Those developed countries which have already met this target will endeavour to ensure that their net resource transfers are maintained and envisage, if possible, an increase in them. Those developed countries which are unable to achieve this target by 1972 will endeavour to attain it not later than 1975.

In recognition of the special importance of the role which can be fulfilled only by official development assistance, a major part of financial resource transfers to the developing countries should be provided in the form of official development assistance. Each economically advanced country will progressively increase its official development assistance to the developing countries and will exert its best efforts to reach a minimum of 0.7 per cent of its gross national product at market prices by the middle of the Decade.

As soon as adequate experience is available on the working of the scheme of Special Drawing Rights, serious consideration will be given to the possibility of the establishment of a link between the allocation of the new reserve assets under the scheme and the provision of additional development finance for the benefit of all developing countries. The question will, in any case, be examined before the allocation of Special Drawing Rights in 1972.

As mentioned earlier, an amendment to the International Monetary Fund's Articles of Agreement establishing the Special Drawing Rights scheme to expand international liquidity — under the scheme members' quotas in the Fund were enlarged without any additional subscription in gold or national currencies — had entered into force on 28 July 1969; and on 1 January 1970 the first allocation of SDRs, equivalent to approximately $3^1/_2$ billion dollars, was made to 104 participants in the Special Drawing Account. But since the major shares of the SDRs went to the developed countries, particularly the United States, with high quotas in the Fund, the developing countries, with low quotas and small shares, were anxious to establish a link between the allocation of the new reserve assets under the scheme and the provision of additional finance for their development; and, as indicated above, the Assembly's resolution on the International Development Strategy declared that serious consideration would be given to the matter.

It should also be noted that in the Assembly's resolution it was emphasised that 'financial and technical assistance should be aimed exclusively at promoting the economic and social progress of developing countries and should not in any way be used by the developed countries to the detriment of the national sovereignty of recipient countries'. Clearly, this implied that multilaterial aid schemes under the auspices of the UN, though mainly financed by developed countries, should not be operated in any way that contravened the Charter's principle of non-interference in matters essentially within the domestic jurisdiction of the recipient countries.

Other policy measures covered in the Strategy were designed to promote, by national and international action, the earnings of developing countries from invisible trade, such as tourism, insurance, and shipping:[72] to provide special assistance to the least developed among the developing countries[73] and land-locked developing countries:[74] and to further international co-operation so that developing countries could expand their capability to apply science and technology for development.[75] A special section on 'Human Development'[76] also prescribed social policies for the developing countries in the fields of employment, education, health and nutrition, housing and related community facilities, the environment, etc., and it was stated in the resolution that 'those developing countries which consider that their rate of population growth hampers their development will adopt measures which they deem necessary in accordance with their concept of development'.

Mention has already been made that a clause was included on the need to protect the national sovereignty of developing countries in connection with the use of external aid. Another clause was inserted to safeguard their sovereignty in the section on measures for expansion and diversification of production.[77] 'Full exercise by developing countries of permanent sovereignty over their natural resources will play an important role in the achievement of the goals and objectives of the Decade,' it read. 'Developing countries will take steps to develop the full potential of their natural resources. Concerted efforts will be made, particularly through international assistance, to enable them to prepare an inventory of natural resources for their more rational utilization in all productive activities.'

As to policy measures prescribed for developing countries to augment production and improve productivity in order to provide goods and services necessary for raising levels of living and improving economic viability, the Assembly's resolution on International Development for the Second Decade included the following:[78]

Developing countries will formulate, early in the Decade, appropriate strategies for agriculture — including animal husbandry, fisheries and forestry — designed to secure a more adequate food supply from both the quantitative and qualitative viewpoints, to meet their nutritional and industrial requirements, to expand rural employment and to increase export earnings. They will undertake, as appropriate, reform of land tenure systems for promoting both social justice and farm efficiency . .

Developing countries will take parallel steps to promote industry in order to achieve rapid expansion, modernization and diversification of their economies. They will devise measures to ensure adequate expansion of the industries that utilize domestic raw materials, that supply essential inputs to both agriculture and other industries, and that help to increase export earnings . . .

As already mentioned, since the Strategy was arrived at by a consensus of all UN members, it was not at variance with the Charter's principle of non-interference in matters essentially within the domestic jurisdiction of states, and it must be realised that the terms of the Strategy constituted no more than the expression of the moral commitment of the governments of the developed and the developing states in favour of measures designed to uplift the economic and social standards of the hundreds of millions of people suffering from poverty, disease, hunger and illiteracy throughout the world. It imposed no international legal obligations on the developed states to implement the measures considered essential to assist the developing countries, and no legal obligations on the latter to carry out the prescribed economic and social reforms, such as the reform of land tenure systems for promoting social justice, where it was applicable. In brief, then the Strategy was not an international treaty or convention, but a declaration of moral intent. Consequently, its unanimous adoption by UN members did not give the UN the authority to make binding decisions on the policy measures prescribed. The competence of the Organisation in economic and social matters remained essentially recommendatory.

Appraisal of Progress in Implementing the International Development Strategy

The first over-all review and appraisal of progress in the implementation of the International Development Strategy in 1973, as required under the Assembly's resolution,[79] — the Economic and Social Council working paper prepared by the Working Group on Review and Appraisal[80] — concluded that 'the International Development Strategy remains much more a wish than a policy. It has not yet taken hold with anything like the force needed. Generally in the developing countries the recognition of the complementarities among the major goals and objectives of development and of the need for economic growth to be accompanied by the qualitative and structural changes in the society as laid down in the International Development Strategy has not yet been adequately reflected in their development programmes and policies. This includes, *inter alia*, the building into the development programme of each country of measures for spreading the benefits of economic growth and for overcoming the under-utilization of production capacity as well as the orientation of educational systems towards development priorities. The developed countries have displayed a lack of implementation or late or imperfect execution of the policy measures embodied in the Strategy. Only some developed countries have so far shown an encouraging response to the provisions of the Strategy. The net contribution of the developed world to the economic and social progress of the developing countries has not yet shown the degree of forward movement envisaged in the Strategy'.[81]

Both developing and developed countries were urged in the report to take steps to implement the International Development Strategy, and all countries were called upon to 'actively promote the achievement of general and complete disarmament through effective measures'. The resources that may be released as a result of effective measures of actual disarmament, it was stressed, should be used for the promotion of economic and social development of all nations.[82]

The report also emphasised that the reform of the international monetary system was vital if the objectives of the International Development Strategy were to be realised. This could hardly be gainsaid, for during 1971 to 1973 there had been a continuing crisis in international monetary relations because of the deterioration in the balance of payments position of the United States resulting from American investments in Western European countries and Japan. In August 1971 the crisis became particularly acute because the United States, facing marked losses in its gold and foreign currency reserves, decided to suspend convertibility for the dollar into gold and to allow the dollar to float, with the result that the central banks of other countries were left holding vast quantities of almost unusable dollars. Indeed, 'in terms of other currencies, this action amounted to a dollar devaluation of about 8%' and 'there were consequential changes in the currency parities of the leading trading nations. . .'[83] In fact, despite subsequent moves in 1972 and 1973 to restore some order into international monetary relations, the question of dollar inconvertibility remained the main reason for the lack of confidence in the dollar, which was devalued by 10% in February 1973, and there was much uncertainty through the precarious practice of floating exchange rates.[84]

In view of the upheaval in international monetary relations between 1971 and 1973, it was not surprising, therefore, that the report of the Economic and Social Council's Working Group on the Review and Appraisal of the International Development Strategy stressed the need for international monetary reform. 'A satisfactory and early settlement of international monetary affairs is in the interests of all countries, developed and developing,' it declared. 'Special attention should be paid to the effect of the international monetary crisis on the developing countries, with particular reference to the adequacy and value of their reserves, sustained growth of their export earnings, the prices of their export products and their terms of trade.' Certainly, the developing countries were particularly vulnerable to the instability of the rates of exchange of the currencies of the main trading nations; since a large proportion of their currency reserves was in dollars, the devaluation of the American dollar led to the depreciation of their reserves.[85] The report thus argued that 'developing countries should be accorded an effective voice in the discussions relating to all aspects of the international monetary system in such a way that the results are fully in consonance with their development needs', and advocated 'a review of the voting system and the quota structure of the International Monetary Fund with a view to making it possible for developing countries to have greater participation in international monetary decisions' and 'the establishment of a link between new allocations of special drawing rights and additional development financing'.[86]

But international monetary problems were made enormously more difficult towards the end of 1973 by the decision of the Organisation of Petroleum Exporting Countries (OPEC) — Saudi Arabia, Libya, Kuwait, Oatar, Abu Dhabi, Algeria, Iraq, Nigeria, Indonesia, Iran and Venezuela — to impose a fourfold increase in the price of oil; for this had an inflationary effect on the price of everything which oil helped to produce or distribute in both the developed and developing oil-importing countries. The dramatic increases in the price of oil thus created considerable balance of payments difficulties for the oil-importing states, whilst it produced huge money surpluses for the oil-exporting states. Consequently, unless measures were taken to recycle these huge surplus sums of money to finance economic activity throughout the world, there was the danger that the balance of payments difficulties of the oil-importing countries would force them to introduce import restrictions of all kinds and devalue their currencies. Indeed, there was a great danger that many countries would become economically paralysed through lack of money circulation.

The World Bank's Annual Report for the period July 1973 to June 1974[87] pointed out that the most significant developments of the recent past had included the realignment and floating of exchange rates; accelerated inflation, associated with rapid rises in the prices of most primary commodities and of industrial exports; dramatic increases in petroleum prices; shortages of foodgrains and of fertilizer; and a slowing of the growth of gross national product (GNP) in industrialised countries. It was expected that GNP growth in many developing countries would fall below 6% over the rest of the 1970s, the report added; the rate of growth in the poorest countries, including the most populous, would be so low that per capita incomes would either stagnate or rise very little between 1974 and 1980.

Among the factors contributing to the need for a larger flow of external assistance to developing countries was the sharp rise in commodity prices, the impact of inflation on the prices of manufactured goods which they imported from industrialised countries, and the terms of financing to meet increases in their current account deficits. Indeed, the Bank's report underlined that the international community needed not only to mobilise more development assistance, but also to direct such assistance immediately to the poorest among and within the developing countries, which included those in the whole of the Indian sub-continent, tropical Africa, parts of Latin America, and the Caribbean.

But help for the poorest developing countries depended not only on the economically developed countries, but also on OPEC countries with rapidly increasing oil revenues. Besides, the ability of the economically advanced countries to play a more generous role in the field of development assistance depended on the negotiation of equitable prices for raw materials and foodstuffs with those developing countries that produced them.

How far the United Nations and its specialised agencies have been able to assist in finding solutions to this question of raw materials and development, and other inter-related problems requiring international action, without trespassing on matters essentially within the domestic jurisdiction of states, is considered below.

The UN Assembly's Special Session on the Problems of Raw Materials and Development, 1974.[88]

The special session of the UN Assembly in April-May 1974 on the problems of raw materials and development, which was called on the initiative of President Boumedienne of Algeria, resulted in the adoption without vote of a Declaration of Principles and Programme of Action that had been formulated by the hundred or so developing countries within the United Nations. These amounted to a reiteration of the main recommendations of the UN Assembly's 1970 resolution on International Development Strategy, which was not at variance with the principle of non-intervention in matters essentially within the domestic jurisdiction of UN states.

The Declaration of Principles, the force of which was of a moral nature, recognised that 'current events have brought into sharp focus the realization that the interests of the developing countries can no longer be isolated from each other; that there is close inter-relationship between the prosperity of the developed countries and the growth and development of the developing countries; and that the prosperity of the international community as a whole depends upon the prosperity of its constituent parts'. But it was significant that it affirmed that the new international economic order should be founded not only on the various principles on which the International Development Strategy was based, but also on 'facilitating the role which producers' associations may play within the framework of international co-operation, and in pursuance of their aims, *inter alia*, assisting in promotion of sustained growth of the world economy and accelerating development of developing countries'.

It was apparent, however, that in the mind of the American Secretary of State, Dr. Henry Kissinger, producers' associations could also pursue policies at variance with the spirit of international co-operation, for in an address to the Assembly,[89] he warned that 'no nation or group of nations can gain by pushing its claims beyond the limits that sustain world economic growth', and he maintained that 'the notion of the northern rich and the southern poor has been shattered. The world is composed not of two sets of interests but many: developed nations which are energy suppliers and developing nations which are energy consumers: market economies and nonmarket economies: capital providers and capital recipients'.

'The world economy is a sensitive set of relationships in which actions can easily set off a vicious spiral of counteractions deeply affecting all countries, developing as well as technologically advanced,' he added. 'Global inflation erodes the capacity to import. A reduction in the rate of world growth reduces export prospects. Exorbitant high prices lower consumption, spur alternative production, and foster development of substitutes.'

But from the viewpoint of the OPEC countries, and even of those developing countries who were suffering from the exorbitant increase in the price of oil, the imposition of higher prices for their commodity exports was a justifiable challenge to the rich developed states who had for so long resisted their pleas within the United Nations for more equitable and stable prices with a view to increasing the foreign exchange earnings of primary products from developing countries. Moreover, there can be little doubt that Arab hostility to the United States and other Western European countries that gave support to Israel in her struggle with Arab countries was a factor of some importance in motivating the exorbitant increase in the price of oil.

The point that needs to be stressed, however, is that the action of the OPEC countries in creating such immense problems for both developed and developing countries, as well as the reluctance of the economically developed states to treat the trade and development problems of the developing countries with a greater sense of urgency, served to underline the need for greater international co-operation and the extension of the competence of the United Nations to intervene in matters essentially within the domestic jurisdiction of its member states in the economic and social fields. But this could be achieved, without contravening the principle of non-intervention under Article 2(7) of the Charter, only if all member nations, developed and developing, producers and consumers, arrived at a consensus on the world-wide arrangements that were necessary, and gave UN organs the authority and the means to carry them out.

The programme of action of most immediate practical importance that was adopted at the Sixth Special Session of the UN Assembly on Raw Materials and Development was the establishment of a special emergency fund, under the auspices of the UN, to help those developing countries most severely affected by the increased prices of their vital imports of oil, foodstuffs, fertilisers and capital goods. The Secretary-General was asked to make arrangements for the operation of the fund in consultation with the various specialised agencies, and to launch an appeal for voluntary contributions to the fund.

The fact that the fund was based on voluntary contributions indicated that no consensus emerged at the Assembly for the cost of the emergency operations to be treated as expenses of the UN under Article 17 of the Charter, and thus subject to binding apportionment by the Assembly. Indeed, the United States opposed the creation of the fund even though it was based on voluntary contributions, but this was not because it disputed the need for emergency aid to those countries hardest hit by the international inflation, but because it considered that such aid should be channelled through existing institutions within the UN system. Subsequently, at the Assembly's regular session in December 1974, the American delegate distributed a statement which maintained that the aid fund proposed by the non-aligned block would merely 'insert yet another layer of bureaucracy between donors and those who so desperately need assistance'. Apparently, the Americans were also irritated by the attitude of the oil producing Arab states towards the emergency fund, stated one UN correspondent. The Arabs maintained that they supported the fund and that they were giving large sums to those countries the fund aimed to help. But they refused to say how much they were giving or to whom, and the recipient nations were too fearful of antagonising the Arabs to talk about it publicly ... Even the World Bank had been unable to find out what the Arabs were giving. The only certainties were that the situation was being politicised by both the Americans and the Arabs; the poor countries were not getting what they needed; and the General Assembly had done little about it.[90]

This account of the response of member states of the United Nations to the Assembly's special emergency fund, referred to above, underlined once again the essentially recommendatory competence of the United Nations in the economic and social fields. Though its resolutions might be supported by substantial majorities, it had no means of compelling member-states to make financial contributions to the economic or social programmes recommended, and this was one of the realities of international life which the developing countries found it difficult to accept.

Conflicting Views on the UN's Competence

The developing countries were also dissatisfied with the limited competence of the United Nations Conference on Trade and Development (UNCTAD). In general, the developing countries, supported by the Soviet bloc, wanted to reform UNCTAD into a comprehensive trade organisation with sufficient authority to make binding decisions on matters designed to improve their terms of trade, such as the fixing of equitable and stable prices for their commodity exports on which developed states were very much dependent, as well as on matters involving the restructuring of the institutional framework of international economic relations so as to ensure a more balanced relationship between developed and developing countries. On the other hand, the United States, the United Kingdom, France, Canada and other developed countries considered that UNCTAD should remain essentially a consultative organ of the Assembly and arrive at its recommendations by consensus and not by majority decisions to which they might be opposed.[91]

The differing interpretations of the *Charter of Economic Rights and Duties of States*, which was approved by the UN Assembly on 12 December 1974, by a vote of 120 to 6, with 10 abstentions,[92] also brought into focus the conflicting views of the developing states and several developed states on the competence of the Assembly in the economic field. The six states that voted against the resolution containing the text of the new Charter were Belgium, Denmark, West Germany, Luxembourg, the United Kingdom and United States, and the ten that abstained were Austria, Canada, France, Ireland, Israel, Italy, Japan, the Netherlands, Norway and Spain.

This Charter, which was based on a recommendation adopted by UNCTAD at its third session at Santiago in May 1972, and the report of a working group established by the UN Assembly in December of the same year, was a declaration of the economic rights and duties of states which reflected the standpoint of developing countries. It affirmed each state's right to exercise full permanent sovereignty, including possession, use and disposal, over all its wealth, natural resources and economic activities: to regulate and exercise authority over foreign investment within its territory in accordance with its laws and regulations: to regulate the activities of transnational corporations, and to nationalise, expropriate or transfer ownership of foreign property, with compensation settled under its domestic law and by its tribunals unless it was mutually agreed by all states concerned that other peaceful means should be sought to resolve the matter.

It was also declared in the charter that states had the right to associate in organisations of primary commodity producers in order to develop their national economies to achieve financing for their development; that it was the duty of states to contribute to the development of international trade by the conclusion of long-term multilateral commodity agreements which took into account the interests of producers and consumers; that all states shared the responsibility to promote the regular flow and access of goods traded at stable, remunerative and equitable prices; and that 'with a view to accelerating the economic growth of developing countries and bridging the economic gap between developed and developing countries, developed countries should grant generalized preferential, non-reciprocal and non-discriminatory treatment to developing countries in those fields of international ecnomic co-operation where it may be feasible'.

The debate on this Charter of Economic Rights and Duties of States in the UN Assembly indicated, as *The Guardian's* UN correspondent pointed out, that the developing countries regarded it as 'a set of legal norms and a first step towards codifying international law',[93] an interpretation which implied that the economically advanced states could no longer regard the duties prescribed in the charter as matters essentially within their domestic jurisdiction. On the other hand, the United States considered the charter 'non-legal and non-binding',[94] and voted against it not because it was opposed to all its articles, but mainly on the ground that its articles on the treatment of foreign investment and compensation for foreign property nationalised by a state did not fully take into account respect for agreements and international obligations, and because it could not accept the endorsement of producer cartels which could fix and hold prices against the normal forces of supply and demand. In fact, the United States delegate to the UN Assembly's Second (Economic and Financial) Committee did not consider that the charter provided for a balanced relationship between developed and developing countries and would discourage the international flow of capital which was so vital for development.[95]

This debate in the Assembly thus showed that there was no consensus between developed and developing countries on several important issues, but at the Assembly's seventh special session in September 1975 both sides displayed a greater measure of compromise than previously, and approved a resolution which represented a new consensus on Development and International Economic Co-operation.[96] Above all, though it did not endorse the establishment of producer cartels which could fix and hold prices against the normal forces of supply and demand, it recognised the need for the improvement of market structures to assist developing countries, as explained below.

The New Consensus on Development and International Economic Co-operation

Section 1 of the Assembly's resolution on Development and International Economic Co-operation, which dealt with international trade, began by affirming that 'concerted efforts should be made in favour of the developing countries towards expanding and diversifying their trade, improving and diversifying their productive capacity, improving their productivity, increasing their export earnings, with a view to counteracting the adverse effects of inflation — thereby sustaining real incomes — and with a view to improving the terms of trade of the developing countries and in order to eliminate the economic imbalance between the developed and developing countries'. It then stated that an important aim of the UN Conference on Trade and Development (UNCTAD) should be 'to reach decisions on the improvement of market structures in the field of raw materials and commodities of export interest to the developing countries', and that such decisions should be concerned with international stocking and other forms of market arrangements, including long-term, and medium-term contracts, and adequate international financing for such arrangements, in order to secure stable, remunerative and equitable prices for commodities of export interest to developing countries. It was also stressed that UNCTAD's decisions should take into account the need for substantially improved facilities for compensatory financing to assist countries hit by a sharp decline in commodity prices. In fact, in Section II of the resolution — *transfer of real resources for financing the development of developing countries and international monetary reforms* — it was stated that the compensatory financing facility available through the International Monetary Fund should be expanded and liberalised and that this should also apply to its buffer stock financing facilities.

The International Monetary Fund, which was given a key role under the Assembly's resolution, had approved a Compensatory Financing for Export Fluctuations scheme in 1963. This scheme, which was intended to help developing countries faced by sudden falls in their export earnings, was liberalised in 1966, when IMF members, particularly developing countries that produced primary products, were allowed to draw up to 50% of their quota in compensation for temporary shortfalls beyond their control. Besides, in 1969 the Fund also decided to allow drawings up to 50% of quota to permit member states to finance participation in commodity buffer stocks organised under international agreements.[97] Later, in February 1975, the International Monetary Fund agreed 'to study the possibility of increasing its assistance to buffer stocks and in so-called "compensatory financing" when a country's foreign earnings from raw materials drop off',[98] and took several decisions to increase its financial resources to provide ready cash for countries with liquidity problems, and long-term credit facilities at low interest rates to the poor developing countries most seriously affected by such difficulties. The special oil facility to assist members in meeting increased oil import costs, which had been established in 1974, was enlarged from SDR 3 billion to 5 billion, or the equivalent of 6.2 billion dollars; financial subscriptions to the Fund were raised by more than 30 per cent; the OPEC members' quotas were doubled and hence their subscriptions; and the Fund was authorised to raise money which would enable it to make loans to developing countries in greatest need at the annual interest rate of about $2^1/_2$ per cent.[99] Moreover, in September 1975 the IMF decided that one third of its gold holdings, then valued at 14 billion dollars, should be sold, that half of the proceeds should be distributed to its members in accordance with their relative quotas, and that the other half should be placed in a trust fund to provide loans at a low interest rate to developing countries with pressing liquidity difficulties.[100]

The establishment of such a trust fund, financed not only through the International Monetary Fund gold sales, but also through voluntary contributions, was recommended in the UN Assembly's resolution on Development and International Economic Co-operation.[101] The Assembly also recommended that 'the establishment of a link between the special drawing rights and development assistance should form part of the consideration by the International Monetary Fund of the creation of new special drawing rights as and when they are created according to the needs of international liquidity'.[102] As mentioned earlier, the object of such a link would be to enable developing countries to obtain a greater percentage of SDRs when they were created in the future, for during the period 1970-75, they received less than 3 per cent of the SDRs which were distributed in accordance with IMF decisions; 'all in all, the developed countries received SDR 100 billion of international reserve credits over these (past) five years (97 per cent) and the less developed countries 2.9 billion (less than 3 per cent)'.[103]

It remains to be seen whether this trend in SDR distribution will be modified to enable developing countries to obtain greater financial resources for development. But since the developing countries (including OPEC countries) control only about a third of the votes under the IMF's weighted system of voting, the developed countries have the voting power to determine decisions on the matter. Needless to say, they would have the last word if decisions were arrived at consensually.

The fact is that although decisions of the IMF are binding on its members, unlike the recommendatory decisions of the UN Assembly and its subsidiary organs, such as UNCTAD and UNDP, they cannot be reached without the support of the major developed countries. In effect, therefore, the question of determining the acceleration of capital exports to the poorest developing countries is a matter within their jurisdiction, and this also applies to decisions relating to the enlargement of financial resources for development assistance by the World Bank and its affiliate, the International Development Association, which was recommended by the UN Assembly in its 1975 resolution on Development and International Economic Co-operation.[104]

The Assembly's 1975 resolution stated that 'the participation of developing countries in the decision-making process in the competent organs of international finance and development institutions should be adequately increased and made more effective without adversely affecting the broad geographic representation of developing countries and in accordance with the existing and evolving rules'.[105] But general agreement on the precise formula for such a development is unlikely to change significantly the dominant position of the major developed countries. Under the agreement reached in January 1976 at the Kingston meeting of the IMF, 'the preponderance of the United States and other western nations will continue even though new voting arrangements will give a greater say to the oil producing countries who have become the new rich of the world system'.[106]

Such being the case, the least that should be expected of the advanced developed states is that they should faithfully implement decisions arrived at with their consent, not at variance with the principle of non-intervention in matters of domestic jurisdiction, which are adopted in the organs of the specialised international agencies and UN development institutions. In brief, this means that they should carry out recommendations in respect of targets relating to the transfer of resources to developing countries, in particular the official development assistance target of 0.7 per cent of gross national product, to which they agreed in the Assembly's 1970 resolution on International Development Strategy for the Second Development Decade, and confirmed in the Assembly's resolution in September 1975 on Development and International Economic Co-operation.[107] It is also imperative that they should make a determined effort, as recommended in the Assembly's 1975 resolution, to ease access of developing countries' exports, especially manufactured goods, into their own markets,[108] expand their assistance to scientific and technological programmes of the developing world,[109] facilitate the development of new policies, including labour market policies, which would encourage the redeployment of their industries that are less competitive internationally to developing countries,[110] and take financial and technical measures to increase rapidly the production of food in the needy countries.[111]

It is also essential that developing countries in a position to do so, as stated in the Assembly's 1975 resolution, should help the poorest nations of the developing world who find great difficulty in coping with shortages of raw materials and food.[112] Besides, it should be recognised by both developing and developed countries, though this was not mentioned in the resolution, that stopping the population explosion as quickly as possible is of fundamental importance, as emphasised by Professor John P. Lewis. He rightly asserts that 'poor countries must do it to aid their scramble for improved welfare, and to improve internal equity. The rich countries must do it to ease the resource-saving adjustments they are going to have to make. It is a global imperative with which virtually all national needs, rationally examined, are consistent'.[113]

But at the World Population Conference in Bucharest in 1974, the majority of the delegates from the 135 countries represented expressed the view 'that population problems could not be solved without economic and social progress which, in turn, required a more equitable international economic order. High fertility rates would not decline merely through the provision of family planning information and means; declines in birth rates and smaller family size generally were associated with development and modernization'.[114] Indeed, the efforts of the advocates of family planning to secure specific commitments by governments to provide information and means of contraception to reduce over-population — measures which are as essential as the expansion of economic development programmes if living standards are to be raised — were unsuccessful.

The fact is that population and environmental policies in general are matters essentially within the domestic jurisdiction of states, so that member states of the United Nations can claim that the Organisation has no authority to intervene in such questions, other than to make general recommendations. International Conventions may be formulated on such matters, but their ratification and implementation depend upon the consent forthcoming from the nation-states.

Conclusions

Since the decisions of the UN Assembly and its subsidiary organs in the economic, social and related fields are of a recommendatory nature, their implementation depends upon the consent of UN member states. Consequently, UN recommendations on questions of international trade and development assistance, which involve arrangements between developed and developing countries, stand little or no chance of being put into effect unless they are arrived at by consensus between both groups. Indeed, there is no guarantee that even consensual decisions, not at variance with the principle of non-intervention in matters essentially within the domestic jurisdiction of states under Article 2(7) of the Charter, will be implemented, for since they are recommendatory, they cannot impose binding obligations on UN members, and this applies to the Assembly's resolution on Development and International Economic Co-operation which was approved unanimously at its seventh special session in September 1975.

It must also be appreciated that although implementation of the Assembly's 1975 resolution on Development and International Economic Co-operation largely depends on decisions by the International Monetary Fund and the World Bank group of agencies, which are binding on their members, unlike the recommendatory decisions of UN development institutions such as UNCTAD and UNDP, they cannot be reached without the support of the major developed countries whether they are arrived at consensually or in accordance with the weighted system of voting that obtains in those bodies.

The Lomé Convention agreed to by the nine developed countries in the

European Economic Community and forty-six developing countries in Africa, the Caribbean and the Pacific, in February 1975, pointed the way to the kind of comprehensive programme on international trade and development assistance that might be arranged on a global scale through UN institutions and the specialised agencies to implement the Assembly's resolution on Development and International Economic Co-operation. Under this convention, provision was made for stabilising foreign exchange earnings of the forty-six developing countries from twelve commodity exports, through compensating them when falling prices reduce such earnings: financial aid totalling £1,700 million was made available to the developing countries for a five-year period: the industrial exports of the developing countries were freed entirely of customs, duties and levies: and most of their agricultural exports given tariff-free entry to the nine EEC states. In return, the latter were assured access to raw materials at predictable prices.[115]

Of course, a global version of the Lomé Convention, under which UNCTAD and the specialised finance agencies could play a co-ordinated role, would require the acceptance of precise international obligations arrived at by consensus between the developed and developing countries, not at variance with the principle of non-intervention in matters within their domestic jurisdiction. So, too, would the Integrated Programme for Commodities, the plan considered at the fourth session of UNCTAD in Nairobi in May 1976, whose implementation depends upon agreement between the developed and developing countries on the establishment of a common fund to stabilise the export earnings of the commodity producing countries by financing stockpiles to help even out price movements and to provide compensation for falls in export earnings if prices fall below a certain level.[116]

VIII. CONCLUSIONS

In the light of the discussions at the San Francisco Conference in 1945, it was the evident intention of those who drafted Article 2(7) of the Charter that United Nations organs should not interfere in matters traditionally regarded within the domestic jurisdiction of states. This principle of non–interference was thus meant to apply to a state's form of government: the treatment of its own subjects, which covered the entire field of human rights: its administration of a non-self-governing territory not placed under the UN trusteeship system: internal conflicts within its territory: the size of its armaments and armed forces: and, in the absence of international treaties, its immigration policies, questions of nationality, and economic policies, such as the imposition of tariffs. The only exception to this general principle of non-interference in matters essentially within the domestic jurisdiction of states was the competence given to the Security Council to authorise enforcement measures to maintain or restore international peace under Chapter VII of the Charter, if it determined that a situation arising out of a matter of domestic jurisdiction constituted a threat to or breach of the peace.

It should be appreciated, however, that nothing was included in Article 2(7) to indicate which organ or authority was to determine whether or not a matter was essentially within the domestic jurisdiction of a state, and this, together with the fact that the criterion of international law was also omitted as a means of deciding the question, conspired to make the article a subject of controversial interpretation. Besides, although it is evident that those who drafted Article 2(7) intended that the term 'non-intervention' should mean 'no interference in any form', the text of the article did not clarify its implications. The organs of the United Nations were thus given the loophole to assert their competence to deal with questions which states could justifiably claim as matters essentially within their domestic juris-diction, and this has certainly been exploited in their handling of human rights and colonial questions.

Human Rights Questions

In several instances United Nations organs have rejected claims by states that the human rights of their subjects, which they have been accused of violating, were matters essentially within their domestic jurisdiction, to which the general principle of non-interference under Article 2(7) was applicable. Not only the Security Council, but also the Assembly, the Economic and Social Council and the UN Commission on Human Rights have assumed the competence to do this to justify their practice of addressing censures to particular governments on human rights violations, though at the same time it has been recognised by the Assembly that states are not bound by international legal obligations in respect of human rights if they have not voluntarily ratified international conventions which remove such matters from the sphere of domestic jurisdiction.

Naturally UN interference in human rights questions has aroused the resentment of those states which have been subjected to this treatment, and created much antagonism between members of the United Nations, which has weakened the Organisation. Besides, many states, themselves guilty of practising various forms of tyranny, have actively supported UN resolutions condemning the human rights violations of other states, and thus exhibited what has been described as 'the indecent spectacle of tyrants condemning tyranny at the United Nations'.[1] There is much to justify the view, therefore, that the organs of the United Nations should cease interfering in human rights questions in respect of which states have not accepted international legal obligations, and that the legal approach to the implementation of human rights, through the voluntary ratification by states of the Assembly's comprehensive International Covenants on Human Rights, should be strictly adhered to i.e. in accordance with the principle of consent which is not at variance with the principle of non-intervention in matters essentially within the domestic jurisdiction of states under Article 2(7) of the Charter.

It is recognised realistically in the Covenant on Economic, Social and Cultural Rights that the implementation of such rights as the right to education and social security can only indicate objectives and standards, for the realisation of these rights depends on the resources available to states and the degree of international co-operation and assistance forthcoming to improve the economic and social conditions in developing countries. In contrast, the obligations which states assume under the Covenant on Civil and Political Rights are meant to be implemented as soon as they ratify it. It should be realised, however, that this offers no guarantee that states will honour their obligations, for the violators of the Covenant can only be exposed to the moral pressure of the international community. Even so, it is possible that states will do something to modify their domestic policies in the field of basic human rights if they are likely to incur the moral condemnation of world opinion for transgressing the International Covenant on Civil and Political Rights which they have voluntarily ratifed.

The UN and the Self-determination of Peoples

Not long after the formation of the United Nations, its political organs began to intervene in colonial questions which colonial powers could justifiably claim were matters essentially within their domestic jurisdiction to which the principle of non-interference under Article 2(7) of the Charter was applicable. For instance, by asserting its competence to make recommendations on economic, social and educational conditions in non-self-governing territories not placed under the UN trusteeship system, and to determine whether or not a territory was self-governing under Article 73 of the Charter, the Assembly assumed a supervisory role in respect of those territories similar to that which it had been authorised to perform, with the aid of the Trusteeship Council, with regard to trust territories.

With few exceptions, the colonial powers yielded to this measure of accountability to the United Nations during the early years of the Organisation, though it had not been intended by the architects of the Charter. But there was more determined opposition on their part to prevent the United Nations from intervening in colonial conflicts, and prior to 1960, with the exception of the Indonesian affair because the United States was prepared to exert pressure against the Netherlands in support of the Security Council's policy of decolonising Indonesia, the UN's role in such conflicts was restricted mainly to recommending the desirability of negotiations between France and her rebellious colonial peoples in North Africa.

But the entry of a large number of former African and Asian colonies into membership of the United Nations served to strengthen the attack against colonialism in the Assembly, and after the adoption of the 1960 Declaration on the Granting of Independence to Colonial Countries and Peoples, the Assembly acted on the assumption that the principle of self-determination imposed a legal obligation on states to grant independent statehood to those non-self-governing peoples under their control, and was a sufficient basis on which to justify UN intervention in colonial conflicts without contravening Article 2(7) of the Charter.

This assumption was of dubious validity. Even the most extreme of anti-colonialist states had recognised that the 'right of self-determination', and other rights which were included in the international covenants on human rights then being drafted, could not be converted into legal obligations until such covenants had been ratified by states. Moreover, the fact that the Soviet Union was anxious that the United Nations should act on this assumption was not consistent with its disrespect for the principle of self-determination of peoples in Eastern Europe, though it was understandable that states in Africa and Asia which had just emerged from colonial rule should have been eager to accelerate the process of decolonisation through UN intervention in colonial conflicts, even if it was difficult to justify its intervention on legal grounds.

Most of those states with non-self-governing territories were not averse to the process of decolonisation being continued, though the pressure exerted by the Assembly's Committee of 24 probably influenced them to speed up their plans to grant independence to colonial peoples. On the other hand, South Africa was determined not to yield control over South West Africa (Namibia), and Portugal held on stubbornly to its African colonies until the fall of the Caetano regime in 1974. The illegal regime in Rhodesia, too, denied the black population in that country the political rights necessary to enable them to elect a government responsive to their wishes in consonance with the principle of self-determination. Consequently, during the 1960s and after, the Assembly concentrated its efforts mainly against those states.

The Assembly justified its recommendation for diplomatic and economic sanctions against Portugal not only because it considered that the principle of self-determination was a legal right against which Article 2(7) of the Charter was no defence, but also on the ground that the conflicts in the Portuguese colonies endangered international peace and security. It is arguable, therefore; that this recommendation was a contravention of Artice 2(7), since the principle of self-determination had not been converted into a legal right which nullified Portugal's domestic jurisdiction over the question of determining when its colonial peoples should obtain independence, and only the Security Council was entitled to authorise enforcement measures in situations arising out of matters of domestic jurisdiction that constituted a threat to international peace. On the other hand, in recommending economic sanctions against South Africa for refusing to comply with its resolutions on Namibia, the Assembly was on sounder ground, for it could reasonably claim that South Africa was accountable to the United Nations for its administration of a former League of Nations mandate, as the International Court of Justice emphasised in 1971 when it advised that the continued presence of South Africa in Namibia was illegal.

The Western powers were thus less justified in refusing to join in the application of economic sanctions against South Africa in response to the Assembly's recommendations on Namibia, and in exercising their veto to prevent the authorisation of such measures by the Security Council under Chapter VII of the Charter, than in preventing such action against Portugal prior to that state's surrender of its African colonies. It would appear that the Western powers, upon whom the effectiveness of economic sanctions against South Africa would largely depend, were afraid that such coercive measures would not only damage their own economies, but also lead to a situation in southern Africa which would give the Soviet Union opportunities to extend its influence in the area.

In the case of Rhodesia the Security Council succeeded in authorising mandatory economic sanctions against a regime which it condemned for pursuing a policy incompatible with the self-determination of the black majority in that country. But even though this action was not a contravention of the non-intervention principle under Article 2(7) of the Charter — it was the sequel to a request by the United Kingdom, the state whose permission was necessary for constitutional changes in Rhodesia — the sanctionary pressure which the UN was able to exert was insufficient to bring about the collapse of the illegal regime. The Rhodesian affair thus demonstrated the limited enforcement capabilities of the Organisation, and not surprisingly gave rise to what Richard A. Falk has described as 'strategies of violent implementation' by those whose claims to self-determination could not be realised through action by the UN.

It should also be noted that though a combination of sanctionary economic pressure by UN members, the adverse effect of the world recession on the Rhodesian economy, and the impact of the guerilla war impelled the Smith regime to seek a settlement with the three internal black nationalist leaders in November 1977, there was no immediate prospect that the architects of the internal settlement of March 1978 and the Patriotic Front guerilla leaders would be prepared to accept a compromise formula based on the Anglo-American proposals which the Security Council had approved in September, 1977. Moreover, there was little hope that the Security Council members would be able to agree to the authorisation of measures to prevent an intensification of the military struggle.

UN Peacekeeping and the Non-intervention Principle

At San Francisco the architects of the Charter agreed that each of the great powers, the permanent members of the Security Council, should possess the right of veto in the field of enforcement action. Though this meant that the Security Council would be unable to authorise enforcement measures against a great power under Chapter VII of the Charter, it was presumed that the great powers would co-operate to enable the Council to do so when they were not directly involved, i.e. authorise enforcement measures against lesser states that threatened or caused a breach of international peace. But the history of the Security Council has shown that great power dis-unity has made it a major failure in this connection, and prevented agreement being reached on making available to the Security Council the armed forces necessary for maintaining international peace and security, in accordance with special agreements under Article 43 of the Charter.

The history of the United Nations has also shown that though the Assembly has been able to recommend sanctionary measures against states whose policies, in the view of the majority, have endangered international peace, its recommendations for the application of such measures have been ineffectively implemented because states whose support was vital were opposed to them.

Notwithstanding the limited capabilities of the United Nations as an agency for the enforcement of peace, however, the Organisation has succeeded in slowing down the impetus of conflict or effecting a cessation of hostilities in some troubled areas. This it has done through some form of UN presence, such as military observer groups or forces armed only for self-defence which have been contributed voluntarily by member-states and established with the consent of those states on whose territory they have been required to operate. The establishment of such peacekeeping personnel has thus not been at variance with the principle of non-intervention in matters essentially within the domestic jurisdiction of states under Article 2(7) of the Charter.

The most effective instance of UN peacekeeping with the consent of states was that conducted by UN observers and UNSF (United Nations Security Force) in West New Guinea (West Irian) in 1962. This was because the Force was given a clear mandate to maintain law and order whilst the United Nations Temporary Executive Authority (UNTEA) took steps, under an agreed political setttlement of the dispute between Indonesia and the Netherlands, to transfer the administration of the territory to Indonesia. But other peacekeeping operations by UN forces established with the consent of states have been embarked upon when there was no immediate prospect of a political settlement between the parties to the conflict, so that any party which considered that the continued presence of the UN Force beyond a reasonable period of time was simply having the effect of freezing the status quo, to the advantage of its adversary, was likely to regard the force as an expedient which had outlived its usefulness. Apparently, this was the case in 1967 when Egypt reached the conclusion that only through collaborating with Syria and Jordan in exercising military pressure against Israel could the Arab-Israeli question be resolved, and demanded the withdrawal of the UN Emergency Force which had been established by the Assembly with Egyptian consent in 1956.

That Egypt was able to secure the withdrawal of the UN force in 1967 without challenge in the political organs of the United Nations, even though this was likely to lead to a resumption of hostilities between Israel and her Arab neighbours, demonstrated the fragile nature of a UN peace-keeping operation whose termination was recognised as a matter within the domestic jurisdiction of the state on whose territory it was being conducted. And though the question of determining the termination of the second UN Emergency Force in the Middle East, which was established by the Security Council with the consent of Egypt and Israel in 1973, appears to be a matter within the jurisdiction of the Council, so that neither Egypt nor Israel may legitimately invoke the non-intervention principle under Article 2(7) of the Charter to justify a demand for its withdrawal, in practice that body has dealt with extensions of the force's mandate as if decisions on such matters depended on the consent of Egypt and Israel. Besides, it has been recognised that Syria and Israel must give their approval before the Security Council can extend UNDOP's mandate. Consequently, the continued presence of UN peacekeeping forces in the Middle East is highly precarious, and without significant progress towards a comprehensive political settlement of the Arab-Israeli question, there is the danger of a recurrence of hostilities which the small sized UN forces armed only for self-defence could not check.

It is difficult to avoid the conclusion, therefore, that the Middle East will remain highly explosive until the great powers, particularly the United

States and the Soviet Union, apply sufficient diplomatic and economic pressure on the parties concerned to induce them to accept a political settlement in consonance with principles considered reasonable by the Security Council, and assist jointly in transforming the existing non-coercive UN forces in the area into forces with effective enforcement capabilities to ensure the observance of such a settlement. Certainly, it is in the interest of the super powers to adopt such an approach, since it is the most sensible way by which they can avoid direct confrontation with each other in areas of conflict outside their military alliance systems.

Indeed, it is difficult to see how the great powers can make a policy of detente credible unless they resist the temptation to exploit such conflicts to extend their own spheres of influence, whether such conflicts involve strife between lesser states or war between rival factions in a single state that constitutes a threat to international peace and security, such as occurred in the Congo in the early 1960s or in Angola in the mid 1970s. Clearly, it is desirable that the great powers should recognise the need for joint action under the auspices of the UN to put an end to such conflicts, and it needs to be understood that such action would not be at variance with the principle of non-intervention in matters essentially within the domestic jurisdiction of states under the Charter.

It is significant that an end to the conflict in the Congo was not effected until after the Security Council had authorised Secretary-General U Thant to take measures against Tshombe's Katanga which approximated more to enforcement measures under Article 42 of the Charter than to provisional, non-enforcement measures under Article 40, which Secretary-General Hammarskjold had attempted to apply in accordance with the principle of self-defence and non-intervention in internal conflicts, constitutional or otherwise. Indeed, had there been great power unanimity in the Security Council to enable that body to authorise enforcement measures in July 1960, it is reasonable to assume that much of the conflict during the years that followed would have been prevented.

From the analysis of peacekeeping operations with UN forces in this study, it would appear logical to infer, therefore, that unless the great powers recognise the need to permit the Security Council to authorise enforcement measures to deal with threats to the peace, breaches of the peace, or acts of aggression which involve lesser states outside their military alliance systems — action permissible under Chapter VII of the Charter without contravening the principle of non-intervention under Article 2(7) — there is little hope of the UN being able to function effectively as a peace-keeping agency with a limited but none the less important role, for UN forces, armed only for self-defence and established with the consent of states, have for the most part proved very fragile instruments of peace-keeping in areas of conflict. Certainly, it is in the interest of the great powers to act in this way to prevent their collision in dangerous storm centres, as well as to exert their influence on lesser states to accept political settlements of their differences, based on principles recommended by the Security Council, in order to prevent the outbreak or recurrence of violent conflicts.

The Reduction and Regulation of National Armaments

Of course, the creation of a UN peacekeeping force, equipped with sufficient strength to deter or coerce any state that challenged it, and without which parties to an international treaty on general disarmament could not be afforded adequate security, must be regarded as a utopian concept, since there is no prospect of transforming the United Nations into a political institution with sufficient powers to establish or control such a force. Consequently, it has to be recognised that it is unrealistic to regard general and large scale disarmament as a serious objective for the foreseeable future, and that the only practicable objectives, in the present context of international politics, are partial measures of arms control and limited reductions of armaments and military personnel.

A basic weakness of the arms control agreements already concluded is the right of states, parties to such agreements, to withdraw from their commitments if they decide that their national interests are jeopardised because of events related to the subject matter of the treaties. For instance, the domestic jurisdiction reservation on withdrawal from the Treaty on the Non-Proliferation of Nuclear Weapons not only gives a loophole to any non-nuclear state, party to it, to embark on a nuclear arms programme if it decides that its national interest dictates such a course of action, but also provides the means for any nuclear power, party to the treaty, to terminate its obligation not to transfer nuclear weapons to a non-nuclear state or to assist that state in their manufacture. It is desirable, therefore, that the domestic jurisdiction reservation on withdrawal should be removed from the Treaty on the Non-Proliferation of Nuclear Weapons and other partial arms control treaties which recognise this reservation.

Another major weakness of these arms control agreements is that China and France are not party to them. Clearly, since both states are permanent members of the Security Council, the body competent under the terms of the Non-Proliferation Treaty, the Sea Bed treaty, and the Convention on Biological Weapons to consider violations and to authorise enforcement measures against violators, their participation in such treaties is vital to their effective implementation. Consequently, it is imperative that the United States, the Soviet Union, and the United Kingdom should make serious diplomatic efforts to encourage their collaboration.

Above all, it has to be recognised that progress towards the conclusion of satisfactory partial arms control and limited disarmament agreements, not at variance with the principle of non-intervention in matters of domestic jurisdiction, depends upon the consent forthcoming from states to accept effective methods of international inspection, where necessary, to ensure that such agreements are observed. Indeed, the safeguards agreements between the International Atomic Energy Agency and non-nuclear weapon states, parties to the Treaty on the Non-Proliferation of Nuclear Weapons, which involves the use of the agency's inspectors to verify whether such agreements are being complied with, may well serve as a pattern for verification procedures in other possible arms control agreements.

The UN's Role in the Economic and Social Fields

Though the UN Assembly and the Economic and Social Council were not given the competence to take decisions on economic and social matters which would be binding on UN member states, it was nevertheless recognised in the Charter that it was desirable for its state-signatories to participate in autonomous economic and social agencies which might possess the competence to take mandatory decisions to enable the process of international economic and social co-operation to be conducted more effectively. Of course, since the obligations accepted by states through the membership of such agencies had to depend on their ratification of multilateral treaties in accordance with the principle of consent, they had no reason to complain that any limitation of their domestic jurisdiction as members of such institutions would conflict with the principle of non-intervention or non-interference in matters essentially within their domestic jurisdiction.

But though the specialised financial agencies related to the UN — the International Monetary Fund and the World Bank group of agencies — have been designed to operate under constitutions which invest them with the authority to take decisions which are binding on their member-states, in contrast to the UN Assembly and its subsidiary organs in the economic and social fields, whose competence is restricted to the approval of recommendatory decisions, it must be appreciated that the binding decisions of the IMF and the World Bank Group cannot be reached without the support of the major developed countries, like the United States, or such groups as the E.E.C., whether they are arrived at consensually or in accordance with the weighted system of voting under the constitutions of those bodies. The fact is that the decision making processes of these agencies-institutions which have vital roles in the implementation of the UN Assembly's recommendations on Development and International Economic Co-operation — do not, in effect, limit the freedom of action of the major economically advanced countries on international monetary matters and the expansion of financial assistance to the poor developing countries.

But it must also be realised that the developing countries, no less than the developed countries, have been prepared to surrender little of their domestic jurisdiction to achieve more effective international action in solving problems of an economic and social character. Indeed, it has to be recognised realistically that progress in uplifting economic and social standards throughout the world largely depends upon the willingness of both developed and developing countries to implement faithfully recommendations arrived at by consensus in UN bodies, which are not at variance with the principle of non-intervention in matters essentially within the domestic jurisdiction of states, through the voluntary acceptance of precise international obligations under multilateral treaties.

To sum up: whilst it is judicious that the organs of the United Nations should refrain from interfering in the affairs of states not covered by precise international legal obligations, it is desirable that UN members should consent to a greater diminution of their domestic jurisdiction in favour of such obligations, in order to make international co-operation more effective in the security, political, economic and social fields.

ABBREVIATIONS TO THE NOTES

UNCIO	United Nations Conference on International Organization, San Francisco, 1945
GAOR	General Assembly Official Records
GA Res.	General Assembly Resolution
A	Document of the General Assembly
A/C	Document of a Committee of the General Assembly
GA(ES)	Emergency Session of the General Assembly
GA(S-)	Special Session of the General Assembly
SCOR	Security Council Official Records
SC Res.	Security Council Resolution
S	Document of the Security Council
ECS Res.	Economic and Social Council Resolution
E	Document of the Economic and Social Council
ICJ Reports	International Court of Justice, *Reports of Judgments, Advisory Opinions and Orders*, Leyden, Sitjhoff
AEC	Atomic Energy Commission
UND	*The United Nations and Disarmament, 1945-70*, New York, United Nations, 1970
CESI	Centre for Economic and Social Information, Geneva, United Nations
YUN	Yearbook of the United Nations

I. INTRODUCTION — FROM THE CONGRESS OF VIENNA TO THE BIRTH OF THE UNITED NATIONS

1. For accounts of the Congress System, see David Thomson, *Europe Since Napoleon* (A Pelican Book), Penguin Books, 1967, first published by Longmans, 1957, pp. 135-40: and Grant and Temperley, *Europe in the Nineteenth and Twentieth Centuries, 1789-1950*, Rev. and Ed. by L.M. Penson, Longmans, New Impression, 1964, pp. 133-44.

2. See Arthur Nussbaum, *A Concise History of the Law of Nations*, Macmillan, 1947, pp. 179-80. The author points out that 'it was only the end of the Napoleonic era which brought an advancement, and a significant one, of the law of nations, namely, by the work of the Congress of Vienna, especially in its Final Act of June 7th, 1815. Signed by the representatives of Austria, France, Great Britain, Portugal, Prussia, Russia and Sweden — the alphabetical order being a salutary innovation in diplomacy — the treaty fixed the grand lines of the political map of Europe for half a century, that is, until the unification of Germany and Italy, and in a measure even for another half century. The new German Confederation which it established in lieu of the defunct Holy Roman Empire, was constructed as a permanent league among sovereigns, hence as an institution of international law. Moreover, the Final Act concerned itself in several important respects with general problems of international law'.

3. A guarantee of the territorial integrity of the Turkish empire was not included in the Vienna settlement because of differences between Russia and Britain ... Castlereagh had wanted such a guarantee, but the Tsar Alexander had refused to consider it unless various conditions were fulfilled, one of which was that the powers should first put an end to Turkish maltreatment of the Serbs, (See F.H. Hinsley, *Power and the Pursuit of Peace*, Cambridge University Press, 1963, pp. 199-200.

4. Temperley H. and Penson L.M., ed. *Foundations of British Foreign Policy from Pitt (1972) to Salisbury (1902)*, Cambridge University Press, 1938, p. 54.

5. Carsten Holbraad, *The Concert of Europe, A Study in German and British International Theory, 1815-1914*, Longman, 1970, p. 33. See pp. 23-33 for an analysis of Metternich's policy.

6. See C.K. Webster, *The Foreign Policy of Castlereagh, 1815-1822, Britain and the European Alliance*, Bell, 1931, p. 322.

7. See Carsten Holbraad, op. cit., pp. 124-25 and pp. 136-7.

8. Quoted in F.H. Hinsley, op. cit., p. 209.

9. F.J.C. Hearnshaw, *Main Currents of European History, 1815-1915*, Macmillan, 1918, p.144.

10. Canning: *The Speeches* ... vi, 422, quoted in Carsten Holbraad, op. cit., p. 126.

11. H. Temperley, *The Foreign Policy of Canning, 1822-27*, Bell, 1925, p. 217, quoted in Carsten Holbraad, op. cit., p. 126.

12. See F.H. Hinsley, op. cit., pp. 211-12.

13. Ibid., p. 199.

14. Ibid., p. 212.

15. Carsten Holbraad, op.cit., p. 136.

16. David Thomson, op. cit., pp. 244-45.

17. This was ratified by the concert of major European powers in 1832.

18. F.H. Hinsley, op. cit., p. 228.

19. Grant and Temperley, op. cit., p. 219. For the full text of the Firman, see Sir Edward Hertslet, *Map of Europe by Treaty*, Vol. II, 1814-75, Butterworths, Harrison, 1875.

20. See Carsten Holbraad, op. cit., pp. 167-68.

21. David Thomson, op. cit., p.466. See also F.H. Hinsley, op. cit., p. 263. Under the Treaty of Berlin, Bosnia and Herzegovina were placed under Austrian rule, and the 'Big Bulgaria' which Russia had demanded under the San Stefano arrangement, was split into three parts: a northern part which was made autonomous: eastern Rumelia which was placed under a Christian governor but subject to the authority of the Sultan: and a southern part, including Macedonia, which was returned to Turkey. As A.J.P. Taylor points out in *The Struggle for Mastery in Europe*, Oxford University Press, 1954, pp. 252-53, 'The Macedonian question haunted European diplomacy for a generation and then caused the Balkan War of 1912. Bosnia first provoked the crisis of 1908, and then exploded the World War of 1914 . . .'

22. Carsten Holbraad, op. cit., p. 169.

23. Ibid., p. 180.

24. Ibid., p. 181.

25. F.H. Hinsley, op. cit., pp. 268-69.

26. The Council consisted of the representatives of the principal allied powers and representatives of four other members of the League.

27. It is interesting to note in this connection moves made by Gladstone during his Second Ministry (1880-85) viz. 'the Conference of Madrid summoned on Great Britain's initiative to deal with the problem of growing disorder in Morocco by introducing reforms there under the supervision of the Powers,' to which F.H. Hinsley refers, and adds: 'The same aspiration underlay Gladstone's insistence on placing the affairs of Egypt under the supervision of the Great Powers after the British occupation of 1882'. See F.H. Hinsley op. cit., pp. 256-57.

28. The Assembly consisted of all members of the League; each member had one vote.

29. F.P. Walters, *A History of the League of Nations,* Vol. 1., Oxford University Press, 1952, p. 174.

30. P.A. Reynolds, *British Foreign Policy in the Inter-War Years,* Longmans, 1954, p. 12.

31. See Philip C. Jessup, *A Modern Law of Nations,* Macmillan, 1949, p. 80. The author points out that 'traditional international law has recognised the right of a state to adopt such tests as it wishes for the admission of aliens'.

32. Under Article 16 of the Covenant, members of the League undertook to subject any Covenant breaker to 'the severance of all trade and financial relations, the prohibition of all intercourse between their nationals and the nationals of the Covenant breaking state, and the nationals of any other state, whether a member of the League or not'; and it was the duty of the Council in such cases 'to recommend to the several governments concerned what effective military, naval or airforce the members of the League shall severally contribute to the armed forces to be used to protect the covenants of the League'.

33. W. Arnold-Forster, *The Victory of Reason*, The Hogarth Press, 1926, p. 24.

34. Sir Alfred Zimmern, *The League of Nations and the Rule of Law, 1918-35*, pp. 244-45.

35. Ibid., p. 245.

36. Ibid.

37. Article 5(1) of the Covenant stated that 'except where otherwise expressly provided in this Covenant, or by the terms of the present Treaty, decisions at any meeting of the Assembly or of the Council shall require the agreement of all Members of the League

represented at that meeting'. As emphasised by Sir Alfred Zimmern, op. cit., p. 413, 'the Council could indeed take action under Article XI, but for such action unanimity, including the votes of the two disputants, was required'. Besides, the vote of a single state, even though a party to a dispute, could prevent the Assembly from taking a decision on the matter.

38. See Arthur Nussbaum, op. cit., pp. 266-67. 'According to the Statute,' it is stated, 'the Court had to apply (1) international conventions recognised by the contesting states; (2) international custom, as evidence of a general practice accepted as law; (3) the general principles of law recognised by civilised nations; (4) subsidiarily, judicial decisions and the teaching of the most highly qualified publicists of the various nations'.

39. See Cecil J.B. Hurst's 'Note on the Court's Opinion', *British Year Book of International Law (1923-24)*, pp. 175-78.

40. See Sir Gerald Fitzmaurice, 'The Law and Procedure of the International Court of Justice, 1954-59; General Principles and Sources of International Law', *British Year Book of International Law, 1959*, pp. 197-98.

41. Cecil J.B. Hurst, op. cit., p. 176.

42. F.P. Walters, op. cit., p.44, states that 'the Assembly did not, and could not, make a democratic constitution one of the conditions of admission; nor was it ever proposed that any of those Members in which democracy was ousted by some form of despotic rule should on that account be precluded from the League'.

43. See Rupert Emerson, 'The United Nations and Colonialism', *The Evolving United Nations*, ed. by Kenneth J. Twitchett, Europa publications, published for the David Davies Memorial Institute of International Studies, 1971, p. 89. The author states that 'according to the older politics and jurisprudence there could be little or no doubt that colonies fell exclusively within the domestic jurisdiction of the administering state unless express treaty or other provisions imposed restrictions, as in the case of the Congo basin. It might be said that this position was further evidenced by the introduction of the mandates system which established a measure of international responsibility for a limited group of territories, thus by implication certifying the non-international status of the remaining dependencies'.

44. See J.L. Brierly, *The Law of Nations*, 6th Edition, ed. by Sir Humphrey Waldock, Oxford, Clarendon, Press, 1963, p. 291. It is stated that 'under customary international law no rule was clearer than that a state's treatment of its own nationals was a matter exclusively within the domestic jurisdiction of that state'.

45. See F.P. Walters, op. cit., p. 91.

46. See Philip C. Jessup, op. cit., p. 80.

47. Ibid., p. 86.

48. The attempts to secure international agreements on tariffs are described in F.P. Walters, op. cit., Vol. 1., pp. 415, 427, 429, and Vol. II, p. 520.

49. M.S. Rajan, *United Nations and Domestic Jurisdiction*, Asia Publishing House, London, Second Edition, 1961, p. 25.

50. Ibid., p. 30.

51. F.P. Walters, op. cit., Vol. 1., p. 427.

52. Ibid., p. 428.

53. See *Encyclopaedia Britannica*, under Minorities II, World War and its Aftermath.

II. THE PRINCIPLE OF NON-INTERVENTION IN MATTERS ESSENTIALLY WITHIN THE DOMESTIC JURISDICTION OF STATES UNDER ARTICLE 2(7) OF THE CHARTER OF THE UNITED NATIONS

1. Under the Covenant it was possible for the Council of the League of Nations to recommend military sanctions against a great power if it (i) refused to submit a dispute, to which it was party, to the Council: (ii) resorted to war in defiance of the unanimous judgment of the Council members not party to the dispute: and (iii) resorted to war before three months had elapsed after the report of the Council.

2. Inis L. Claude, Jnr., *Power and International Relations*, Random House, New York, 1962, p. 280.

3. The membership of the Security Council was increased from 11 to 15 in 1965, but there was no change in the composition of the permanent members.

4. This question is dealt with in chapter V of this study. See also Goodrich, Hambro and Simons, *Charter of the United Nations: Commentary and Documents*, Third and Rev. Edition, Columbia University Press, 1969, pp. 125-27. In 1962, as pointed out, 'the International Court of Justice stated that "the kind of action referred to in Article 11(2) is coercive or enforcement action". The term "action" must mean "such action as is solely within the province of the Security Council". The last sentence of Article 11(2) "has no application where the necessary action is not enforcement action".' In 1950 however, when the UN Assembly adopted its 'Uniting for Peace' plan, the majority of UN members interpreted Article 11(2) differently, as indicated in chapter V of this study.

5. Goodrich, Hambro and Simons, op. cit., p. 448.

6. See Articles 10, 13 and 62(2) of the Charter.

7. See Leland M. Goodrich, *The United Nations*, Stevens & Sons Ltd., 1960, pp. 282-83.

8. See H. Lauterpacht, *International Law and Human Rights*, Stevens & Sons Ltd., pp. 147-48.

9. Leland M. Goodrich, op. cit., p. 260.

10. Goodrich and Hambro, *Charter of the United Nations, Commentary and Documents*, World Peace Foundation, Boston, 1946, p. 64.

11. The text of the Dumbarton Oaks Proposals is given in Goodrich, Hambro and Simons, op. cit., pp. 665-74.

12. See *UNCIO, Documents*, Vol. 3, under countries referred to.

13. Ibid., p. 136.

14. Ibid., p.371.

15. See Ruth B. Russell, Assisted by Jeanette E. Muther, *A History of the United Nations Charter, The Role of the United States*, 1940-45, The Brookings Institution, Washington, D.C., 1958, pp. 901-2.

16. *UNCIO Documents Committee I/1, Verbatim Minutes of Seventeenth Meeting, June 14th, 1945, Running Number 4.*

17. *Annex A, Consultation of the United States, United Kingdom, Soviet Union and China on their Amendments to the Dumbarton Oaks Proposals (US Gen 58), May 3, 1945.* Original Records, Harley Notter File, National Archives & Records Service, Washington, D.C., p. 5.

18. Section A(3) dealt with the methods of pacific settlement which the parties to a dispute might employ when called upon by the Security Council to settle it.

19. Section B dealt with the *Determination of Threats to the Peace or Acts of Aggression and Action with Respect Thereto.*

20. *Annex B, Domestic Jurisdiction (US Gen 53), May 3, 1945*, Original Records, Harley Notter File, National Archives and Records Service, Washington, D.C.

21. See *Foreign Relations of the United States, Diplomatic Papers, 1945, Department of State Publication 8294*, Washington, 1967, pp. 582-83.

22. *UNCIO Documents 1945,* Vol. 3, *Document 215, 1/1/10. (Documentation for Meetings of Committee I/1), May 11, 1945,* p. 567.
23. Leland M. Goodrich, op. cit., pp. 75-6.
24. See Ruth B. Russell & Jeanette E. Muther, op. cit., Chapters XXIV and XXXV.
25. See four-power statement referred to under note 20 above.
26. H. Lauterpacht, op. cit., pp. 167-68.
27. See Goodrich, Hambro and Simons, op. cit., p. 67.
28. See *Foreign Relations of the United States, Diplomatic Papers, 1945, Dept. of State Publication 8294,* Washington, 1967, p. 583.
29. *UNCIO Documents, Committee I/1, Verbatim Minutes of Eighth Meeting,* May 17, 1945, Nos. 3-6.
30. Prior to the submission of the Australian amendment, a sub-committee of Committee I/1 had made a slight change in the text, viz. that 'the state concerned' should read 'any state'.
31. *UNCIO Documents, Committee I/1, Verbatim Minutes of Eighth Meeting,* May 17, 1945, Nos. 29-31.
32. *Document 969, 1/1/39, June 14, 1945, (Memorandum by Dr. H.V. Evatt on behalf of the Australian delegation), UNCIO,* Vol. 6, pp. 436-40.
33. *UNCIO Documents, Committee I/1, Verbatim Minutes of Sixteenth Meeting, June 13, 1945, Nos. 24-6.*
34. Ibid., Nos. 15-16.
35. Ibid., No. 32.
36. See Goodrich, Hambro and Simons, op. cit., pp. 208-9, for a commentary on the non-binding nature of recommendations by the Security Council under the Charter, which confirms this interpretation.
37. *UNCIO Documents, Committee I/1, Verbatim Minutes of Seventeenth Meeting, June 14, 1945,* Nos. 1-5.
38. Ibid., Nos. 5-6.
39. Ruth B. Russell and Jeanette E. Muther, op. cit., p. 960.
40. *UNCIO Documents Committee, I/1, Verbatim Minutes of Seventeenth Meeting, June 14, 1945,* Nos. 15-16.
41. Ibid., Nos. 14-15.
42. Ibid., Nos. 29-30. His amendment to substitute 'solely' for 'essentially' was defeated by 28 to 6. So, too, was his attempt to add the words 'in the judgment of the Organisation' by 27 to 7; and though his amendment to include 'according to international law' secured a vote of 18 to 14, it failed to get the required two-thirds majority.
43. Goodrich and Hambro, *Charter of the United Nations: Commentary and Documents,* 2nd Rev. Edition, World Peace Foundation, Boston, 1949, p. 120.
44. H. Lauterpacht, op. cit., p. 214.
45. M.S. Rajan, *United Nations and Domestic Jurisdiction,* Asia Publishing House, London, 2nd Edition, 1961, pp. 74-5.
46. Cf. L. Preuss, 'Article 2, paragraph 7, of the Charter of the United Nations and Matters of Domestic Jurisdiction', *Recueil des Cours de L'Academie de Droit International, 74 (1949),1,* Chapter II,4. 'Discussion and Recommendation with regard to Domestic Matters', pp. 579-87.
47. Though it was agreed at the San Francisco Conference in 1945 that Spain could not be admitted to membership of the United Nations on the ground that the Franco regime had been installed with the help of the Axis Powers (See *UNCIO, Vol. 1, pp. 615-16),* and the General Assembly of the UN recommended in 1946 'that the Franco Government of Spain be debarred from membership in international agencies established by or brought into relationship with the United Nations, and from participation in conferences or other activities which may be arranged by the United Nations or by these agencies, until a new and acceptable government is formed in Spain', and also recom-

mended 'that all Members of the United Nations immediately recall from Madrid their Ambassadors and Ministers Plenipotentiary' (*GA Res. 39 (1), 12 December 1946*), Spain was accepted as a member of the United Nations in 1955 when the Franco regime was still in power. (For an account of 'The Question of the Existence of the Franco Regime in Spain' and the United Nations, see M.S. Rajan, op. cit., pp. 111-21.)

48. Article 2(4) reads: 'All Members shall refrain in their international relations from the threat or use of force against the territorial integrity or political independence of any state, or in any other manner inconsistent with the Purposes of the Charter'.

49. *UNCIO* Documents, Vol. 13, p. 709.

III. THE APPLICATION OF THE NON-INTERVENTION PRINCIPLE IN CASES OF ALLEGED VIOLATIONS OF HUMAN RIGHTS

1. *UNCIO* Documents, Doc. 215, 1/1//10, May 11, 1945, pp. 536, 545-51, 552 and 560.
2. *UNCIO* Documents, Vol. 6, p. 456.
3. *UNCIO* Documents, Vol. 10, pp. 271-72.
4. See *E/800*, 28 June, 1948.
5. *GA Res. 217(III)*, 10 December 1948.
6. *YUN, 1948-49*, p. 535.
7. See ibid., pp. 526-34.
8. Jorge Castaneda, *Legal Effects of United Nations Resolutions*, Columbia University Press, New York & London, 1969, p. 193.
9. *GA Res. 2200 (XXI)*, 16 December 1966.
10. By the end of 1975 these covenants had been ratified by 35 states, thus enabling them to come into force. But the large majority had not ratified either the Covenant on Economic, Social and Cultural Rights or the Covenant on Civil and Political Rights. See *Press Release, BR/75/49, 23 December 1975*. UN Information Centre, London.
11. Morris B. Abram, 'The United Nations and Human Rights', *Foreign Affairs*, January 1969, p. 367.
12. See Djura Nincic, *The Problem of Sovereignty in the Charter and in the Practice of the United Nations*, Martinus Nijhoff, The Hague, 1970, Chapter XVI.
13. See *YUN*, 1946-47, pp. 144-48.
14. Ibid., p. 148.
15. *GA Res. 44(I)*, 8 December 1946.
16. After its admission to the United Nations in September 1947, Pakistan had joined India as a party in the case in protesting against South Africa's discriminatory measures towards people of Pakistani origin in South Africa.
17. For the debate in the Political Committee in May 1949, see *YUN, 1948-49*, pp. 305-7.
18. *GA Res. 265(III)*, 14 May 1949.
19. See *YUN, 1950*, pp. 398-407.
20. *GA Res. 395(V)*, 2 December, 1950.
21. *GA Res. 615(VII)*, 5 December 1952.
22. See *YUN, 1948-49*, pp. 327-34.
23. See Article 13(2) and 16(3) of the final Declaration.
24. *ESC Res. 154(VIII) D*, 23 August 1948, deplored 'the legislative or administrative provisions which deny to a woman the right to leave her country of origin and reside with her husband in any other'.
25. *GA Res. 285(III)*, 25 April, 1949.
26. See *YUN, 1948-49*, pp. 316-21.
27. *GA Res. 272(III)*, 30 April 1949.
28. See *YUN, 1948-49*, pp. 321-27.
29. *GA Res. 294(IV)*, 22 October 1949.
30. *ICJ Reports, 1950*, pp. 70-1.

31. Ibid., p.70.
32. Rosalyn Higgins, *The Development of International Law through the Political Organs of the United Nations*, Oxford University Press, 1963, p. 128, footnote 49.
33. For a summary of the Court's Opinion on the First Two Questions (30 March 1950) and the Third Question (18 July 1950), see *YUN, 1950*, pp. 386-92.
34. *GA Res. 385(V)*, November 1950.
35. This question and that of *The Treatment of People of Indian and Pakistan origin in South Africa* were dealt with as separate items by the Assembly until they were combined into one item in 1962 as *The Policies of Apartheid of the Government of the Republic of South Africa.*
36. Afghanistan, Burma, Egypt, India, Indonesia, Iran, Iraq, Lebanon, Pakistan, Philippines, Saudi-Arabia, Syria and Yemen.
37. See *YUN, 1952*, pp. 297-306.
38. *GA Res. 616A(VII)*, 5 December 1952.
39. *GA Res. 616B(VII)*, 5 December 1952.
40. *GA Res. 721(VIII)*, 8 December 1953.
41. *See YUN, 1955*, pp. 69-70.
42. *SC Res. 4300*, 1 April 1960. For an account of the Council's consideration of the question, see *YUN, 1960*, pp. 142-47.
43. *GA Res. 1958(XV)*, 13 April 1961. For an account of the debate, see *YUN, 1961*, pp. 147-51.
44. *GA Res. 1761(XVII)*, 6 November 1962. See *YUN, 1962*, pp. 93-100.
45. *GA Res. 377(V)*, 3 November 1950.
46. *SC Res. 5471*, 4 December 1963.
47. For an account of the debate on this question, see *YUN, 1963*, pp. 13-23.
48. Goodrich and Hambro, *Charter of the United Nations: Commentary and Documents*, World Peace Foundation, Boston, 1946, p.86.
49. For a summary of the proceedings in the Assembly which led to the adoption of the resolution on 11 November 1975, see *Keesing's Contemporary Archives*, December 15-21, 1975, pp. 27487-89.
50. *ESC Res. 75(V)*, 5 August 1947.
51. See *Repertory of Practice of United Nations Organs*, Vol. III,258-60.
52. *ESC. Res. 728(XXVIII)*, 1959.
53. See *YUN, 1967*, pp. 507-8.
54. Ibid., pp. 509-12.
55. See *YUN, 1968*, pp. 548-52.
56. See ibid., 552-53.
57. For useful accounts of debates on Human Rights questions in UN bodies, see *UN Monthly Chronicle*, sections on Human Rights.
58. See 'A Conspiracy to Oppress' by William Shawcross, et al. in *The Sunday Times Weekly Review*, 14 March 1976. For reasons stated in this chapter, it is erroneous for the writers to assert, however, that 'the Declaration on Human Rights which the Commission drew up and which is now, through the UN Charter, binding on all members'.
59. Evan Luard, *Peace and Opinion*, Oxford University Press, 1962, p.119.
60. See Information release, WS/78/12, 22 March 1978, United Nations Information Centre for the United Kingdom.
61. See Evan Luard, 'Promotion of Human Rights by Political Bodies', *The International Protection of Human Rights*, ed. by Evan Luard, Thames and Hudson, 1967, pp. 140-41.

241

IV. THE UNITED NATIONS AND COLONIAL QUESTIONS CLAIMED AS MATTERS OF DOMESTIC JURISDICTION

1. Eleven territories were placed under the UN trusteeship system: Togoland(Br.). Tanganyika, Cameroons(Br.) under United Kingdom administration: Cameroons(Fr.) and Togoland(Fr.) under French administration: Ruanda-Urundi under Belgian administration: Nauru and New Guinea under Australian administration: Somaliland under Italian administration: Western Samoa under New Zealand administration: and the trust territory of the Pacific Islands (composed of the former Japanese mandated islands of the Marshalls, Marianas, except Guam, and Carolines) which was a strategic trust territory administered by the United States under an agreement approved by the Security Council in 1947. South West Africa, now referred to by the UN as Namibia, was the only one of the seven African Territories, which had been held under the League of Nations Mandate system, not placed under the UN Trusteeship system. The Union of South Africa refused to do this though the International Court of Justice gave an advisory opinion in 1950 which stated that South Africa continued to have international obligations for the territory and the United Nations should exercise supervision over its administration.

2. *Foreign Office Reconstruction File, F.O. 371/50723, U4957, 25 June 1945*, paragraph 10, (Released in 1972).

3. *A Commentary on the Charter of the United Nations, signed at San Francisco on the 26th June, 1945, Cmd.6666*, HMSO, 1945, p.11.

4. Ruth B. Russell & Jeanette E. Muther, *A History of the United Nations Charter, The Role of the United States, 1940-45*, The Brookings Institution, Washington, 1958, p.821.

5. Ibid., pp. 821-22, note 24.

6. Ibid., p. 821.

7. See Summary Report of Sixth Meeting of Committee II/4, Doc. 404, II/4/17, May 18, 1945, *UNCIO Documents*, Vol. 10, pp. 453-54.

8. See Summary Report of the Eleventh Meeting of Committee II/4, Doc. 712, II/4/30, May 31, 1945, *UNCIO Documents*, Vol. 10, pp. 496-7.

9. Ibid., p. 497.

10. E.H. Carr, *Conditions of Peace*, Macmillan, 1942, p.38.

11. Anne Winslow, Editor-in-Chief, *International Conciliation*, in a foreword to 'Self-Determination and Colonial Areas' by Benjamin Rivlin, *International Conciliation*, No. 501, January 1955, p. 193.

12. Russell and Muther, op. cit., p. 811.

13. Ibid., pp. 811-12, and note 10 on p. 812.

14. Doc. 343, I/I/16, May 15, 1945 Summary Report of Sixth Meeting of Committee I/1, San Francisco Conference, 1945, *UNCIO Documents*, Vol. 6, p. 296. See also *Committee I/1, Verbatim Minutes of Sixth Meeting, May 15, 1945*, Nos. 1-27.

15. Report of the Rapporteur of Committee 1 to Commission I, Doc. 944, I/1/34(1), June 13, 1945, *UNCIO Documents*, Vol. 6, p. 455.

16. Benjamin Rivlin, 'Self-Determination and Colonial Areas', *International Conciliation*, No. 501, January 1955, p. 199.

17. See *UNCIO, Co-ordination Committee, Verbatim Minutes of Twenty Second Meeting, June 15, 1945*.

18. Sir Francis Vallat, Editor, *An Introduction to the Study of Human Rights*, Europa Publications, London, 1972, p. xiv (introduction).

19. See Quincy Wright, 'Recognition and Self-Determination,' *Proceedings of the American Society of International Law, 48th meeting, 22-4 April 1954*. See also Djura Nincic, op. cit., p. 244.

20. See *YUN, 1951*, p. 485.

21. *GA Res. 545(VI)*, 5 February 1952.
22. See *YUN, 1955*, pp. 153-58, for an account of the debate on the question and the text of the article approved by the Third Committee of the Assembly.
23. *GA Res. 2200(XXI)*, 16 December 1966.
24. See chapter III of this study.
25. *GA Res. 9(I)*, 9 February 1946.
26. See *Non-Self-Governing Territories: Summaries of Information Transmitted to the Secretary-General during 1946*, New York, UN, 1947, chapter VI.
27. See *YUN, 1946-47*, pp. 208-11.
28. *GA Res. 66(I)*, 13 December 1946.
29. *GA Res. 146(II)*, 3 November 1947.
30. *GA Res. 144(II)*, 3 November 1947.
31. See *YUN, 1948-49*, pp. 720-21.
32. Ibid., p. 721.
33. *GA Res. 327(IV)*, 2 December 1949. The voting was 33 to 9, with 11 abstentions.
34. See *YUN, 1948-49*, pp. 723-24.
35. *GA Res. 222(III)*, 3 November 1948.
36. See *YUN, 1948-49*, pp. 730-31.
37. Ibid., 731-32.
38. *GA Res. 334(IV)*, 2 December 1949.
39. In January 1952 the Special Committee became the 'Committee on Information from Non-Self-Governing Territories'.
40. *GA Res. 742(VIII)*, 27 November 1953.
41. *GA Res. 748(VIII)*, 27 November 1953.
42. *GA Res. 849(IX)*, 22 November 1954.
43. *GA Res. 945(X)*, 15 December 1955.
44. *GA Res. 1469(XIV)*, 12 December 1959.
45. Under *GA Res. 1542(XV)*, 15 December 1960, the Assembly declared that Portugal's African territories were non-self-governing and that Portugal was obliged to transmit information about them under Article 73(e).
46. *GA Res. 1468(XIV)*, 12 December 1959.
47. See *YUN, 1946-47*, pp. 338-40.
48. See *YUN, 1947-48*, pp. 362-65.
49. Under Article 40 the Security Council may, before deciding on enforcement measures, call upon the parties to comply with such provisional measures as it deems necessary or desirable.
50. *SC Res. 459*, 1 August, 1947.
51. See chapter II of this study.
52. *SC Res. 487*, 12 August 1947.
53. *SC Res. 525(1)*, 25 August 1947.
54. *SC Res. 525(II)* 25 August 1947.
55. See *YUN, 1948-49*, pp. 212-13.
56. *SC Res. 1150*, 24 December 1948.
57. See *YUN, 1948-49*, p. 213 et.seq.
58. *SC Res. 1234*, 28 January 1949.
59. S. Windass, 'Indonesia and the UN, Legalism, Politics and the Law', *International Relations*, Vol. III, No.8, Nov. 1969, The Journal of the David Davies Memorial Institute of International Studies, p. 587.
60. Ibid., p. 593.
61. Ibid., p. 589.
62. See *YUN, 1952*, pp. 278-85.
63. *GA Res. 612(VII)*, 19 December 1952.
64. See *YUN, 1953*, p.198.
65. See *GA Res. 812(IX)*, 17 December 1954 and *GA Res. 911(X)*, 3 December 1955.

66. See *YUN, 1952*, p. 266 et. seq.
67. *GA Res. 611(VII)*, 17 December 1952.
68. See *YUN, 1953*, pp. 208-13.
69. 31 voted for the draft resolution, 18 against, and 10 abstained.
70. *GA Res. 813(IX)*, 17 December 1954.
71. See *YUN, 1955*, pp. 65-9 for an account of the Algerian question in 1955.
72. *GA Res. 1012(XI)*, 15 February 1957.
73 *GA Res. 1184(XII)*, 10 December 1957.
74. See *YUN, 1958*, pp. 79-81. The voting on the draft resolution was 35 votes in favour, 18 against, with 28 abstentions.
75. See *YUN, 1954*, pp. 94-6.
76. See *YUN.1957*, pp. 72-6.
77. *GA Res. 1287(XIII)*, 5 December 1958.
78. *YUN. 1955*, p. 158.
79. Ghana, Guinea, Jordan, Khmer Republic, Laos, Libyan Arab Republic, Malaysia, Nepal, Tunisia, Sudan, Sri Lanka (formerly Ceylon), and Morocco.
80. Central African Republic, Cameroon, Chad, Congo, Dahomey, Gabon, Ivory Coast, Madagascar, Mali, Niger, Nigeria, Senegal, Somalia, and Togo.
81. *GA Res. 1514(XV)*, 14 December 1960.
82. See *YUN, 1960*, pp. 44-50, for an account of the debate on the Declaration and its full text.
83. See *GA Res. 1724(XVI)*, 20 December 1961.
84. See *YUN, 1961*, pp. 47-57.
85. *GA Res. 1654(XVI)*, 27 November 1961. It was approved by 97 to 0, with 4 abstentions.
86. For accounts of the work of the Special Committee, see 'Situation with regard to the implementation of the Declaration on the Granting of Independence to Colonial Countries and Peoples' in *YUN 1962* and subsequent *YUN*s.
87. See I.S. Djermakoye, Under-Secretary General for Trusteeship and Non-Self-Governing Territories, *The United Nations and De-colonization*, UN Office of Public Information, New York, 1970, p.8.
88. *GA. Res. 1603*, 20 April 1961.
89. *SC Res. 4835*, 9 June 1961. (See *YUN.1961*, pp. 89-95 for an account of the Angolan question).
90. *GA Res. 1819(XVII)*, 18 December 1962.
91. *SC Res. 180*, 31 July 1963.
92. *GA Res. 2107(XX)*, 21 December 1965.
93. See *YUN*, 1966, pp. 608-18.
94. *GA Res. 65(I)*, 14 December 1946; *GA Res.141(II)*, 1 November 1947; *GA Res. 227(III)*, 26 November 1948.
95. *ICJ Reports*, 1950, pp. 128, 138-40, 144; or see *YUN.1950*, pp. 807-14.
96. *ICJ Reports*, 1955, pp. 67-8, or *YUN,1955*, pp. 265-72; and *ICJ Reports*, 1956, p. 32, or *YUN,1956*, pp. 304-13.
97. *GA Res. 1702(XVI)*, 19 December 1961.
98. *ICJ Reports*, 1966, p.6, et. seq., or *YUN. 1966*, pp. 648-52, and p. 623 et. seq.
99. *GA Res. 2145(XXI)*, 28 October 1966.
100. *GA Res. 2248(XXII)*, 19 May 1967.
101. *GA.Res. 2325(XXII)*, 16 December 1967.
102. For an account of the question of Namibia before the Security Council in 1969, see *YUN. 1969*, pp. 675-701.
103. *SC Res. 283*, 29 July 1970. For an account of the proceedings which led to its approval, see *YUN, 1970*, pp. 733-58.
104. *SC Res. 284*, 29 July 1970.
105. See *YUN. 1971*, pp. 581-86.

106. *SC Res. 301,* 20 October 1971, See *UN Monthly Chronicle,* November 1971, pp. 13-34, for debate on Namibia in the Security Council.

107. *SC Res. 366,* 17 December 1974. See 'Situation in Namibia', *UN Monthly Chronicle,* January 1975, pp. 15-27.

108. See *The Times,* 2 September 1977.

109. See *The Times,* 4 April 1978.

110. What follows on the question of Namibia is based on (i) reports in *The Times* on 29 July 1978: 4, 12, 22 and 31 August 1978: 11, 18, 20, 21, 23, 27 and 30 September 1978: 6, 14, 18, and 20 October 1978: and 14, 16 and 24 November 1978; (ii) *The Guardian,* 23 December 1978; and (iii) the following releases by the UN Information Centre, London:- BR/78/31, 31 July 1978: WS/78/36, August 1978: WS/78/37, WS/78/38, WS/78/39 and WS/78/40, September 1978: BR/78/41, WS/78/40, WS/78/43 and WS/78/44, October 1978: WS/78/47, 24 November 1978: and BR/78/46, 23 November 1978. Reports in *The Guardian,* 12 & 13 March 1979, also consulted.

111. *GA Res. 1747(XVI),* 28 June 1962.

112. *GA Res. 2022(XX),* 7 November 1965.

113. *SC Res. 216,* 12 November 1965.

114. *SC Res. 217,* 20 November 1965.

115. *GA Res. 2105(XX),* 20 December 1965.

116. *GA Res. 2151(XXI),* 17 November 1966. See *YUN, 1966,* pp. 94-117, for an account of the proceedings which led to the adoption of the resolution.

117. *SC Res. 232,* 16 December 1966.

118. See *YUN. 1967,* pp. 99.-119.

119. *GA Res. 2262(XXII),* 3 November 1967.

120. *GA Res. 2326(XXIII),* 16 December 1968.

121. *SC Res. 253,* 29 May 1968.

122. See Richard A. Falk, 'The United Nations: Various Systems of Operation', *The United Nations in International Politics,* Ed. by Leon Gordenker, Princeton University Press, 1971, pp. 193-4.

123. *The Sunday Times,* 7 March 1976, p.10.

124. For an account of Dr. Kissinger's Lusaka speech, see *The Times,* 28 April 1976, p.1 and p.6.

125. See *The Times,* 'Rhodesia White Paper', 2 September 1977.

126. See U.K. United Nations Information Centre Press release, BR/77/39, 30 September 1977.

127. *The Times,* 3 September 1977.

128. For the text of Mr. Smith's statement, see *The Times,* 25 November 1977.

129. *The Times,* 2 March 1978.

130. For the text of the agreement, see *The Times,* 4 March 1978.

131. See *The Times,* 9 March 1978.

132. See *The Times,* 15 March 1978.

133. SC Res. 423, 14 March 1978.

134. Nr. Nkomo, joint leader of the Patriotic Front, said in an interview with James Pringle of *Newsweek,* published on 6 March 1978, that the Russians and Cubans had already been giving all necessary help, and that they could become more involved. See report by *The Times* correspondent in New York, Michael Leapman, *The Times,* 7 March 1978.

135. See *The Times,* 17 April 1978.

136. See *The Times,* 26 April, 1978.

137. Since 1975 Arab and Eastern European countries, and a wide range of Third World states, have secured the adoption of several resolutions by the UN Assembly to impress upon the Security Council the need for measures to bring about Palestinian statehood. On 10 November 1975 the Assembly, by a vote of 101 to 8, with 25 abstentions, re-affirmed its resolution 3236 (XXIX) of 22 November 1974, which had recognised 'the

inalienable national rights of the Palestinian people', decided to establish a Committee on the Exercise of the Inalienable Rights of the Palestinian People, and authorised that Committee to submit a report, with recommendations, to the Secretary-General not later than 1 June 1976 to enable him to transmit the report to the Security Council. Also on 10 November 1975, the Assembly, by a vote of 93 to 18, with 27 abstentions, called for 'the invitation of the Palestine Liberation Organisation, the representative of the Palestine people, to participate in all efforts, deliberations and conferences on the Middle East; which are held under the auspices of the United Nations, on an equal footing with other parties, on the basis of resolution 3236(XXIX)'.

The United States and other states that voted against these resolutions took the view that the Palestine Liberation Organisation's refusal to accept the existence of Israel and its rejection of Security Council resolutions on the Middle East disqualified it as a participant in conferences on the Middle East.

Since Israel was a state which had been established by the United Nations, there was justification for their opposition to the Assembly's call for the PLO to participate in UN conferences on the Middle East, but it is difficult to justify United States action in vetoing a resolution before the Security Council on 27 January 1976, which would have affirmed that the Palestinian people should be enabled to exercise its right to establish an independent state in Palestine, that Israel should withdraw from all Arab territories occupied since 1967, and that there should be arrangements guaranteeing the right of all states in the area to peaceful existence within secure and recognised boundaries. The United States delegate asserted that his delegation's negative vote was not based on antipathy to the aspirations of the Palestinians, but because it did not consider that the draft resolution was the most effective way of addressing the problem of their future in the context of an over-all settlement.

It is difficult to see how a settlement of the Middle East question can be effected, as the delegate for France recognised during the debate in the Security Council, unless provision is made for Israeli withdrawal from the occupied territories, recognition of the right of the Palestinian Arabs to an independent homeland, and reaffirmation of the right of all states in the region, including Israel, to secure and recognised boundaries.

The report submitted to the Security Council in May 1976 by the Committee on the Exercise of the Inalienable Rights of the Palestinian People, which was set up by the Assembly in November 1975, called for the return of displaced Palestinians to their homes and recommended that the Security Council should set a deadline of 1 June 1977 for the complete withdrawal by Israel from the areas occupied in 1967, and that the evacuated territories should be taken over by the UN, in co-operation with the League of Arab States, which would subsequently hand them over to the Palestine Liberation Organisation. But the report had nothing to say about the need for the PLO to recognise the existence of the state of Israel, and it was not surprising that it had no chance of being accepted by the United States and other Western Countries.

(The following 'UN Centre for the UK' releases were useful in the compilation of the above: WS/75/46, November 1975, BR/75/43, November 1975, WS/76/3, January 1976, WS/76/5, February 1976, and WS/76/21, May 1976).

V. THE NON-INTERVENTION PRINCIPLE AS AN ISSUE IN PEACE-KEEPING OPERATIONS WITH UN FORCES

1. For an account of great power differences on this subject, see D.W. Bowett, *United Nations Forces*, Stevens and Sons Ltd., 1964, pp. 12-18.
2. Linda Miller, *World Order and Local Disorder*, Princeton University Press, 1967, p.28.
3. See *SC Res. 1501*, 25 June 1950. It was adopted by 9 to 0, with 1 abstention (Yugoslavia). For an account of the Korean affair in 1950, see *YUN, 1950*, p. 230, et.seq.

4. See *SC Res. 1511*, 27 June 1950. It was adopted by 7 votes to 1 (Yugoslavia), with 2 abstentions (Egypt and India).
5. See *SC Res. 1588*, 7 July 1950. It was adopted by 7 votes to 0, with 3 abstentions (Yugoslavia, Egypt and India).
6. See Rosalyn Higgins, *United Nations Peacekeeping 1946-67, Documents and Commentary, II. Asia*, Oxford University Press for Royal Institute of International Affairs, p. 176.
7. *SCOR*, 5th year, 482nd meeting, p.7.
8. *GA Res. 377(V)*, 3 November 1950. It was adopted by 52 votes to 5.
9. See *GAOR*, 5th session, 299th and 302nd Plenary meetings, November 1-3, 1950.
10. *GA Res. 500(V)*, 18 May 1951. It was adopted by 47 votes to 0, with 5 abstentions.
11. James M. Boyd, *United Nations Peace-keeping Operations, A Military Appraisal*, Praeger Publishers, New York, 1971, pp. 104-5 and Note 5, p. 115.
12. Gabriella Rosner, 'The United Nations Emergency Force', *From Collective Security to Preventive Diplomacy, Readings in International Organization and the Maintenance of Peace*, ed. by Joel Larus, John Wiley and Sons, 1965, p. 455.
13. For an account of UN military observer groups established with the consent of states, see Rosalyn Higgins, op. cit., Vols. I and II.
14. The General Assembly met in emergency session from November 1-10, 1956.
15. Evan Luard, 'United Nations Peace Forces', *The Evolution of International Organization*, Ed. by Evan Luard, Thames and Hudson, 1966, p. 147.
16. Units from the five permanent members of the Security Council and from states which, because of their geographical position, or for other reasons might be considered as having a special interest in the situation, were excluded from the force, and it was agreed that states contributing units, in order to protect the organisational strength of the force, would inform the Secretary-General in advance of a decision to withdraw their contingents.
17. Hammarskjold outlined the basic principles and rules that governed the establishment, structure and functioning of the Force in his *Summary Study of the UNEF experience*. See *A/3943*, 9 October 1958, paragraphs 154-193 and Annex 1.
18. See *A/3302*, 6 November 1956.
19. *GA Res. 1001(ES-1)*, 7 November 1956.
20. The 'Uniting for Peace' resolution, under which the Suez question was transferred to the Assembly by a procedural vote on 21 October 1956, when the Security Council had failed to act, did not exclude appropriate recommendations for collective measures other than the use of armed forces for coercive measures to maintain or restore international peace and security.
21. *A/3302*, paragraph 9.
22. See *GAOR*, 1st *ES.*, 567th meeting, 7 November 1956, paragraphs 291-7.
23. See *A/3375*, Report of the Secretary-General on basic points for the presence and functioning in Egypt of UNEF, 20 November 1956, Annex.
24. *GA Res. 1121(XI)*, 24 November 1956.
25. This resolution noted with satisfaction the first report of the Secretary-General on his plan for an emergency international UN force (*A/3289*) and established a UN command for the force to secure and supervise the cessation of hostilities.
26. *A/3943*, 9 October 1958, paragraph 158.
27. Mona Harrington Gagnon, 'Peace Forces and the Veto: the Relevance of Consent', *International Organization*, Vol. XXI, 1967, p.827.
28. For text, see Rosalyn Higgins, *United Nations Peacekeeping, Documents and Commentary, 1946-67*. Vol. I, The Middle East, pp. 363-66.
29. Ibid., p. 366.
30. Ibid.
31. When the union of Egypt and Syria took place in 1958 the new state was called the

United Arab Republic, but in 1961, when the union was dissolved, Egypt retained the name of United Arab Republic for herself.

32. *A/6730. Add. 3*, Report of the Secretary-General on the withdrawal of the Emergency Force, 26 June 1967, paragraph 73.
33. Mona Harrington Gagnon, op. cit., p. 826. 'Since the memorandum was not included in any report on the negotiations of the good faith agreement,' she asserts, 'it is frivolous to suggest that it establishes the meaning that Hammarskjold and President Gamal Abdel Nasser intended the agreement to convey.'
34. Ibid., p. 827 and footnote 33 on p. 827.
35. *A/6730/Add.3*, paragraph 22.
36. Ibid.
37. Ibid.
38. Ibid., paragraph 37.
39. Ibid., paragraph 23.
40. Ibid., paragraph 24.
41. Ibid., paragraphs 26 and 27.
42. Ibid., paragraph 44.
43. *S/7896*, 19 May 1967.
44. At the San Francisco Conference in 1945 it was decided that the Secretary-General should not be given the authority to bring such a matter before the Assembly on the ground that 'applying the provision explicitly to the General Assembly would violate the primary responsibility of the Security Council'. See Goodrich, Hambro and Simons, op. cit., p. 589.
45. Alan James, *The Politics of Peace-keeping*, Chatto and Windus, for the Institute for Strategic Studies, 1969, p. 310. For the author's comments on UNEF's withdrawal see pp. 306-13.
46. *ICJ Reports*, 1962, pp. 164-65, or see *YUN,1962*, pp. 476-77.
47. Accounts of the Congo affair, with UN documentation, are given in *YUNs*, 1960-64.
48. *S/4382,1*.
49. *S/4382,1 1*.
50. *SC Res. 4387*, 14 July, 1960. It was adopted by 8 to 0, with 3 abstentions.
51. *S/4389 and Add.1-6*. First report by the Secretary-General on the implementation of *SC Res. 4387*, 14 July 1960.
52. *SC Res. 4405*, 22 July 1960. It was adopted unanimously.
53. *S/4389.Add.5*.
54. See *S/4417, Add.2*. Second report of the Secretary-General on the implementation of *SC Res.4387*, 14 July 1960, and *SC Res.4405*, 22 July 1960.
55. See *SCOR*, 884th and 885th meetings, 8 August 1960.
56. See *SCOR*, 920th meeting, 13-14 December 1960, pp. 14-25.
57. See *SCOR*, 885th meeting, 8 August 1960.
58. *SC Res.4426*, 9 August 1960. It was adopted by 9 votes to 0, with 2 abstentions (France and Italy).
59. See *S/4417*, Add. 6, 12 August 1960.
60. See *S/4417,* Add. *7(II)*, 14 August 1960.
61. Brian Urquhart, *Hammarskjold*, The Bodley Head, 1972, p.428. This author's account of the Congo affair draws upon unpublished sources.
62. See *SCOR*, 887th, 888th and 889th meetings, 21-22 August 1960.
63. Brian Urquhart, op. cit., p. 438.
64. Ibid., p. 444.
65. Ibid., p. 445.
66. Ibid., p. 442.
67. See *S/4482*, paragraph 12, Fourth report of the Secretary-General.
68. See *S/4523*, 14 September 1960.

69. *GA Res. 1474(ES-IV)*, 20 September 1960. It was adopted by 70 votes to 0, with 11 abstentions (the Soviet bloc states, France and the Union of South Africa).
70. See *GA Res. 1498(XV)*, 22 November 1960. It was approved by 53 votes to 24, with 19 abstentions.
71. See *S/4573*, 6 December 1960.
72. This would appear to be the conclusion that can be drawn from the Secretary-General's statements to the Security Council at its 920th meeting in December 1960. See *SCOR*, 920th meeting, paragraphs 56-59; *S/987 and Add. 1*, 13 December 1960.
73. See *SCOR*, 935th meeting, 15 February 1961, paragraphs 3-37.
74. *SC Res. 4741*, 21 February 1961. It was adopted by 9 votes to 0, with 2 abstentions (France and the Soviet Union).
75. See *S/4742* (Letter of 21 February 1961) and *S/4743* (Cable of 22 February 1961) from the representative of the Republic of the Congo.
76. See *S/4753 and Corr.1.*, Report of 27 February 1961 from Special Representative of the Secretary-General in the Congo on incidents in Leopoldville involving UN personnel.
77. See *S/4761 and Corr.1.*, Report of 8 March 1961 from Special Representative of the Secretary-General in the Congo.
78. See *S/4775*, Exchange of Correspondence between the Secretary-General and President of Congo on Matadi.
79. See *GA Res. 1600(XV)*, 15 April 1961.
80. See *S/4807 and Add. 1. Annex 1*, 17 May 1961.
81. See Brian Urquhart, op. cit., pp. 549-50.
82. See *S/4940 and Add. 1-12, and Add. 12/Corr. 1.*, Report of 14 September 1961 by Officer-in-Charge of United Nations Operation in Congo relating to implementation of paragraph A-2 of Security Council resolution of 21 February 1961.
83. See unpublished cable from Hammarskjold to Sture Linner, Officer in charge of United Nations Operation in the Congo, quoted by Brian Urquhart, op. cit., pp. 555-6.
84. See *S/4940*, quoted in Note 82.
85. For an account of the plan, see Brian Urquhart, op. cit., pp. 562-69. For Conor Cruise O'Brien's version, see O'Brien, *To Katanga and Back*, Hutchinson, 1962, p.266, et.seq.
86. For an account of the British government's reaction to UN operations in Katanga in August and September 1961, see *The Parliamentary Debates (Hansard)*, Vol. 234, House of Lords Official Report, Col. 446, and House of Commons, Debates, Vol. 646, Cols. 19-22.
87. See Alan James, op. cit., p. 418.
88. *SC Res. 5002*, 24 November 1961. It was adopted by 9 votes to 0, with 2 abstentions (France and United Kingdom).
89. See *S/4940/Add.14. 15 and Corr. 1, 16-19*. Reports of 29 November — 22 December 1961 by Officer-in-Charge of United Nations Operation in Congo, relating to implementation of paragraph A-2 of Security Council resolution of 21 February 1961 including Report relating to incident of 28 November 1961 in Elisabethville (*S/4940/Add. 15 and Corr. 1*) and Reports concerning situation in Elisabethville (*S/4940/Add. 16-19*).
90. See *S/5025*. Note verbale of 11 December 1961 from permanent Representative of Belgium communicating text of three cables from Minister for Foreign Affairs of Belgium to Acting Secretary-General, and replies of 8 and 15 December 1961.
91. See *S/5038*, Report of 21 December 1961 by Secretary-General concerning negotiations at Kitona between Prime Minister Cyrille Adoula and Mr. Tshombe.
92. Alan James, op. cit., p. 420.
93. See *S/5053/Add. 13, Annex 1*, for text of the Secretary-General's plan.
94. See *S/5053/Add. 14, Annex XXXIV*.
95. See *S/5053/Add. 14 and 15*.
96. See *S/5053/Add. 15*.

97. Mona Harrington Gagnon, op. cit., pp. 830-31.
98. D.W. Bowett, op. cit., p. 197.
99. Richard N. Gardner, *In Pursuit of World Order*, Frederick A. Praeger, pp. 79-80.
100. Inis L. Claude, Jnr., 'The United Nations and the Use of Force', *International Conciliation*, No. 532, March 1961, p. 579. (Quoted by Linda B. Miller, op.cit., p.82.)
101. See Rosalyn Higgins, *United Nations Peacekeeping, 1946-47, Documents and Commentary, II, Asia*, pp. 93-110, for background and commentary.
102. Ibid., pp. 101-6.
103. Ibid., pp. 111-13.
104. *GA Res. 1752 (XVII)*, 21 September 1962
105. See the *Secretary-General's Annual Report for 1963*, for an account of how the UN Security Force in West Irian carried out its tasks.
106. Rosalyn Higgins, op. cit., II. Asia, p. 128.
107. For a summary of the Cyprus affair, see M.D. Donelan and M.J. Grieve, *International Disputes, Case Histories*, Europa Publications, 1973, pp. 116-22.
108. *SC Res. 5575*, 4 March 1964.
109. *S/5634*, 31 March 1964, Report of the Secretary-General on the organisation and operation of UNFICYP (Containing exchange of letters constituting an agreement between United Nations and Government of the Republic of Cyprus concerning status of UNFICYP).
110. *S/5653*, 11 April 1964, Note by the Secretary-General.
111. *S/5671*, 29 April 1964, Report by Secretary-General on Operation of United Nations Peacekeeping Force in Cyprus.
112. See *Report of the Secretary-General on the Organization and Operation of UNFICYP, 8 May 1964*, Special Release SPL/43.
113. See S/5688, Letter of 7 May 1964 from the Representative of Cyprus to the President of the Security Council.
114. Goodrich, Hambro and Simons, op. cit. p. 306.
115. For accounts of UNFICYP, see *YUN* and *UN Monthly Chronicle* from 1964 onwards.
116. *SC Res. 353*, 20 July 1974.
117. See *S/11353/Add. 24 and 25* for Secretary General's Report on developments in Cyprus, which was considered by the Security Council on 15 August 1974.
118. See *S/11473*, which was considered by the Security Council on 29/8/74.
119. *The Observer*, Editorial, 18 August, 1974, p.8.
120. *SC Res. 340*, 25 October 1973.
121. *SC Res. 341*, 27 October 1973.
122. See *UN Monthly Chronicle*, August 1975, for the record of the proceedings in the Security Council on extending the mandate of UNEF.
123. See 'Race against the Clock to get Golan Agreement', *The Times*, 1 December 1975.
124. For the text of the Israel-Egypt Agreement, signed on 1 September 1975, see *The Times*, 3 September 1975.
125. *SC Res. 425*, 19 March 1978.
126. Secretary-General's Report on the Implementation of Security Council Res. 425/78, *S/12611*, 19 March 1978.
127. Report by David Watt, *The Times*, 4 April 1978.
128. The Secretary-General's report (*S/12611*, 19 March 1978), stated that appropriate agreements on the status of the Force would have to be concluded with the parties to cover such matters as freedom of movement and communication.

VI. THE DOMESTIC JURISDICTION LIMITATION ON THE COMPETENCE OF THE UNITED NATIONS TO INTERVENE IN MATTERS RELATING TO THE REGULATION AND REDUCTION OF ARMAMENTS.

1. Inis L. Claude, Jnr., *Power and International Relations*, Random House, New York, 1962, p. 162.
2. See the report of the Military Staff Committee, *SCOR*, 2nd year, 1947, Supplement 1.
3. *GA Res. 1(1)*, 24 January 1946. It was adopted by 51 to 0.
4. Canada, which was not a member of the Security Council when the Atomic Energy Commission was formed, was invited to become a member because of her partnership with the United States and Britain in atomic energy research.
5. For an account of the discussions in the Atomic Energy Commission and UN documentation, see *The United Nations and Disarmament, 1945-70*, United Nations, New York, 1970, pp. 11-24. (This work of reference is referred to as *UND* in subsequent notes.)
6. *UND*, p. 16.
7. Ibid., p. 17.
8. Andrew Martin, *Collective Security*, UNESCO, Paris, 1952, p. 67.
9. Atomic Energy Commission, Official Records, Special Supplement, No. 10: *First Report to the Security Council*, 31 December 1946.
10. See *YUN, 1946-47*, p. 451.
11. Atomic Energy Commission, *Third Report to the Security Council, 1948*, AEC/Rev.1. See *YUN, 1947-48*, p. 471.
12. See *YUN, 1948-49*, pp. 346-50.
13. *GA Res. 191(III)*, 4 November 1948.
14. Evan Luard, *Conflict and Peace*, University of London Press, 1970, p. 207.
15. See *UND*, pp. 25-34.
16. *GA Res. 41(1)*, 14 December 1946.
17. *GA Res. 502(VI)*, 11 January, 1952.
18. See *UND*, pp. 37-77.
19. See *GAOR*, Sixth Session, Annexes, agenda item 67, *A/C.1/698*.
20. See *Official Records of the Disarmament Commission*, Supplement for April to December 1955, Annex 15, DC/SC.1/26/Rev. 2.
21. See *UND*, pp. 57-62.
22. *Cmnd. 228, July 1957*, HMSO.
23. *GA Res. 1148(XII)*, 14 November 1957.
24. For the text see *UND*, Appendix IV, pp. 441-46.
25. *GA Res. 1378*, 20 November 1959.
26. Quoted in *UND*, pp. 87-8.
27. See *YUN. 1961*, pp. 11-15, for the debate on this issue in the UN Assembly.
28. For an analysis of these matters, see Leonard Beaton, *The Reform of Power*, Chatto and Windus, 1972, pp. 90-8.
29. The Eighteen-Nation Committee on Disarmament was established under *GA Res. 1722(XVI)*, 20 December 1961. Its members were Brazil, Bulgaria, Burma, Canada, Czechoslovakia, Ethiopia, France, India, Italy, Mexico, Nigeria, Poland, Romania, Sweden, USSR, United Arab Republic, United Kingdom, and United States.
30. For the text, including amendments accepted after its presentation to the Eighteen-Nation Disarmament Committee, see *UND*, pp. 392-412.
31. For the text, including amendments after it had been presented to the Eighteen-Nation Disarmament Committee in April, 1962, see *UND*, Appendix III, pp. 413-40.
32. *Stage 1.G(3c)* of the United States draft treaty, See also Article V of the draft treaty sub-

mitted in the Eighteen Nation Committee on Disarmament on 10 December 1962, the text of which is reproduced in *UND*, p. 437.

33. See *Stage 1,G(c)* of the United States draft treaty.
34. See *United Nations Review*, December 1962, p. 11.
35. Ibid., p. 47.
36. Quoted by Leonard Beaton, op. cit., p. 92.
37. See United States draft treaty, *Stage III, H(3)*.
38. See USSR draft treaty, *Article 37*.
39. United States draft treaty, *Stage I, H(5)*.
40. Ibid., *Stage III, H(3)*.
41. Ibid., *Stage II, G(1b)*.
42. Ibid., *G(2a)*.
43. Ibid., *G(2b)*.
44. See *United Nations Review*, December 1962, pp. 44-5.
45. Arthur I. Waskow, 'Conflicting National Interests in Alternative Disarmed Worlds', *Security in Disarmament*, Ed. by Richard J. Barnet and Richard A. Falk, Princeton University Press, New Jersey, 1965, pp. 362-63.
46. Ibid., p. 363.
47. Inis L. Claude, Jnr., op. cit., p. 280.
48. In 1969 the Eighteen-Nation Disarmament Committee, which had been formed in 1962, was enlarged to 26, and re-named the Conference of the Committee on Disarmament.
49. For the text of 'Treaty Banning Nuclear Weapon Tests in the Atmosphere, in Outer Space and Under Water', see *UND*, Appendix VI, pp. 450-52.
50. See *GA Res. 1910(XVIII)*, 22 November 1963. It was approved by 104 votes to 1 (France), with 3 abstentions.
51. See David W. Wainhouse, et. al., *Arms Control Agreements*, The John Hopkins Press, Baltimore, Maryland, 1968, p. 107, viz. 'Under the external concept, each state might monitor the activities of other states by any means short of those requiring physical intrusion. For example, compliance with limited test ban treaty might be verified by electronic reconnaissance, by seismic, acoustic and hydro-acoustic monitoring, by analysis of air samples, and other methods.'
52. See Ibid., p. 108.
53. Article IV.
54. For full text, see *The Times*, 4 July 1974.
55. See *The Times* leader, 4 July 1974. The Soviet-American treaty on peaceful nuclear explosions for such purposes as diverting rivers, designed to complement the Treaty on the Limitation of Underground Nuclear Weapons Tests, was signed in Moscow and Washington on 28 May 1976. Clearly, as *The Times* leader asserted on 29 May 1976, the treaty will not 'noticeably curb the development of nuclear weapons, even though it will bring into effect the threshold test ban treaty which was signed in July, 1974. Both treaties provide single explosions with a yield of more than 150 kilotons. The atom bomb which devastated Hiroshima in 1945 had a yield of 20 kilotons'. But whilst this has to be recognised, *The Times* was right to point out that since provision was made in the treaty for 'on-site verification in certain circumstances', the conclusion of the treaty was 'mildly encouraging'.
    For an account of the main provisions of the Soviet-American treaty on peaceful nuclear explosions, see *The Times*, 29th May 1976, p. 4.
56. The text of this treaty is reproduced in *UND*, Appendix VII, pp. 453-58.
57. *GA Res. 2222(XXI)*, 14 December 1966.
58. See *Article 15* of the Soviet draft treaty and *Stage 1,D3* of the United States draft treaty.
59. For the text of this treaty, see *Disarmament, Negotiations and Treaties, 1946-71*, Keesing's Research Report 7, pp. 281-88 and 299-300.
60. *GA Res. 2660(XXV)*, 7 December 1970. Adopted by 104 to 2, with 2 abstentions.

61. Article VIII of the Sea Bed Treaty.
62. See *UND*, Appendix IV, pp. 474-82, for the text of this treaty.
63. *GA Res. 2373(XXII)*, 12 June 1968.
64. At the end of the first conference to review the Non-Proliferation Treaty (Geneva, 1975), 94 states had ratified the treaty, 15 states had signed but not ratified it, and 37 had not even signed. (See *Keesing's Contemporary Archives*, July 28 — August 3, 1975. p. 27249).
65. See *The Structure and Content of Agreements between the Agency and States required in connection with the Treaty on the Non-Proliferation of Nuclear Weapons*, International Atomic Energy Agency, Vienna, May 1971.
66. See *Keesing's Contemporary Archives*, July 28-August 3 1975, pp. 27249-27250.
67. Quoted in *Treaty on the Non-Proliferation of Nuclear Weapons*, Office of Public Information, United Nations, New York, 1969, p.10.
68. William Shawcross, 'The Nuclear Queue', *The Sunday Times*, 30 June 1974.
69. See *UND*, pp. 300-2.
70. *SC Res. 255(1968)*. It was adopted by 10 votes to 0, with 5 abstentions.
71. See *Conference of Non-Nuclear Weapon States*, UN Office of Public Information, 1968, and *YUN,1968*, pp. 31-2.
72. The Non-Proliferation Treaty was debated in the Assembly during April, May and June, 1968. See *YUN, 1968*, pp. 3-20.
73. For the text of the communique on the Strategic Arms Limitation Agreement on 3 July 1974, see *The Times*, 4 July 1974.
74. See *Keesing's Contemporary Archives*, 1974, p. 26869A.
75. See report on Nuclear Non-Proliferation Conference, *Keesing's Contemporary Archives*, 1975, pp. 27249-27250.
76. For the text of this treaty, see *Arms Limitation and Disarmament, Notes on Current Developments, No.11, September 1972, Annex 1,* Foreign and Commonwealth Office.
77. Ibid., No.12. December, 1973, p.4.
78. *Conference of the Committee on Disarmament, Record of the Six Hundred and Forty First Meeting (Doc. CCD/PV. 641), 9 July 1974*, p.11. Document supplied by the Foreign and Commonwealth Office.
79. For the text of the communique, see *The Times*, 4 July 1974, p.7.
80. Sir Michael Wright, *Disarm and Verify*, Chatto and Windus, 1964, p.90.
81. Ibid., p.91.
82. Ibid., pp. 91-2.

VII. THE ROLE OF THE UN AND ITS SPECIALISED AGENCIES IN THE ECONOMIC, SOCIAL AND RELATED FIELDS, WITH SPECIAL REFERENCE TO THE NON-INTERVENTION PRINCIPLE

1. See Article 55 and 56 of the Charter.
2. *UNCIO, Documents, Vol. 10, pp. 271-72.*
3. See *chapter II of this study.*
4. See *Opinion of the International Court of Justice in the 'Certain Expenses' case, ICJ Reports, 1962,* p.168, and John G. Stoessinger, 'The World Court Advisory Opinion', in Maurice Waters, *The United Nations,* The Macmillan Co., New York, 1962, p.244. For Summary of the Court's opinion see *YUN*, 1962, pp. 473-77.
5. See Article 18 of the Charter.
6. See chapter II of this study.
7. See Article 67 of the Charter.

8. The number of members was originally 18, but this was increased to 27 in 1965, and to 54 in 1971.
9. See Chapter III of this study.
10. See Georg Schwarzenberger, *A Manual of International Law*, Fourth Edition, Vol.1, Stevens and Sons, London, 1960, p.316. For the rules underlying the principle of consent, see ibid., pp. 138-41.
11. Inis L. Claude, Jr., *Swords into Ploughshares*, Third Edition, University of London Press, 1964, p.61.
12. For an account of the structure and powers of these specialised agencies, see Max Sorensen, 'Institutionalized International Co-operation in Economic, Social and Cultural Fields', *Manual of Public International Law*, Edited by Max Sorensen, Macmillan, 1968, pp. 605-71.
13. For the text of the constitution of WHO, see *Chronicle of the World Health Organization*, Vol. 1, Nos. 1-2, 1947, pp. 29-43.
14. See Michael Virally, 'The Sources of International Law', *Manual of Public International Law*, Edited by Max Sorensen, p.163.
15. See *Articles of Agreement, International Monetary Fund*, Washington, D.C., United States, and *United Nations Monetary and Financial Conference, Bretton Woods, U.S.A., July 1 to July 22, 1944, Final Act, (Cmd. 6546, 1944,* HMSO).
16. See *Encyclopaedia Britannica*, 'International Monetary Fund'.
17. Susan Strange, 'IMF: Monetary Managers', *The Anatomy of Influence, Decision-Making in International Organization*, Robert W. Cox and Harold K. Jacobson, Yale University Press, 1973, p. 282.
18. See ibid., pp. 282-3.
19. For the background to this, see *YUN, 1968*, pp. 323-26, p.388, and p.373. See also *Encyclopaedia Britannica* under 'International Monetary Fund' and 'International Payments — Monetary Agreement'.
20. See *What it is — What it does*, International Monetary Fund, Washington, D.C.
21. See 'Monetary Pact seen as start of new era', *The Times*, 10 January 1976.
22. See *United Nations Monetary and Financial Conference, Bretton Woods, U.S.A. July 1 — to July 22, 1944, Final Act, Cmd.6546, 1944,* HMSO.
23. See Edward Yemin, *Legislative Powers in the United Nations and Specialized Agencies*, A.W. Sitjhoff, Leyden, 1969, p.25.
24. Max Sorensen, *Manual of Public International Law*, p. 653.
25. Leland M. Goodrich, *The United Nations*, Stevens and Sons Ltd., 1960, p.23.
26. See *United Nations, Conference on Trade and Employment, Final Act and Related Docs., Havana, E/Conf.2/78. 2 April 1948.* (Sales No. 1948, II. D4.EF). See also *YUN.1947-48*, pp. 973-75 and *YUN.1948-49*, pp. 1107-8.
27. Gerard and Victoria Curzon. 'GATT: Traders' Club', *The Anatomy of Influence*, (q.v.), p.300.
28. See *YUN.1947-48*, pp. 976-7. The following countries participated in the 1947 negotiations: Australia, Belgium, Brazil, Burma, Canada, Ceylon, Chile, China, Cuba, Czechoslovakia, France, India, Lebanon, Luxembourg, Netherlands, New Zealand, Norway, Pakistan, Southern Rhodesia, Syria, Union of South Africa, United Kingdom and United States.
29. See *Instruments and Selected Documents Series*, Vol. IV, GATT publications.
30. Richard N. Gardner, 'The United Nations Conference on Trade and Development', *International Organization*, Winter, 1968, p.102.
31. At the second session of the FAO Conference in Copenhagen, September 1946. See G.D.H. Cole, *The Intelligent Man's Guide to the Post-War World*, Victor Gollancz, 1947, pp. 1009-11.
32. Quoted by John MacLaurin, *The United Nations and Power Politics*, George Allen and Unwin, 1951, p.320.

33. G.D.H. Cole, op. cit., p. 1010.
34. Susan Strange, 'The United Nations and International Economic Relations', *The Evolving United Nations*, Edited by Kenneth J. Twitchett, Europa Publications, London, for David Davies Memorial Institute of International Studies, 1971, p. 107.
35. See Sir W. Arthur Lewis, *The Evolution of Foreign Aid*, (The Inaugural David Owen Memorial Lecture given on 19 November 1971 at University College, Cardiff), p.10.
36. See International Court of Justice, 'Certain Expenses of the United Nations (article 17, paragraph 2, of the Charter), Advisory Opinion of 20 July 1962, *ICJ Reports, 1962*. For an analysis of the Court's Opinion, see John S. Stoessinger, op. cit., pp. 242-53. See also *YUN.1962* pp. 473-77.
37. Established under *GA Res. 57(I)*, 11 December 1946.
38. Established under *GA Res. 304(IV)*, 16 November 1949.
39. See Ralph Townley, 'The Economic Organs of the United Nations', *The Evolution of International Organization*, Edited by Evan Luard, Thames and Hudson, 1966, p.262.
40. See *UN Bulletin*, November 1949.
41. Andrew Shonfield, 'The World Bank', *The Evolution of International Organization* (q.v.), p.233.
42. *Report on Special United Nations Fund for Economic Development. E/2381, (UN Sales No. 1953, II.B.1)*.
43. See *YUN.1953*, pp. 294-300 for an account of the debates in the Economic and Social Council and the Assembly.
44. See *GA Res. 724(VIII),A*, which was adopted by 44 votes to 0 with 6 abstentions.
45. Ibid., Part B, which was adopted by 46 votes to 5, with 5 abstentions.
46. See *GA Res. 1240(XIII)*, 14 October 1958. It was adopted by 77 votes to 0, with 1 abstention. See *YUN.1958*, pp. 137-41.
47. See Ralph Townley, op. cit., p. 262.
48. Ibid., p. 269.
49. Andrew Shonfield, op. cit., pp. 236-7.
50. *GA Res. 1710(XVI)*, 19 December 1961. See *YUN.1961*, pp. 23-32, for further details.
51. See *UN Development Decade-Proposals for Action, E/3613 and Corr.1, Report of the Secretary-General, YUN.1962*, p. 230.
52. See *GA Res. 1827(XVII)*, 18 December, 1962.
53. Richard N. Gardner, op. cit., p. 100.
54. See *Proceedings of United Nations Conference on Trade and Development, Geneva, 23 March — 16 June 1964, Vol.1, Final Act and Report*.
55. *Ibid., Section on Institutional Arrangements*.
56. *GA Res.1995(XIX)*, 30 December 1964.
57. Richard N. Gardner, op. cit., p.116.
58. Joseph Nye, 'UNCTAD: Poor Nations Pressure Group', *The Anatomy of Influence* (q.v.), p. 336.
59. Established by *GA Res. 2029(XX)*, 22 November 1965.
60. See Walter M. Kotschnigg, 'The United Nations as an Instrument of Economic and Social Development', *International Organization*, Winter 1968, pp. 32-3.
61. See *GA Res. 2152(XXI)*, 17 November 1966.
62. Walter M. Kotschnigg, op. cit., p.33.
63. *YUN.1968*, p.413.
64. See *GA Res. 2186(XXI)*, 13 December 1966. It was adopted by 76 votes to 19, with 14 abstentions.
65. See *YUN.1966*, pp. 285-7.
66. See *YUN.1967*, p.370.
67. *GA Res. 2626(XXV)*, 24 October 1970. (For an account of the background of its adoption, see *YUN.1970*, pp. 305-33).
68. Ibid., see paragraphs 13-18 of the resolution.

69. Ibid., see paragraphs 21-37 of the resolution.
70. *YUN.1968,* p.371.
71. *GA Res.2626(XXV),* 24 October 1970, paragraphs 41-52.
72. Ibid., paragraphs 53-5.
73. Ibid., paragraphs 56-7.
74. Ibid., paragraph 59.
75. Ibid., paragraphs 60-4.
76. Ibid., paragraphs 65-72.
77. Ibid., paragraph 74.
78. Ibid., paragraphs 75 and 76.
79. Ibid., paragraphs 79-83.
80. See *Development Forum, Supplement, ECOSOC, October 1973, CESI*, United Nations, Geneva, pp. V-VIII.
81. Ibid., p. VII.
82. Ibid., p. VIII.
83. See *Encyclopaedia Britannica,* 'International Monetary Fund'.
84. For an analysis of international monetary relations, from 1971-74, see Peter Coffey, *The World Monetary Crisis,* The Macmillan Press Ltd., 1974, Chapter 3.
85. See Oleg Bogdanov, 'Monetary Crisis and Development', *Development Forum, CESI April 1974,* p.5.
86. *Development Forum, Supplement, ECOSOC, October 1973, CESI,* p. VIII.
87. See World Bank Supplement, Annual Report 1974, *Development Forum, CESI September-October 1974.*
88. See *GAOR,* Sixth Special Session, 9 April-2 May 1974.
89. The address was delivered on 15 April 1974.
90. See Report by Jane Rosen, United Nations (NY), *The Guardian,* 19 December 1974.
91. See *Proceedings of the Conference on Trade and Development, Third Session, 13 April, — 21 May 1972, Vol. 1. Report and Annexes,* United Nations, 1973, p. 27, p. 67, and p. 299.
92. *GA Res. 3281,* 12 December 1974. The Charter of Economic Rights and Duties of States was drafted by a working group of UNCTAD. (See *UN Monthly Chronicle,* January 1974, pp. 57-8).
93. *The Guardian,* 13 December 1974.
94. Ibid.
95. See *Keesing's Contemporary Archives,* February 3-9, 1975, p. 26956, and Report of the Assembly's Second Committee on the Charter of Economic Rights and Duties of States, *A / 9946,* December 1974.
96. *GA Res. 3362(S-VII),* September 1975.
97. See *International Monetary Fund, What it is, What it Does,* IMF, Washington, D.C.
98. See 'Making the Money go Round', *Development Forum, March 1975, CESI,* p.3.
99. Ibid.,
100. See 'More Cash and Credit', *Development Forum, October 1975, CESI,* p.3.
101. See *GA Res. 3362(S-VII),* September 1975, Section II(3).
102. Ibid.
103. This was stated by Professor Robert Triffin of Yale University at a conference, as quoted by William Lineberry in an article on 'Monetary Reform and Development', which appeared in *Action UNDP,* September-October 1975, UNDP, New York, p.1.
104. See *GA Res. 3362(S-VII)* September 1975, Section II(4a).
105. Ibid., Section II(13).
106. See leader on 'Modest Realism about Money', *The Times,* 10 January 1976.
107. See *GA Res. 3362(S-VII),* September 1975, Section II(2).
108. Ibid., Section I(8-10).
109. Ibid., Section III.

110. Ibid., Section IV(2).
111. Ibid., Section V.
112. Ibid., Section V (2 & 6).
113. John P..Lewis, 'Oil, Other Scarcities, and the Poor Countries', *World Politics*, Vol. XXVII, Number 1, October 1974, p.71.
114. 'What happened at Bucharest', *Development Forum, September — October 1974, CESI*, p.3.
115. See *The Times*, 3 February 1975.
116. It was agreed at the fourth session of UNCTAD in Nairobi in May 1976, that an integrated commodity programme was in the interests of all countries: that steps would be taken towards the negotiation of a common fund: that other steps could include international stockpiles, pricing arrangements, export quotas and compensatory financing facilities: and that UNCTAD should convene a negotiating conference open to all its 154 member-states by March 1977. See *The Times*, 30 May 1976. p.1 and p.4.

VIII. CONCLUSIONS

1. Bernard Levin, 'The Indecent Spectacle of Tyrants Condemning Tyranny at the United Nations', *The Times*, 22 October 1975, p.10.

BIBLIOGRAPHY

I. INTRODUCTION: FROM THE CONGRESS OF VIENNA TO THE BIRTH OF THE UNITED NATIONS

Arnold-Forster, W. *The Victory of Reason*, London, The Hogarth Press, 1926.

Brierly, J.L. *The Law of Nations,* ed. Sir Humphrey Waldock, 6th ed., Oxford, Clarendon Press, 1963.

Canning, George, *The Speeches of the Right Honourable George Canning.* With a Memoir of his Life by R. Therry, London, Ridgeway, 1828.

Emerson, Rupert. 'The United Nations and Colonialism', *The Evolving United Nations: A Prospect for Peace?* London, Europa Publications for the David Davies Memorial Institutute of International Studies, 1971.

Fitzmaurice, Sir. Gerald. 'The Law and Procedure of the International Court of Justice, 1954-59: General Principles and Sources of International Law', *British Year Book of International Law, 1959*, London, Oxford University Press for Royal Institute of International Affairs, 1960.

Goodrich Leland M. and Hambro, Edvard. *Charter of the United Nations, Commentary and Documents*, Boston, World Peace Foundation, 1946.

Grant, A.J. and Temperley, H. *Europe in the Nineteenth and Twentieth Centuries (1789-1950)*, rev. and ed. by Lillian M. Penson, Longmans, 6th ed. 1952, new impression 1964.

Hearnshaw, F.J.C. *Main Currents of European History, 1815-1914*, London, Macmillan, 1918.

Hertslet, Sir Edward. *Map of Europe by Treaty, 1814-75, Vol. II* London, Harrison, Butterworths, 1875.

Hinsley, F.H. *Power and the Pursuit of Peace, Theory and Practice in the History of Relations between States*, Cambridge University Press, 1963.

Holbraad, Carsten. *The Concert of Europe, A Study in German and British International Theory, 1815-1914*, London, Longman, 1970.

Hurst, Cecil J.B. Note on 'Interpretation of Article 15, paragraph 8, of the Covenant of the League of Nations, Matters solely within the domestic jurisdiction of a state', *British Year Book of International Law, 1923-4*, London, Henry Frowde & Hodder & Stoughton, 1924.

Jessup, Philip C. *A Modern Law of Nations*, New York, Macmillan, 1949.

Lauterpacht, H. *International Law and Human Rights*, London, Stevens & Sons Ltd., 1950.

Nussbaum, Arthur. *A Concise History of the Law of Nations*, New York, Macmillan, 1947.

Rajan, M.S. *United Nations and Domestic Jurisdiction*, London, Asia Publishing House, second ed. 1961.

Reynolds, P.A. *British Foreign Policy in the Inter-War Years*, London, Longmans, 1954.

Taylor, A.J.P. *The Struggle for Mastery in Europe, 1848-1918*, Oxford University Press, 1954.

Temperley, H. *The Foreign Policy of Canning, 1822-27*, London, Bell. 1925.

Temperley, H. and Penson, L.M. ed. *Foundations of British Foreign Policy from Pitt (1792) to Salisbury (1902) or Documents, Old and New,* Cambridge University Press, 1938.

Thomson, David. *Europe Since Napoleon*, London, A Pelican Book, Penguin Books, 1967, first published by Longmans, 1957.

Walters, F.P. *A History of the League of Nations, Vols. 1 & 2*, Oxford University Press, 1952.

Webster, C.K. *The Foreign Policy of Castlereagh. 1815-22, Britain and the European Alliance*, London, Bell, 1925.

Zimmern, Alfred, *The League of Nations and the Rule of Law, 1918-35*, London, MacMillan, 1936.

II. THE PRINCIPLE OF NON-INTERVENTION IN MATTERS ESSENTIALLY WITHIN THE DOMESTIC JURISDICTION OF STATES UNDER ARTICLE 2(7) OF THE CHARTER OF THE UNITED NATIONS.

Official Records, Reports and Papers

Documents of the United Nations Conference on International Organization, San Francisco, 1945, Vols. 3, 6 and 13.

Verbatim Minutes of Committee I/1 of the San Francisco Conference, 1945: (i) Eighth Meeting, May 17, 1945; (ii) Fifteenth Meeting, June 11, 1945; (iii) Sixteenth Meeting, June 13, 1945; and (iv) Seventeenth Meeting, June 14, 1945. Copies supplied by Archives Section, United Nations, New York.

Annex A, Consultation of the United States, United Kingdom, Soviet Union and China on their Amendments to the Dumbarton Oaks Proposals (US Gen 58) and *Annex B, Domestic Jurisdiction (US Gen 53), May 3, 1945.* Copies supplied by National Archives and Records Service, Washington, D.C.

Foreign Relations of the United States, Diplomatic Papers, 1945, Vol. 1, Department of State Publication 8294, Washington, D.C.

Other Works Consulted

Claude, Inis L. Jnr. *Power and International Relations*, New York, Random House, 1962.

Goodrich, Leland M. *The United Nations*, London, Stevens & Sons, Ltd., 1960.

Goodrich, Leland M. and Hambro, Edvard. *Charter of the United Nations Commentary and Documents*, Boston, World Peace Foundation, 1946; and 2nd rev. ed. 1949.

Goodrich, Leland M., Hambro, Edvard, and Simons, Anne Patricia, *Charter of the United Nations: Documents and Commentary*, New York and London, Columbia University Press, Third and Rev. Ed. 1969.

Lauterpacht, H. *International Law and Human Rights*, London, Stevens & Sons Ltd., 1950.

Luard, Evan, *Peace and Opinion*, London and New York, Oxford University Press, 1962.

Preuss, L. 'Article 2, Paragraph 7 of the Charter of the United Nations and Matters of Domestic Jurisdiction' *Recueil des Cours de L'Academie de Droit International*, 74(1949),I, pp. 553-652.

Rajan, M.S. *United Nations and Domestic Jurisdiction*, London, Asia Publishing House, Second Ed. 1961.

Russell, Ruth B. and Muther, Jeanette E. *A History of the United Nations: The Role of the United States, 1940-45*, Washington D.C., The Brookings Institution, 1958.

III. THE APPLICATION OF THE NON-INTERVENTION PRINCIPLE IN CASES OF ALLEGED VIOLATIONS OF HUMAN RIGHTS

Official Records, Reports and Papers

Documents of the United Nations Conference on International Organization, San Francisco, 1945, Vols. 3, 6 and 10.

General Assembly, Official Records.

Economic and Social Council, Official Records.

Repertory of Practice of United Nations Organs, Vol. III, New York, United Nations Office of Public Information.

Yearbooks of the United Nations, 1946-64. New York, Columbia University Press in co-operation with the United Nations; 1965- New York, United Nations Office of Public Information.

UN Monthly Chronicle, New York, United Nations Office of Public Information.

International Court of Justice, *Reports of Judgments, Advisory Opinions and Orders,* 1950, Leyden, Sitjhoff.

Press Releases, BR/75/49. 23 December 1975, and WS/78/12, 22 March 1978, London United Nations Information Centre.

Other Works Consulted

Abram, Morris B. 'The UN and Human Rights', *Foreign Affairs,* January, 1969.

Castaneda, Jorge. *Legal Effects of United Nations Resolutions,* Columbia University Press, New York and London, 1969.

Goodrich, Leland M. and Hambro, Edvard. *Charter of the United Nations: Commentary and Documents,* Boston, World Peace Foundation, 1946.

Higgins, Rosalyn, *The Development of International Law through the Political Organs of the United Nations,* London, Oxford University Press, 1963.

Korey, William, 'The Key to Human Rights Implementation', *International Conciliation,* No. 570, November 1968.

Luard, Evan *Peace and Opinion,* London and New York, Oxford University Press, 1962. 'Promotion of Human Rights by Political Bodies', *The International Protection of Human Rights,* ed. Evan Luard, London, Thames and Hudson, 1967.

Nincic, Djura. *The Problem of Sovereignty in the Charter and in the Practice of the United Nations,* The Hague, Martinus Nitjhoff, 1970.

Shawcross, William, Terry, Antony, and Pringle, Peter. 'A Conspiracy to Oppress', *The Sunday Times Weekly Review,* 14 March 1976.

IV. THE UNITED NATIONS AND COLONIAL QUESTIONS CLAIMED AS MATTERS OF DOMESTIC JURISDICTION

Official Records, Reports and Papers

Documents of the United Nations Conference on International Organization San

Francisco, 1945, New York and London, United Nations Information Organization, 1945, Vols. 6 and 10.

Verbatim Minutes of Committee I/1 of the San Francisco Conference, 1945, Sixth Meeting, May 15, 1945.

Verbatim Minutes of the Co-ordination Committee of the San Francisco Conference, 1945, Twenty Second Meeting June 15 1945.

Non-Self-Governing Territories: Summaries of Information Transmitted to the Secretary-General during 1946, New York, United Nations, 1947.

Yearbooks of the United Nations

UN Monthly Chronicle

International Court of Justice, *Reports of Judgments, Advisory Opinions and Orders,* (1950, 1955, 1956, 1966, 1971), Leyden, Sitjhoff.

Foreign Office Reconstruction File. F.O. 371/50723, U 4957, 25 June 1945, Public Records Office, London, Released in 1972.

A Commentary on the Charter of the United Nations, Signed at San Francisco 1945, Cmd. 6666, HMSO, 1945.

Newspaper Reports and Opinion — The Times

Press Releases, BR/75/43 and WS/75/46, November 1975; WS/76//3, January 1976; WS/76/5, February 1976; WS/76/21, May 1976; and BR/77/39, 30 September 1977: London, United Nations Information Centre.

Other Works Consulted

Carr, E.H. *Conditions of Peace,* London, Macmillan, 1962.

Castaneda, Jorge, *Legal Effects of United Nations Resolutions,* New York and London, Columbia University Press, 1969.

Djermakoye, I.S. Under-Secretary General for Trusteeship and Non-Self-Governing Territories, *The United Nations and De-colonization,* New York, UN Office of Public Information, 1970.

Emerson, Rupert. 'The United Nations and Colonialism', *The Evolving United Nations,* Ed by Kenneth J. Twitchett, London, Europa Publications (published for the David Davies Memorial Institute of International Studies, 1971.)

Falk, Richard A. 'The United Nations: Various Systems of Operation' *The United Nations in International Politics,* Edited by Leon Gordenker, Princeton University Press, 1971.

Higgins, Rosalyn. *The Development of International Law through the Political Organs of the United Nations,* London, New York and Toronto, Oxford University Press, 1963.

Nincic, Djura. *The Problem of Sovereignty in the Charter and in the Practice of the United Nations,* The Hague, Martinus Nijhoff, 1970.

Rivlin, Benjamin. 'Self-Determination and Colonial Areas', *International Conciliation,* No. 501, January 1955, Edited by Anne Winslow.

Russell, Ruth B. & Muther, Jeanette E. *A History of the United Nations Charter: The Role of the United States, 1940-45,* . Washington, D.C., The Brookings Institution, 1958.

Vallat, Sir Francis. Editor, *An Introduction to the Study of Human Rights*, London, Europa Publications, 1972.

Windass, S. 'Indonesia and the UN: Legalism, Politics and Law', *International Relations*, Vol. III, No. 8, November 1969, The Journal of the David Davies Memorial Institute of International Studies, Edited by M.M. Sibthorp.

Wright, Quincy. 'Recognition and Self-Determination', *Proceedings of American Society of International Law*, 48th Meeting, 22-24 April 1954.

V. THE NON-INTERVENTION PRINCIPLE AS AN ISSUE IN PEACEKEEPING OPERATIONS WITH UN FORCES

Official Records, Reports and Papers

General Assembly Official Records, New York, United Nations.

Security Council Official Records, New York, United Nations.

Yearbooks of the United Nations

UN Monthly Chronicle

International Court of Justice, *Reports of Judgments, Advisory Opinions and Orders*, (1962), Leyden, Sitjhoff.

Parliamentary Debates (Hansard), HMSO, London: (i) House of Lords Official Report, Vol. 234, and (ii) House of Commons, Debates, Vol. 646.

Newspaper Reports and Opinion

The Times

The Observer

Other Works Consulted

Bowett, D.W. *United Nations Forces*, London, Stevens & Sons, 1964.

Boyd, James M. *United Nations Peace-keeping Operations: A Military and Political Appraisal*, New York, Praeger Publishers, 1971.

Claude, Inis L. Jnr. 'The United Nations and the Use of Force', *International Conciliation*, No. 532, March 1961.

Donelan, M.D. & Grieve, M.J. *International Disputes, Case Histories, 1945-70*, London, Europa Publications for the David Davies Memorial Institute of International Studies, 1973.

Gagnon, Mona Harrington, 'Peace Forces and the Veto: The Relevance of Consent', *International Organization*, Vol. XXI, 1967.

Gardner, Richard N. *In Pursuit of World Order*, New York, Frederick A. Praeger, 1964.

Goodrich, Leland M. Hambro, Edvard, & Simons, Anne Patricia. *Charter of the United Nations: Documents and Commentary*, Third and Rev. ed., New York and London, Columbia University Press, 1969.

262

Higgins, Rosalyn. *United Nations Peacekeeping, 1946-67, Documents and Commentary, 1.* The Middle East, London, Oxford University Press for R.I.I.A., 1969; II, Asia, 1970.

Higgins, Rosalyn & Harbottle, Brigadier M. *United Nations Peacekeeping: Past Lessons and Future Prospects,* London, The David Davies Memorial Institute of International Studies, 1971.

James Alan, *The Politics of Peacekeeping,* London, Chatto and Windus for the Institute for Strategic Studies, 1969.

Luard, Evan. 'United Nations Peace Forces', *The Evolution of International Organization,* Ed. Evan Luard, London, Thames and Hudson, 1966.

Miller, Linda S. *World Order and Local Disorder,* Princeton, N.J., Princeton University Press, 1967.

O'Brien, Conor Cruise. *To Katanga and Back,* London, Hutchinson, 1962.

Rosner, Gabriella. 'The United Nations Emergency Force', *From Collective Security to Preventive Diplomacy: Readings in International Organization and the Maintenance of Peace,* New York, John Wiley & Sons Inc., 1965.

Urquhart, Brian. *Hammarskjold,* London, The Bodley Head, 1972.

VI. THE DOMESTIC JURISDICTION LIMITATION ON THE COMPETENCE OF THE UNITED NATIONS TO INTERVENE IN MATTERS RELATING TO THE REGULATION AND REDUCTION OF ARMAMENTS

Official Records, Reports and Papers

Security Council Official Records, New York, United Nations.

General Assembly Official Records, New York, United Nations.

The United Nations and Disarmament, 1945-70, New York, United Nations, 1970. (This contains an account of negotiations as well as texts of international agreements).

Yearbooks of the United Nations

UN Monthly Chronicle

United Nations Review (1962)

The Conference of Non-Nuclear-Weapon States, 1968, New York, United Nations Office of Public Information, 1968.

Treaty on the Non-Proliferation of Nuclear Weapons, New York, UN Office of Public Information, 1969.

The Structure and Content of Agreements between the Agency and States required in connection with the Treaty on the Non-proliferation of Nuclear Weapons, International Atomic Energy Agency, Vienna, 1971.

Conference of the Committee on Disarmament (CCD/PV.641), Geneva, Final Record of the Six Hundred and Forty First Meeting, 9 July 1974, Supplied by Foreign and Commonwealth Office, U.K., London.

Arms Limitation and Disarmament: Notes on Current Developments, Nos. 1-12 (1967-73), Foreign and Commonwealth Office, U.K. London.

Keesing's Research Report 7, Disarmament, Negotiations and Treaties, 1946-71, New York, Charles Scribner's Sons, 1972.

Text of Communique on Nixon-Brezhnev Talks, Moscow, 3 July 1974, The Times, 4 July 1974.

Report on Nuclear Non-Proliferation Conference, Geneva, May 5-30, 1975, Keesing's Contemporary Archives, 28 July-3 August 1975.

Other Works Consulted

Beaton, Leonard. *The Reform of Power*, London, Chatton and Windus, 1972.

Claude, Inis L. Jnr. *Power and International Relations,* New York, Random House, 1962.

Luard, Evan, *Conflict and Peace*, London, University of London Press, 1970.

Martin, Andrew. *Collective Security*, Paris, UNESCO, 1952.

Shawcross, William. 'The Nuclear Queue', *The Sunday Times*, 30 June 1974.

Wainhouse, David W. et. al. *Arms Control Agreements*, Baltimore, Maryland, The John Hopkins Press, 1968.

Waskow, Arthur I. 'Conflicting National Interests in Alternative Disarmed Worlds', *Security in Disarmament*, ed. by Richard J. Barnet and Richard A. Falk, New Jersey, Princeton University Press, 1965.

Wright, Sir Michael, *Disarm and Verify*, London, Chatto and Windus, 1964.

VII. THE ROLE OF THE UN AND ITS SPECIALISED AGENCIES IN THE ECONOMIC, SOCIAL AND RELATED FIELDS, WITH SPECIAL REFERENCE TO THE NON-INTERVENTION PRINCIPLE.

Official Records, Reports and Papers

Documents of the United Nations Conference on International Organization, San Francisco, 1945, Vol. 10.

United Nations Monetary and Financial Conference, Bretton Woods, U.S.A., July 1 to July 22, 1944, Final Act, Cmd. 6546, 1944. HMSO.

Chronicle of the World Health Organisation, Vol. 1, 1947, WHO, Geneva.

UN Bulletin, 1949, United Nations, New York.

United Nations Conference on Trade and Employment, Final Act and Related Documents, Havana, E/Conf. 2/78.2, April 1948, UN Publications No. 1948, II. D4 EF.

Instruments and Selected Documents Series, Vol. IV, GATT publications.

Report on Special United Nations Fund for Economic Development, E/2381, 1953, UN Sales No. 1953. II. B1.

Proceedings of United Nations Conference on Trade and Development Geneva, 23 March-16 June 1964, Vol.1. Final Act and Report, UN Sales No. 64. II. BII.

Proceedings of the Conference on Trade and Development, Third Session, 13 April — 21 May 1972, Vol. 1. Report and Annexes, United Nations, 1973.

General Assembly Official Records, New York, United Nations.

Economic and Social Council Official Records, New York, United Nations.

Yearbooks of the United Nations

UN Monthly Chronicle

Keesing's Contemporary Archives, Report on Charter of Economic Rights and Duties of States, Feb 3-9, 1975.

Development Forum and *Supplements*, Centre for Economic and Social Information, Geneva, United Nations.

International Court of Justice, *Reports of Judgments, Advisory Opinions and Orders* (1962), Leyden, Sitjhoff.

The Guardian, 13 & 19 December 1974.

The Times, 10 January 1976.

Other Works Consulted

Bogdanov, Oleg. 'Monetary Crisis and Development', *Development Forum, CESI*, United Nations, Geneva, April 1974.

Claude, Inis L. Jnr. *Swords into Ploughshares*, Third Edition, London, University of London Press, 1964.

Coffey, Peter, *The World Monetary Crisis*, London, The Macmillan Press Ltd., 1974.

Cole, G.D.H. *The Intelligent Man's Guide to the Post-War World*, London, Victor Gollancz, 1947.

Curzon, Gerard and Victoria. 'GATT: Traders' Club', *The Anatomy of Influence: Decision-making in international Organization*. Robert W. Cox and Harold K. Jacobson, et.al. New Haven and London, Yale University Press. 1973.

Encyclopaedia Britannica, 'International Monetary Fund' and 'International Payments'.

Gardner, Richard N. 'The United Nations Conference on Trade and Development', *International Organization*, Winter 1968.

Goodrich, Leland M. *The United Nations*, London, Stevens & Sons, 1960.

Goodrich, Leland M., Hambro, Edvard, and Simons, Anne Patricia, *Charter of the United Nations: Commentary and Documents*, Third and Revised Edition, New York and London, Columbia University Press, 1969.

Kotschnigg, Walter M. *The United Nations as an Instrument of Economic and Social Development', International Organization*, Winter 1968.

Lewis, John P. 'Oil, Other Scarcities, and the Poor Countries', *World Politics*, Vol. XXVII. Number 1, October 1974.

Lewis, Sir W. Arthur. *The Evolution of Foreign Aid*, The Inaugural David Owen Memorial Lecture, 19 November 1971, University College, Cardiff.

MacLaurin, John. *The United Nations and Power Politics*, London, George Allen & Unwin, 1951.

Nye, Joseph, 'UNCTAD: Poor Nations Pressure Group', *The Anatomy of Influence* (q.v.)

Schonfield, Andrew. 'The World Bank', *The Evolution of International Organization*, Ed. by Evan Luard, London, Thames and Hudson, 1966.

Schwarzenberger, Georg. *A Manual of International Law*, Fourth Edition, Vol. 1, London, Stevens & Sons Ltd., 1960.

Sorensen, Max, 'Institutionalized International Co-operation in Economic, Social and Cultural Fields', *Manual of Public International Law*, Ed. by Max Sorensen, London, Macmillan, 1968.

Stoessinger, John G. 'The World Court Advisory Opinion', *The United Nations* by Maurice Waters, New York, The Macmillan Co., 1962.

Strange, Susan. 'IMF: Monetary Managers', *The Anatomy of Influence* (q.v.); and

'The United Nations and International Economic Relations', *The Evolving United Nations*, Edited by Kenneth J. Twitchett, Europa Publications, London, for The David Davies Memorial Institute of International Studies, 1971.

Townley, Ralph. 'The Economic Organs of the United Nations', *The Evolution of International Organization*, Ed. by Evan Luard, London, Thames and Hudson, 1966.

Virally, Michael. 'The Sources of International Law', *Manual of Public International Law*, Edited by Max Sorensen, London, Macmillan, 1968.

Yemin, Edward. *Legislative Powers in the United Nations and Specialised Agencies*, Leyden, A.W. Sitjhoff, 1969.

VIII. CONCLUSIONS

Levin, Bernard. 'The Indecent Spectacle of Tyrants Condemning Tyranny', *The Times*, 22 October 1975.

****

INDEX

Note numbers in Arabic numerals are preceded by the chapter numbers in Roman numerals, and the letter *n*, e.g., *IVn. 1, 10*.

Dayal, Rajeshwar, 132, 134.
Dean, Arthur H., 172.
Decolonisation, The UN and, (see United Nations).
Disraeli, Benjamin, 6.
Djermakoye, Y.S., *IVn.87.*
Domestic Jurisdiction of States,
    criterion of international law for determining matters within,
        under Article 15(8) of the League of Nations Covenant, 9-10;
        referred to in opinion of Permanent Court of Justice on Tunis-Morocco nationality
        decrees, 10-11;
        included in Dumbarton Oaks proposals (1944), 18-19;
        omitted in sponsoring powers' amendment to Dumbarton Oaks proposal at San
        Francisco Conference (1945), 19-22;
        failure of attempts to include it in Article 2(7) of the Charter at San Francisco
        Conference, 29;
    scope of during League of Nations period, 11;
    matters traditionally regarded within at the birth of the United Nations, 31;
    nothing in UN Charter to indicate which organ or authority was to determine matters
    within, 29;
    principle of non-intervention in matters within (i) under the League of Nations
    Covenant, (See League of Nations): and (ii) under the UN Charter, (See United Nations,
    Charter of, Article 2(7)). See also Concert of Europe, and question of non-intervention
    in matters of domestic jurisdiction.
    extent to which limited under (i) arms control treaties, 166-167, 173-176: (ii) constitutions of
    specialised agencies related to the UN, 188-192.
Donelan, M.D. and Grieve, M.J., *Vn.107.*
Dulles, John Foster, 20, 21, 26-29, 80-81.
Dumbarton Oaks Conference (1944),
        domestic jurisdiction reservation agreed to by four great powers at, 18-19;
        subsequent changes in that proposal, 19-23;
        reason for such changes, 28;
        also mentioned on 69.

Eban, Abba, 123.
Economic, social and related matters, The UN and, (See United Nations).
Eden, Sir Anthony, 21.
Eisenhower, President Dwight D., 165
Emerson, Rupert, *In.43.*
Ennals, David, 182.
European Economic Community (EEC), 223, 232.
European Convention on Human Rights, 37.
Evatt, Dr. H.V.. 24-25.

Falk, Richard A., 109.
Fitzmaurice, Sir Gerald, *In.40.*

Gagnon, Mona H., 122, 123, 140.
Gardner, Richard N., *Vn.99*; *VIIn.30,53,57.*
Gizenga, Antoine, 133,138,139,142.
Gladstone, W.E., 5,6,8,12,31.
Godber, J.B., 171.
Golunsky, Sergei A., 21.
Goodrich, Leland M., *IIn.7,9,23*; *VIIn.25.*

Goodrich, Leland M. and Hambro, Edvard, 30; *IIn.10*; *IIIn.48*.
Goodrich, Leland M., Hambro, Edvard, and Simons, Anne Patricia, 151; *IIn.4,5,11,27,36*; *Vn.44*.
Grant, A.J. and Temperley, H.rev. and ed. by L.M. Penson, *In.1,19*.
Guardian, The, 218; *IVn.110*; *VIIn.90*.

Hague Conference (1899), 7-8.
Hammarskjold, Dag,
       and UNEF operation in the Middle East, 120-123;
       and UN operation in the Congo, 126-137, 141-142;
       also mentioned on 146, 150, 158
Havana Charter (1948), 192-194.
Hearnshaw, F.J.C., *In.9*.
Higgins, Rosalyn, 51,117,145-146.
Hinsley, F.H., *In.3,13,14,18,25,27*.
Holbraad, Carsten, *In.5,15,20,22,24*.
Human Rights, The UN and, (See United Nations).
Hurst, Cecil J.B., *In.39*.

Ileo, Joseph, 132,133,135.
Indonesia, The UN and, 78-83,114.
International Court of Justice,
       Statute of, 16; and interpretation of the Charter, 32; proposals on at San Francisco Conference, 19; John Foster Dulles on, 28-29; mentioned in cases of alleged violations of human rights, 39-40,41,43,44,46-47,63; advisory opinion on interpretation of peace treaties with Bulgaria, Hungary and Romania (1950), 49-52; advisory opinion on 'Certain Expenses of the United Nations (Article 17(2) of the Charter (1962), 197-198; advisory opinion on the status of South West Africa (1950), 100; subsequent opinions on UN's competence to exercise supervision over the administration of South West Africa (1955 and 1956), 100; ruling on the legal standing of Ethiopia and Liberia to petition it that South Africa had violated mandate obligations with regard to South West Africa (Namibia), 1966, 101; advisory opinion on the legal implications for the UN of the continued presence of South African authorities in Namibia (1971), 102-103; also mentioned on 63,80,81,84,85,88,125,167,172.

James, Alan, *Vn.45,87,92*.
Jessup, Philip C., *In.31,46,47*.

Kalonji, Albert, 133.
Kasavubu, President Joseph, 126,132,133,134,135,136,138,141,142.
Katanga, Question of, (See United Nations, peacekeeping operation in the Congo).
Khiary, Mahmoud, 137.
Khrushchev, Nikita S.,95.
Kissinger, Dr. Henry, 109,215.
Korean affair (1950-53), 116-117.
Kotschnigg, Walter M., *VIIn. 60,62*.

Lauterpacht, Sir H., 23,27,30,40,41,52; *IIn.8*.
League of Nations,
       and the principle of non-intervention in matters of domestic jurisdiction, 8-12, 26; system more in consonance with the concept of Castlereagh and Salisbury than that of Gladstone, 8; its competence discussed in relation to that of the United Nations, 15, 38; and national minorities, 8,13; mandates system, 8, 65.

Leapman, Michael, *IVn.134.*
Lebanon, UN Force in, (See United Nations, peacekeeping operations).
Levin, Bernard, *VIIIn.1.*
Lewis, Professor John P., 221.
Lewis, Sir W. Arthur, *VIIn.35.*
Lineberry, William, *VIIn.103.*
Lomé Convention (1975), 222-223.
Luard, Evan, 119-20; *IIIn.59,61.*
Lumumba, Patrice, 126,128,131,132,134,141,142.

MacLaurin, John, *VIIn.32.*
Makarios, President, 147,148,150,151.
Malkin, Sir William, 21.
Marshall plan, 197; suspension of Marshall aid to Netherlands, 82.
Martin, Dr. Andrew, 162.
McCloy, J.J., 167,169.
Metternich, Prince von, 2,3.
Miller, Linda, *Vn.2.*
Mobutu, Col. (later President) Joseph Désiré, 132,133,134.
Molotov, V.M., 21.
Monroe doctrine, 4.
Morocco, The UN and, 1951-56, 83-86, 89-90, 114-115.
Mugabe, Robert, 111, 112.
Muzorewa, Bishop Abel, 111

Namibia, The UN and, 100-107, 227.
Nasser, President Gamal Abdel, 121,122.
Nincic, Djura, *IIIn.12.*
Nkomo, Joshua, 111,112.
Nuclear Suppliers' Group, 177.
Nussbaum, Arthur, *In.2,38.*

O'Brien, Dr. Conor Cruise, 136,137; *Vn.85.*
Observer, The, 152.
Organisation of African Unity (OAU), 59, 100.
Organisation for European Economic Co-operation (OEEC), 197.
Organisation of Petroleum Exporting Countries (OPEC), 213,214,215,219.
Orr, Lord John Boyd,
        advocacy of World Food Board, 195-196.
Owen, Dr. David, 112.

Palestinian question, 60, 153; *IVn.137.*
Pasvolsky, Leo, 23-24.
Peacekeeping operations with UN forces (See United Nations).
Permanent Court of International Justice,
        role in determining matters of domestic jurisdiction under League of Nations
        Covenant, 10,38; advisory opinion on Tunis-Morocco nationality decrees, 10-11;
        Statute of, *In.38,* 16; mentioned in connection with the question of Morocco, 84.
Political Rights of Women, Convention on, 1952, 36.
Population, World Conference on, 1974, 221-222.
Portuguese colonies, The UN and question of, 98-100, 227.
Prem Chand, Major-General, 111.
Preuss, Lawrence, *IIn.46.*

270

Rajan, M.S., 30; *In.49,50*; *IIn.47*.
Reynolds, P.A., *In.30*.
Rivlin, Benjamin, 70.
Rosner, Gabriella, 119.
Rosen, Jane, *VIIn.90*.
Russell, Ruth B. and Muther, Jeanette E., 22,69; *IIn.15,39, IVn.4,5,6.12*.

Salisbury, 3rd Marquess of, 6,7,8,12,13.
San Francisco Conference (1945),
    drafting of domestic jurisdiction reservation at, 19-29; and the question of human rights, 33-34;
    drafting of Charter's provisions on dependent territories, 65-71;
    decisions on international economic and social co-operation, 186;
    concept of international security envisaged at, 116.
Sampson, Nicos, 151.
Self-determination, Principle of, 13,68-71,88,91,92,93-97,99,107,225-228.
Shawcross, William, *IIIn.58;VIn.68*.
Shonfield, Andrew, *VIIn.41,49*.
Sithole, Rev. Ndabaningi, 111.
Smith, Ian, 111; also Smith regime, 107,108,112,113.
Soong, Dr. T.V., 21.
Sorensen, Max, *VIIn.12,24*.
South West Africa People's Organisation (SWAPO), 104, 105, 106.
Southern Rhodesia, The UN and, 107-113, 227-228.
Specialised Agencies related to UN — See United Nations.
Sukarno, President Achmed, 83.
Stalin, Joseph V., 197.
Stassen, Harold, 171.
Stettinius, Edward R.Jr., 21.
Steyn, Justice M.T., 105.
Stoessinger, John G., *VIIn.4*.
Strange, Susan, *VIIn.17,34*.
Strategic Arms Limitation Talks (SALT), 180.

Taylor, A.J.P., *In.21*.
Temperley, H., *In.11*.
Thant, U
    and termination of UNEF in the Middle East in 1967, 122-125;
    and UN operation in the Congo, 138-140;142.
    and UN operation in West Irian, 143;
    and UN operation in Cyprus, 149-150;
    on dangers of nuclear proliferation, 176-177.
Thomson, David, *In.1.16,21*.
Times, The
    on 'Brakes on the Nuclear Spread', 177; on 'Treaty on the limitation of underground nuclear weapons tests', *VIn.55*; on voting arrangements in the IMF, *VIIn.106*;
Townley, Ralph, *VIIn.39,47,48*.
Triffin, Professor Robert, *VIIn.103*.
Tshombe, Moise, 126,131,135,136,137,138,139,140,141.
Tunisia, The UN and, 1952-56, 86-90, 114-115.

United Nations,
    Charter of,
        Articles cited,
        1(1): 16; 1(2): 16,54,68,69,70,78,79,83,85,88,90,92,93,113-114.

and the regulation and reduction of armaments,
Charter's provisions on, 159-160; questions considered by Atomic Energy Commission, 160-164; Commission for Conventional Armaments, 164; Disarmament Commission's search for agreement on plan for comprehensive system of disarmament, 164-166; US-Soviet statement on principles for general and complete disarmament (1961), 167-170; analysis of US and Soviet draft treaties on general and complete disarmament (1962), 170-173; General Assembly's resolution on partial measures of disarmament and arms control (1957), 166; Antarctic treaty (1959), 166-167; Nuclear test ban treaty (partial) 1963, 174; treaty on limitation of underground nuclear weapon tests (1974), 174; Outer space treaty (1966), 174-175; treaty on non-proliferation of nuclear weapons (1968), 175-180; Sea-bed treaty (1970), 175; Convention on bacteriological (biological) and toxin weapons (1972), 181-182; question of a convention on the prohibition, production and stockpiling of chemical weapons discussed, 182; need for all the permanent members of the Security Council to be involved in the implementation of arms control agreements, 180-81, 185; matters raised at Conference of Non-Nuclear-Weapon States in Geneva (1968) discussed, 179; conclusions, 182-185, 231-232.
specialised agencies related to,
International Monetary Fund (IMF), 188-190, 192, 194, 209, 213, 219-220, 232. International Bank for Reconstruction and Development (IBRD), 190-191, 192, 194,199,206,213-214,216,232; International Finance Corporation (IFC), 191,200,206; International Development Association (IDA), 191,201,206; International Labour Organisation (ILO), 36,192; Food and Agriculture Organisation (FAO), 196; United Nations Educational, Scientific and Cultural Organisation (UNESCO), 192; World Health Organisation (WHO), 188; General Agreement on Tariffs and Trade (GATT), 194-195; International Atomic Energy Agency (IAEA), 176,184,232.
Urquhart, Brian, *Vn,63,64,65,66,81,83,85.*

Vallat, Sir Francis, 70-71.
Vandenberg, Senator Arthur W., 23.
Virally, Michael, *VIIn.14.*
Vorster, John, 105.

Wainhouse, David W. *VIn.51,52.*
Waldheim, Dr. Kurt,
and UN peacekeeping operation in Cyprus, 152;
and UN peacekeeping operation in Lebanon (referred to as Secretary-General), 154-155; proposals for UN force in Namibia (referred to as Secretary-General), 105.
Walters, F.P., *In.29,42,45,48,51,52.*
Wang Chia-chen, 21.
Waskow, Arthur I., 172-173.
Watt, David, *Vn.127.*
Webster, Sir C.K., *In.6.*
Welensky, Sir Roy, 136.
Wellington, Duke of, 3.
West Irian, UN operation in, (See United Nations, peacekeeping operations).
Wilson, President Woodrow, 13.
Windass, S., *IVn.59,60,61.*
Winiarski, Judge Bohdan, 198.
Winslow, Anne, *IVn.11.*
Wright, Sir Michael, 183.
Wright, Quincy, *IVn.19.*